S0-ASO-643

Bible Student's Commentary

Deuteronomy

Bible Student's Commentary

Deuteronomy

Translated by Ed M. van der Maas

J. Ridderbos

Western Bible College Library
16075 West Belleview Ave.
Morristown, Co. 80465

Regency
Reference Library
Zondervan Publishing House
Grand Rapids, Michigan

4193

COLORADO CHRISTIAN COLLEGE LIBRARY

THE BIBLE STUDENT'S COMMENTARY—DEUTERONOMY
Originally published in 1950-51 in Dutch under the title *Korte Verklaring der Heilige Schrift—Deuteronomium* by J. H. Kok, Kampen, The Netherlands.
Copyright © 1984 by The Zondervan Corporation
Grand Rapids, Michigan

REGENCY REFERENCE LIBRARY is an imprint of Zondervan Publishing House,
1415 Lake Drive, S.E., Grand Rapids, Michigan 49506.

Library of Congress Cataloging in Publication Data

Ridderbos, J. (Jan)
    Bible student's commentary—Deuteronomy.

    Translation of: Korte Verklaring der Heilige Schrift—Deuteronomium
    Includes bibliographical references
    1. Bible. O.T. Deuteronomy—Commentaries. I. Bible. O.T. Deuteronomy.
English. 1984. II. Title.
BS1275.3.R5313   1984   222'.15077   84–17420
ISBN 0-310-45260-0

The Scripture text used is that of the New International Version (North American Edition), copyright 1978 by the International Bible Society. Used by permission.

All rights reserved. No part of this publication may be reproduced, stored in a retrieval system, or transmitted in any form or by any means—electronic, mechanical, photocopy, recording, or any other—except for brief quotations in printed reviews, without the prior permission of the publisher.

Edited by Ben Chapman and Laura Weller
Designed by Ed Viening

Printed in the United States of America

84 85 86 87 88 89 / 10 9 8 7 6 5 4 3 2 1

Contents

Foreword

The leading evangelical commentary on the whole Bible among Dutch-speaking people is the *Korte Verklaring Der Heilige Schrift,* a set of sixty-two volumes written by prominent Dutch scholars and exegetes. Unfortunately, the *Korte Verklaring* has not been widely known in the English-speaking world, although a number of the contributors and editors have made contributions to biblical and theological studies that have been widely acknowledged outside the Netherlands.

Publication of the *Korte Verklaring* began in the 1920s and continued, with occasional additions and updating, into the 1960s. It was designed to be a commentary for the lay reader who does not have a knowledge of Hebrew and Greek or a detailed knowledge of critical questions. It has admirably fulfilled this purpose and at the same time is highly regarded and frequently used by scholars because of its exegetical insights.

The Bible Student's Commentary at last will make the *Korte Verklaring* available to the English-speaking world. It has been adapted for English use by incorporating the text of the New International Version into the commentary discussion. Where appropriate, the original contributor's discussion has been edited to reflect the wording of the NIV and translation issues among the other English versions. The *Bible Student's Commentary* is a work of enduring value because of the exegetical material it makes available to the serious student of Scripture.

The Publisher

Introduction

I. NAME, CONTENTS, AND CHARACTER

In the Hebrew Bible, the first words of each of the first five books (collectively called the Pentateuch) are used as their respective titles. Thus, the fifth book is called "And These Are the Words" or, in shortened form, "The Words."

Some of the rabbis also called Deuteronomy "The Book of Exhortations," while others called it "The Repetition of the Law." The latter name is based on what is in our opinion an incorrect understanding of Deuteronomy 17:18, which states that the king must write "a copy of this law"; some Jewish exegetes took this phrase to mean "a repetition of the law," which they then understood to refer to our Book of Deuteronomy. The translators of the LXX adopted this view and rendered the phrase *to deuteronomion touto,* "this second law"; they used *Deuteronomion* as the title for the book. The Vulgate adopted this title and Latinized it: *Deuteronomium,* the title we still use.

★ The use our Savior made of this book should indicate to us that its contents are important. When tempted, He quoted Deuteronomy in all three instances to rebuff the Tempter (8:3; 6:16; 6:13; cf. Matt. 4:4, 7, 10), and in Matthew 22:37–38 it is again Deuteronomy from which He derived what He called "the first and greatest commandment" (Deut. 6:5; 10:12; 30:6). Of the more specific provisions in Deuteronomy He quoted those regarding the need for two or three witnesses (Matt. 18:16; John 8:17; cf. Deut. 17:6; 19:15) and discussed those concerning the certificate of divorce (Matt. 19:8; cf. Deut. 24:1) and the levirate (Matt. 22:24; cf. Deut. 25:5ff.).

Deuteronomy consists almost entirely of Moses' farewell speeches to the people, given "east of the Jordan in the territory of Moab" (1:5) to

1

impress the Lord's laws on Israel before they entered Canaan. The second and longest of these discourses includes a number of separate laws, which may be called the actual law code of Deuteronomy (ch. 12–26). The final chapters (31–34) have a different character. The broad divisions of the book are then as follows:

Chapters 1–4	First (preparatory) discourse a. Historical survey (1–3) b. Exhortation to keep the law (4)
Chapters 5–26	Second discourse a. Foundational part (historical reminders of the giving of the law at Horeb and exhortations and commandments of a general nature) (5–11) b. Specific laws (12–26)
Chapters 27–30	Concluding words, including extensive pronouncements of blessing and curse
Chapters 31–34	Moses' final arrangements, his farewell address, and the narrative of his death; included here are the Song of Moses (32) and Moses' blessing (33)

Deuteronomy takes us to the boundary between two worlds and thus speaks of both past and future. It speaks of the past in a manner entirely in keeping with its hortatory nature: it does not present a continuous narrative of past events, but reminds of selected events (especially Israel's experiences during the Exodus and the wilderness journey) to provide a basis for its exhortations and warnings.

But more than on the past, the book focuses on the future. Its laws clearly bear the mark of being intended for the time Israel will live in Canaan; it warns the people against the dangers to which they will be exposed there. Its purpose is to ensure that Israel will walk in obedience and thus live long in the land promised to their forefathers, enjoying the rich blessings the Lord wants to bestow on them there.

Deuteronomy is Moses' exposition of the law to the people (1:5: "Moses began to expound"; KJV, "declare"; RSV, "explain"; Heb. *ba'ar,* "to make distinct, plain"). Accordingly, the book is popular rather than technical in nature, and it is "this law" that is to be read every seven years during the Feast of Tabernacles (31:10–13).

The law that Moses here presents to and impresses upon the people is *in substance* the law that was given at Sinai, and as such the name "second law," understood in the sense of "repetition of the law," is not inappropriate for this book. But we must emphasize the words "in substance," because Deuteronomy is far from a verbatim copy of the preceding books of the Law, or even of parts of these books, but has its own character, both in form and content.

Viewed as a whole, Deuteronomy bears a prophetic and religious rather than a juridical stamp. The instruction in the law presented here does not limit itself to the presentation of a number of laws and regulations, but also contains a prophetic sermon concerning the principles on which the law is based and the only foundations on which the keeping of the law can rest.

In all this Deuteronomy clearly accentuates a concept that is basic to the entire Old Testament: The Lord is Israel's God and Israel is the Lord's people—the words "the LORD your God" are repeated numerous times. Furthermore, the fact that this special relationship has acquired the more specific character of a covenant is placed in the foreground.

The unity of God receives strong emphasis (6:4), even as the love and grace which God has shown to the patriarchs and Israel (4:37; 7:8; 10:15; et al.). Love occupies an important place among those things that are required of Israel (6:5; 11:1; 13:3; et al.); the fear of the Lord is not in conflict with this love—it is mentioned several times alongside it.

All this is dealt with more extensively in the last section of this introduction, where we shall discuss in more detail the relationship between the Lord and Israel as seen in Deuteronomy.

These matters are presented, not on an abstract level, but in several series of historical reminiscences and exhortations, all of which serve to impress upon Israel the commandments of the Lord. The reminiscences and exhortations give the book the character of a sermon, all the more impressive because delivered by Moses, the man of God, at the end of his life, to Israel on the verge of crossing the Jordan.

The human element is also clearly in the foreground in this book: Moses speaks like a father who before his death earnestly and in love exhorts, admonishes, and warns his children.

But this human aspect is the vehicle for a divine content. Moses speaks of God's work, of the awesome revelation of God on Mount Horeb, of what God has done for Israel (and for the forefathers), and of what He will do for Israel in the future. Moses' fatherly words express the love of Him who is Israel's Father, and his minatory earnestness draws Israel's attention to the holiness of the Lord, who cannot tolerate evil in His people. In the whole book, the God of the covenant speaks to Israel with His love and grace, with the strict demand of His law, with His promise of blessing and threat of curse.

These historical reminiscences and exhortations show that Deuteronomy is something other than a verbatim repetition, and the same is true of the law code proper (ch. 12–26). The latter differs not only from the priestly laws in Exodus and especially those in Leviticus and Numbers but also from the other collections of laws that are specifically related to the making of the covenant at Sinai (the so-called Book of the Covenant of Exod. 20:22–23[1]) or to the renewal of the covenant after the sin with the golden calf (the small collection of laws in Exod. 34:10–26).

When we compare Deuteronomy with these nonpriestly laws, we find that the latter contain much that is not found in Deuteronomy, and also much that the laws in Deuteronomy treat in a somewhat different manner. Conversely, Deuteronomy contains a number of provisions that are not found in the older laws at all, thus frequently supplementing the older laws.[2]

We can only conjecture as to why not all laws were included in Exodus. It has been suggested that Exodus 21:1ff. was intended primarily for use by judges and heads of families and had to be memorized, the reason why these laws had to be brief.[3]

The specific purpose of Deuteronomy was that it should be read to the people; this would explain why provisions and formulations for which there was no place in Exodus with its different purpose were included in Deuteronomy, especially those that were designed to influence public opinion. Nor must we forget that Israel's imminent transition from the wilderness to Canaan apparently was reason to clarify or supplement the law with a view to certain aspects of the future life in Canaan.

---

[1]The name is based on the assumption that this is the "Book of the Covenant" Moses read to the people according to Exodus 24:7.

[2]Although Moses does state that he received the commandments recorded here from the Lord on Mount Horeb (5:31ff.; cf. 6:20–25), this does not necessarily mean that they are identical to those identified as such in Exodus 20:22ff. There is no reason why Moses could not have received more laws on Mount Horeb than are recorded in Exodus. It is also possible that here in 5:31ff. Moses incorporates supplements and clarifications, added under divine inspiration, in the laws that were given him on the mountain.

[3]H. M. Wiener, *Pentateuchal Studies* (London, 1912), p. 181.

Furthermore, it is natural that the majority of the priestly laws did not find a place in Deuteronomy. This is true of the commands that applied only once in a specific situation (those concerning the initial consecration of the priests and the building of the tabernacle), but also of provisions that had continuing application. The latter include not only the laws that were intended only for the priests (e.g., the laws that specified the manner in which the various offerings were to be brought and those that regulated the organization of the priestly tribe and in particular the distinction between priests and Levites), but also regulations that were of such a technical nature that only the priests could instruct the people in them (e.g., the law concerning leprosy, marriage laws, etc.).

Those matters with which the law code of Deuteronomy does deal focus, like the rest of Deuteronomy, on the time when Israel will be living in Canaan. The law code even deals with Israel's kings (17:14–20), and the regulation concerning the centralization of the cultus with which the law code opens (ch. 12) presupposes a later period in Israel's life in Canaan (12:10). The primary purpose of this law is to keep Israel from participating in Canaan's idolatry, a purpose that also underlies various other regulations.

The law of chapter 12 is of no mean importance for the history of God's revelation (see commentary on ch. 12). It is worth noting that this one, central place of cultic worship gives expression to both the unity of Israel's God and the unity of Israel as a nation. Furthermore, we should mention that the ideal presented in chapter 12 was bound to involve a drastic reduction in the offerings and paved the way for their abolition; the ceremonial law thus contains the seed of its own abrogation. The fact that the offerings are not the highest that the Lord asks of Israel also finds expression in Deuteronomy in the way in which the great religio-ethical demands are placed in the foreground.

A characteristic feature of the cultic laws of Deuteronomy is the accentuation of the concept of joy, the "eating and drinking in the presence of the LORD" (cf. 12:7; et al.). It is also important that the servants as well as the Levites, widows, orphans, and aliens are to share in this joy.

The civil laws also repeatedly champion the servants, the poor, widows, orphans, Levites, and aliens. The demand for mercy, fairness, and a gentle and brotherly attitude toward all these groups is enjoined upon Israel—even the ox that is treading out the grain has a right of fair treatment (25:4).

In general, many of the civil laws in Deuteronomy have an ethical rather than juridical character. Nevertheless, Deuteronomy is important for an understanding of legal relationships as such. It contains (especially in ch. 20–25) a number of regulations that could formally serve as a basis for the administration of justice. These regulations are apparently intended to supplement earlier laws (see above).

It is of special interest that Deuteronomy contains rather detailed provisions for the administration of justice and the various juridical organs, concerning the king and his duties, and concerning the prophets.

The laws of Deuteronomy, like other laws of the Pentateuch, frequently display a great measure of similarity, both in form and in content, with those of Hammurabi; the differences, however, are much more pronounced.

II. AUTHORSHIP: THE CRITICAL PROBLEM

A. *The theory of the school of Wellhausen*

According to its own witness, the main contents of the Book of Deuteronomy are of Mosaic origin (see below, sec. 3). Various arguments have been brought against this Mosaic origin, but we shall limit ourselves to the most important one—the argument based on the demand of Deuteronomy 12 that there be only one place of sacrifice, the so-called *centralization of the cultus.*

Following two publications by De Wette in 1805 and 1806, the view became dominant among critical scholars that the Book of the Law that was found in the temple during the reign of King Josiah (621 B.C.; 2 Kings 22) contained the substance of Deuteronomy, and that this book had come into being only a short time before it was found; Deuteronomy then did not acquire its present form until after Josiah's time.

This view has become one of the pillars of the theory about the origin of the Pentateuch that was constructed by the critical school during the nineteenth century and that is generally known by the name of one of its most prominent spokesmen: the school of Wellhausen. This approach held virtually unlimited sway among critical scholars until the end of the last century, while its theses, in spite of changes in the climate of opinion since, continue to exert considerable influence.

As we shall see, the idea that the Book of the Law found during Josiah's reign was (or was closely related to) Deuteronomy had already been suggested before De Wette, and there is in our opinion some support for this view. But the critical theory links this with the idea that the book in question was not an ancient law code of Mosaic origin, but rather a book that (at least where its main contents, contained in ch. 12, are concerned) supposedly dates from a much later time. Some think the book dates from Josiah's own time (i.e., it was written shortly before it was "found"), while others go back to a slightly earlier period, e.g., the time of Hezekiah, who would then have used it as the basis for his own reforms.

Underlying this approach is the idea that the primary emphasis in the law code of Deuteronomy falls on the demand in chapter 12 that the offerings be brought only at the central sanctuary—in other words, the demand to cease offering on the "high places," which is precisely what characterized Josiah's reformation.

This legislation directed against the worship on the "high places" then would not date from Moses' time, but would rather be the result of the ministry of the earliest prophets as reflected especially in the prophecies of Hosea, who so sharply condemned the paganized worship on the "high places." Under the influence of these prophetic voices, but also due to the impression made by the fall of Samaria (722 B.C.), a movement would have sprung up in Judah that was related to the prophets in its seeking salvation for Judah by a return to the pure worship of Jahweh; the movement differed from that of the prophets, however, in that it also sought support from the law in its struggle to reach its goal, and sought to use the law in its attempt to eradicate especially the worship on the "high places" that had been adopted from the Canaanites. The way had, of course, been paved for this course of events by the building of the temple and the efforts of the kings of Judah to make the temple the center of the cultus, efforts that had no chance of succeeding until after the fall of Samaria, when only the small kingdom of Judah remained.

In order to prove the thesis of the late origin of Deuteronomy 12, appeals are made to various data that are supposed to show that Israel could not have had a law like this since ancient times. These data are of three kinds.

1. The stipulation of Exodus 20:24, "Make an altar of earth for me and sacrifice on it your burnt offerings and fellowship offerings, your sheep and goats and your cattle. Wherever I cause my name to be honored, I will come to you and bless you." This command is thought to belong to Israel's oldest laws (the "Book of the Covenant"). It is

7

then pointed out that this law speaks of bringing offerings pleasing to the Lord in *various* places. This ancient lawgiver thus knew nothing of the demand to sacrifice in only one place.

2. The practice of ancient Israel, it is claimed, also agrees with this. The oldest historical books show that the bringing of offerings in various places (the "high places") was not only common practice in ancient times, but was also considered lawful, since it was done by men who were representatives of Israel's legitimate religion. *Gideon,* at the Lord's command, built an altar "on the top of [the] bluff" at Ophrah (Judg. 6:26); *Samuel* offered in a number of places (Bethel, Gilgal, Mizpah, Ramah); *Solomon* offered sacrifices "on the most important high place" at Gibeon (1 Kings 3:4–5); *Elijah* offered on Mount Carmel (1 Kings 18:32) and complained that the altars of the Lord (i.e., the altars on the "high places") had been broken down (1 Kings 19:10).

3. The earliest writing prophets (i.e., those before the time of Josiah) do not condemn the worship on the "high places" as such.

B. *Counterarguments*

Although the theory outlined above was dominant for a long time, it ran into opposition from the very beginning. It was, of course, rejected in principle by Bible-believing scholars. More conservative critics imposed limitations on the critical theory by assuming that Deuteronomy contained a core that dated from the time of the Judges or even from Moses' time.

But more recently opposition has arisen from within the critical camp against the premise of the theory—the close connection between Deuteronomy and Josiah's reform. This connection has been disputed from several angles. While some would ascribe the law code of Deuteronomy to a time considerably earlier than Josiah's reign, others have suggested that Deuteronomy is of even more recent origin and cannot have come into being until shortly after the Captivity. But in either case arguments are advanced that undermine the theory that for so long was considered to be beyond question.

We begin the presentation of our own view by noting that the theory of the school of Wellhausen is in direct contradiction to the testimony of the Scriptures. The record of the finding of the Book of the Law in 2 Kings 22 clearly assumes that the book in question had existed and had been authoritative since ancient times (cf. vv. 13, 16). The critical theory must assume that the author of this chapter did not understand what really took place (or that he falsified the record).

The critical theory also rejects entirely all that the Book of Deuteronomy itself says concerning the origin of its contents (see below, sec. 3). Some have simply assumed that deceit was involved: The author, in order to make his creation carry weight, gave it the imprint of a Mosaic and divine origin (the same could also have happened after the Captivity with the priestly laws). In addition, the historical tradition was then reworked in the spirit of this spurious legislation. Thus it is understandable that the radical critics have declared the entire Old Testament to be a falsification, done in such a subtle and cunning way that it has fooled the world for centuries.

Less radical critics have, of course, pronounced a much milder verdict on the same set of supposed facts. Thus, one of them still speaks of deceit but calls it "pious deceit" because of the good intentions behind it; this "piousness" would then, in fact, be based on the principle that the end justifies the means. Others say that we cannot speak of deceit here; they claim that among less-developed peoples a new law is often proclaimed under the name of an ancient lawgiver without deceit being involved, since everyone knows what is being done. But the examples used to support this view are less than convincing. Furthermore, Israel's laws are so interwoven with the historical narrative that the latter then must also be considered little more than embellishment. All this certainly contradicts the intent of the Scriptures. For example, when according to 2 Kings 22:13 Josiah speaks of the Lord's anger that "burns against us because our fathers have not obeyed the words of this book," the antiquity of the book is presented as an awesome reality that has nothing to do with "style" or "form." And there can be no doubt that the author of 2 Kings is in agreement with Josiah's statement.

There is thus no need to elaborate on the fact that the critical view is entirely unacceptable to anyone who accepts the authority of the Scriptures. Nevertheless, the question remains whether there are arguments (apart from the argument from the authority of the Scriptures) that show that the critical view is untenable and challenges the reliability of the Scriptures on inadequate grounds. We would point to the following:

1. The contents and character of Deuteronomy (see above, sec. 1) reflect the distinctive features of Moses' time to a much greater degree than those of Josiah's time and thus confirm in more than one

way the testimony of the book concerning its own origin. Moses is generally the speaker—a fact the critics claim to be mere embellishment. But the later author who supposedly put these words into Moses' mouth then must have been able to enter into Moses' thought world with exceptional skill.

The content and tone of Moses' words are generally entirely in accord with what could be expected at this particular time, when the wilderness journey lay behind and Canaan before Israel. We point to the following specifics:

a. The frequent reminders of Egypt (5:15; 7:15; 11:10; 15:15; 16:12; et al.) bear the stamp of authenticity. We note especially the curious comparison between Egypt and Canaan in 11:10.

b. The regulations of 7:1ff., which forbid the Israelites to make a treaty with the Canaanites or to mix with them, while enjoining Israel to "totally destroy" them, would be meaningless in the time of Josiah or of Hezekiah. The same is true of the manner in which Israel is exhorted not to fear the strength of the nations (7:17ff.).

c. Very important also is the collection of laws in chapters 12–26. There is not much room here for the concept of embellishment. These laws are intended for concrete situations, and a number of them could not very well have originated in the time of Josiah.

d. The severe punishment imposed on idolatry (13:6–11; 12–15) would have been impossible to carry out at a time when that sin was rampant. The critics therefore allow for the possibility that not all laws recorded in Deuteronomy date from a late period, but that some had existed for a long time as common law; some conservative critics would go as far back as the time of the Judges or even of Moses.

e. In the law concerning the king (17:14ff.), the stipulation that the king must not be a foreigner certainly does not reflect Josiah's time when the hereditary succession of David's house had been established for many centuries.

f. We also find in these chapters the commands to exterminate the Canaanites (20:16–18) and the Amalekites (25:17–19), neither of which fits Josiah's time.

2. In the days of Josiah, according to the critical view, a book of laws of recent origin but attributed to Moses was successfully introduced as Mosaic, so successfully that this falsification became the basis for a drastic reform of the cultus throughout the land. It is surprising that this could happen and that no one apparently raised any doubts as to the authenticity of the book, all the more so because there were many who

stood to gain by exposing the fraud, such as the idol priests and the priests of the "high places" who were affected by this reformation.
3. The specific connection between Josiah's reformation and the law of Deuteronomy 12 is highly debatable. Even if we could be certain that the Book of the Law of 2 Kings 22 was indeed Deuteronomy or contained its substance (which we do indeed consider probable; see below), this would still not justify the critical position in the least. For although in our opinion it cannot be denied that Deuteronomy 12 envisions the abolition of the worship in the "high places" (see below), and although Josiah's reform also was in part directed against the "high places" (cf. 2 Kings 23:8–9), it is incorrect to see this abolition as dominating Josiah's reformation to the extent the critical theory assumes, or to hold that his reformation was the result of an action against the "high places" that then would have found expression in Deuteronomy 12.[4] The biblical narrative concerning Josiah's reform efforts focuses rather on the abolition of idol worship,[5] and indicates that his efforts had begun prior to the finding of the Book of the Law— the book was found during the cleaning and restoring of the temple. Furthermore, according to 2 Chronicles 34, Josiah's reforms had already begun in the eighth and twelfth years of his reign.

4. The appeal to history—the law of Exodus 20:4, the actions of Samuel and others, and the attitude of the earlier prophets towards the "high places"—to prove that the law of Deuteronomy 12 did not exist in ancient times does not take into consideration the prophetic character of this law. It was given for the time when the Lord would not only have brought Israel into Canaan, but when they would have rest from their enemies and would live in peace (v. 10). This law was thus intended for a time when an orderly situation would exist. Until then a central sanctuary as the only cultic center was an impossibility, and the offering on the "high places" remained excusable (1 Kings 3:2–3).

It is easy to understand that the requirement of one place of sacrifice was not an absolute command. Deuteronomy 12 itself indicates that

---

[4]Also important is Oestreicher's observation that the transfer of the priests to Jerusalem, mentioned in 2 Kings 23:8, is not based on Deuteronomy, nor the fact that these priests are barred from serving at the altar (v. 9); *Das deuteronomische Grundgesetz* (Gütersloh, 1923), pp. 35ff.

[5]The fact that Deuteronomy 12 speaks in the first place against the *idolatrous* cultus on the "high places" does not diminish the force of this argument (see commentary on Deut. 12:4–7). At issue is whether Josiah's reformation was based specifically on Deuteronomy 12. This cannot be said of his struggle against idolatry, since idolatry is certainly not condemned only in Deuteronomy 12.

this demand was subordinate to a higher goal—the prevention of idolatry. The cultus on the "high places" could thus still be excused to the extent that it was practiced without pagan admixtures (see commentary on 12:4–7). The historical data to which the critics appeal acquire a different meaning when viewed in this light. Because of their importance we shall discuss these matters in more detail.

C. *Deuteronomy 12 and history*

We begin by noting that according to the Scriptures the entire cultus was centered around the tabernacle during the wilderness period. But the same is therefore not necessarily true after Israel entered Canaan. Besides, this argument has little force against the critics, since they declare most of what the Scriptures say concerning the tabernacle to be unhistorical.

But there are other testimonies, accepted as historical also by the critics, that say that *ancient Israel in Canaan had a central sanctuary*—even though this sanctuary did not function as the *only* cultic center. The Book of the Covenant, which the critics acknowledge to be of ancient origin, points to this fact when it stipulates that all men must appear before the Lord three times per year (Exod. 23:14–17). This clearly points to a central sanctuary. Furthermore, the context speaks of "the house of the LORD your God" (v. 19).

The data in the historical books are also in agreement with this. According to nondisputed historical data, there was a "house of the Lord" in *Shiloh* during the period of the Judges that was the recognized center of worship (1 Sam. 1:7). We add immediately that, according to the Scriptures, this sanctuary was the tabernacle, which had been placed here in Joshua's day (Josh. 18:1); it was later moved, first to Nob and then to Gibeon.

In Saul's time there was a sanctuary at *Nob* with the bread of the Presence and the ephod; a large number of priests served here, whose head was Ahimelech (1 Sam. 21:6, 9; 22:9ff.). We can assume that the priests of Shiloh had been transferred to Nob together with the tabernacle, perhaps by Saul, who may have wanted the sanctuary to be close to him.

At the beginning of his reign, Solomon went to *Gibeon* to bring offerings, "for that was the most important high place" (1 Kings 3:4). Elsewhere we find that the tabernacle was already there in David's time (1 Chron. 16:39; 21:29; 2 Chron. 1:3).

It is clear that this sanctuary, located first at Shiloh and later at Nob and Gibeon, had a unique importance among the cultic places of ancient Israel. Shiloh was a place of national importance also for other reasons: Here Joshua had his headquarters for quite some time; here he cast the lot for the division of the land "in the presence of the LORD" (Josh. 18:8ff.); here the towns of the Levites were chosen (Josh. 21:2). The faithful went to the house of the Lord in Shiloh annually (1 Sam. 1:3; 2:14). We also hear of an annual festival at Shiloh, celebrated in honor of the Lord (Judg. 21:19) and of an organized priesthood that brought offerings here. At Nob we also hear of the bread of the Presence and of the ephod. The national significance of the sanctuary at Nob also appears from the fact that the sword of Goliath, captured by David, was placed here as a votive offering (1 Sam. 21:9). This sanctuary, located first at Shiloh and later at Nob and Gibeon, was in fact the *only legitimate sanctuary.*[6]

A certain duality developed when the tabernacle and the ark were separated. While the tabernacle was moved to Nob and later to Gibeon,[7] the ark, after it had been captured by the Philistines and returned, was stored in Beth Shemesh and later in Kiriath Jearim (1 Sam. 6:12, 21); still later it was brought to Zion by David (2 Sam. 6; 1 Chron. 15–16). In Zion it was placed in a new tent built for the purpose (2 Sam. 6:17; 1 Chron. 16:1; 2 Chron. 1:4). Offerings were brought on this occasion, and David instituted observances that were to be carried out daily by the Levites and priests (1 Chron. 16:4ff.); the description of these observances, however, mentions only singing and music. Apparently no offerings were instituted (but see Keil on 1 Chron. 16:39); at least, specific mention is made of the daily offerings at Gibeon on the altar of burnt offering that stood by the tabernacle (1 Chron. 16:39–40).

On the other hand, we must admit that the existence of such a central sanctuary does not necessarily mean that *all* offerings had to be brought there as required in Deuteronomy 12. The practice of ancient Israel, and also the divine revelations on which this practice was in part based, show that *this* ideal had at that time not as yet found fulfillment. Besides the central sanctuary at Shiloh (and later at Nob and Gibeon),

---

[6]The private cultus place of Micah in Judges 17:5, which included a "shrine" (NIV; lit., "house of *'elohim*"), had a distinctly illicit character; it is the origin of the cultus at Dan (Judg. 18).

[7]The tabernacle was moved to the temple after it was built and was probably stored in one of the side rooms as a sacred relic (1 Kings 8:4; 2 Chron. 5:5).

there were several other places where, after Israel's settling in Canaan, Jahweh was worshiped for shorter or longer periods.[8] Two of these—at Gibeah and Ramah—are specifically called "high places" (as is also the place of sacrifice at Gibeon, mentioned above, where the tabernacle stood at that time), even though no mention is made of a sanctuary. When on *Mount Ebal* Joshua wrote the law of Moses on large stones (cf. Deut. 27:2), he also built an altar there at the Lord's command and offered on it (Josh. 8:31–32). At the end of his life he gathered the tribes of Israel at *Shechem* "before God" (Josh. 24:1) and at the end of the proceedings took a large stone and set it up "under the oak near the holy place of the LORD" (Josh. 24:26); it was undoubtedly customary at that time to bring offerings at this "holy place" where one appeared "before God." It may have been the same place where Abraham built an altar (Gen. 12:6–7) and where Jacob buried the foreign idols "under the oak at Shechem" (Gen. 35:2, 4; cf. also Judg. 9:6).

In Judges 2:5 we read of an offering brought by the people at *Bokim*, and in the days of Jephthah there appears to have been a cultus place at *Mizpah in Gilead,* as indicated by the statement that Jephthah spoke there "before the LORD" (Judg. 11:11).

Gideon built an altar to the Lord, which he called "The LORD is Peace," in *Ophrah* under the oak where the angel of the Lord had appeared to him; this altar was still there when the narrative was written (Judg. 6:24; cf. v. 19). He also built at the Lord's command an altar "on the top of this bluff" to replace his father's altar to Baal (Judg. 6:26). Manoah sacrificed on a rock near *Zorah* in Dan when an angel of the Lord appeared to him (Judg. 13:19–20). The people gathered "before the LORD" at *Mizpah west of the Jordan* (Judg. 20:1; 21:5); later Samuel gathered the people there to pray for them and offered to the Lord (1 Sam. 7:5, 9–10). There he also cast the sacred lots "before the LORD" and deposited the document containing the regulations for the kingship (1 Sam. 10–19ff.).

Bethel is also mentioned as a place where the people "inquire of God" (Judg. 20:18),[9] where they gathered "before God," and where they brought offerings (Judg. 20:26; 21:2). In Samuel's time there is still mention of "going up to God at Bethel" (1 Sam. 10:3).

In Samuel's time we also hear of a "high place" near *Gibeah,* hence

---

[8]We do not refer here to the worship of the Baals and Astartes or to the mixing of the Jahweh cultus and Baal worship that probably emerged relatively early.

[9]An alternative view is that the reference is not to Bethel, but to the "house of God" (the literal meaning of "Bethel") in Shiloh.

called "Gibeah of God" (1 Sam. 10:5). Saul is made king "in the presence of the Lord" at *Gilgal,* where sacrifices were brought on this occasion, as well as at other times (1 Sam. 11:15; 13:9; 15:21; cf. 15:33). On a hill outside *Ramah* was a "high place" where under Samuel's direction an offering feast was held (1 Sam. 9:12ff.); the altar Samuel built at Ramah probably also stood here (1 Sam. 7:17). We also read that Samuel went to *Bethlehem* to sacrifice, inviting Jesse and his sons together with the elders of the town (1 Sam. 16). Later we hear of a sacrifice brought annually at Bethlehem, "made there for his [David's] whole clan" (1 Sam. 20:6, 29).

During David's reign we hear of a place of sacrifice in *Hebron.* Absalom requested permission to fulfill a vow (2 Sam. 15:7–9) and held an offering feast there (v. 12). In this light we should also understand the fact that David had earlier made a "compact" with the elders of Israel "before the LORD" (2 Sam. 5:3). In David's time the summit of the *Mount of Olives* was another place "where people used to worship God" (2 Sam. 15:32); it is, however, possible that, since we do not hear of a place of sacrifice here, this expression refers to the custom of worshiping God who dwelt in the sanctuary on Mount Zion. David's son Adonijah also sacrificed near *En Rogel* (1 Kings 1:9).

It is not equally clear in all the above references that a fixed place of sacrifice is in view. It is possible that a temporary altar was built in a given place in response to a special event. No further mention of its use as a cultic place of sacrifice is made in connection with Joshua's offering on Mount Ebal, the people's offering at Bokim, or Manoah's offering on the rock of Zorah—this in contrast to one of Gideon's altars. But it is probable, also in view of the statement "wherever I cause my name to be honored" (Exod. 20:24–26; RSV, "in every place where . . ."), that the special events that were the reason why these places were used for offerings in the first place would also be a reason for them to be dedicated as permanent places of sacrifice. But since the reader would be familiar with them there was no need to make special mention of this.

It should be noted that the speaking or gathering "before God" or "before the LORD," mentioned several times in the above references, could simply mean that the people placed themselves before the Lord in a solemn ceremony, especially in prayer or by the swearing of an oath (cf. Keil on Judg. 11:11). But in several of the references quoted it is clear that the expression relates to the presence of an altar where offerings were brought to the Lord. And usually this appears to be not merely an altar built for a specific occasion, but rather a more permanent cultus place.

Besides these cultus places that are known by name, there were undoubtedly others that were also dedicated to the true worship of Jahweh. We have few data concerning this from the time of the Judges, but during the period of the kings there were apparently many "high places," especially when they had become unlawful, i.e., after the building of the temple (1 Kings 3:2); the cultus on these "high places" usually was of a paganized nature.

We have thus seen that ancient Israel worshiped Jahweh in places other than those where the central sanctuary stood. This practice undoubtedly found some legal basis in the law of Exodus 20:24–26, which speaks of offering "in every place where I cause my name to be remembered" (RSV). It would appear to us that it cannot be denied that this speaks of various coexisting places of sacrifice. An alternative view would be that Exodus 20:24–26 speaks of the various places where the central sanctuary stood in succession; but this seems unlikely, both because of the wording and because of the facts of later history. Exodus 20 specifies that the altar must be built of earth or undressed stones, which justifies the opinion that the lawgiver does not have the altar of the central sanctuary in mind here but a simpler altar: an elevated platform of earth or rocks on which the wood for the offering is placed. This is what the altars of the patriarchs probably looked like as well as the altars of the Israelites before the building of the tabernacle, including the altars Moses built at Rephidim (Exod. 17:15) and at Sinai (Exod. 24:4). The later altars on Mount Ebal (Deut. 27:5; Josh. 8:31) and on Mount Carmel are described similarly. Exodus 20 thus codified an ancient custom. And even though the laws concerning the tabernacle would be given shortly after this law, it was nevertheless not without significance. For one thing, Moses would have to build such an altar before the tabernacle was built (Exod. 24:4). But also, the provision of Exodus 20 could remain in force even after the tabernacle was built and even after Moses had given the law of Deuteronomy 12. In order to understand this we must keep in mind the intent of this law.

As we saw, Deuteronomy 12:5 and 14 limit offering to the central sanctuary, and thus do indeed state a different rule than Exodus 20:24–26. But we must not lose sight of the prophetic character of Deuteronomy 12 (see sec. 1), which presupposes an orderly situation. As long as this had not become a reality only the broader regulation of

Exodus 20 could be applied. It is from this perspective that the above-mentioned historical facts to which the critical school has made their appeal must be viewed. A situation like that presupposed in Deuteronomy 12 did not become a lasting reality until the reign of David, who then took the initiative toward the building of the temple, which was completed by Solomon. Until that time, therefore, the offering on the "high places," although outside the norm, could be excused.

It is true that even before David's time Israel knew periods during which the supposition of Deuteronomy 12 that Israel would have rest from its enemies had become a partial reality; during these periods the central sanctuary at Shiloh occupied an important place in Israel's religious life. But it is understandable that during these periods no attempt was made to make this sanctuary into the *only* place of sacrifice—the conditions were too uncertain and the national unity too precarious for this. Indeed, those periods of peace did not last. Especially after the rejection of Eli and his sons a period of great confusion began. The ark was carried away, and the Philistines were supreme. It is precisely from this period that the critics derive their seemingly strongest arguments. But it is quite natural (and does not contradict Deut. 12) that Samuel had to make do with local altars during this period. It has been pointed out that Samuel continued to sacrifice in various locations even after the ark had been returned, and that the previous condition of relative stability was not immediately restored; the ark first found a temporary home in Kiriath Jearim to wait for a better time when the Lord would give Israel rest—a time that came with David and Solomon.

It is true that the law of Deuteronomy 12 was not put into practice as soon as Solomon had built the temple. The remarks in 1 Kings 3:3 that Solomon "offered sacrifices and burned incense on the high places" may refer to the time before the building of the temple (cf. v. 2) and thus would prove nothing. We are not told, on the other hand, that Solomon sought to abolish the cultus on the "high places" after the building of the temple. But this cannot prove that the law of Deuteronomy 12 did not exist at that time. There were undoubtedly problems in immediately making the temple the only place of sacrifice as soon as the temple had been completed. Furthermore, Solomon, who to please his wives did not keep himself entirely from pagan practices, may very well have fallen short on this point, as is even more true of his successors.

On the other hand, we must note that of none of the God-fearing kings after Solomon is it said that he sacrificed "on the high places" (although this *is* said of the people during their reigns). But we also have testimony concerning various kings before Josiah that they opposed the cultus on the "high places." The fact that these statements are found primarily in Chronicles is no justification for simply setting them aside. Mention is made of a cultus reform by Asa (1 Kings 15:12–13) that included the removal of the "high places," the sacred stones, and the Asherah poles (2 Chron. 14:2–4). Of Jehoshaphat it is said that he again removed the "high places" and the Asherah poles from Judah (2 Chron. 17:6; 19:3). The statements that in the days of these kings the "high places" did not disappear (1 Kings 15:14; cf. 2 Chron. 15:17; 20:33) do not necessarily mean anything more than that these two reformations did not have any lasting success in this respect.

In 2 Kings 18:4 (cf. v. 22) it is said of Hezekiah that he removed the "high places," smashed the sacred stones, and cut down the Asherah poles, while those who celebrated the Passover that Hezekiah organized afterward went out and destroyed the "high places" and the altars, a reaction that reached even into Israel. This reformation was followed by that of Josiah. The historicity of the reformations cannot be challenged on the grounds that they have left little trace in history, as indicated by the fact that the old evil returned also after Josiah's death. Only after the Captivity was the ideal of Deuteronomy 12 realized.

Elijah is the first among the prophets to whom the critics appeal. But he, even more than Samuel, lived under highly abnormal conditions. The temple, it is true, had been built, but the division of the kingdom had separated the northern tribes from the temple in Jerusalem, not only politically, but also with respect to the cultus. The Northern Kingdom developed an illegitimate and paganized cultus—and under Ahab even a Baal cultus. It is understandable that in his struggle against Baal, Elijah complained about the tearing down of the altars of the Lord without entering into the question whether they were fully legitimate, as we can also understand that he made use of an altar on Mount Carmel with divine approval.

It cannot be proven that the *writing prophets* from before Josiah's time approved of the cultus on the "high places"; rather, they most strongly disapproved of it. All that can be said is that as a rule they condemned this cultus on the basis of its paganized character rather than on the consideration that it was in formal conflict with the regulation concerning one central sanctuary. On the other hand, we should note the following:

1. Hosea found himself in the northern kingdom in a position similar to that of Elijah.
2. The prophets were in general not primarily concerned with the implementation of the law in its formal aspects—this was the concern of the priests. But apart from this, it is quite understandable that they placed full emphasis on the greatest evil: the *paganized character* of this cultus.
3. When Hosea says that Ephraim built many altars "for sin offerings" (8:11), he does make a connection between this sinning and the multitude of altars. No less important is the fact that Hosea and the other prophets before Josiah consider Zion to be the place where the Lord dwells and reveals Himself (Hos. 3:5; Amos 1:2; Mic. 4:2).

III. AUTHORSHIP: A POSITIVE APPROACH

In the preceding section we have attempted to explain that the arguments presented by the school of Wellhausen against the self-witness of Deuteronomy concerning its Mosaic origin cannot be considered valid. We shall now take a closer look at this self-witness and seek to determine what conclusions may be drawn from it.

Deuteronomy presents a clearer self-witness concerning its authorship than any of the other books of the Pentateuch. The outline of the contents given earlier (see sec. 1) shows that the book presents itself as largely Mosaic—it contains mostly discourses by Moses (cf. 1:5; 5:1; 29:2). But also the actual writing down of the material is expressly attributed to Moses. In 31:9 we read, "So Moses wrote down this law and gave it to the priests, the sons of Levi, who carried the ark of the covenant of the LORD, and to all the elders of Israel" (cf. v. 24). Although it is not entirely clear precisely what is meant by "this law," we are convinced that this expression, when found in Deuteronomy (cf. 1:5; 4:8, 44; 17:8–9; 27:3, 26; 29:20, 28; 30:10; 32:46), is always restricted to Deuteronomy and does not in some cases (including 31:9) refer to the whole Pentateuch (as Keil believes). In some instances this restricted meaning is indisputable (e.g., 1:5), and in none of the other cases is there any reason to adopt a different meaning.

On the other hand, it is uncertain whether "this law" begins with 1:6 or later (5:1 or even 12:1). In this respect the expression appears not to have been used in the same sense throughout. In 1:5 ("Moses began to expound this law") the intent appears to be that "this law" begins in 1:6. It is possible to argue on the basis of the verb "explain" that we should take the first four (or the first eleven) chapters not as a law but as an explanation or exposition of the law. But "this law" can scarcely be a law the author does not state until almost four (or eleven) chapters later. The only natural explanation is that "this law" begins immediately after 1:5; the Hebrew verb rendered "expound" in the NIV should thus be taken in the sense of "unfold" or "declare" (KJV, ASV) rather than "explain" (RSV). Furthermore, "law" is thus to be understood in the broader sense of the prophetic instruction in the law by Moses, which encompasses not only commands but also exhortations and historical reminiscences.

But 4:44, in contrast to 1:5, appears to indicate that "the law" begins in 5:1; similarly, the end of 4:8 ("this body of laws I am setting before you today") seems to imply that the law is yet to follow, while the equation of "this body of laws" with "decrees and laws" cannot well refer to chapters 1–4.

In 27:3 Moses gives instructions that "all the words of this law" be written on large stones coated with plaster. Here we can think of the possibility—since these instructions follow immediately after chapter 26—that this refers only to the collection of laws of chapters 12–26. But it is in our opinion more likely that the earlier discourses (beginning with either 1:6 or 5:1) are also in view; especially the Ten Words (5:6–22) could scarcely be omitted from such a record.

It is in our opinion also unlikely that the "law" that was written down according to 31:9, 24 would have included only chapters 12–26; the mere fact that this statement is not made until chapter 31 would point in a different direction. On the other hand, we cannot be certain whether the "law" of 31:9 and 24 begins with 1:6 or 5:1, considering the difference in wording between 1:5 and 4:44. There is thus room for the possibility that chapters 1–4 were added by someone else, yet in such a manner that the essential content of these chapters represents what Moses said, which means that this person must have had access to adequate information.

With respect to the end of "this law," it is most natural to limit the statement of 31:9 to what precedes it. This means that we do not have any testimony regarding chapter 31, which consists mostly of words spoken by Moses himself or by the Lord to Moses; however, someone else could have recorded these.

On the other hand, the Song of Moses mentioned in chapter 31 and recorded in chapter 32 is expressly said to have been written down by Moses (31:22). Moses' blessing (ch. 33) is said to have been pronounced by Moses, but no mention is made of his writing it down; there are even reasons for conjecturing that it was written down in its entirety by a later hand (see commentary). Any indication of authorship is lacking with respect to chapter 34 (the story of Moses' death); we may conjecture that this was written by, e.g., Joshua, and then probably later in his life (see commentary).

All this would indicate that Moses is named as the author of chapters 5–30 (or 1–30) and chapter 32. However, this does not necessarily apply to the very letter of those chapters, but rather to their main contents. After all, the fact that Moses wrote down "this law" does not of necessity mean that he also wrote a historical note such as 4:41–43, or that the various superscriptions are from his hand (1:1–5; et al.). There are even reasons for thinking that this is not the case; one of these is the variation in meaning of the expression "across the Jordan." In the two passages just mentioned this phrase means "east of the Jordan" (1:1, 5; 4:41, 46, 47, 49), while it usually means "west of the Jordan" when used by Moses (3:20, 25; 11:30), which would reflect Moses' actual perspective.[10] This would seem to indicate that 1:1–5 and the historical section in 4:41–43 were written by someone else, someone who lived west of the Jordan.[11]

But neither do we have to assume that the discourses and the laws of chapters 12–26 were written down by Moses in the exact form in which they lie before us, down to the last letter. In the first place, we have already noted that chapters 1–4 (or more precisely, 1:6–4:40) are not necessarily included in "this law" that Moses wrote down according to 31:9. Yet we should not place too much emphasis on this; the agreement in language and style between these and the following chapters argue for one author. Furthermore, since the testimony of the Scriptures that Moses *spoke* these words is valid for us, it is most probable that he would also have *written* them down.

On the other hand, several verses in these chapters would appear not to be from Moses' hand. In 2:10–12 the conclusion, "just as Israel did in the land the LORD gave them as their possession," points to an author from the time when Israel lived in Canaan (the NIV places these verses in parentheses). Also, the historical data in these verses do not fit well

---

[10]The NIV renders the phrase literally in 3:20, 25; 11:30 ("across the Jordan," "beyond the Jordan"), but interpretatively in 1:1, 5; 4:41, 46, 47, 49; and in 3:8 ("east of the Jordan"). For a more detailed discussion of this phrase, see Appendix 1 in the commentary on Joshua in this series—TRANS.

[11]In 3:8, where Moses is the speaker, the expression refers to the land east of the Jordan. If this is not due to a later redaction, we have to assume that the expression here is a fixed term for the land east of the Jordan.

in an address of Moses to the people; they interrupt the recounting of the Lord's words to Moses. There is thus every reason to assume that these verses are of later origin. We find a similar historical note in 2:20–23, which leads to the same supposition. And it is no different with 3:9, 11—especially the observation concerning Og's sarcophagus (cf. NIV mg.) would not have made much sense coming from Moses, who was Og's contemporary; the same is true of "to this day" in 3:14.

It goes without saying that we assume such additions to have found a place in the Scriptures under God's special providence and that they are therefore indeed part of the Holy Scriptures. But the manner in which these later additions found a place in Deuteronomy can be viewed in a number of ways. If we assume that 1:6–4:40 was added to the rest of the book by a later redactor, then it would also be possible that this same redactor inserted the various observations just mentioned into the text. On the other hand, they may have been glosses (annotations in the margin) that were later incorporated into the text.

But there is also no reason to deny the possibility of later additions or clarifications in chapters 5–30, to which the statement in 31:9 definitely applies; not only is this true of the discourses, but also of the special laws of chapters 12–26. When we consider that the law of chapter 12 concerning the centralization of the cultus consists of three parts, each presenting the demand of one place of sacrifice in its own way, then the question arises whether these might not originally have been three independent versions of this law, which were placed side by side to complement one another. It then becomes probable that we can see here the hand of Moses as well as that of a later redactor.

IV. DEUTERONOMY AND THE BOOK OF THE LAW OF JOSIAH

As we have seen, the starting point of the theory of the school of Wellhausen as to the time of the origin of the Pentateuch is the idea that the Book of the Law that was found in the temple during Josiah's reign contained the main contents of Deuteronomy. However, the identification of this Book of the Law with Deuteronomy is not entirely unique to the school of Wellhausen; it is, e.g., already found in some of the church fathers. It would therefore appear that this question deserves to be considered separately, apart from the critical theory that came to be connected with it later. We want to state at the outset that the identification of Josiah's Book of the Law with Deuteronomy has, in our opinion, the weight of probability on its side, even though we cannot decide this with absolute certainty.

We must agree that the threats of curse in chapters 27–29 were suited to bring about a dismay such as that described in 2 Kings 22:13, and also that the abolition of the worship "on the high places" was a part of Josiah's reformation (2 Kings 23:8). Nor can we deny that this abolition is demanded in Deuteronomy 12 (see above). But these arguments per se are insufficient.

The threats of curse in Deuteronomy could also have had their effect if the Book of the Law that was found in Josiah's time had been the entire Pentateuch. And if the book in question was a collection of laws unknown to us (a collection that was probably used in the temple), it can be assumed that this collection also contained threats of curse, since these threats are not unique to Deuteronomy but are also found elsewhere in the Pentateuch (Lev. 26:14ff.). The appeal to Deuteronomy 12 (cf. 2 Kings 23:8) loses much of its force when we consider that the abolition of the worship on the "high places" was certainly not the main thrust of Josiah's reformation (see above); rather, the emphasis was on the abolition of idolatry, which was not an implementation of specifically Deuteronomic demands.

And when 2 Kings 23:8 speaks of the breaking down of the "high place of the satyrs,"[12] it should be noted that this demon worship is prohibited only in Leviticus 17:7 and not at all in Deuteronomy. However, the latter does not prove that the Book of the Law of Josiah must have contained more than Deuteronomy. It is not necessary to assume that the ignorance concerning the Lord's service was so profound among Josiah and his contemporaries that the king needed a definite statement from the Book of the Law for each and every one of his reform measures. It is much more probable that the direct impact of the Book of the Law was limited to the generating of a general impression.

We are thus of the opinion that we cannot draw definite conclusions concerning the precise contents of the Book of the Law on the basis of Josiah's measures, and that we therefore cannot identify Deuteronomy with this Book of the Law on the basis of its contents.

The first reason we nevertheless prefer the identification of the Book of the Law with Deuteronomy is that Deuteronomy 31:26 states that "this Book of the Law" (which in our opinion refers to Deuteronomy rather than the Pentateuch) was to be placed beside the ark. It would

---

[12]I.e., demons represented as a goat. This reading is based on an emendation of the text (cf. NEB, TEV, JB). The NIV renders this phrase "the shrines at the gates"—TRANS.

therefore be highly probable that the Book of the Law that was found was a copy of Deuteronomy, which had been placed in the Most Holy Place of the temple to satisfy this command and had been moved from its proper place during the period of apostasy.

Another reason why it is less likely that Josiah's Book of the Law contained the entire Pentateuch lies in what is said about its reading. The statements that Shaphan read it, first himself (2 Kings 22:8) and later in the presence of the king (v. 10), can be understood in a limited sense (cf. "read from it" in 2 Chron. 34:18).[13] But when according to 2 Kings 23:2 the king (we may assume by means of the priests) "read in their hearing [i.e., of 'all the people from the least to the greatest'] all the words of the Book of the Covenant, which had been found in the temple of the LORD," this cannot but mean that the book was read in its entirety; we should therefore think of a book of lesser size than the Pentateuch.

The view that the expression "the Book of the Law" in 2 Kings 22:8 can only refer to the Pentateuch (Keil) is in our opinion incorrect, if only because in Hebrew idiom "the book of the law" can mean "that particular book of the law that I have found," in which case the expression would be more accurately rendered "a book of the law." But even if we retain "the Book of the Law" (as we prefer), a reference such as Deuteronomy 31:26 (see above) indicates that it may very well refer to Deuteronomy.

Finally, there is little room for the view that would see the Book of the Law of Josiah as a collection of laws not known to us if we consider Deuteronomy, and especially the regulation of Deuteronomy 31:26, to be Mosaic.

V. DEUTERONOMY AND THE COVENANT

For an understanding of the character of the Old Testament revelation of God, it is instructive to examine the relationship between the Lord and Israel as it is described in Deuteronomy.

A. *Israel, the Lord's People*

The special relationship between the Lord and Israel that forms the basis of the entire Old Testament revelation is very much in the

---

[13]The NIV inserts "from it" also in 2 Kings 22:10; the Hebrew reads "read it" — TRANS.

foreground in Deuteronomy: The Lord is the God of Israel, Israel is the Lord's people. This does not mean that this relationship involves only the nation as a whole and not its individual members. Rather, the members of the nation are included in the covenant to the fullest extent also for their personal lives. The singular "you," which addresses Israel as a nation, is continually interchanged with the singular or plural "you" that addresses the Israelites more individually. But this personal aspect always stands against the background of belonging to Israel, the nation that as a whole has been placed in a special relationship to the Lord. This Israel is called "the assembly of the LORD" in 23:1; in light of the full revelation we can say that Israel is the church of God in its Old Testament form.

But this does not alter the fact that Israel is a national-political entity, i.e., a nation in the full sense of the word, a fact that is especially prominent in Deuteronomy. Even when Israel is called "the assembly of the LORD" this national-political character is not negated, as we can see from the stipulation that certain nations (the Ammonites and Moabites) are excluded from joining this "assembly" (23:3). Again and again Israel is called the seed of Abraham, Isaac, and Jacob, and the fact that members of other nations could also be admitted into Israel cannot nullify its character as a people in a national-political sense. The latter comes to light very clearly in the laws that relate especially to the national-political or the civil life; we mention only the laws concerning the king (17:14ff.), the military, jurisprudence, marriage, and the laws of a social nature.

It is important to note immediately in connection with this the manner in which Deuteronomy (more so than some other parts of the Law) places the earthly-temporal in the foreground. Blessing and curse, reward and punishment, life and death are mentioned, but always in an earthly-temporal sense (a point to which we shall return), and this is intimately linked with the fact that these laws relate to Israel as a people in a national-political sense.

It is to this Israel that the words are spoken, "I am the LORD your God, who brought you out of Egypt, out of the land of slavery" (5:6). The Lord is Israel's God. And Israel is thus the Lord's people, His "treasured possession" (7:6; 14:2; 26:18). The same thought is implied in the expression "a people holy to the LORD" (7:6; 14:2, 21; 26:19; 28:9). This does not reflect in the first place a religious and moral quality of Israel, but rather the fact that Israel belongs to the Lord; indeed, the expressions "treasured possession" and "a people holy to the L<small>ORD</small>'' are sometimes placed side by side and are essentially synonymous. The relationship between the Lord and Israel reflected in these terms is the reason why Israel must refrain from idolatry, the worship of images, etc. (7:6; 14:2, 21).

B. *This relationship as covenant relationship*

The fact that the Lord is Israel's God and that Israel is His people is also stated in a more specific manner. Several times the Lord is called Israel's Father or the Father of the Israelites: "You are the children of the L<small>ORD</small> your God" (14:1). In the Song of Moses, the people as a whole are asked the question, "Is he not your Father, your Creator, who made you and formed you?" (32:6; cf. vv. 18, 20). The Lord is also seen as King over Israel in Moses' blessing (33:5).

But Deuteronomy also emphasizes the fact that this relationship between the Lord and Israel has the formal character of a *covenant* relationship. The exposition of the meaning of this covenant (we think especially of the covenant of particular grace) according to the Scriptures presents its own peculiar problems.[14] The problems begin with the Hebrew word for "covenant," for which we use the not-quite-equivalent terms "covenant" and "testament." The reason for this lies in the fact that we are dealing with the Hebrew *berît* and the Greek *diathēkē*, words that do not have an identical meaning, while our word "covenant" is an imperfect rendering used for both. However, "covenant" is the most suitable for lack of a better word and can be used, as long as we remember that we cannot draw conclusions on the basis of the English term.

The Hebrew *berît*, when applied to a covenant between two people, indicates primarily a legal relationship (or the arrangement that creates this relationship), although it is not always limited to a legal sense. When Jonathan made a covenant of friendship with David, he gave him his robe, his tunic, his sword, bow, and belt and thereby expressed his intimate relationship with David (1 Sam 18:4).

When the concept "covenant" is applied to the relationship between God and man, two things should be noted. On the one hand, the legal character of the word, which is dominant when applied to human relationships, is also important here, as we shall see below. On the other hand, there is of course a modification because the relationship

---

[14]Cf. *Het Godswoord der Profeten*, 3:150–56.

between God and man has a unique character that can never find a perfect analogy in human relationships. One aspect of this uniqueness is the inequality between the two parties: one of the parties in the relationship is absolutely dominant. Another aspect is the content of the covenant, specifically when that content is not limited to a single obligation God assumes (Gen. 8:21–22) but rather involves God entering into a relationship with human beings as *their* God. The latter undoubtedly also involves a legal relationship; this is particularly true in the case of the national covenant made with Israel, a covenant that acquires a legal character also in the sense that the permanence of the words "I am your God" is made contingent upon Israel's fulfilling certain conditions. But taken in its full meaning, the statement "I am your God" has an absolute purport: it not only creates a legal relationship, it also creates or confirms (in a much higher sense than the covenant of friendship between Jonathan and David) an all-encompassing relationship in which God with all His virtues links Himself to man with an unbreakable tie. This is why from the very beginning this covenant is called an "eternal covenant" (Gen. 17:7) and why it finds a richer disclosure in prophecies such as that of Isaiah 54:10 (the "covenant of peace" that will not be removed) and Jer. 31:31ff. (the "new covenant" the Lord will make by putting His law in their minds and hearts), and finally in the revelation of the New Testament.

We can distinguish in Scripture between references that speak explicitly of the covenant and others that state the essence but make no reference to its formal aspects or to the word *covenant*. The covenant of (particular) grace is formally mentioned for the first time in connection with Abraham, and later in relation to Israel. In both cases it is not the beginning, but rather a further confirmation and particularization of the relationship between God and those who are His. In Abraham's case, the covenant was made when he had been walking the path of faith for some time. Israel already was God's people when they left Egypt (Exod. 4:22; 5:1), and the covenant was not made until they reached Horeb. Thus, the covenant is not the beginning of Israel's special relationship with God, but rather its confirmation and formalization or particularization.[15]

Taken in its formal sense, we cannot say that the covenant concept

---

[15]Nevertheless, we can say that Israel became the Lord's people at Horeb, provided that we understand this in the above-mentioned relative sense. The Scriptures themselves even say this (of course, in a relative sense) of the making of the second covenant in the plains of Moab (Deut. 27:9).

dominates the Old Testament revelation. Indeed, the word "covenant" is entirely absent in large portions of the Old Testament. It is true that the special relationship between God and Israel underlies the Old Testament throughout, but this relationship is described in many ways. Frequently the description is limited to the general idea that the Lord is Israel's God and Israel the Lord's people. And even when the Old Testament is more specific it does not always describe the relationship as a covenant; sometimes the relationship is described as that between the Father and His child, between the Husband and His wife, or between the Shepherd and His flock.

But when we ask where the covenant of grace is present *in essence* the situation is different. From the aforementioned all-encompassing content of the covenant, and also from what is said concerning the "new covenant" in Jeremiah 31:31ff. and in the New Testament, we can infer that the covenant in its essence exists wherever God enters into a relationship of saving grace with fallen man, and that it thus went into effect immediately after the Fall (Gen. 3:15).

Viewed from this perspective, the Scriptures speak of the covenant on every page. We might add that the Scriptures also speak everywhere of God's (saving) kingship, fatherhood, etc., even though these particular *words* are not always used. The covenant, God's kingship, and His fatherhood each show an aspect of the gracious relationship of God to those whom He leads to blessedness; at the same time, each of these concepts encompasses the relationship as a whole and thus includes in essence the others as well.

It is clear that the specific covenant concept occupies an important place in Deuteronomy. For a time the critical school even held that it was Deuteronomy (which was then more or less equated with the Book of the Law found under Josiah, assumed to have been written shortly before Josiah's time) that introduced the concept of the relationship between the Lord and Israel as a covenant in order to replace the ancient concept of a primitive, natural relationship. This is, of course, in direct contradiction to what is stated in Deuteronomy itself and elsewhere in the Scriptures, viz., that the covenant was actually made at Horeb with Israel (before that it was with the patriarchs). For that matter, many critical scholars still accept the fact to a greater or lesser degree that the concept of the covenant between the Lord and Israel (apart from the question of its historical reality) dates from the beginning of Israel's history and not from Josiah's time. The fact that the impressive ceremony of the making of the covenant described in

Exodus is reviewed extensively in Deuteronomy implies that the specific covenant concept occupies an important place in our book. Deuteronomy also speaks of a "covenant" made by the Lord with the forefathers (4:31; et al.), and mentions several times the "oath" He swore to the forefathers (7:8). This "oath" is the same as the covenant it confirmed (7:12; 8:18). The covenant made at Horeb is usually distinguished from that made with the forefathers as a separate covenant; it is said to have been made "not with our fathers" but "with us" (5:3).

Nevertheless, this covenant with Israel is based on that made with the forefathers: The Lord led Israel out of Egypt "because the LORD loved you and kept the oath he swore to your forefathers" (7:8). Fundamentally it is one and the same covenant. If Israel pays attention to these laws and keeps them, then the Lord "will keep his covenant of love with you, as he swore to your forefathers"—and He will love Israel and bless them (7:12). Keeping the covenant made under oath with the forefathers is the same as keeping the covenant made with Israel (see also 8:18). In the light of the revelation as a whole it becomes even clearer that these two covenants are fundamentally one and could therefore be called two phases of the same covenant.

Deuteronomy mentions yet another covenant, "the covenant the LORD commanded Moses to make with the Israelites in Moab, in addition to the covenant he had made with them at Horeb" (29:1; cf. 26:17–19; 27:9). But it is clear that this is essentially but a confirmation of the covenant made at Horeb.

C. *Grace and* heil[16]

When we examine what, according to Deuteronomy, the relationship between the Lord and Israel (whether specifically characterized as a

---

[16]The Dutch *heil*, like its German cognate, does not have an exact equivalent in English. In some contexts, "salvation" and "redemption" are acceptable renderings, while in others "blessing" might be better. The reason for this is that *heil* encompasses all that God gives to man and does for man, the love and goodness of God focused in His dealings with His creation. Thus, where the English word "salvation" tends to have the connotation "from" ("salvation from sin"), *heil* connotes the *Source* of salvation and would therefore be more appropriately rendered "God's salvation." In a sense, salvation, redemption, blessing, etc., are specific aspects of *heil* in the full sense of the word. In some instances the word *heil* has not been translated, in order to avoid interpretive choices of meaning or unwieldy paraphrases, all of which would of necessity be less than accurate— TRANS.

"covenant" or not) essentially encompasses, we take as our starting point the *heil* that Israel is given or promised and the free grace the Lord bestowed on Israel in doing this. Deuteronomy itself (and indeed the whole Law) has this same perspective. Even though Deuteronomy consists to a large extent of laws, it places those laws in the framework of salvation history (*heilsgeschiedenis*). We only mention the fact that the Ten Words are introduced with, "I am the LORD your God, who brought you out of Egypt, out of the land of slavery" (5:6).

The relationship between the Lord and Israel is a *heils*-relationship; the covenant is a covenant of *heil* that is founded in grace. For Israel (i.e., for Israel as a *nation*—we shall speak of Israel as church later) all this can turn into its opposite. But *heil* and grace are the foundation, the starting point. This is why "covenant" and "love" can be placed side by side as synonymous (7:9, 12 KJV, RSV; NIV, "covenant of love").

The earthly-temporal blessings of this *heil* are prominent (in part because Israel is always seen as a nation in the political-national sense). With regard to the past there is the recurring reminder of the liberation from Egypt and the preservation in the wilderness. In the future the Lord will, if Israel keeps His commandments, drive out the nations of Canaan before them (11:23ff.), grant Israel long life (4:40; 5:16; 16:20; 22:7; cf. 17:20), and give them "the ability to produce wealth" (8:18); He will make Israel numerous (13:17) and bless them in all the work of their hands (14:29; 15:10, 18; 23:20), so that they "will lend to many nations but will borrow from none" (28:12); He will make Israel "the head, not the tail" (28:13) and set her "in praise, fame and honor high above all the nations" (26:19). The often repeated "that it may go well with you" (4:40; 6:3; et al.) is, of course, also to be understood in this earthly-temporal sense.

All this does not mean that the earthly exhausts the blessings given to Israel. Thus, 8:10 says, "When you have eaten and are satisfied, praise the LORD your God for the good land he has given you," which contains the clear implication that for Israel the enjoyment of earthly goods must not be the highest good. The ultimate purport of all earthly things is, of course, that in these things Israel may enjoy the goodness and favor of her God; the repeatedly used phrase "rejoice in the presence of the LORD your God" points in the same direction.

Furthermore, all *heil* is contained in the truth, repeated over and over again, that the Lord is Israel's God. Also, Moses speaks in the final analysis of more than an external treasure when he points out to Israel that no other great nation has such "righteous decrees and laws" as those he sets before them (4:8). And for the future the Lord promises Israel a prophet like Moses, in whose mouth He will put His words (18:18). But in the further description of what Israel possesses in this God and in His laws and words, it is always the earthly-temporal blessings that are mentioned. The receiving or retaining of these blessings, however, is in many ways tied to Israel's obedience. But this is only one side; the other is that Israel *has already received* the beginnings of this *heil* and that there is the *certain* prospect of more to come. The Exodus from Egypt *has* taken place; Israel, the people of the covenant, is also the people that *has* been redeemed. But the fulfillment of what has been promised for the future, the inheriting of Canaan, is equally certain. It is possible for a given generation or for individuals to be excluded from this fulfillment due to unbelief and sin, a point that is very important in that it shows that the Lord links the receiving of the promise to the obedience of faith. Also for Israel as a whole the entering of Canaan is tied to the careful observance of "all these commands I am giving you to follow" (11:22ff.). But this does not mean that it is therefore uncertain whether Israel will possess Canaan. Deuteronomy is pervaded by the certainty that Israel will live in Canaan and that it will there enjoy abundantly the Lord's blessing. This implies that, to the extent that the Lord ties the entrance into Canaan to the obedience of faith (which is, of course, not found in every individual), it is certain beforehand that He will also take care that this obedience will be present in His people.

Great emphasis is placed on the fact that the special relationship between the Lord and Israel rests on the Lord's *free elective grace.* This relationship is not a necessity, given in the nature of things, nor is it based on any excellence or merit on Israel's part, whether past or present. The former is shown, e.g., in the making of the covenant, since there the relationship is characterized as based on an act of free will, first and foremost on the Lord's part, and as tied to the fulfillment of certain requirements that take on the character of conditions.

But this has a deeper background. The Lord is not a national god, whose existence coincides with that of a certain nation (Israel). He is the great God who made all nations (26:19). He does not stand beside the gods of the nations as their equal, but He gave those nations their gods (i.e., the worship of all these gods has come into being under His sovereign governance); confronting these gods, He brought Israel out of the iron-smelting furnace, out of Egypt, to be His own people (4:19–20). To the Lord belong the heavens, the earth, and everything that is in them, "yet the LORD set his affection on your forefathers and loved them, and he chose you, their descendants, above all the nations, as it is today" (10:14–15). Thus it is the Lord's *free elective love* toward the forefathers and their descendants that is the source of Israel's *heil;* it is important to note that the word "choose" ("elect") is used repeatedly in this connection (4:37; 7:6; 10:15; 14:2).

Before this God, who in the fullness of His riches does not need Israel, stands Israel in her poverty and unworthiness, reasons why she has to receive everything from Him. The Israelites must confess that their forefather Jacob was a "wandering Aramean" in danger of perishing (26:5). Now the people have come out of the land of slavery in Egypt, led by the Lord (5:6). Soon they will inherit Canaan with its large and beautiful cities they have not built and houses filled with all kinds of goods they did not provide (6:10–11). When Israel becomes prosperous in Canaan it will not be because of their own strength but due to the Lord, who gives Israel power and strength because He remembers the covenant He made with their forefathers (8:17–18).

Israel receives all of this without being able to make any claim to it on the basis of excellence or merit. The Lord did not choose Israel "because [they] were more numerous than other peoples, for [they] were the fewest of all peoples. But it was because the LORD loved [them] and kept the oath he swore to [their] forefathers" (7:6–8). Again and again His free love toward the forefathers is named as the source of Israel's blessing (10:15; et al.).

When Israel reaches Canaan in the near future it is not because of her righteousness, but because of the wickedness of the nations of Canaan and because the Lord wants to keep the promise He made to the forefathers under oath (9:5). It is certainly not because of Israel's righteousness; they are a stiff-necked people, who have again and again incurred the Lord's wrath during the wilderness journey, as is pointed out at length (9:6ff.).

D. *Demands or conditions; blessing and curse*

The gracious favor the Lord showed Israel in making her His own people, a holy people (i.e., a people set apart for Him), does not have as its only purpose to let Israel live in peace and prosperity in Canaan. The words "I am the LORD your God, who brought you out of Egypt, out of the land of slavery" (5:6) are the introduction to the Ten Words, which contain the essence of what the Lord commands Israel. Indeed, the larger part of Deuteronomy contains laws, decrees, and requirements (together with exhortations to keep them) in which the Lord makes known, both to Israel as a whole and to the individual members of the nation, His will with respect to the general religio-ethical, cultic, political, and social realms. Thus the Lord's relationship to Israel has, besides its character of grace and *heil*, also a *demanding* character. The latter did not become part of the relationship only when it was formalized in the covenant (it can also be deduced from His fatherhood and the fact that He is King or Lord; cf. Mal. 1:6); we cannot even say that it is implied in the Old Testament concept of covenant per se (cf. Gen. 9:9ff.). But the covenant form lends itself to express in a unique and especially powerful manner the two-sided character of the relationship, the giving and the demanding.

In the covenant made with Israel this is seen in the manner in which the making of the covenant and the giving of the law are related. The covenant made at Horeb acquires in strong measure (much more so than the covenant made with the forefathers, which is always seen as a *promise* made by the Lord under oath) the character of an *obligation* or *law* imposed on the people. Thus, the Ten Words are simply called "the covenant" in 4:13 (cf. 4:23; 5:2).

It is characteristic of the Mosaic law, furthermore, that this divine demand is particularized in a large number of "laws," "decrees," and "requirements," all of which Israel is enjoined to observe carefully, while at the same time it is emphasized that the life and well-being of the nation depend on the keeping of this obligation. The Lord "shows love" (5:10) or "keeps his covenant of love" (7:9) to those who love Him and keep His commandments. Again and again the thought is repeated that life and well-being depend on the keeping of the laws and commands proclaimed by Moses. Deuteronomy begins with the history of Israel's rebelliousness and unbelief—the reason why this present generation cannot enter Canaan (ch. 1). Accordingly, the entering of Canaan is for the new generation dependent on the hearing and obeying of the decrees and laws that Moses teaches them (4:1), and in numerous places the exhortation to keep these commandments is linked with the consideration that this is the only way to remain in Canaan and to enjoy the good things there (4:26-27, 40; 6:2, "that you may enjoy long life"; 6:3, "that it may go well with you and that you may increase greatly"; et al.)

Although the Lord made Israel a holy nation long ago (see above), nevertheless it is said (28:9) that *if* Israel listens to the Lord and keeps His commandments, then the Lord *will* establish them as His holy people, which, in the light of the preceding, means that this privilege then will be *confirmed* and *made manifest* to all (cf. 28:10) by the prosperity that Israel as the Lord's people will receive from Him. Thus it would appear at times that the relationship between the Lord and Israel depends on a contract, on a quid pro quo. For example, in 7:12 we read, "If [lit., and it shall be because] you pay attention to these laws and are careful to follow them, then the LORD your God will keep His covenant of love with you, as he swore to your forefathers." The first words of this verse seem to present the Lord's keeping of the covenant as a return for Israel's keeping of the law. Also noteworthy in this respect is the statement in 26:17–19, where the Lord and Israel join themselves to each other with a mutual declaration of what they will do for each other and what they expect from each other.

Finally, it should be noted that the *curse* in case of disobedience is emphatically placed over against the *blessing* that is linked with obedience. And as the blessing is summed up in life, so the curse culminates in Israel's destruction and perdition (6:15; 7:4; 8:19; 11:26–27). Toward the end of Deuteronomy this is stated in an imposing manner (chs. 27–28; cf. also 30:15-20); the emphasis in these chapters falls mostly on the curse, and it is made clear that, at least for a time, the curse will have the upper hand (30:1–10; cf. 4:29–31).

We cannot deny that all this puts a legal stamp on the covenant made at Horeb, which distinguishes it from the new covenant (and to a lesser degree also from the covenant made with Abraham). It is true that, also according to the New Testament, participation in God's *heil* requires conversion and a holy walk. But three things are prominent in the New Testament requirement. In the first place, this holy walk is the fruit of faith focused on God's free grace that justifies the ungodly. Furthermore, the holiness of our walk on earth always remains very much imperfect, so that even the most "holy" individual has had only "a small beginning of this obedience" (Heidelberg Catechism, A. 114). And finally, this "small beginning" and the faith from which it springs are the fruit of God's working in the heart and cannot be lost again; those who participate in it can also be assured of their salvation. It is clear that these elements are rather in the background in this facet of Deuteronomy. The requirement of the law is emphasized, the law is divided into a virtually endless number of decrees and requirements, and the keeping of *all* of these is made necessary for a continued possession of the *heil*. As a result, faith as a decisive factor, the possibility of keeping the law *in principle*, and the truth of the decisive work of God in the heart are very much in the background. The statements concerning temporal goods and a *heil* that can be lost appear to know nothing of the certainty of salvation. The covenant appears to be as much a covenant of curse as of blessing, and at the end of the book the blessing is even overshadowed by the curse.

But it has already become clear that this legal aspect is only one side of the Book of Deuteronomy. As we saw in the preceding section, Deuteronomy also has another side. The relationship between the Lord and Israel is clearly described as a *heil* relationship: Israel has already been redeemed from Egypt and will certainly inherit Canaan. The Lord's free elective grace, which is the foundation of the covenant made with Abraham and his descendants, is extolled, and it is because of this grace that Israel inherits Canaan—not because of her righteousness but rather in spite of the rebelliousness she displayed throughout the wilderness journey.

However, we should not understand the quid-pro-quo statements of Deuteronomy in as strictly a legalistic sense as might be supposed when these statements are viewed in isolation. In the first place, what is said about the gracious character of the covenant is of essential importance for the keeping of the law *in principle*. The proofs of God's grace to Israel did not begin after Israel began keeping the law. Rather, the reverse is true: God's grace comes first, and Israel is exhorted to obey on the basis of this grace. Deuteronomy sees the keeping of the law as an act of *gratitude;* the love God has shown to the forefathers and the blessings He has bestowed on Israel (Israel's election, the Exodus from Egypt, the entrance into Canaan) must motivate Israel to honor only Him as God and to keep His commandments (4:37ff.; cf. 4:20; see also 6:1–9:6). The Lord has made Israel His own and therefore a holy people (i.e., a people set apart for Him)—this is why Israel is called to keep His commandments (7:6; 14:2; 26:19).

Seen in this light, the individual laws and regulations take on an entirely different meaning. They point out to Israel how in all aspects of life they can show the Lord their God their gratitude for all the demonstrations of His mercy and love they have received.

Concerning the *character* of the law we also note that, while it contains a large number of commands, decrees, and requirements, underlying its pluriformity is an *inner unity*. The Ten Words, the great religio-ethical demands that were an integral part of the making of the covenant, are placed in the foreground, and their special position as the "constitution" of the covenant is strongly emphasized (see comments on 5:22). It is no less significant (and characteristic of Deuteronomy) that principles such as love, faithfulness, humility, and gratitude are mentioned repeatedly, principles in which the religio-ethical demands are summed up and shown to be related to Israel's inner disposition. Thus, in the general exhortations of 6:1–9:6 Israel is encouraged to be grateful and humbly faithful to the Lord, who has revealed and still reveals Himself to them as a God of faithfulness and love. Especially peculiar to Deuteronomy is the emphasis on the demand to love the Lord. The express description of the relationship to the Lord as "love" is rare in the Old Testament, even in the Pentateuch. Love to the Lord is also mentioned in the Decalogue in Exodus 20:6, and Leviticus speaks of love for the neighbor, but only Deuteronomy speaks again and again of loving (and holding fast to) "the LORD your God" (often with the addition, "with all your heart and with all your soul and with all your strength," 5:10; 6:5; 10:12; 11:1, 13, 22; 13:3; 19:9; 30:6, 16, 20).

Nor must we forget that in Deuteronomy, as throughout the Old Testament laws, the first thing that is asked of Israel (even when not expressly stated) is always faith—faith in Him who has given the law with its blessing and curse. But also—and indeed first and foremost—faith in Him who will fulfill the promise made under oath to the forefathers. The sin in chapter 1, the reason why the then-living generation could not enter Canaan, was in the final analysis a sin of unbelief.

Finally we should point out that, even though curse and blessing are found side by side and the former at times appears to be dominant, the curse never has the final word. Deuteronomy also announces that when Israel, after having been scattered among the nations, turns to the Lord, she shall be brought back to the land of her inheritance (4:29ff.; 30:1–6), again on the basis of the covenant made with the forefathers (4:31). The grace of the covenant is thus not exhausted even when Israel initially brings the curse of the covenant on herself. Even a circumcision of the heart, performed by the Lord, is mentioned in this context (30:6). But the work of God as the first and decisive factor is not yet shown here with the clarity with which it is presented later in Jeremiah 31:31ff. Everything is still conditional on returning to the Lord (30:1–2), and the truth that this returning, this conversion, is the result of God's work thus does not yet find expression. We can also say that conversion is described in legalistic terms, because it is linked to all that Moses commands (30:2). But this does not take away from the fact that these statements clearly show that there is a mercy of the Lord that is stronger than the curse of the law and that the Lord does not withdraw His hand from His people in spite of Israel's disobedience.

When all this is placed in the context of the Scriptures as a whole, we must come to the conclusion that the temporal form of the covenant at Horeb is dominant in the legal pronouncements, while in the other statements it is the immutable nature of the covenant as a covenant of grace that becomes evident.

As long as both categories are viewed in isolation from one another they constitute a contrast. The legalistic principle, expressed in the complementary statements, "The man who does these things will live by them" (Gal. 3:12; cf. Lev. 18:5) and "Cursed is everyone who does not continue to do everything written in the Book of the Law" (Gal. 3:10; cf. Deut. 27:26), contradicts, when taken by itself, the principle that the righteous shall live by faith. From this perspective the law was not able to give life but could serve only to include everything under sin, and thus the best that could be said of it was that it was "put in charge to lead us to Christ" (Gal. 3:21ff.).

But Christ Himself was present in the covenant made at Horeb; this is why the legal principle (which was a constituent element of the covenant) must *not* be viewed in isolation, but rather in the context of all of the Scriptures (and, as seen above, also in the context of all of Deuteronomy). The covenant in all its stages, including Horeb, is ultimately and essentially a covenant of grace.

Seen in this light all acts of obedience to the law are expressions of faith, a faith that takes hold of and holds on to the grace of the covenant. Thus there is a justification based on actions (James 2:20–24) that is ultimately nothing but justification by faith. Of this the psalmists also speak when they infer their righteousness before God from their living in accordance with the law; this godliness does bear a legalistic stamp, but it is nevertheless in essence a living out of grace.

VI. THE SIGNIFICANCE OF DEUTERONOMY FOR THE CHURCH OF
THE NEW COVENANT

Already in the prophecies of the Old Testament, a "new" covenant is placed over against the covenant made at Horeb. This is done most clearly by Jeremiah in his well-known statement in 31:31–33. The new covenant he announces is described with the words, "I will put my law in their minds and write it on their hearts. I will be their God, and they will be my people.''

The New Testament is even more clear. The people of God of the new dispensation do not constitute a national-political entity but the church gathered from among all nations. And this church is the heir, not only of the name Israel, but also of all that is permanent and essential in what was given or promised to Israel.

The relationship in which this church stands to God is indicated by various names: In the foreground now stands God's name "Father," the church is also called the body of Christ, etc. But also the specific covenant concept is not absent, although it receives less emphasis than in the Old Testament.[17] Especially in the Epistle to the Hebrews this New Testament covenant concept is closely related to Jeremiah 31:31–33 (see Heb. 8:8–13; 10:16–17).

It is important to note here that the contrast made by Jeremiah and in Hebrews between the old and new covenants should not be understood in an absolute sense. This is already implicit in much that has been quoted above, especially in the fact that God's sovereign grace is the foundation of the Sinaitic covenant. But more should be said here.

Besides Jeremiah's *new* covenant, which takes the place of the old, there are also other statements, according to which the Lord's covenant with Israel shall continue to exist even during the Captivity and shall never be abolished (Isa. 50:1; 54:10). Therefore, if we want to do justice to the whole of the Scriptures, we must say that the covenant of the future is new in one sense, while in another sense it is a continuation of the old.

This is also related to the fact that we see two things in Israel: the nation and the church. The national covenant is also the covenant of God with the church in its Old Testament form. But church and nation are not identical, and the church covenant reaches deeper and higher than the national covenant. This is also the reason why the Sinaitic covenant is ultimately and essentially one with the new covenant of Jeremiah's prophecy, even as it is one with the covenant God made with the patriarchs and, indeed, one with what has been ever since Paradise (although not explicitly called a covenant) the only source from which flowed saving grace for sinful people (Gen. 3:15). The

---

[17]The emphasis must fall on the covenant *concept*. The Greek word used in the New Testament, *diathēkē*, which we render "covenant" (or occasionally "testament") is not the exact equivalent of the Old Testament *berît*, but represents (as the rendering "testament" indicates) rather a divine arrangement or ordinance.

peculiarity of the Sinaitic covenant is that it (more so than the covenant with the patriarchs, although we can see the beginnings already there) intertwines, as it were, this ancient and everlasting covenant with a temporary national covenant and thus places the covenant of grace more or less in the framework of a covenant of works.

The contrast made in the Scriptures between the old and the new covenant thus has a relative character: it holds true only when the Sinaitic covenant is viewed from a certain perspective, i.e., when it is seen as a national covenant with a legal character, with temporary, ceremonial aspects, etc.

The relative nature of this contrast is reinforced when we contrast the Sinaitic covenant, not with the new covenant as predicted in Jeremiah 31:31-33, but with the new covenant as it has become a reality in the first coming of Christ, the dispensation of grace, usually called the New Covenant or New Testament. We are of the opinion that the latter cannot be simply equated with the "new covenant" of Jeremiah 31. Although it is true that Hebrews 8 and 10 teach that the coming of this new dispensation is in fulfillment of Jeremiah 31:31-33, this does not necessarily mean that this is its only and complete fulfillment. In our opinion, the fulfillment of this prophecy comes about in stages (as is true of so many Old Testament prophecies). Something of the *initial* fulfillment is already seen in the renewal of the covenant after the return from the Captivity, the fulfillment *in principle* came at Christ's first coming, while the *final* fulfillment still awaits the end of time. The latter follows from the words of Jeremiah 31:34, "they will all know me." Do these words find their complete fulfillment in the church of the New Testament? Certainly not in the visible church, of which it is still true that "they are not all Israel, which are of Israel" (Rom. 9:6 KJV). The tendency is therefore to apply the words "they will all know me" to the invisible church, to the elect or believers. But it is nothing new that these *all* know the Lord—this was also true under the old covenant. It appears to us that the statement "they will all know me" is meaningful only when applied to a visible church. But then it is clear that this will be true in its full sense only in the future, when, in the dispensation of glory all evil and all evil persons will have been removed from the church.

The church of the new dispensation of which we are a part occupies a mediating position between the church of the old covenant and the church of the state of glory. Because of the outpouring of the Holy Spirit, and because it has been detached from the ties with Israel's national existence, it stands much closer to the state of perfection depicted in Jeremiah than the Old Testament church, and its appearance fulfills Jeremiah's prophecy in principle. But on the other hand, the church has not yet achieved perfection and there are those in her midst who do not belong to her.

The character of the new covenant under which the church now lives accords with this. The duality of the old covenant—on the one hand an impermanent national covenant, on the other an eternal covenant with the church elected for salvation by God—has been overcome in principle but has not yet been fully shed. This new covenant also still has an internal and an external aspect, which are not fully identical, corresponding to the visible and invisible aspects of the church with which this covenant has been made. In the church, and thus also within the sphere of the covenant, there are still hypocrites. This incongruence is reinforced by the fact that this church is still a church that is "in the making," a church that grows because, among other things, the seed of the believers is included in the covenant and in the church in accordance with the ancient covenant principle (although with respect to their spiritual disposition the principle remains in effect that not all are Israel who are of Israel).

Attempts have been made to overcome this duality that can still be observed in both church and covenant. Some have spiritualized, rejecting infant baptism and, when admitting adults into the church, wanting to sit in judgment on the heart in order to achieve in this manner a (visible) church consisting of saints only. Others have approached it from the opposite direction by taking both church and covenant in an externalized sense, teaching that believers as well as unbelievers are included in both *in the same sense*. The first solution is a premature anticipation of the state of glory, the second a denaturing of the concepts of church and covenant. An "external" covenant that consists of nothing but a (nonsaving) de jure position and provides nothing but the *possibility* of salvation not only stands below the new, but also stands below the old covenant. In the old covenant, as the opening of the Ten Words shows (Deut. 5:6), the *heil* of the covenant (for Israel as a nation a transitory, for Israel as the church an everlasting *heil*) is a gift, already given and received in principle and in incipient actuality.

Thus, the contrast between the old and the presently existing new covenant is limited in two respects. In the first (and most important) place, the contrast is limited because the old covenant is ultimately and essentially also a covenant with the church, and thus in essence one with the new covenant. And second, also in the new covenant we must still distinguish between an external and an internal aspect, aspects that are not fully identical as long as the "they all" of Jeremiah 31 has not found its final fulfillment.

The church of the new dispensation recognizes the Book of Deuteronomy as part of the Holy Scriptures; the revelation of God given in this book is indeed given to the church of all future ages. But this book, even as the whole Old Testament, must be understood in the light of the New Testament. This means that the national, ceremonial, and legal aspects—in short, all that is specific to the Old Testament—fall away and many things take on new meanings. "I am the LORD your God, who brought you out of Egypt, out of the land of slavery" is also addressed to the New Testament church; the difference is that the church understands these words to speak of her redemption from the slavery of sin.

What is stated with so much emphasis and clarity in Deuteronomy concerning God's free elective love and grace by which He bound Himself to the patriarchs and Israel (Israel is the people of the *covenant* because it is the *elect* people) acquires its full meaning in the eternal covenant made in Christ with those who are elect unto eternal life by God's sovereign good pleasure.

It is therefore also clear that in the New Testament (and already in the prophecies of the Old Testament that speak of the "new covenant") the character of the covenant as a covenant of *grace* is revealed more richly and fully than in the law. In Jeremiah 31:31ff., the covenant of God is described with virtual New Testament clarity as being based *entirely* (also in what is asked of man) on God's work. The fact that it is Jeremiah who says this may be related to the fact that he twice experienced a reformation under Josiah, while also experiencing that such a reformation is of no avail if it is limited to externals and does not touch the heart (cf. 3:10). Thus we see on the one hand Jeremiah's appeals to Israel for a conversion of the heart, but on the other hand the promise of chapter 31 that God *Himself* will effect that change of heart. In view of the fact, already evident back then, that the external law cannot give life, Jeremiah announced the new covenant, which consists in the Lord's putting His law in their minds and writing it on their hearts. As we already saw, the contrast established here with the old covenant is valid only when the covenant is viewed from a specific perspective, viz., in its external aspect.

41

The *transitory* nature of the old covenant stands over against the *permanence* of the new in the same sense. Jeremiah speaks of this in 31:35ff.; his words here (even more clearly than in vv. 31ff.) are tied to the forms of Israel's national existence. But also this part of his prophecy finds its *complete* fulfillment (it found an initial fulfillment when Israel returned from the Captivity and Jerusalem was rebuilt, cf. vv. 38ff.), not in the national covenant with Israel, but in the "eternal covenant of grace and reconciliation" with the church of all ages.

The permanent character of this covenant is based on what is announced in vv. 31ff. The foundation of this new covenant, including what is expected and demanded of man, is solely the work of the Lord (as was in the final analysis also true of the old covenant). Of course, this does not mean at all that this covenant can exist *without* man's keeping the law, *without* his knowing the Lord, and *without* faith (the basis of both covenants). Jeremiah's words imply the opposite. But what is stated is that this keeping of the law and this knowing of the Lord are not uncertain factors that may or may not be present so that the covenant may be nullified, or at least the blessing of the covenant may be withheld if they are absent. The Lord Himself *writes* the law in the inner man and causes man to know Him; this is why this covenant is imperishable and its blessings never end.

The fact that man's action is described as the result of God's grace does not keep it from being *commanded* by God; although Jeremiah does not say this explicitly here, it is nevertheless clear from the Scriptures as a whole. And Jeremiah does speak of the *law* of the Lord. It has been said that a law that is written on the heart is no longer a law, but this is an unfounded assertion. The authority with which the law speaks and commands continues to exist, even when the heart conforms to its demands and any conflict with its authority is thus precluded.

Furthermore, our intellect cannot grasp how these two can coexist: on the one hand the effectual, all-decisive work of God in the heart, and on the other hand the divine demand and the human responsibility it implies. But the Scriptures clearly teach both, and the fuller revelation of the *heil* and grace of the covenant found in the prophets and in the New Testament thus does not in any way detract from the forcefulness with which the *demand* of the covenant is set before man. Also for the church of today the words "I am the LORD your God" are followed by "you shall."

But, while the old and new covenant are one in essence, there are nevertheless many differences. First of all, they are different in what is demanded. The ceremonial, civil, and political laws are no longer binding in the form in which they are given, although this does not mean that they have lost their significance. In the religio-ethical law, the positive command to *love* (which already finds clear expression in Deuteronomy) is now central, and consequently *faith* as the root of any keeping of the law and as the primary demand of the covenant stands much more in the foreground.

All this is related to a difference in the *manner* in which the demand of the covenant is urged on man. Hebrews 12:18–24 states that the church of the new covenant has not come to a tangible mountain and a burning fire, but to "Mount Zion, to the heavenly Jerusalem, the city of the living God. . .to Jesus the mediator of a new covenant, and to the sprinkled blood that speaks a better word than the blood of Abel.'' The much fuller revelation of God's grace in Christ Jesus gives the demand of the covenant an entirely different tone.

It has been a subject of much debate whether the eternal and indestructible covenant of Jeremiah leaves room for speaking of a *breaking* of the covenant and of the *curse* and *retribution* of the covenant. We note the following:

1. Although conservative Reformed scholars have held different opinions, they are essentially in much closer agreement than might appear on the surface, since all agree that the Scriptures clearly teach the perseverance of the saints. On the other hand, no one can deny that the Scriptures nevertheless warn the church against falling away. The Epistle to the Hebrews is here also the *locus classicus*. It is precisely the purpose of the section just quoted (12:18ff.), which so strongly accentuates the gracious character of the new covenant as opposed to the old, to warn against falling away. This warning is preceded by, among other things, a warning against following the example of Esau, who sold his birthright for food and was rejected (vv. 16–17), and is followed by the words, "See to it that you do not refuse him who speaks . . ." (v. 25). The section concludes with the awesome words, "for our God is a consuming fire" (v. 29). We find similar warnings again and again in Hebrews; we only mention 3:11–19, which contains an explicit reminder of the events described in Deuteronomy 1.

2. The reason this warning is necessary in spite of the certainty of the perseverance of the saints is the still imperfect state of the church. There are those in the church who do not have saving faith and who will bring Esau's judgment on themselves if they do not repent. But the

exhortation and warning are addressed to all and are important for all. We think of the fact that the Canons of Dort (v. 14) also say concerning perseverance that God "preserves, continues, and perfects" the work of grace in us "by the hearing and reading of His Word, by meditation thereon, and by the exhortations, threatenings, and promises thereof . . ."—although we must add that anyone who has the confidence of faith knows that these "threatenings" can never imply a complete rejection.

3. Concerning the "breaking," the "curse," and the "retribution" of the covenant, it is clear that none of these can have a place in the covenant as described in Jeremiah 31, which is the invincible and indestructible work of God. Those who participate in the covenant in the sense of Jeremiah 31, i.e., in the fullest sense, can and will transgress the covenant again and again, but are kept from a final breaking of the covenant by God's grace, in accordance with His promise.

But we must not forget that as long as this earthly dispensation lasts, the covenant still has an aspect that is not included in Jeremiah's description: Among those who (as "children of the covenant") have entered into the sphere of the covenant there are also those who do not participate in the covenant in the sense of Jeremiah 31. Nevertheless, the relation to the covenant and to the God of the covenant into which they have been brought is such that their unbelief and impenitence can justly be called a leaving of the God of the covenant and a breaking of the covenant, and the resulting punishment can be called "curse" and "retribution" of the covenant.

4. As far as I can see, the concept of breaking the new covenant in its specific sense is presented most clearly in the New Testament in Hebrews 10:29, which speaks of him who "has treated as an unholy thing the blood of the covenant that sanctified him"; the author quotes in this connection the words from Deuteronomy, "It is mine to avenge; I will repay." What is said here is virtually the same as using the words "breaking" of the covenant and "retribution" of the covenant. Nevertheless, these *words* ("breaking," "curse," "retribution") are not used of the covenant in the New Testament, although their *substance* is by no means absent. This is an indication of the extent to which the New Testament, when it explicitly speaks of the covenant, places its gracious character in the foreground.

5. But this certainly does not mean that the *substance* is therefore de-emphasized in the New Testament. On the contrary, the fuller

revelation of grace is accompanied by a more severe announcement of judgment on those who reject this grace (cf. Heb. 2:3; 10:28ff.; 12:25). And when we compare the temporal judgments announced in Deuteronomy with the statement concerning the worm that does not die and the fire that is not extinguished, we see immediately that the fuller light of the New Testament *heil* revelation has a correspondingly deeper shadow in the announcement of greatly intensified punishment.

VII. OUTLINE OF DEUTERONOMY

Superscription (1:1–5)

Part One—Moses' First (Preparatory) Discourse (1:6–4:40)
  I. Historical Survey (1:6–3:29)
    A. Advance to Canaan! (1:6–8)
    B. The Appointment of Leaders (1:9–18)
    C. Kadesh Barnea: The People's Unbelief (1:19–33)
    D. Kadesh Barnea: The Punishment (1:34–46)
    E. From Kadesh South and Along the Border of Edom (2:1–8)
    F. Along Moab and Ammon to the Border of the Amorites (2:9–25)
    G. Conquest of the Kingdom of Sihon (2:26–37)
    H. Conquest of the Kingdom of Og (3:1–7)
    I. The Division of the Land East of the Jordan (3:8–20)
    J. Joshua to Be Moses' Successor (3:21–29)
  II. Exhortation to Keep the Law (4:1–40)
    A. In Praise of the Law (4:1–8)
    B. Against the Worship of Images and Idolatry; Captivity and Deliverance (4:9–31)
    C. The Lord Alone Is God (4:32–40)

Interlude: The Three Cities of Refuge East of the Jordan (4:41–43)

Part Two: Moses' Second Discourse (4:44–30:20)
  I. Superscription (4:44–49)
  II. Foundational Part (5:1–11:32)
    A. Introduction (5:1–5)
    B. The Giving of the Law at Horeb (5:6–33)
      1. The Ten Words (5:6–22)

47

Deuteronomy
Commentary

Superscription
(1:1–5)

These verses constitute a superscription, or introduction, to the whole Book of Deuteronomy and serve to fix the place and time of the contents of the book.

1:1 *These are the words Moses spoke to all Israel in the desert east of the Jordan—that is, in the Arabah—opposite Suph, between Paran and Tophel, Laban, Hazeroth and Dizahab.*

The phrase "these are the words" refers to what follows; the view that the expression refers back to the preceding material (Numbers) is untenable. The similar phrase in Numbers 36:13, "These are the commands and regulations," clearly marks a conclusion, while this verse indicates a new beginning. The expression "to all Israel," which occurs a number of times in this book, emphasizes that the people of Israel as a whole is addressed and included in the covenant of God. Then follows a statement as to the place where Moses spoke these words. The geographical reference is clear in substance but not in detail. It took place (lit.) "across the Jordan," i.e., "east of the Jordan" (cf. Introduction, p.21). Israel had not yet crossed the Jordan and entered Canaan. "In the desert" (or, "steppe") characterizes this region and contrasts it to the arable land west of the Jordan. "In the Arabah" means literally "in the steppe" or "in the plain," but the word is used here, as frequently elsewhere, of the depression that includes the Jordan Valley and the Dead Sea and stretches south to the Gulf of Aqaba. Thus far, the geographical indicators are very general,

51

but we are in the dark concerning the specifics that follow. We know from other sources that the locale in question was east of the Dead Sea (in the land of Moab, v.5), and more specifically east of the northern end of the Dead Sea ("in the land of Sihon," which was situated north of the Arnon, and "near Beth Peor," 4:46; cf. 3:29). But the rest of the geographical references in this verse are obscure to us. "Suph" has sometimes been thought to refer to *Yam Suph,* the Sea of Reeds or Red Sea, but it is too far away and was never called merely *Suph.* The identification with Suphah (Num. 21:14) is unfounded. The words that follow place the location between Paran on one end and Tophel, Laban, Hazeroth, and Dizahab on the other. Paran is usually equated with the desert of Paran, the northern or northeastern part of the Sinai Peninsula; but its mention here would be rather meaningless. Laban may be the same as el-Libben, east of Jericho; Hazeroth is mentioned in Numbers 33:17 as a stopping-place in the desert, but this does not fit in well with the situation here, and we must probably assume that it refers to a different place of the same name.

1:2–4 *(It takes eleven days to go from Horeb to Kadesh Barnea by the Mount Seir road.)*

³In the fortieth year, on the first day of the eleventh month, Moses proclaimed to the Israelites all that the Lᴏʀᴅ had commanded him concerning them. ⁴This was after he had defeated Sihon king of the Amorites, who reigned in Heshbon, and at Edrei had defeated Og king of Bashan, who reigned in Ashtaroth.

Having stated the place, the author goes on to mention the time when Moses spoke: the fortieth year. However, he first reminds his hearers that it did not need to have taken the Israelites forty years to reach Canaan. They had been at Canaan's border long before this—at Kadesh Barnea (cf. v.19)—and from Horeb to where Israel is now is only an eleven-day journey. The words that follow have been interpreted in different ways; they read literally, "along the road to Mount Seir to Kadesh Barnea," which we understand to mean that the people went first in the direction of Mount Seir and then to Kadesh, whether by traveling along the mountains and then westward to Kadesh or by going, e.g., to Ezion Geber and from there directly to Kadesh. In view of the "eleven days," the latter seems more probable. Uncertainties remain, however, also because the data we find elsewhere concerning this part of the wilderness journey are not clear to us.

Because of their unbelief Israel could not enter Canaan from Kadesh

Barnea (see vv. 19ff.); thus it was much later, in the fortieth year following the Exodus, after many wanderings and toward the end of his career, that Moses finds himself with the Israelites east of the Jordan, where he addresses them. The exact date is given: the first day of the eleventh month. The year began with the month of the Passover (Exod. 12:2–3; et al.), first called Abib and after the Captivity Nisan, which was approximately the same as our April. The eleventh month was thus approximately our February. Moses proclaimed "all that the Lord had commanded him concerning them." We should not see this and similar expressions (e.g., 4:5; 6:1) as referring to the laws recorded in the preceding books but rather to what the Lord has commanded Moses now; the latter is in substance, but not in all details, the same as the former, and Moses' words are also here based fully on the revelation given him for this purpose.

Verse 4 complements verse 3a by stating that this took place after the defeat of Sihon and Og (cf. 2:4 – 3:8; Num. 21:21–35), the kings of the two Amorite kingdoms east of the Jordan. The southernmost of the two was that of Sihon, who resided in Heshbon; Israel now finds itself in his former territory, which extended southward to the Arnon (4:46). According to verse 5, Moses addressed the people "in the territory of Moab" (the same region that is elsewhere called "the plains of Moab," Num. 36:13). This apparent discrepancy can be explained by the fact that this region once belonged to Moab and retained its name even after the Amorites invaded it from the north. Edrei is also mentioned in Joshua 12:4; 13:12, 31 as Og's second residence;[1] it was the place where he was defeated (3:1; Num. 21:33).

1:5 *East of the Jordan in the territory of Moab, Moses began to expound this law, saying:*

The author repeats "East of the Jordan" (lit., "across the Jordan"; cf. v. 1) and adds "in the territory of Moab" (see comments on vv. 1, 4). Moses now begins his discourse. "This law" is the law that follows immediately in 1:6, rather than in 5:1 or 12:1 (see Introduction, p. 000). The fact that this law is essentially one with the law in the preceding books is not explicitly stated but not thereby denied.

---

[1]This is based on an alternate rendering of verse 4: "Og the king of Bashan, who lived in Ashtaroth and in Edrei" (RSV). Another variation is "which dwelt at Astaroth in Edrei" (KJV).

Part One

Moses' First (Preparatory) Discourse
(1:6–4:40)

I. Historical Survey
(1:6–3:29)

After the superscription (1:1–5) follow Moses' words. Since 5:1 constitutes a new beginning, 1:6–4:40 must be considered a separate discourse (or series of discourses). The first part of Moses' address contains a historical survey of the events from the breaking up of the camp at Horeb to the time this discourse is given.

A. ADVANCE TO CANAAN! (1:6–8)

The first thing Moses mentions is God's command to the people to break camp and enter Canaan. This command is not recorded explicitly in the preceding books, although we do read of divine regulations that prepared Israel for this departure (Num. 1–4; 9:15–10:10), and we are also told that the cloud lifted from above the tabernacle (Num. 10:11). All this essentially implies a command to break camp (cf. also Exod. 32:34; 33:1).

1:6 *The LORD our God said to us at Horeb, "You have stayed long enough at this mountain.*

54

"The LORD our God" is the Lord (Jahweh) who made a covenant with Israel "at Horeb," the name Deuteronomy uses for the mountain that is elsewhere called Sinai. "Long enough": there is no reason why Israel should stay here any longer, since the purpose of the stay has been accomplished. The journey to Canaan, Israel's destination, must now begin.

1:7 *Break camp and advance into the hill country of the Amorites; go to all the neighboring peoples in the Arabah, in the mountains, in the western foothills, in the Negev and along the coast, to the land of the Canaanites and to Lebanon, as far as the great river, the Euphrates.*

"Break camp and advance" is literally "turn and take your journey, and go" (RSV); "turn" indicates both the preparation for the journey, further specified in "take your journey" (i.e., break camp), and its beginning.

"Into the hill country of the Amorites [Heb., Amorite]; go to all the neighboring peoples": thus Moses describes Canaan. The Amorites were one of the chief tribes that inhabited Canaan, which is the reason they are placed first here. In 1:4 we saw that there were also Amorites living east of the Jordan. But, as the following description indicates, these are not in view here. The land west of the Jordan was Canaan proper, and according to the original plan Israel would have entered Canaan from the south rather than the east. The land west of the Jordan consists of mountains, flanked by the coastal plain in the west and the Jordan valley in the east; these mountains were occupied primarily by the Amorites, which is why Canaan is referred to as "the hill country of the Amorites."

The addition "and all the [lit., 'its'] neighboring peoples" serves to complete the description, while the following statements further specify this by listing the various divisions of the land west of the Jordan. Beginning in the east, Moses first names the Arabah (cf. v. 1), which here refers exclusively to the Jordan valley. Then he mentions the "mountains"; he had referred to these earlier ("the hill country" is the same word rendered "mountains" here) as the habitat of the Amorites, but other "neighbors," i.e., other tribes, also lived here. Third, he mentions "the western foothills," a phrase that usually refers to the land of the Philistines, generally including the hilly strip west of the mountains of Judah (although the latter is sometimes distinguished from the former, Josh. 10:40; 12:8). The "coast" mentioned later probably refers to the plain of Sharon to the north, perhaps with inclusion of the narrow Phoenician seacoast. Between these two is mentioned the Negev (lit., "steppe"; the name later came to mean "south," cf. KJV), the arid region south of the mountains of Judah. All this is finally summarized in the words, "the land of the Canaanites." The Canaanites and the Amorites were the two most important tribes among the pre-Israelitic population of Canaan; "Canaanites" is used here as a collective name for all those tribes. The words that follow extend this territory by including the Lebanon (and the surrounding region) "as far as the great river, the Euphrates." This is the widest extent of the territory promised to Israel (cf. 11:24; Gen. 15:18; Exod. 23:31); Israel's power did indeed reach this far in David's time.

1:8 *See, I have given you this land. Go in and take possession of the land that the LORD swore he would give to your fathers—to Abraham, Isaac and Jacob— and to their descendants after them."*

The Lord adds to the command to enter Canaan the assurance that He gives them the land (lit., "I have set before your face," i.e., it lies before you as something for the taking). Therefore, enter the land and take possession of it. The ancient promise of God, given to the forefathers and confirmed with an oath, guarantees that it cannot elude them (cf. Gen. 12:7; 13:15; et al.; concerning the oath, see Gen. 22:16). Verse 8b reads literally, "the land which the Lord swore to your fathers, to Abraham, to Isaac, and to Jacob, to give to them and to their seed after them" (cf. RSV); the latter explains the former: "to them, i.e., to their descendants after them." The patriarchs themselves did not receive the land but their descendants did, and thus the patriarchs received it indirectly in that they live on in their descendants (cf. the use of "to you" and "to your descendants" in Gen. 15:7, 18).

B. THE APPOINTMENT OF LEADERS (1:9–18)

Moses reminds Israel that, before they set out from Horeb, he appointed leaders (vv. 9–15) whom he gave instructions concerning the administration of justice (vv. 16–17). At that time he told the people all that they were to do (v. 18). He apparently mentions these things here to make it clear that Israel had been fully prepared to settle in Canaan; perhaps we should also think in this context of the military organization necessary for the conquest (see comments on v. 15).

What Moses states here is essentially the same as what is described in Exodus 18:13ff. According to Exodus 18, Moses acted on the advice of his father-in-law, Jethro. The fact that this is not explicitly mentioned in Deuteronomy does not prove that Deuteronomy and Exodus do not deal with the same event. Nor is the circumstance that Exodus places the story of Jethro's visit (and thus also the appointment of the judges) before the giving of the law an insurmountable problem; we merely have to assume that the words "at that time" (v. 9) do not indicate that verse 9 follows after verses 6–8 chronologically, but rather are meant in a broader sense. This assumption finds support in verse 18, which also speaks of things that preceded the events mentioned in verses 6–8.

1:9–12 *At that time I said to you, "You are too heavy a burden for me to carry alone. ¹⁰The Lord your God has increased your numbers so that today you are as many as the stars in the sky. ¹¹May the Lord, the God of your fathers, increase you a thousand times and bless you as he has promised! ¹²But how can I bear your problems and your burdens and your disputes all by myself?*

Moses had said that the burden of responsibility for the people was too much for him alone because of their large numbers. The people were numerous as a result of God's blessing, as He had promised to the forefathers (Gen. 12:2; 15:15ff.; et al.). Moses would not think of complaining about this blessing (v. 11); on the contrary, his prayer was that the Lord might continue to increase their numbers and might (in this as well as in other respects) continue to bless the people "as he has promised" (lit., "promised you," i.e., in the promise to the forefathers). But this was all the more reason not to consider their large numbers something temporary but rather to draw the conclusion that Moses alone could not bear the full burden (v. 12).

"Your problems and your burdens and your disputes" refers in general to everything with which Moses as the leader of the people had to concern himself. The "disputes" are mentioned separately, since these called for a juridical decision (vv. 16ff.).

1:13–15 *Choose some wise, understanding and respected men from each of your tribes, and I will set them over you."*

¹⁴You answered me, "What you propose to do is good."

¹⁵So I took the leading men of your tribes, wise and respected men, and appointed them to have authority over you—as commanders of thousands, of hundreds, of fifties and of tens and as tribal officials.

Moses thought it necessary that leaders over the people be appointed under him. He left the choice of leaders to the people, but those designated by the people would receive their official appointment from Moses. "From each of your tribes": verse 15 gives a more detailed structure, but it is a structure based on the ancient tribal divisions. After the people voiced their agreement (v. 14) the plan was executed (v. 15). The words "I took" should probably be understood in the sense that Moses accepted the men who had been chosen beforehand by the people; he officially appointed them as leaders with varying responsibilities: "commanders of thousands, of hundreds of fifties and of tens."

Nothing is said explicitly concerning the task of these leaders. In Exodus 18:25 the same organization is applied specifically to judges, and the emphasis here appears to be similar (cf. vv. 9, 12, 16). Numbers 31:14 mentions commanders of thousands and commanders of hundreds in the army; it is not necessary to limit the function of the leaders mentioned in Deuteronomy to being judges. Also mentioned are "officials"; the Hebrew word indicates any official whose task involved writing; in legal matters a clerk, perhaps also notaries who drew up contracts (cf. 16:18), but also administrative military personnel (20:5ff.). "Tribal officials" is literally "officials according to your tribes" (the same expression is rendered "from each of your tribes" in v. 13).

1:16–17 *And I charged your judges at that time: Hear the disputes between your brothers and judge fairly, whether the case is between brother Israelites or between one of them and an alien. ¹⁷Do not show partiality in judging; hear both small and great alike. Do not be afraid of any man, for judgment belongs to God. Bring me any case too hard for you, and I will hear it.*

Moses then gave instructions to the "judges" (i.e., the "leaders" of the preceding verses to the extent that they were charged with the administration of justice). They must hear both sides of any dispute and must judge fairly. "Your brothers" are fellow Israelites; this is expanded in the last part of the verse: they must not only judge between Israelites, but also between an Israelite and "an alien" (*gēr*), or more precisely, "his alien" (RSV, "the alien that is with him"), who lives under his protection. The "alien" is a "semi-citizen" (in contrast to a foreigner), who is subject to Israelite law. The judges (v. 17) must judge fairly without respect of persons—they must not make a distinction between "small" and "great," between unimportant and important. They must not "be afraid of any man," because "judgment belongs to God." In the final analysis, God is the Judge and the earthly judge acts only as His representative and in His name. The administration of justice is therefore a sacred work and must not be corrupted by partiality or fear of people. And finally, those cases that were too difficult for them were to be brought before Moses, who thus remained, as far as earthly justice was concerned, the final court of appeal.

1:18 *And at that time I told you everything you were to do.*

Verse 18 is not a summary of the preceding but a separate topic. The appointment of leaders was not the only thing Moses did "at that time," i.e., before the people set out on their further journey to Canaan. He told the people "everything [they] were to do," i.e., he taught them God's decrees and laws, as is also stated in Exodus 18:20 in the same context.

C. KADESH BARNEA: THE PEOPLE'S UNBELIEF (1:19-33)

The Lord had done everything that was necessary for Israel to live in Canaan as a blessed nation. But now comes the story of the stay at Kadesh Barnea, where Israel herself through unbelief and disobedience blocked the way into the Promised Land (cf. Num. 13-14).

1:19 *Then, as the LORD our God commanded us, we set out from Horeb and went toward the hill country of the Amorites through all that vast and dreadful desert that you have seen, and so we reached Kadesh Barnea.*

In keeping with the command of verse 7, Israel set out from Horeb and traveled toward the hill country of the Amorites, i.e., toward Canaan. Moses emphatically reminds his hearers how they traveled through "all that vast and dreadful desert" (cf. 8:15; the desert *et Tih*). The difficulties they endured on their journey and especially the help of God they experienced (cf. v. 31) cast the folly of their later attitude into sharp relief. Thus they reached Kadesh Barnea on the border of the Promised Land (cf. Num. 13:26); verse 2 stated that the distance between Horeb and Kadesh Barnea is an eleven-day journey. Numbers 11 and 12 record that the people rebelled against God's guidance as soon as they reached the first stopping places, but Moses does not mention this in order to focus the attention entirely on what happened at Kadesh Barnea.

1:20-21 *Then I said to you, "You have reached the hill country of the Amorites, which the LORD our God is giving us. ²¹See, the LORD your God has given you* *the land. Go up and take possession of it as the LORD, the God of your fathers, told you. Do not be afraid; do not be discouraged."*

Here, at Kadesh, Moses pointed out to the people that they had reached the border of the Promised Land, and, reminding them of the old and new promises of God, he repeated God's command to "go up" (into the hill country) and to take possession of the land (cf. vv. 7–8). He concluded with the strong exhortation to set aside any fear.

1:22–25 *Then all of you came to me and said, "Let us send men ahead to spy out the land for us and bring back a report about the route we are to take and the towns we will come to."*
²³The idea seemed good to me; so I selected twelve of you, one man from each tribe. ²⁴They left and went up into the hill country, and came to the Valley of Eshcol and explored it. ²⁵Taking with them some of the fruit of the land, they brought it down to us and reported, "It is a good land that the LORD our God is giving us."

The decision was postponed. The people wanted to send out spies first—in itself a reasonable request (cf. Num 13:1). Moses then took one man from each tribe, a total of twelve men, who explored especially the Valley of Eshcol near Hebron and brought back with them some of the fruit of the land. They reported that it was a good land. True, this was not all they said—with the exception of two of them, they shared in the unbelief of the people (see comments on v. 28)—but Moses here only shows the bright side, in order to present the contrast with the people's unbelief in the next verses.

1:26–28 *But you were unwilling to go up; you rebelled against the command of the LORD your God. ²⁷You grumbled in your tents and said, "The LORD hates us; so he brought us out of Egypt to deliver us into the hands of the Amorites to destroy us. ²⁸Where can we go? Our brothers have made us lose heart. They say, 'The people are stronger and taller than we are; the cities are large, with walls up to the sky. We even saw the Anakites there.'"*

The people refused to go up. Even as in the preceding verses, Moses addresses the people directly: "*You* were unwilling," even though he is speaking to a new generation that is not directly responsible for what happened then. But it is the same nation, and the fact that Moses addresses this new generation implies both a warning that they may fall into a similar sin and an indirect exhortation to guard against it. Moses emphatically characterizes the people's refusal as rebellion against the command of the Lord, "your God," who had so much reason to expect obedience. The root of this rebellion is identified as unbelief in verse 27 (cf. v. 32). They did not believe in the Lord's love for them; they even, in blasphemous unbelief, recast the Exodus from Egypt, the great evidence of the Lord's love for Israel, into its opposite: they saw it as the result of the Lord's hate, which sought to destroy them. "Grumbled in your tents" (cf. Num. 14:1): they believed, of course, that they had grounds for their grumbling. They appealed to their brothers, the spies, who had taken away their courage by emphasizing the dangers they would face (cf. Num. 13:28ff.). The only exceptions were Caleb (Num. 13:30; cf. Deut. 1:36) and Joshua (Num. 14:6). "Where can we go?" — if we go against so powerful a nation we are going toward our destruction. "With walls up to the sky" is hyperbole, entirely in line with their fear and natural under the circumstances. To the eyes of those standing at the foot of the city walls built on the slopes, it would appear that the walls touch the sky. On "taller," cf. Numbers 13:32. In Numbers 13:33, the "Anakites" are said to belong to the Nephilim (KJV, "giants"); see also comments on 2:10–11 and Numbers 13:22.

1:29–31 *Then I said to you, "Do not be terrified; do not be afraid of them.* [30]*The LORD your God, who is going before you, will fight for you, as he did for you in Egypt, before your very eyes,* [31]*and in the desert. There you saw how the LORD your God carried you, as a father carries his son, all the way you went until you reached this place."*

Moses encouraged them to set aside their fear. The Lord "your God," who had gone before them on their journey and would continue to do so, would Himself fight for them and be with them in no lesser measure than before. The first thing Moses mentioned of the past was what the Lord had done for Israel in Egypt (cf. v. 27); then he reminds them of what the Lord had done for them during the wilderness journey with its troubles and perils (v. 31; cf. v. 19). In the wilderness He carried Israel like a man carries his son (cf. 8:5), i.e., He surrounded Israel with the tenderest of care (cf. v. 33).

1:32–33 *In spite of this, you did not trust in the LORD your God,* [33]*who went ahead of you on your journey, in fire by night and in a cloud by day, to search out places for you to camp and to show you the way you should go.*

In spite of the acts of God of which Moses reminded them, Israel continued to refuse to trust "the LORD your God." And again (v. 33) Moses reminded Israel of God's care during the wilderness journey: God went ahead of them, at night in a column of fire and during the day in a pillar of cloud, to show them a place to camp and to guide them (cf. Exod. 13:21–22; Num. 9:15ff.; 10:34).

D. KADESH BARNEA: THE PUNISHMENT (1:34–46)

The disobedience was followed by punishment (for this section, cf. Num. 14:21–45).

1:34–38 *When the LORD heard what you said, he was angry and solemnly swore:* 35*"Not a man of this evil generation shall see the good land I swore to give your forefathers,* 36*except Caleb son of Jephunneh. He will see it, and I will give him and his descendants the land he set his feet on, because he followed the LORD wholeheartedly."*

37*Because of you the LORD became angry with me also and said, "You shall not enter it, either.* 38*But your assistant, Joshua son of Nun, will enter it. Encourage him, because he will lead Israel to inherit it.*

The people's expressions of disobedience (vv. 27–28), in which they persisted even after Moses' speech (v. 32), aroused the Lord's anger. He swore that no one of this generation would enter the Promised Land.

An exception was made for Caleb, one of the spies, because he remained faithful to the Lord and encouraged the people to enter Canaan in obedience to God's command (cf. Num. 13:30). Joshua, who is also mentioned in Numbers 14:6, is not spoken of here, since he will be mentioned later in a somewhat different context.

On the other hand, the Lord was also angry with Moses (v. 37), who will not enter Canaan either. According to Numbers 20:1–13 (cf. Deut. 32:51) this event took place later, during the second stay at Kadesh, when Moses (and Aaron) did not honor the Lord at Meribah. Deuteronomy does not mention the second stay at Kadesh at all, and Moses links the story of his punishment directly to Israel's refusal to enter Canaan ("because of you"). The occasion for Moses' sin was the rebellion of the people against the Lord. The fact that Moses emphasizes this without mentioning his own sin directly indicates how much he wants to show the full extent of the sin and guilt of the people in order that his hearers may guard against doing the same thing. Because of God's displeasure Moses was told that he could not enter Canaan. In his place, Joshua, Moses' assistant (lit., "who stands before you," cf. KJV, RSV) will be Israel's leader when they take possession of Canaan; Moses must therefore "encourage him" (lit., "strengthen him"), i.e., through instruction and encouragement prepare him for his great task (v. 38).

1:39–40 *And the little ones that you said would be taken captive, your children who do not yet know good from bad—they will enter the land. I will give it to them and they will take possession of it. ⁴⁰But as for you, turn around and set out toward the desert along the route to the Red Sea."*

But the Israel that will take possession of Canaan will be a new generation. The Lord told the "evil generation," whom He had rejected (v. 35), that not they but their children would enter the land. The same children about whom the people in their unbelief had wailed that they would fall prey to the enemy will receive the fulfillment of the promise in their parents' stead. Thus their unbelief is both punished and exposed in its folly: when God will give Canaan to those who were then small, helpless children, it will be a striking evidence of His power and faithfulness. The addition "who do not yet know good from bad" (i.e., who do not yet have understanding—a child reaches for fire, walks into the water, etc.) serves to throw their helplessness, and thus God's work, into bolder relief. The unbelieving generation, by contrast, received another command (v. 40). They must turn around and go back into the wilderness, back toward the Red Sea (here the Gulf of Aqaba; cf. 2:2; Num 14:25). "Set out," cf. verse 7. According to Numbers 14:25 they were to set out the next day.

1:41–42 *Then you replied, "We have sinned against the LORD. We will go up and fight, as the LORD our God commanded us." So every one of you put on his weapons, thinking it easy to go up into the hill country.*
⁴²But the LORD said to me, "Tell them, 'Do not go up and fight, because I will not be with you. You will be defeated by your enemies.'"

The divine punishment did not fail to make an impression on the people. They admitted that they had sinned against the Lord and now declared themselves prepared to obey God's command to go up and fight. But there was no true repentance. They were still the same people, going again against the Lord's command (vv. 40, 41)—self-willed Israel who did not want to go when they were allowed to and who want to go when they no longer may. "We will go up": not our children, but we. They put on their weapons and were ready to go up; their fear had turned into rashness, which is as alien to true faith in God as fear. Moses, in the Lord's name, emphatically forbade the people to go up and fight (v. 42)—they were assured that they would most certainly be defeated because the Lord would not be with them as when things were well (cf. Josh. 5:13ff.; 2 Sam. 5:24; Ps. 44:10). Numbers 14:44 indicates that the Lord's not going with them was also manifested externally by the ark's remaining in the camp. The Lord is a forgiving God, but this does not mean that He must be moved by the cry of the people, "We have sinned," to revoke the sentence pronounced in verse 35. Although the Lord could have removed the sentence, He remains sovereign also in this. Besides, He knew that the attitude of the people had not fundamentally changed (cf. also 1 Sam. 28:6; Hos. 5:6).

1:43–45 *So I told you, but you would not listen. You rebelled against the* LORD'*s command and in your arrogance you marched up into the hill country.* ⁴⁴*The Amorites who lived in those hills came out against you; they chased you like a swarm of bees and beat you down from Seir all the way to Hormah.* ⁴⁵*You came back and wept before the* LORD, *but he paid no attention to your weeping and turned a deaf ear to you.*

Again the people rebelled against God's command (cf. v. 26) and marched up, but they had to suffer the consequences (v. 44). The Amorites came out and defeated the Israelites; they chased them (lit.) "as the bees do" (cf. RSV), so fierce and so numerous were they. The Amorites beat the Israelites (lit.) "in Seir, to Hormah." Hormah is the later name of the city of Zephath (Judg. 1:17) and is thus used proleptically here; it is perhaps the present es-Sebaita, north-northeast of Kadesh (see also Num. 14:45). "In Seir" (NIV, "from Seir") is unclear, since other data at our disposal place Seir farther to the east; but it is possible that the name is used here in a broader sense.¹ They came back to the camp (v. 45) and went "before the Lord," i.e., in front of the tabernacle, to invoke His mercy and help. But God does not let Himself be swayed by the weeping of a people that still rebels against His command.

1:46 *And so you stayed in Kadesh many days—all the time you spent there.*

We see this verse as a summary description of the entire period of time Israel stayed in Kadesh, which began in verse 19. It is clear that the sending out of the spies alone would involve quite some time. Others take this verse in the sense that *after* the defeat Israel stayed

---

¹Some would delete "in Seir" as a later addition (Num. 14:45 has only "to Hormah"). Others, like the NIV, read "from Seir," i.e., from the western border to Seir to Hormah.

many days in Kadesh. But this is in our opinion less likely, since the command of verse 40 appears to indicate an imminent departure (cf. Num. 14:25, "tomorrow"); this departure had been delayed by the people's disobedience, and it probably took some time after the defeat before the people could set out, but if the people had wanted to remain there "many days," Moses would undoubtedly have objected, of which we hear nothing. "All the days you spent there": Moses does not deem it necessary to say exactly how long; we might paraphrase, "exactly how many days is irrelevant." Another possible interpretation of the phrase is, "many days, equal to the days you had already spent there." But this presupposes that after the defeat Israel stayed at Kadesh for many more days, which we consider unlikely for reasons already stated.

E. FROM KADESH SOUTH AND ALONG THE BORDER OF EDOM (2:1–8)

2:1 *Then we turned back and set out toward the desert along the route to the Red Sea, as the LORD had directed me. For a long time we made our way around the hill country of Seir.*

After the stay in Kadesh the journey was resumed—not directly to Canaan but into the desert, in the direction of the Red Sea, in accordance with the command of 1:40 (cf. Num. 14:25). They traveled along (the western and southern edge of) the hill country of Seir. "For a long time": according to 2:14, the journey from Kadesh to the crossing of the brook Zered (KJV; NIV, "Zered Valley") took thirty-eight years. Much happened during that period, including a second stay at Kadesh (Num. 20:1); none of these events are mentioned here. In a simplified description Moses presents all that took place during those years as a single journey from Kadesh to the Red Sea.

2:2–7 *Then the LORD said to me,* *³"You have made your way around this hill country long enough; now turn north.* *⁴Give the people these orders: 'You are about to pass through the territory of your brothers the descendants of Esau, who live in Seir. They will be afraid of you, but be very careful.* *⁵Do not provoke them to war, for I will not give you any of their land, not even enough to put your foot on. I have given Esau the hill country of Seir as his own.* *⁶You are to pay them in silver for the food you eat and the water you drink.' "*
    ⁷The LORD your God has blessed you in all the work of your hands. He has watched over your journey through this vast desert. These forty years the LORD your God has been with you, and you have not lacked anything.

From the Gulf of Aqaba they traveled north, along the border of Edom to the region of Moab. Finally they received the Lord's command to turn north (from the northern tip of the Gulf of Aqaba, where they found themselves, v. 3; cf. Num. 21:4, 10ff.). "Long enough" (here and in 1:6) indicates that a new period is about to begin. After all the wandering, Israel was finally headed for Canaan. They would meet (v. 4) "the descendants of Esau," i.e., the Edomites, and God gave them instructions how to behave toward them. The Edomites are called "your brothers" because Esau was Jacob's brother; this reminder of their common ancestry contains a motive for the attitude towards them that the Lord asks from Israel (cf. also 23:7; but cf. Amos 1:11; Obad. 10). Neither here nor in verse 8 is mention made of Edom's refusal to let Israel pass through its territory (underlined in the threat of military action; Num. 20:14-21; cf. Judg. 11:17); Moses recounts here simply what finally did happen. The Edomites "will be afraid of you," i.e., they will not initiate a confrontation. But Israel must not be led by a sense of superiority and attack Edom: the hill country of Seir (v. 5) had been given to Edom by the Lord Himself (cf. v. 12), albeit not in perpetuity (cf. Num. 24:18; et al.). The Israelites thus must not take anything from the Edomites by force (v. 6) but must obtain the necessary food and water (cf. Num. 20:17, 19) by peaceful means, i.e., by purchase. Verse 7 speaks of the blessing Israel experienced in the wilderness; the verse begins with "for" (omitted in the NIV), which can be taken to mean, "You *can* pay all this because you have money as a result of the blessing bestowed" (money acquired by selling the products of their labor to the Arabs). "All the work of your hands" probably refers primarily to the keeping of flocks and herds, an enterprise they continued during the wilderness journey (Exod. 19:13; Num. 20:19; 32:1ff.) and of which they could sell some products (e.g., wool and the fabric made with it).

Moses then elaborates on that blessing. God "watched over your journey through this vast wilderness" (lit., He "knew your journey," i.e., cared for all your needs on the journey). During that entire forty-year period (see comments on vv. 1, 14) the Lord was with them so that they lacked nothing. It is clear that in the second half of this verse the mention of God's blessing no longer serves to point out that they are able to pay but rather that God's blessing must be a motivation to obey His instructions and to be generous toward their Edomite brothers. (It is also possible that both parts of the verse should be interpreted in this sense, so that the above explanation, "You *can* pay," would be dropped; this has the advantage of a more unified sense. We cannot be certain, but it is possible that Moses shifted from one emphasis to the other.)

2:8 *So we went on past our brothers the descendants of Esau, who live in Seir. We turned from the Arabah road, which comes up from Elath and Ezion Geber, and traveled along the desert road of Moab.*

The Israelites traveled on in a northerly direction in accord with the command of verse 3. But here they are not said to have gone *through* the territory of the Edomites, as in verse 4, but rather *past* it, ("away from our brethren," RSV). But there is no indication that this is intended as a contrast with verse 4; verse 29 also states that the Israelites came in contact with the Edomites. The intent of this verse is thus that Israel did not cross Edom's territory but rather went around the southern edge of its territory (which extends to the vicinity of the Gulf of Aqaba), and continued to travel along its border in a northerly direction. Israel thus bypassed Edom but traveled so near to it that verse 4 can say that they traveled "through" it and so close that they could transact business with the Edomites (v. 6). The "Arabah road" (cf. v. 1) probably went through Edom's territory; Israel thus also bypassed this road, leaving it to their left. Elath and Ezion Geber were on the Gulf of Aqaba (called Yam Suph, "Sea of Reeds," in v. 1; cf. NIV mg.). They also bypassed these cities and here they turned north. And thus they traveled "along the desert road of Moab" or "in the direction of the steppe of Moab" (cf. KJV), i.e., the steppe east of Moab (northeast of Edom); cf. Numbers 21:11.

F. ALONG MOAB AND AMMON TO THE BORDER OF THE AMORITES
(2:9–25)

The Moabites and Ammonites are descendants of Lot, Abraham's nephew (Gen. 19:37); they were thus related to Israel, albeit less closely than the Edomites, who are called Israel's "brothers" (2:4). This is one of the reasons why Israel must "not harass" them and not "provoke them to war" (vv. 9, 19).

2:9 *Then the LORD said to me, "Do not harass the Moabites or provoke them to war, for I will not give you any part of their land. I have given Ar to the descendants of Lot as a possession."*

The Israelites first reached Moab. Moses received the divine command to treat them kindly (cf. v. 5). "Ar" is in the first place the name of the capital of Moab, but here the name apparently refers to the Moabite territory as a whole (cf. v. 18). Israel will not receive any portion of this land because the Lord has given it to the Moabites, who are here called "the descendants of Lot," reminding Israel of their blood ties with this nation.

2:10–12 *(The Emites used to live there—a people strong and numerous, and as tall as the Anakites.* [11]*Like the Anakites, they too were considered Rephaites, but the Moabites called them Emites.* [12]*Horites used to live in Seir, but the descendants of Esau drove them out. They destroyed the Horites from before them and settled in their place, just as Israel did in the land the* LORD *gave them as their possession.)*

Here a historical note is inserted in the narrative concerning the previous inhabitants of the Moabite territory to illustrate that the Moabites and Edomites did not always live there but received this land from the Lord (v. 9; cf. v. 5). He is not only the God of Israel, but He also guides the lot of the nations and determines their habitat (cf. 32:8; Amos 9:7). The Emites used to live in Moab (v. 10; cf. Gen. 14:5); like the Anakites (1:28), they were tall people and a branch of the Rephaites (cf. Gen. 14:5; 15:20), whose size is also elsewhere mentioned as their chief characteristic (v. 21; 3:11). Verse 12 adds that the Horites (cf. Gen. 14:6; 36:20, 29) once lived in Seir (cf. vv. 4–5). The Edomites drove them out and destroyed them and took possession of their land, just as the Israelites took possession of the land the Lord gave them. As we already saw, both the Edomites and the Moabites received their land from the Lord (vv. 5, 9; cf. vv. 21–22); this, of course, is not to deny that this was true of Israel in a different sense than of these nations. The question arises how verse 12 can speak of the land the Lord "gave" Israel "as their possession," when the land west of the Jordan was yet to be conquered at the time of Moses' discourse. The solution that the land east of the Jordan is in view here is unsatisfactory; this land had indeed been given as a "possession" (3:20), but only to Reuben, Gad, and the half-tribe of Manasseh, while verse 12 speaks of "Israel." It is in our opinion more likely that verses 10–12 are not part of Moses' discourse but a later interpolation (the NIV indicates this by placing these verses in parentheses). The context also supports this view. It is difficult to see how these verses can be part of God's command that begins in verse 9; rather, they seem to interrupt it (v. 12

speaks of the Lord in the third person). We can of course assume that such interpolations have found their way into the Scriptures under God's special providence (cf. Introduction).

2:13-15 *And the LORD said, "Now get up and cross the Zered Valley." So we crossed the valley.* *[14]Thirty-eight years passed from the time we left Kadesh Barnea until we crossed the Zered Valley. By then, that entire generation of fighting men had perished from the camp, as the LORD had sworn to them. [15]The LORD's hand was against them until he had completely eliminated them from the camp.*

The divine command of verse 9 is continued. Israel must cross the Zered Valley;[2] its location is uncertain (see Noordtzij on Num. 21:12-13 in the *Bible Student's Commentary*). According to verse 8, Israel was east of Moab; they apparently traveled in a generally northerly direction, but in such a way that they went through the edge of Moab's territory (see below, v. 18).

Israel obeyed God's instructions, and here is the point where Moses observes that thirty-eight years have passed since Israel left Kadesh Barnea (i.e., since the first time they left, cf. Num. 14:20ff.). The wilderness journey lasted forty years in all (v. 7); the remaining two years cover the time from the Exodus to the first departure from Kadesh. In those thirty-eight years the entire generation whom the Lord had under oath denied entrance into Canaan perished (1:34-35). The reference is specifically to the "fighting men," i.e., the men twenty years of age and older (cf. Num. 1:3; 14:29). They did not all die a natural death; some perished as a result of the Lord's judgment (v. 15; cf. Num. 14:37; 16:35; 17:13; 21:6; 25:9).

2:16-19 *Now when the last of these fighting men among the people had died, [17]the LORD said to me, [18]"Today you are to pass by the region of Moab at Ar. [19]When you come to the Ammonites, do not harass them or provoke them to war, for I will not give you possession of any land belonging to the Ammonites. I have given it as a possession to the descendants of Lot."*

Across the Zered Valley Moses received new instructions for the people, this time with regard to Ammon. First they were told that they would "pass by the region of Moab" (RSV, "pass over the boundary of

---

[2]KJV, RSV: "the brook Zered." The Hebrew *nachal* can mean "wadi" or "stream bed," but also "stream" or "torrent," due to the fact that the wadis are dry most of the year but become "torrents" during the rainy season.—TRANS.

Moab"). Verse 29 indicates that the Moabites (even as the Edomites) did not place obstacles in the way of their peaceful passage; Israel probably passed through only the edge of their territory, as they did in the case of Edom. But their journey will thus take them into the vicinity of the Amorites, who lived northeast of Moab (v. 19; lit., "you shall draw near, across from the sons of Ammon") i.e., they will approach them in such a manner that Ammon will not be straight ahead but off to their side; this means that Israel does not have to cross the territory of the Ammonites (also descendants of Lot) as they did with regard to the Moabites (cf. v. 9).

2:20–23 *(That too was considered a land of the Rephaites, who used to live there; but the Ammonites called them Zamzummites. ²¹They were a people strong and numerous, and as tall as the Anakites. The LORD destroyed them from before the Ammonites, who drove them out and settled in their place. ²²The LORD had done the same for the descendants of Esau, who lived in Seir, when he destroyed the Horites from before them. They drove them out and have lived in their place to this day. ²³And as for the Avvites who lived in villages as far as Gaza, the Caphtorites coming out from Caphtor destroyed them and settled in their place.)*

Again a historical note is inserted (cf. vv. 10–12), perhaps also from a later hand; its content is similar to that of verses 10–12. The Rephaites who once lived here were called Zamzummites (probably the same as the Zuzites of Gen. 14:5). Here it is stated explicitly that the Lord destroyed them so that the Ammonites could settle their territory. Verse 22 refers once again to the Horites who were driven out by the Edomites (cf. v. 12). Verse 23 mentions still another tribe that once lived here, the Avvites (cf. Josh. 13:3). They lived in (tent) villages as far as Gaza and were displaced by the Caphtorites who invaded Canaan from Caphtor (Crete; cf. also Gen. 10:14).

2:24–25 *"Set out now and cross the Arnon Gorge. See, I have given into your hand Sihon the Amorite, king of Heshbon, and his country. Begin to take possession of it and engage him in battle. ²⁵This very day I will begin to put the terror and fear of you on all the nations under heaven. They will hear reports of you and will tremble and be in anguish because of you."*

God's instructions of verse 9 are continued. Israel must cross the Arnon, which was at that time the northern boundary of Moab. Thus they approached the two kingdoms the Amorites had established east of the Jordan. The southernmost was the kingdom of Sihon, who resided in Heshbon. In spite of the fact that the land east of the Jordan was not specifically part of the land promised to the patriarchs (cf. 2:29), Israel was told to have a different attitude towards the Amorites than towards the Edomites and the Moabites (although the Amorites are treated differently than the population of Canaan proper; see comments on 2:26–29). The Amorites are an offshoot of the nations of Canaan who are destined for judgment. Thus, the Lord promised that He would give Sihon (and later also Og) into Israel's power; they must engage him in battle and thus take the first step toward the conquest of the land. The Lord also took the first step (v. 25) by putting the "terror and fear" of Israel on the nations. "Under heaven" is a hyperbolic expression indicating first of all that whatever nations Israel might encounter, none would be able to resist (cf. 11:25; Exod. 23:27), but also that other nations who might hear reports of Israel's advance would tremble.

G. CONQUEST OF THE KINGDOM OF SIHON (2:26–37)

2:26–29 *From the desert of Kedemoth I sent messengers to Sihon king of Heshbon offering peace and saying, 27"Let us pass through your country. We will stay on the main road; we will not turn aside to the right or to the left. 28Sell us food to eat and water to drink for their price in silver. Only let us pass through on foot— 29as the descendants of Esau, who live in Seir, and the Moabites, who live in Ar, did for us—until we cross the Jordan into the land the LORD our God is giving us."*

Moses began by requesting Sihon to allow Israel peaceful passage through his territory (cf. Num. 21:21ff.). In spite of the command of verse 24b, Israel (probably on the Lord's instructions) did not initiate the hostilities. The territory God had promised to the forefathers lay west of the Jordan as an "extra." This also was in accord with God's counsel and the promise given to Moses (v. 24; see also v. 30). But Sihon would bring his fate on himself by his attitude toward Israel; and thus Moses made his request in good faith, even though he knew what the outcome would be (v. 24).

The desert of Kedemoth (v. 26), named for the city of Kedemoth in what would later be Reuben's territory (Josh. 13:18; 1 Chron. 6:79), lay north of the eastern reaches of the Arnon, which marks the southeasterly border between the Amorites and Moab (Judg. 11:18). Moses promised that they would stay on the main road and not cross the fields and farmlands of Sihon's kingdom (v. 27; cf. Num. 20:19). He promised that they would pay for food and water (cf. v. 6). "Only let us pass through on foot" is a descriptive expression that accentuates the fact that Israel requested permission to merely pass through. We have not been told before that Edom and Moab granted this request (v. 29; see vv. 4, 9, 18). In 23:4 Moab and Ammon are reproached for not having met them "with bread and water"; this does not contradict verse 29, but rather indicates a lack of spontaneous support, which would have gone well beyond what is stated in verse 29. On "in Ar," cf. verse 18 (Ar here refers to the territory of Moab). "Until we cross the Jordan. . ." indicates the reason why Israel made this request: it wanted to go to the Promised Land. Sihon is here given the opportunity to save his life and his kingdom.

2:30-31 *But Sihon king of Heshbon refused to let us pass through. For the* LORD *your God had made his spirit stubborn and his heart obstinate in order to give him into your hands, as he has now done.*
    ³¹The LORD *said to me, "See, I have begun to deliver Sihon and his country over to you. Now begin to conquer and possess his land."*

But Sihon refused to let Israel pass through. The Lord, the God of Israel, had made "his spirit stubborn and his heart obstinate": he was insensitive to the peaceful offer of Israel and the offer of grace of Israel's God implicit in Israel's request. What is said here of the hardening caused by God shows us that the Lord's counsel was fulfilled through Sihon's refusal; thus the Lord wanted to give him and his kingdom into Israel's hand. This does not negate Sihon's responsibility. On the basis of what the Scriptures teach elsewhere concerning the history of sin, we must assume that this hardening does not function mechanically but allows for a choice of the human will; the fact that we cannot harmonize God's counsel and work on the one hand and man's freedom and responsibility on the other does not make either of them less real.

"As he has now done" (v. 30), i.e., at the time of Moses' discourse Sihon had been defeated by Israel and his kingdom was in Israel's possession; this in itself was proof that God had thus willed and worked it. "I have begun to deliver . . ." (v. 31), i.e., by hardening Sihon's heart. The Lord then urged Moses and Israel to begin the conquest by taking Sihon's territory.

2:32-36 *When Sihon and all his army came out to meet us in battle at Jahaz,* *³³the* LORD *our God delivered him over to us and we struck him down, together* *with his sons and his whole army.* ³⁴*At that time we took all his towns and completely destroyed them—men, women and children. We left no survivors.* ³⁵*But the livestock and the plunder from the towns we had captured we carried off for ourselves.* ³⁶*From Aroer on the rim of the Arnon Gorge, and from the town in the gorge, even as far as Gilead, not one town was too strong for us. The* LORD *our God gave us all of them.*

Sihon engaged in battle at Jahaz and was defeated (cf. Num. 21:23–26). The Lord (v. 33) decided the battle in Israel's favor: Sihon was "struck down" together with his sons and his whole army (lit., "people"), which indicates not only that he was defeated, but also that he and his sons and army were killed. All his cities were "completely destroyed" (put under the ban, *cherem*; cf. NIV mg.), specifically the people in them. "We left no survivors" does not have to be taken literally; expressions like this are frequently used hyperbolically (cf. 2 Chron. 14:13). The "ban" (*cherem;* Lev. 27:28–29; Num. 21:2) means that something is devoted to God, frequently as part of a vow; the devoted thing may be turned over to the priests (Num. 18:14) or to the sanctuary (Josh. 6:24), or it may be destroyed. The latter implies complete dedication to a divine judgment. This was true of the Canaanites, although the purpose of the *cherem* in that case also included the preservation of Israel (Deut. 20:1). The ban of destruction was enjoined on Israel with respect to the Canaanites in general but was applied in its strict sense only to Jericho, where not only the people and the cattle were killed, but the city itself with everything in it was burnt, except for the metal objects, which were given to the sanctuary (Josh. 6:24). The other cities of Canaan were left standing, but the inhabitants were killed and the property divided as spoils. Cattle were dealt with differently on different occasions (Josh. 8:21ff.; 10:28ff.; 11:11ff.).

In this case the livestock was divided along with the plunder (v. 35). Verse 36 implies that this principle applied to the entire territory of Sihon, from the Arnon to Gilead; we find elsewhere that the southernmost half of Gilead (south of the Jabbok) was also included (Num. 21:24; Josh. 12:2; Judg. 11:22). Aroer lies on the middle reaches of the Arnon, on the north side, and is thus also included in the conquest. "The town in the gorge" is also mentioned alongside Aroer in Joshua 13:9, 16, and 2 Samuel 24:5, and probably refers to a part of Aroer that lay in the Arnon Gorge. The entire territory mentioned here was conquered along with its fortified cities: none of them was "too strong" (lit., "too high" or "too steep").

2:37 *But in accordance with the command of the LORD our God, you did not encroach on any of the land of the Ammonites, neither the land along the course of the Jabbok nor that around the towns in the hills.*

On the other hand, Moses notes that Israel did not "encroach on any of the land of the Moabites" (cf. v. 19). "The land along the course of the Jabbok" refers to the east bank of the upper reaches of the Jabbok, while "the hills"are the hills farther to the east. (When it is said in Josh. 13:25 that the tribe of Gad received "half the Ammonite country as far as Aroer" we should understand this to refer to a region between the Arnon and the Jabbok that the Amorites had captured from the Ammonites and that is thus included in the territory the Israelites took from the Amorites; cf. Judg. 11:13ff.)

H. CONQUEST OF THE KINGDOM OF OG (3:1–7)

3:1–3 *Next we turned and went up along the road toward Bashan, and Og king of Bashan with his whole army marched out to meet us in battle at Edrei. ²The LORD said to me, "Do not be afraid of him, for I have handed him over to you with his whole army and his land. Do to him what you did to Sihon king of the Amorites, who reigned in Heshbon."*
³So the LORD our God also gave into our hands Og king of Bashan and all his army. We struck them down, leaving no survivors.

The report of the conquest of the kingdom of Og here is almost identical to the report in Numbers 21:33–35. His kingdom is called Bashan (cf. also v. 4). In the narrower sense, Bashan is the land from the Yarmuk to the Hermon in the north and to the Hauran mountains in the east. It is a fertile plain, famous for its fat cows (Amos 4:1) and its oak forests (Isa. 2:13). But since according to verse 13 Og's territory also included northern Gilead (south of the Yarmuk; see comments on 2:26), "Bashan" here is apparently used in a broader sense to include northern Gilead. This time the hostile initiative was more on Israel's side (in contrast to 2:26). Even though they should have turned west to reach their goal (cf. 2:29b), they went north toward Bashan; it was apparently assumed that, since the southern kingdom had been conquered, peace with the northern kingdom was an impossibility. Og immediately marched out against Israel with his entire army and met them at Edrei (cf. 1:4). Here also Moses was encouraged by God's promise, which was fulfilled in the destruction of Og and his army (v. 3; "leaving no survivors," see comments on 2:34).

3:4–7 *At that time we took all his cities. There was not one of the sixty cities that we did not take from them—the whole region of Argob, Og's kingdom in Bashan. ⁵All these cities were fortified with high walls and with gates and bars, and there were also a great many unwalled villages. ⁶We completely destroyed them, as we had done with Sihon king of Heshbon, destroying every city—men, women and children. ⁷But all the livestock and the plunder from their cities we carried off for ourselves.*

After the battle all fortified cities were captured, sixty cities in all. The region is here called Argob (cf. vv. 13-14; 1 Kings 4:13). Besides the sixty fortified cities there were also many unwalled villages. All cities were also "utterly destroyed" in the same manner as Sihon's (vv. 6–7; see comments on 2:34–35).

I. THE DIVISION OF THE LAND EAST OF THE JORDAN (3:8–20)

Moses here reminds Israel how he assigned the conquered territory east of the Jordan to Reuben, Gad, and the half tribe of Manasseh (cf. Num. 32:34–38).

3:8–11 *So at that time we took from these two kings of the Amorites the territory east of the Jordan, from the Arnon Gorge as far as Mount Hermon. ⁹(Hermon is called Sirion by the Sidonians; the Amorites call it Senir.) ¹⁰We took all the towns on the plateau, and all Gilead, and all Bashan as far as Salecah and Edrei, towns of Og's kingdom in Bashan. ¹¹(Only Og king of Bashan was left of the remnant of the Rephaites. His bed was made of iron and was more than thirteen feet long and six feet wide. It is still in Rabbah of the Ammonites.)*

First, the combined territory of the two defeated kings is described; it stretches from the Arnon Gorge in the south to Mount Hermon in the north. "East of the Jordan" is literally "across the Jordan" (see comments on 1:1, 5). Verse 9 interjects the fact that the Sidonians call Mount Hermon "Sirion," while the Amorites call it "Senir." Verse 10 lists the regions from south to north: first, the plateau (Heb., *mīshōr*), then Gilead, and finally Bashan. Verse 11 adds an archaeological-historical footnote: he was the last of the Rephaites (2:11) who once inhabited Bashan (v. 13; Gen. 14:5); as such he was a gigantic man, which accentuates the greatness of the victory God gave the Israelites. As proof of this the reader is referred to his "sarcophagus made of basalt" (cf. NIV mg.), which could still be seen in Rabbah of the Ammonites. The phrase is also rendered "bed made of iron," which is indeed the normal meaning of the words; but the fact that the object was preserved makes it more likely that a coffin or sarcophagus is in view here, especially because such enormous sarcophagi made of basalt can still be found east of the Jordan. Basalt is a ferrous rock that is like iron in color and hardness. Since such an archaeological comment would make little sense coming from Moses, who was a contemporary of Og, we take this verse to be a later addition, that found a place here under God's special providence (cf. Introduction).

3:12–17 *Of the land that we took over at that time, I gave the Reubenites and the Gadites the territory north of Aroer by the Arnon Gorge, including half the hill country of Gilead, together with its towns. ¹³The rest of Gilead and also all of Bashan, the kingdom of Og, I gave to the half tribe of Manasseh. (The whole region of Argob in Bashan used to be known as a land of the Rephaites.) ¹⁴Jair, a descendant of Manasseh, took the whole region of Argob as far as the border of the Geshurites and the Maacathites; it was named after him, so that to this day Bashan is called Havvoth Jair. ¹⁵And I gave Gilead to Makir. ¹⁶But to the Reubenites and the Gadites I gave the territory extending from Gilead down to the Arnon Gorge (the middle of the gorge being the border) and out to the Jabbok River, which is the border of the Ammonites. ¹⁷Its western border was the Jordan in the Arabah, from Kinnereth to the Sea of the Arabah (the Salt Sea), below the slopes of Pisgah.*

Moses divided the southern part, from Aroer north to the Jabbok (thus including half of Gilead), between Reuben and Gad. The northern part of Gilead, together with Bashan or Argob (cf. v. 4) was given to the half tribe of Manasseh. "The whole region of Argob . . . ," see comments on 2:20.

Verses 14–17 mention further details, first concerning the territory assigned to Manasseh. Verse 14 (cf. Num. 32:41) specifies the territory Jair "took," i.e., conquered and hence received from Moses in the division. Jair was the grandson of a daughter of Makir, the son of Manasseh (1 Chron. 2:21–22). He received Argob (Bashan) "as far as the border of the Geshurites and Maacathites," Aramean tribes south of the Hermon, where they still had independent kingdoms in David's time (Absalom's mother was a daughter of the king of Geshur. Josh. 13:11; 2 Sam. 3:3; 10:6; 15:8; 1 Chron. 19:6–7). Jair's territory is here first called "the whole region of Argob" and then "Havvoth Jair" ("Settlements of Jair"). Since in verse 13 Argob refers to all of Bashan, it is logical to assume that it has the same meaning here. The "settlements of Jair" are apparently the same as the sixty cities of Bashan; the same is true in Joshua 13:30. On the other hand,

1 Chronicles 2:22–23 assigns to Jair only twenty-three of the "sixty cities" (which must be the sixty cities of Bashan; v. 22 places these twenty-three cities in Gilead, but the name apparently refers to the entire region east of the Jordan). The other thirty-seven are "Kenath with its surrounding settlements." We must compare this with Numbers 32:42, where besides Jair is also mentioned Nobah, who captured Kenath and its surrounding settlements. According to these references in 2 Chronicles and Numbers, Bashan was thus divided among two Manassite clans. When our text assigns all of Bashan to Jair, we must understand this in the sense that Jair was the more important of the two clans; perhaps Nobah was a branch of the clan of Jair. Concerning the use of "Settlements of Jair" in later times, see Judges 10:3–5 and 1 Kings 4:13, where Argob and Havvoth Jair are distinguished, indicating that the two names are not always used synonymously. The words "to this day" make little sense coming from Moses and are best understood as a later addition (see comments on 2:10–12 and Introduction, p. 22).

Verse 15 adds that Makir, another Manassite clan (Gen. 50:23; Num. 26:29), received Gilead (cf. Num. 32:40). This must then be the part of Gilead north of the Jabbok, since the southern part of Gilead was given to Reuben and Gad (vv. 12–13).

Verses 16–17 give a further description of the territory given to Reuben and Gad and are thus an elaboration of verse 12. "From Gilead down to the Arnon Gorge," includes all of Gilead south of the Jabbok (v. 12). The southern border of this region is the Arnon Gorge, more specifically the middle of the gorge rather than its northern rim. The eastern border is the upper reaches of the Jabbok, across from which are the Ammonites.

These tribes also received the Arabah, the Jordan Valley (cf. 1:1), with the Jordan itself as the border, so that their territory includes only the eastern part of the valley from the Sea of Galilee in the north to the Dead Sea in the south. Kinnereth is sometimes the name of a city (at least in Josh. 19:35) in the territory of Naphtali, probably west of the Sea of Galilee. In 1 Kings 15:20 it refers to the region around the Sea of Galilee, and this is probably its meaning here (Josh. 11:2). Hence the name, Sea of Kinnereth (Num. 34:11; Josh. 13:27; its later name is Gennesar, 1 Macc. 11:67, or Gennesaret, Luke 5:1). "Sea of the Arabah" and "Salt Sea" are names for the Dead Sea, which lies "below the slopes of Pisgah," the mountains east of the north end of the Dead Sea and the southern part of the Jordan Valley; elsewhere

Pisgah is called "Abarim Range" (32:49; Num. 27:12; 33–47). Mount Nebo is one of its peaks (Num. 21:20). (The NIV omits "on the east" at the end of v. 17; cf. RSV.)

3:18–20 *I commanded you at that time: "The LORD your God has given you this land to take possession of it. But all your able-bodied men, armed for battle, must cross over ahead of your brother Israelites. ¹⁹However, your wives, your children and your livestock (I know you have much livestock) may stay in the towns I have given you, ²⁰until the LORD gives rest to your brothers as he has to you, and they too have taken over the land that the LORD your God is giving them, across the Jordan. After that, each of you may go back to the possession I have given you."*

Added to the description of the division is a reminder of the obligation Moses imposed on the trans-Jordan tribes: they were to cross the Jordan ahead of the other tribes and participate in the conquest of Canaan proper (Num. 32 gives a more extensive description of this). This historical note was important for the future to confirm the bond between the tribes on both sides of the Jordan. "Across the Jordan" reflects Moses' perspective prior to the conquest (see comments on 2:10–12 and Introduction, p. 19).

J. JOSHUA TO BE MOSES' SUCCESSOR (3:21–29)

The occupation of the land east of the Jordan was only a prelude to the conquest of Canaan proper. The charge to the tribes that were to settle east of the Jordan (vv. 18–20) already referred to the conquest and God's appointment of Joshua as Moses' successor was a further preparation for it (cf. Num. 27:12ff.).

3:21–22 *At that time I commanded Joshua: "You have seen with your own eyes all that the LORD your God has done to these two kings. The LORD will do the same to all the kingdoms over there where you are going. ²²Do not be afraid of them; the LORD your God himself will fight for you."*

These verses contain a charge to Joshua that anticipate what follows; Joshua is not formally introduced as Moses' successor until verse 28 (at least in this context; see also 1:38). Moses records his speech to Joshua here in verse 21 because his words to Joshua tie in closely with the conquest of the land east of the Jordan that has just been mentioned. What Joshua had seen here with his own eyes would be repeated on the other side of the Jordan; neither he nor Israel must be afraid, since none less than the Lord "your God" (the God who has allied Himself to you, on whom you can depend) will fight for them (cf. 1:29-30).

3:23-28 *At that time I pleaded with the LORD:* ²⁴*"O Sovereign LORD, you have begun to show to your servant your greatness and your strong hand. For what god is there in heaven or on earth who can do the deeds and mighty works you do?* ²⁵*Let me go over and see the good land beyond the Jordan—that fine hill country and Lebanon."*
²⁶*But because of you the LORD was angry with me and would not listen to me. "That is enough," the LORD said. "Do not speak to me anymore about this matter.* ²⁷*Go up to the top of Pisgah and look west and north and south and east. Look at the land with your own eyes, since you are not going to cross this Jordan.* ²⁸*But commission Joshua, and encourage and strengthen him, for he will lead this people across and will cause them to inherit the land that you will see."*

It is now explained why Joshua is placed in the foreground in verse 21. Moses' prayer to be allowed to enter Canaan was not granted (this incident is not mentioned in Num. 27:12ff.). Moses' plea (vv. 24–25) was based on God's earlier statement to him that he would not enter Canaan, but that Joshua would replace him (1:37-38). He pleaded (v. 24) not on the basis of anything he might have done or might deserve, but on what the "Sovereign Lord" (lit., "Lord LORD," *Adonai Jahweh*) had done. God had begun to show Moses (who calls himself respectfully "your servant") His "greatness" and His "strong hand." Based on this, Moses adds a doxology, in which he extols the Lord as the One to whom no other god in heaven or on earth can compare (cf. 4:7, 33-34; Exod. 15:11; Ps. 86:8). This way of looking at things assumes that there are many gods that are worshiped (whereby a distinction is made between heavenly gods and earthly gods), and Moses places the Lord high above all of these. The fact that the Lord is the *only* God is not expressly stated, but is certainly not denied (cf. 4:35, 39). The words "you have begun to show" refer especially to what the Lord had done in the conquest of the land east of the Jordan; this was the beginning of the great task of the conquest, and Moses wanted to see its completion in order to be able to rejoice in the full vision of the Lord's greatness.

Verse 25 contains the express plea to be allowed to cross over and to see "the good land beyond the Jordan." The word "good" (*tob*) is used twice in Moses' request (the "good" land, the "fine" hill country), underlining his plea. Moses characterizes Canaan as a "hill country" in contrast to the low-lying trans-Jordan region. The Lebanon is mentioned separately, both because it is the northern border and because of its beauty and majesty. But the Lord remained angry with Moses for Israel's sake (see comments on 1:37); "anger" here means that the Lord refuses to grant Moses his request. He also forbids Moses to speak of the matter any further and commands him to climb Mount Pisgah to view the land from there—a small compensation for what he is not granted (cf. 32:48–52). In the light of the New Testament, we know that the principle "My grace is sufficient for you" (2 Cor. 12:9) also was true for Moses. Numbers 27:12 uses "Abarim range" instead of "Pisgah" (the latter is the northernmost part of the Abarim range). Moses must also instruct and encourage Joshua (v. 28; cf. vv. 21–22; 1:38; 31:7; Num. 27:23), the man who would "lead this people across and will cause them to inherit the land."

3:29 *So we stayed in the valley near Beth Peor.*

After the event just described, Israel "stayed in the valley near Beth Peor" (cf. Num. 25:1ff.), i.e., in the land of Moab. Beth Peor (cf. Josh. 13:20) was situated across from Jericho; the name means "House [temple] of [Baal] Peor," i.e., of the Baal who is worshiped on Mount Peor (cf. 4:3; Num. 25).

II. Exhortation to Keep the Law
4:1–40

This second part of Moses' first discourse is entirely hortatory in nature. Its purpose is to encourage Israel to keep the law Moses had given them. From verse 9 on, Moses warns especially against the worship of idols and images; the punishment for this is exile (vv. 25–28). But deliverance from this exile is possible if Israel turns again to the Lord (vv. 29–31). Finally, Moses emphasizes that Israel's experience has shown the Lord to be the only God, the reason why they should serve only Him and keep His commandments.

A. IN PRAISE OF THE LAW (4:1–8)

4:1 *Hear now, O Israel, the decrees and laws I am about to teach you. Follow them so that you may live and may go in and take possession of the land that the LORD, the God of your fathers, is giving you.*

Verses 1–8 contains a general encomium of the law. Verse 1 begins with an exhortation to listen to the instruction of the law that is about to follow (5:1ff.; cf. also 1:5). "Hear now" constitutes, as it does frequently, the transition of the exhortation; it characterizes the exhortation as a conclusion that follows from the preceding historical survey and could be paraphrased, "And now, remembering all that the Lord has shown us of His greatness and goodness. . . ." "Decrees and laws" is the usual expression in Deuteronomy for the various laws and regulations. We may assume that this expression includes all the laws, both the major religio-ethical laws and the political and cultic laws. It is doubtful that each of the two words refers to a special type of law. The same is true of the terms "commands" (8:11; 11:1; 30:16) and "stipulations" (4:45; 6:17, 20), which are sometimes added to the list. "I am about to teach you. Follow them" (lit., "teach you to do")— Moses' instruction in the law is not abstract and theoretical but has the practical aim that Israel will keep the law. As happens not infrequently, there is a shift from the plural ("Hear") to the singular ("you"). "So that you may live" is explained by the following words, "may go in and take possession of the land." The primary meaning of "live" is thus that they, unlike the men of the unbelieving generation, will not die in the wilderness (cf. also v. 4), but will live long enough to enter and occupy Canaan (cf. 8:1). If the words "Follow them" are taken to refer to what Israel must do in Canaan, then the subsequent "so that you may live . . ." is not connected with "follow," but is rather a continuation of "Hear" (cf. rsv); "hearing" in the true sense includes obedience to the law and can thus be linked to the promise of life. On the other hand, "Follow them" and "that you may live" can also be taken together (as does the niv) because, although the law can be fully kept only in Canaan (cf. v. 5), a beginning must be made here and now (cf. 8:1). It would not be correct to limit the sense of "that you may live" to its primary meaning "that you may live to take possession of the land" (see above). Similar promises are found repeatedly in the Old Testament in connection with the keeping of God's law; as a rule, the promise involves life in Canaan, in prosperity and for a long time (5:31; cf. 4:40; 6:2; 11:21; 25:15; 30:6, 15 ["life and prosperity"], 19 ["life and death," synonymous with "blessing and curse"]; 32:47). "Life" in the full sense of the word is the enjoyment of the blessing and favor of the Lord[3] —which is ultimately the sense intended here. When this

---

[3]Cf. *Het Godswoord der Profeten,* 4:111.

promise of life is here, as elsewhere, distinctly linked to the hearing (and keeping) of the law, we must not forget that also under the old covenant God always deals with His people on the basis of grace (cf. Introduction). This is why life is found through faith (Hab. 2:4) and through seeking the Lord (Amos 5:4) and why there is no essential difference when this verse links it to the hearing of the law. The law given to Israel is the law of the covenant of grace, and the keeping of that law is a holding fast to that covenant—and thus ultimately an act of faith.[4] On the other hand, this emphasis on the keeping of the law as a requirement for life indicates that at Sinai the old covenant, although remaining in essence a covenant of grace, acquired a legal character that makes its grace–character less obvious.

4:2 *Do not add to what I command you and do not subtract from it, but keep the commands of the* LORD *your God that I give you.*

The hearing of the law and the submission to the law shown in this hearing imply that the law is accepted as given. Israel must therefore neither add to nor subtract from what Moses commands them in the Lord's name (which are thus the inviolable words of God; cf. 12:32; Prov. 30:6; Jer. 26:2; Rev. 22:18–19). Since "subtract from" refers, of course, to a lessening of God's demands, it is most logical to see in "add to" an increasing of God's demands by means of additional human commandments—both errors detract from the majesty of God's law. The additions can also have the direct purpose of nullifying God's command (Matt. 15:6; cf. also Isa. 10:1–2; 29:13; Jer. 8:8; Zeph. 3:4).

4:3–4 *You saw with your own eyes what the* LORD *did at Baal Peor. The* LORD *your God destroyed from among you everyone who followed the Baal of Peor,* [4]*but all of you who held fast to the* LORD *your God are still alive today.*

To illustrate the words "that you may live" of verse 1, Moses reminds Israel of a very recent experience (Num. 25). Baal Peor was the Baal who was worshiped on Mount Peor by the Moabites (Num. 23:28). The Lord punished Israel's participation in that shameful idolatry with a severe plague that killed twenty-four thousand Israelites (Num. 25:9). Moses says here that all the guilty ones were destroyed, while those who remained faithful to the Lord are still alive.

---

[4]The contrast between law and faith in Galatians 3:12 therefore does not apply to the law as it is ultimately intended in the Old Testament.

4:5–8 *See, I have taught you decrees and laws as the LORD my God commanded me, so that you may follow them in the land you are entering to take possession of it. ⁶Observe them carefully, for this will show your wisdom and understanding to the nations, who will hear about all these decrees and say, "Surely this great nation is a wise and understanding people." ⁷What other nation is so great as to have their gods near them the way the LORD our God is near us whenever we pray to him? ⁸And what other nation is so great as to have such righteous decrees and laws as this body of laws I am setting before you today?*

Moses once again emphasizes that the "decrees and laws" he teaches them were commanded by the Lord.⁵ The purpose of his instruction is for Israel to keep these laws when they have entered Canaan. Observing these decrees and laws will show Israel's wisdom and understanding in the eyes of the nations. The phrase "great nation" reflects the respect the nations will have for Israel for this reason. Israel's missionary task vis-à-vis the pagan world is indicated in a veiled manner: This respect for Israel implies respect for Him from whom Israel received these laws. This missionary task is later further unfolded in prophecy, especially where Israel is prophetically described as the servant of the Lord, His messenger whom He sends (Isa. 42:19) to proclaim His praise (43:21), who is called to be His witness (43:10), in whose mouth He has put His words (51:16).⁶ The statement in our text can be fulfilled in the first instance only to the extent that Israel actually fulfilled the law. And indeed, the law was fulfilled to some extent: the many proselytes who joined Israel in later centuries were in part undoubtedly motivated by what they saw in Israel—a godly walk in accordance with God's commands. But this was only a partial fulfillment, which is why the Old Testament points beyond Israel, the servant and messenger of the Lord, to the one Servant, who is in truth the light of the nations (Isa. 42:1; 49:1).⁷

Verses 7–8 indicate that there is every reason for such admiration of Israel on the part of the nations. There is no other nation that can be called "great" in the same sense as Israel, not only because its laws are so righteous (v. 8), but also, as verse 7 interjects, because it is so much

---

⁵The first verb in verse 5 is usually rendered "I have taught you" (thus NIV, KJV, et al.). This is possible if the antecedent is taken to be the laws Moses gave to Israel in the Lord's name at Sinai (cf. 1:18). But it is more natural to take these words as referring to the instruction that is about to begin (cf. v. 1) and that is also the subject of this introductory address (cf. v. 8). We therefore agree with those who would render the verb as a present tense (see *Gesenius' Hebrew Grammar*, ¹ 106i).

⁶Cf. *Het Godswoord der Profeten* 2:313–14.

⁷Ibid., 2:361, 369ff.

the object of divine protection. The continuity of the argument is somewhat interrupted by verse 7; but at the same time, God's protection is another reason for Israel to keep the law. "Their gods": in reality the Lord is the only God (v. 35); concerning this kind of statement, see comments on 3:24. Verse 8 singles out the *righteousness* of the laws here. "This body of laws" (lit., "all this law") refers to what follows from 5:1 on (cf. 4:44 and comments on 1:5). There is nothing strange in the fact that Moses extols this law before it is even given; his hearers were already familiar with its main contents.

B. AGAINST THE WORSHIP OF IMAGES AND IDOLATRY; CAPTIVITY AND DELIVERANCE (4:9–31)

4:9–14 *Only be careful, and watch yourselves closely so that you do not forget the things your eyes have seen or let them slip from your heart as long as you live. Teach them to your children and to their children after them. ¹⁰Remember the day you stood before the LORD your God at Horeb, when he said to me, "Assemble the people before me to hear my words so that they may learn to revere me as long as they live in the land and may teach them to their children." ¹¹You came near and stood at the foot of the mountain while it blazed with fire to the very heavens, with black clouds and deep darkness. ¹² Then the LORD spoke to you out of the fire. You heard the sound of words but saw no form; there was only a voice. ¹³He declared to you his covenant, the Ten Commandments, which he commanded you to follow and then wrote them on two stone tablets. ¹⁴And the LORD directed me at that time to teach you the decrees and laws you are to follow in the land that you are crossing the Jordan to possess.*

The warning against the worship of images and idolatry (the focus of vv. 9–31) is introduced by a reminder of what Israel saw at Horeb (see esp. v. 12). Verse 9 begins with the general exhortation not to forget these things. "Only" links verse 9 to the preceding. What is stated in verse 8 will be a blessing to Israel only if the people take to heart the exhortation that follows: "Be careful, and watch yourselves closely" (lit., "Be on guard for yourself and guard your soul exceedingly"). If they fail to do so they will lose their "soul," or life (cf. vv. 15, 26). "Do not let them slip from your heart"; the heart is *inter alia* the seat of thought and reflection and of memory. "To your children and their children after them": the duty to instruct one's children is impressed upon Israel repeatedly in Deuteronomy (cf. v. 10; 6:7, 20ff.; 11:19; 32:46).

Verses 10–14 then state what it is that must not be forgotten: the events described in Exodus 19–24, summarized in verse 10 as "the day you stood before the LORD your God at Horeb," when Moses had assembled them at the Lord's command (Exod. 19:9ff.). Thus they came near (v. 11) and stood at the foot of the mountain "while it blazed with fire to the very heavens" (because the Lord descended in fire, Exod. 19:18), with "black clouds and deep darkness" (the smoke described in Exod. 19:18).

Verse 12 reminds the people of the fact that on this occasion they heard the voice of the Lord, "but saw no form." This is the main point here, since it is the basis for the warning against the worship of images in verse 15. "The LORD spoke to you out of the fire": in Exodus the Lord's speaking to Moses is more prominent, not only later (Exod. 20:18ff.; Deut. 5:23ff.), but from the very beginning (Exod. 19:19). Nevertheless, the people heard the voice of God, not only in the thunder and in the sound of the trumpet, but initially also when He spoke to Moses (Exod. 19:19; cf. also Deut. 5:4–5; 10:4). But they "saw no form": The people saw the glory of the Lord, which "looked like a consuming fire" (Exod. 24:17), but this was not a "form" (see Deut. 4:16–17). Nor was the fire itself the Lord—He spoke *from* the fire. Moses does not say that it would have been impossible to see a form of God (e.g., because God is Spirit or immaterial); Exodus definitely speaks of a seeing of God.[8] Moses simply observes that this did not happen, and draws from this the conclusion in verses 15–16 that Israel must not make any image of the Lord (a fact that was already known to them, Exod. 20:4). Behind this prohibition lies without doubt the idea that the making (and worshiping) of such an image would detract from God's Being. We should hereby not only think of God's immaterial nature (which the Old Testament does not explicitly mention), but rather of the fact that all the forms in which the nations represented their gods (see vv. 16–19) would defame God's majesty (cf. Rom. 1:23; this would be true no matter what kind of image would be used to represent the Lord).

Before going on to the conclusion concerning the worship of images, Moses briefly describes in verses 13–14 the content of the divine

---

[8]In Exodus 24:10–11 Moses and those with him are said to have seen God. Numbers 12:8 states that Moses "sees the form of the LORD." And according to Exodus 33:20, 23 no one can see the "face" of the Lord and live, which is the reason why Moses saw only His "back." We believe that these were special revelatory "forms" in which God wanted to reveal Himself. In this sense it would also have been possible for the people to see the "form" of God.

revelation on Horeb. This content, in summary, was "his covenant, the Ten Commandments" (lit., "ten words"); these "Ten Words" (10:4; Exod. 34:28) are recorded in Exodus 20:1–17 and Deuteronomy 5:6–21. When these "Ten Words" are equated with the covenant (cf. Exod. 34:28, where they are called "the words of the covenant"), the covenant is predominantly characterized as obligation. Although the Ten Words must be viewed in the light of the introduction (Exod. 20:2; Deut. 5:6) and although they contain words of promise (Exod. 20:6, 12b; Deut. 5:10, 16b), they are nevertheless commandments. And when the covenant is equated with these Ten Words, it is strongly characterized as law, as is also evident from the addition "which he commanded you to follow." The "decrees and laws" Moses was to teach the people (v. 14; cf. 4:1) are apparently the laws that were given to Israel in addition to the Ten Words (Exod. 21ff.).

4:15–24 *You saw no form of any kind the day the LORD spoke to you at Horeb out of the fire. Therefore watch yourselves very carefully, ¹⁶so that you do not become corrupt and make for yourselves an idol, an image of any shape, whether formed like a man or a woman, ¹⁷or like any animal on earth or any bird that flies in the air, ¹⁸or like any creature that moves along the ground or any fish in the waters below. ¹⁹And when you look up to the sky and see the sun, the moon and the stars—all the heavenly array—do not be enticed into bowing down to them and worshiping things the LORD your God has apportioned to all the nations under heaven. ²⁰But as for you, the LORD took you and brought you out of the iron-smelting furnace, out of Egypt, to be the people of his inheritance, as you now are.*

²¹The LORD was angry with me because of you, and he solemnly swore that I would not cross the Jordan and enter the good land the LORD your God is giving you as your inheritance. ²²I will die in this land; I will not cross the Jordan; but you are about to cross over and take possession of that good land. ²³Be careful not to forget the covenant of the LORD your God that he made with you; do not make for yourselves an idol in the form of anything the LORD your God has forbidden. ²⁴For the LORD your God is a consuming fire, a jealous God.

Then comes the main point of this section, for which the foundation was laid in verses 9–14: the warning against the worship of images and idolatry. What follows is the conclusion drawn from the preceding, especially verse 12, of which the salient point is repeated here. "Therefore watch yourselves very carefully" (lit., "watch over your souls exceedingly)—in other words, "your life depends on it" (cf. vv. 9, 26).

Verses 16–18 then state the conclusion: they must not make for themselves "an image of any shape" (referring to an image of God, made, of course, with the purpose of worshiping it, as appears from vv. 12, 15), whether in the shape of a human being or of any kind of animal. Verses 19–20 warn against worship of the heavenly bodies, i.e., against a specific form of idolatry. There is no real change of subject here. The worship of images is not necessarily idolatry in the formal sense; it is possible to erect a statue in order to serve the true God through it (the golden calf at Sinai and the calves at Bethel and Dan). But the reality is different. Since in practice the image is identified with the deity, it nevertheless takes on the character of an idol, so that Jeroboam's golden calves are sometimes characterized as "other gods" (1 Kings 14:9; cf. Hos. 8:5 [9]).

Moses had already warned against idolatry in this sense in verses 16–18; he probably did not only think of the golden calf, but in general of participation in the idol worship of the nations (cf. v. 28). We can thus say that Moses here mentions one form of paganism by name (a form that is also accompanied by the worship of images): the worship of the heavenly bodies, in ancient times practiced by the Arabs, the Assyrians, and in Babylonia, and later also in Israel, especially due to Assyrian influences (cf. Jer. 8:2; et al.). "When you look up to the sky and see the sun, the moon and the stars, . . . do not be enticed": the special beauty of the eastern sky at night inspires wonder and worship but it also presents to the error-prone heart the strong temptation to worship the creature instead of the Creator. "Things the LORD your God has apportioned to all the nations under heaven": even though idolatry is a transgression of God's will and command, it (like all sin) occurs in accordance with His plan and providential governance—"He let all nations go their own way" (Acts 14:16). By contrast, He led Israel out of Egypt "to be the people of his inheritance" (v. 20); this is why it would be in a very special sense unconscionable and unreasonable if Israel were to participate in the idolatry of the nations. "Iron-smelting furnace": the heat of such an oven is an image of the oppression in Egypt but it can also be seen as representing the idea of the refiner's fire—the oppression in Egypt was to prepare Israel to be the Lord's own people. "The people of his inheritance": this is Israel's privilege (it can be assured of the Lord's help and protection) but it also brings with it the solemn duty to serve Him alone, which is what is emphasized here.

---

[9]Cf. *Het Godswoord der Profeten* 1:184–85.

In verses 21–24 Moses once again reminds Israel (cf. 1:37; 3:23ff.) that he himself will not cross the Jordan (here only is stated that the Lord "solemnly swore" this). Israel will thus enter Canaan without Moses, which is a reason for Moses to warn them one last time and to impress on them the heavy responsibility that will rest on their shoulders. They must not forget the covenant (v. 23; cf. v. 13), specifically by falling into idolatry (cf. vv. 16ff.). Verse 24 adds a threat to the exhortation. The Lord is (for those who oppose Him) a "consuming fire" (cf. Heb. 12:29). "A jealous God" (cf. Exod. 20:5): He will not allow the honor due Him to be given to another, to an idol, or to an image that is in fact an idol (see comments on v. 19).

4:25–28 *After you have had children and grandchildren and have lived in the land a long time—if you then become corrupt and make any kind of idol, doing evil in the eyes of the LORD your God and provoking him to anger, 26I call heaven and earth as witnesses against you this day that you will quickly perish from the land that you are crossing the Jordan to possess. You will not live there long but will certainly be destroyed. 27The LORD will scatter you among the peoples, and only a few of you will survive among the nations to which the LORD will drive you. 28There you will worship man-made gods of wood and stone, which cannot see or hear or eat or smell.*

Moses elaborates the threat of verse 24 by telling Israel that if they fall into idolatry they will be scattered among the nations—the Captivity. He thus assumes that it is possible that Israel will succumb to the temptation of idolatry after they "have lived in the land a long time" (and thus have forgotten what they owe the Lord).[10] "As witnesses" (v. 26) refers back to the threat just stated; heaven and earth remain while the generations succeed one another, and they can thus testify later against Israel that they had been warned. The rhetorical expression is designed to impress upon Israel the responsibility this threat brings with it. They will "perish from the land," in part by being "destroyed," in part by being removed from the land and being scattered among the peoples (v. 27).

The fact that there are only "a few of you" is the result of the destruction mentioned in verse 26. While living among the nations they will serve "man-made gods of wood and stone" (either seduced or

---

[10]"Have lived in the land a long time," literally means, "have become old in the land." The phrase has no negative connotations such as "degenerated" or "declined" (as it may have in Lev. 26:10, where it is used of last year's harvest).

forced into idolatry by their pagan environment), the very images whose worship caused their guilt. The punishment answers to the sin, which is a revelation of God's justice. This is the most severe punishment imaginable for the people who know the living God—to be allowed to fall into the service of inanimate gods. Moses' words do not imply that God's grace could not keep them from idolatry while in captivity; he does not mention this here because he wants to depict God's judgment in its most terrible form (but see vv. 29–31). "Manmade gods of wood and stone": the false god and the image are seen as identical (cf. Isa. 44:9ff.); this is what happens in practice in paganism, even though the theory may be different (the image is in theory merely a symbol of the deity). Furthermore, these images are the only real aspect of these false gods; indeed, of these gods can be said what is said of the images: they are dead gods in contrast to the living God of Israel (cf. Isa. 44:9ff.; Ps. 115:4ff.). They cannot "see" the needs of their worshipers, nor "hear" their prayers, and they cannot "eat or smell" the sacrifices that are brought to them.

4:29–31 *But if from there you seek the LORD your God, you will find him if you look for him with all your heart and with all your soul.* ³⁰*When you are in distress and all these things have happened to you, then in later days you will return to the LORD your God and obey him.* ³¹*For the LORD your God is a merciful God; he will not abandon or destroy you or forget the covenant with your forefathers, which he confirmed to them by oath.*

Moses, like the later prophets, shows that there is a better future after stating the threat of punishment (cf. 30:1-10), lest Israel should think too little of the Lord's mercy and His faithfulness to the covenant. Verse 29 is almost identical to Jeremiah 29:13. "From there" (i.e., from the nations to which they were taken) they will "seek" the Lord and "find him"—they will call to Him and He will hear them. Moses adds emphatically that in order to "find" Him they must "look for him" with all their heart and all their soul (in contrast to honoring Him with the lips only, Isa. 29:13). Verse 30 further describes this: in the distress of the Captivity, Israel will return to the Lord and listen to His voice, i.e., obey Him. The latter says, by implication, that He will also speak to them there among the nations; in 30:2 this is explained by the addition "according to everything I command you today," which may also be the intent here. The fact that the Lord continues to speak is proof of His mercy, which is extolled in verse 31. "In later days": elsewhere the Hebrew expression is frequently used to refer to the great consummation of all things (cf. KJV, "in the latter days"), but in some instances, including here, it appears to refer merely to "a later time," or "the future."[11]

Verse 31 reminds Israel of the mercy and covenant faithfulness of the Lord their God. "For" indicates that the ground and source of the preceding promise is this faithfulness. It is because of this mercy and faithfulness that He lets Himself be found when Israel seeks Him wholeheartedly. But also the fact that He will continue to speak to Israel even during the Captivity can be explained only on this basis— and even the fact that Israel will listen and repent is (although not explicitly stated here) ultimately His doing (cf. also Introduction, VI).

C. THE LORD ALONE IS GOD (4:32–40)

This section is closely connected with the preceding (v. 32 begins with "for," omitted in the NIV; cf. KJV). The praises of verse 31 are expanded with a reminder of what the Lord has done for Israel. The conclusion, stated twice, that He is the only God (vv. 35, 39) is reminiscent of the preceding warning against idolatry (which is not repeated here). Moses again extols the law (cf. vv. 1–8; cf. esp. vv. 7–8 with vv. 32–34).

4:32–35 *Ask now about the former days, long before your time, from the day God created man on the earth; ask from one end of the heavens to the other. Has anything so great as this ever happened, or has anything like it ever been heard of?* [33]*Has any other people heard the voice of God speaking out of fire, as you have, and lived?* [34]*Has any god ever tried to take for himself one nation out of another nation, by testings, by miraculous signs and wonders, by war, by a mighty hand and an outstretched arm, or by great and awesome deeds, like all the things the LORD your God did for you in Egypt before your very eyes?*

[35]*You were shown these things so that you might know that the LORD is God; besides him there is no other.*

Let Israel search history, beginning with the day God created man, let them ask all the nations—nowhere else has occurred what God has done for Israel. No nation has heard a god speak from the fire as Israel did at Horeb (v. 33; cf. vv. 10ff.) "and lived"; the emphasis falls on the speaking from the fire, but "and lived" is added to bring out the greatness of the miracle Israel witnessed. God Himself says, "No one

---

[11]Concerning this expression, cf. *Het Godswoord der Profeten* 4:329.

may see me and live'' (Exod. 33:20; cf. Isa. 6:5), and we might expect the same to apply to the hearing of His voice (cf. Deut. 5:24–26). This "and lived" thus is a miracle in itself—it reveals the miracle of the speaking of God as a miracle of grace and salvation (*heils*miracle; see footnote p. 29).

Verse 34 adds that no other god has ever "achieved"[12] to take one nation out of the midst of another as the Lord took Israel out of Egypt, and certainly not by "displays of power" (NIV, "testing"[13]), etc. (cf. 7:19). This word and those that follow all refer to the miracles of the Exodus, and this in the first place to the plagues on Egypt (cf. "in Egypt"). But this is not all Moses thinks of; "war" points to the destruction of Pharaoh's army at the crossing of the Red Sea (Exod. 14:14; 15:3). On "mighty hand and outstretched arm," cf. Exodus 6:6. All these terms emphasize the display of God's omnipotence: no god has ever done anything like this. Moses' words here (and already in v. 33) would appear to allow for the existence of other gods (cf. 3:24; 4:7), but verse 35 makes clear that this is not the intent. Israel has been shown these miracles that they might know that the Lord is the *only* God. "You were shown": "you" is emphatic and implies "and to no other nation." The Egyptians did indeed see the same miracles, but only Israel did experience that miraculous power as saving power, which is what is implied here. Only for Israel is the purpose of these miracles "that you might know that the LORD is God" (cf. v. 39).[14] The fact that He alone has shown His power and favor to His people in such a manner shows that He is the only God. However, this truth is not presented as something that can be arrived at by purely logical reasoning;[15] rather, the knowledge of this truth is always a matter of faith. The revelatory acts that are designed to elicit this understanding that is based on faith are therefore not only revelations of the Lord's

---

[12]The word usually means "to test" but should be understood here in a slightly different sense: to test successfully, i.e., to achieve.

[13]The usual rendering is "testing," "trials" (when used of Pharaoh in his attitude toward the Lord). In our opinion this concept does not fit well here (cf. also 7:19). Furthermore, the word is etymologically closely related to the verb in the beginning of this verse (see preceding note) and is probably to be understood in the same sense: "Has any god ever achieved to take . . . by achievements [i.e., by displays of power]. . . ."

[14]Exodus 7:5 (cf. 14:18) states that "the Egyptians will know that I am the LORD," they will realize the fact. This is not the same as Israel's "knowing," which involves a relationship.

[15]Cf. *Het Godswoord der Profeten* 2:286ff.; the references in Isaiah 40ff. discussed there are in general closely related to this part of Moses' discourse.

omnipotence, but also of His love for Israel (cf. v. 37). "That the LORD is God": the only true God, which is explicitly stated in the words, "besides him there is no other" (cf. v. 39; 32:39; Isa. 44:6, 8; 45:5, 21).

4:36–40 *From heaven he made you hear his voice to discipline you. On earth he showed you his great fire, and you heard his words from out of the fire. ³⁷Because he loved your forefathers and chose their descendants after them, he brought you out of Egypt by his Presence and his great strength, ³⁸to drive out before you nations greater and stronger than you and to bring you into their land to give it to you for your inheritance, as it is today.*

³⁹Acknowledge and take to heart this day that the LORD is God in heaven above and on the earth below. There is no other. ⁴⁰Keep his decrees and commands, which I am giving you today, so that it may go well with you and your children after you and that you may live long in the land the LORD your God gives you for all time.

Once again Israel is exhorted to understand, know, and acknowledge this truth. To this end Israel is first of all reminded again of the revelation at Horeb (v. 36: cf. vv. 10ff., 33). Moses mentions a speaking of God "from heaven" (the same expression is used in Exod. 20:22) and then God's showing them "on earth. . .his great fire." This should not be understood as indicating a sharp distinction, since Moses adds that God spoke "from out of the fire," i.e., on earth. On the other hand, both the manifestation and the voice came from heaven, since the Lord "descended to the top of Mount Sinai" from heaven (Exod. 19:20), and the manifestation remained connected with heaven, since the blaze of fire reached "to the very heavens" (v. 11). The intent of the sentence is thus, "He made you hear his voice from heaven on earth. . .and showed you his great fire." The reason why "from heaven" and "on earth" are mentioned becomes apparent in verse 39, where Moses draws the conclusion that "the LORD is God in heaven above and on the earth below." "To discipline you": the verb *yasar* can mean "to instruct" (cf. KJV) or "to discipline," but this disciplining is always intended to result in instruction. The Lord instructs and disciplines like a father who brings up his child (cf. 8:5; 11:2). The emphasis here falls on the religio-ethical, on the Ten Words as designed to mold Israel spiritually (the statement in v. 35, "the LORD is God; besides him there is no other" has the same purpose; cf. also 8:5 with vv. 2–4).

Verses 37–38 are a long introductory statement that leads up to the exhortation of verse 39, describing once again the favors the Lord has bestowed on Israel. Moses goes back to before the Exodus: the Lord loved the forefathers and therefore "chose" (out of all the nations) their descendants. Not Israel's merit, but the Lord's free elective grace is the basis for the blessings (*heil*, see footnote p. 29) bestowed on Israel (cf. 10:15). Moses mentions one specific aspect: the Exodus. "By his Presence," cf. Exodus 33:14; the "Presence of the Lord" is the pillar of cloud and fire, in which the Lord is present in a special sense. Verse 38 states the purpose of the Exodus: to give to Israel the land of great and powerful nations. If the words "as it is today" were spoken by Moses, "their land" would be the territories of Og and Sihon; it is more probable, however, that Moses includes also (and primarily) the land west of the Jordan, in which case "as it is today" is a later addition.

Verse 39 is the conclusion and states the same truth as verse 35, but in the form of an exhortation. "Take to heart": the heart is the seat of thought and reflection (cf. v. 9). For "in heaven above and on the earth below," see comments on verse 36. Verse 40 expands the exhortations to include the keeping of the decrees and commands Moses is about to give them (cf. vv. 1-8). "Gives you for all time": the promise is implicitly contingent upon Israel's keeping of these commandments.

Interlude

The Three Cities of Refuge East of the Jordan
(4:41–43)

4:41–43 *Then Moses set aside three cities east of the Jordan, ⁴²to which anyone who had killed a person could flee if he had unintentionally killed his neighbor without malice aforethought. He could flee into one of these cities and save his life. ⁴³The cities were these: Bezer in the desert plateau, for the Reubenites; Ramoth in Gilead, for the Gadites; and Golan in Bashan, for the Manassites.*

Between Moses' first and second discourse is this brief interlude, dealing with the setting aside of three cities of refuge east of the Jordan. This was a matter of such importance that it could not be postponed until after the land west of the Jordan would have been conquered as well. The reason why this incident is mentioned here is probably simply that it took place at this time.

The institution of the "cities of refuge" (as they are called in Num. 35:6; Josh. 20:2; et al.) was very important. Blood revenge was known since ancient times even in Israel. In case of murder, the closest (male) relative of the victim was responsible for killing the slayer. The law does not abolish blood revenge, but rather acknowledges it as the means to keep the command of Genesis 9:6. At the same time, the law seeks to prevent the excesses to which blood revenge could lead; it imposes a significant limitation on the right and duty of the avenger of blood. Not every one who is instrumental in the death of another person must be punished with death. Exodus 21:13–14 already mentions places to which a person who had killed someone unintentionally could flee. One such place is the altar (of course not as a permanent place of refuge, but as a place of safety until the matter has been adjudged); we find examples of the use of the altar as a place of refuge in 1 Kings 1:50; 2:28; 1 Maccabees 10:43. But the slayer could be in a place from which it would be difficult to reach a (lawful) altar, especially in the future when there would be only one central altar in the entire country. In view of this, the cities of refuge are instituted (cf. Deut. 19BL,ff.; Num. 35:9–15; Josh. 20BL,ff.). There is no basis for the view that would see a contradiction between those references and this text (which would then be a later addition). In 19BL,ff. Moses demands that in the future Israel set aside three cities of refuge, to which three more could be added (v. 9); this command refers to the land west of the Jordan (the three additional cities were never set aside). Numbers 35:9–15 and Joshua 20BL,ff. speak of six cities of refuge, three on either side of the Jordan, and state that Moses only commanded them to be set aside and that Joshua actually carried out this command; but this should be taken as a more general description, which strictly speaking applies only to the land west of the Jordan. The text here indicates that Moses himself set aside the three cities east of the Jordan, an action that was then probably later confirmed by Joshua.

"East of the Jordan" means literally, "across the Jordan toward the sunrise" (v. 41). "Unintentionally" (v. 42) is further explained by "without malice aforethought"; the sense of the Hebrew is "and did not hate him in time past" (cf. RSV). In 19:5 this is illustrated by the example of a man killed accidentally while cutting wood. It is clear that accidental killing and killing as a result of existing enmity are the two extremes of a spectrum, between which a number of other cases are possible (e.g., someone who kills in a suddenly erupting argument, without any prior hate, and possibly even without wanting to do so). These intermediate situations are not discussed—the law does not regulate every possible situation (Num. 35:16–24 gives some more specific regulations; cf. also Exod. 21:23).

The cities are listed from south to north (v. 43): Bezer "in the desert plateau," i.e., in the plains of Moab (see comments on 3:10), Ramoth in Gilead, and Golan in Bashan.

Part Two

Moses' Second Discourse
(4:44–30:20)

The fact that 4:44–49 is a new superscription indicates that what follows constitutes a new discourse of Moses. The first discourse was a historical survey with exhortations, and was preparatory in nature. This second discourse presents a number of specific laws beginning in chapter 12. The earlier chapters are foundational in nature (especially the Ten Words) and also contain general exhortations; historical reminiscences are interwoven throughout.

I. Superscription
4:44–49

4:44–49 *This is the law Moses set before the Israelites.* [45]*These are the stipulations, decrees and laws Moses gave them when they came out of Egypt* [46]*and were in the valley near Beth Peor east of the Jordan, in the land of Sihon king of the Amorites, who reigned in Heshbon and was defeated by Moses and the Israelites as they came out of Egypt.* [47]*They took possession of his land and the land of Og king of Bashan, the two Amorite kings east of the Jordan.* [48]*This land extended from Aroer on the rim of the Arnon Gorge to Mount Siyon (that is, Hermon),* [49]*and included all the Arabah east of the Jordan, as far as the Sea of the Arabah, below the slopes of Pisgah.*

This is a new superscription; in a sense these verses contain two superscriptions. The first of these (v. 44) characterizes what follows as "law"; it emphasizes the unity of what Moses says and may refer specifically to the first part (ch. 5–11). The second one (vv. 45–49) speaks of "stipulations, decrees and laws," and thus refers to the specific laws as given from chapter 12 on; this second superscription also gives a broad, historically oriented, statement of the place where Moses and Israel were at this point. This reiteration of the locale indicates the importance of the discourse. Because of its great importance as a pledge of what Israel is yet to receive, the victory over Sihon and Og is mentioned again. "Stipulations": the Hebrew word indicates something that has been solemnly declared; it is used in the sense of "law," sometimes specifically the law of the Ten Commandments, but in Deuteronomy for all kinds of regulations; here "stipulations" is synonymous with the following words, "decrees and laws" (see comments on 4:1). "When they came out of Egypt": Israel's "coming out of Egypt" would last until they reached Canaan proper, the land west of the Jordan. "East of the Jordan" refers to the valley across from Beth Peor (v. 46; cf. 1:1, 5; 3:29).

Concerning vv. 46–49, see 1:4; 2:31–3:17. Instead of "Sirion" (according to 3:9, the Sidonian name for Hermon) we read here "Siyon," still another name for these mountains (unless this is a scribal error and should read "Sirion").

II. Foundational Part
(5:1–11:32)

A. INTRODUCTION (5:1–5)

After the superscription (4:44–49) follows the introduction to Moses' second discourse. These verses are primarily intended to introduce the entire discourse; verse 5, however, is a special introduction to the restatement of the Ten Commandments. The "decrees and laws" of verse 1 include more than the Ten Commandments, even though the latter are presented first and occupy a special place among all that follows.

5:1 *Moses summoned all Israel and said: Hear, O Israel, the decrees and laws I declare in your hearing today. Learn them and be sure to follow them.*

Moses summons all Israel (to the place stated in 4:45) and begins to speak. He first exhorts Israel to listen ("Hear, O Israel," cf. 4:1; 6:4) and to take to heart. For "decrees and laws," see comments on 4:1.

5:2 *The L*ORD *our God made a covenant with us at Horeb.*

Moses first of all reminds Israel that the Lord made a covenant with them at Horeb (cf. 4:13, 23). By doing so, Moses places all that follows in the framework of the covenant, and the discourse is thus dominated by the covenant concept (see Introduction). The Ten Commandments that Moses will present next are also called "the words of the covenant" (Exod. 34:28), written on "the tablets of the covenant" (Deut. 9:11, 15). Furthermore, it is clear that the covenant of Horeb is thus predominantly characterized as an obligation imposed by God on Israel, i.e., as law, although it remains true that this law is given on the basis of grace (see comments on 4:13; 5:6; and Introduction). "The LORD our God": He did not become Israel's God at Horeb but was already their God when Israel left Egypt (cf. 5:6 and Introduction).

5:3 *It was not with our fathers that the L*ORD *made this covenant, but with us, with all of us who are alive here today.*

Moses says of the covenant made at Horeb that the Lord did not make it with the forefathers but "with us," with those who are assembled here. The purport is clear: Moses wants to impress on the assembled people that the demands of this covenant are binding on *them.* There is difference of opinion as to the exact meaning of the words; in our opinion they cannot mean that the covenant was made with *this* generation—all those twenty years of age and older of the Horeb generation had died with the exception of Moses, Joshua, and Caleb (cf. 2:16), and a new generation had taken their place, the generation Moses now addresses. But since the covenant was made not with individuals but with the people as a whole, Moses can ignore this distinction between the two generations: this is the same people as that which once stood at the foot of Horeb. From this it also follows that the phrase "not with our fathers" does not refer to the generations before the Exodus but to the patriarchs (cf. 4:31, 37). The fact that the Lord also made a covenant with them is beside the point, since Moses here speaks of "this covenant" that includes the Ten Words and all that was added to them at Horeb. The fact that this covenant was essentially one with the covenant the Lord made with the patriarchs falls outside the scope of Moses' statement here.

5:4-5 *The LORD spoke to you face to face out of the fire on the mountain. ⁵(At that time I stood between the LORD and you to declare to you the word of the LORD, because you were afraid of the fire and did not go up the mountain.) And he said:*

"Face to face" in verse 4 is not used in the special sense that applies only to the unique, intimate manner in which the Lord revealed Himself to Moses (Exod. 33:11) but is rather a general reference to the fact that the Lord spoke to the people with an audible voice (cf. 4:12; 10:4). The phrase thus refers only to the proclamation of the Ten Commandments (vv. 6ff., 22); after this proclamation the people no longer had to hear God's voice (5:23ff.).

The parenthetical sentence in verse 5 is not entirely clear. There is some support for the view that Moses here refers to his mediation that began after the proclamation of the Ten Commandments (5:23ff.). "At that time" must then be understood in a broader sense. It would be more logical if verse 5, like verse 4, referred to the proclamation of the Ten Commandments, which is indeed possible. Verse 5 then states that the speaking of God to the people must be understood in a limited sense even in the proclamation of the Ten Words. Even though the further limitation described in vv. 23ff., had not yet gone into effect, when the Ten Commandments were given Moses was the only one who climbed the mountain (because the people were afraid of the fire), so that he stood between the Lord and the people; the Lord thus spoke more directly to Moses than to the people (see comments on 4:12), which also explains why Moses had to "declare" (in the sense of "clarify") the Lord's words to the people.[1]

B. THE GIVING OF THE LAW AT HOREB (5:6-33)

1. The Ten Words (5:6-22)

5:6-21

"I am the LORD your God, who brought you out of Egypt, out of the land of slavery.

---

[1]It is also possible, but in our opinion not preferable, to take the last words of verse 5, "and he said" (lit., "saying"), as a continuation of "declare" (the parentheses then should be omitted): "to declare to you the word of the LORD. . .saying."

⁷"You shall have no other gods before me.

⁸"You shall not make for yourself an idol in the form of anything in heaven above or on the earth beneath or in the waters below. ⁹You shall not bow down to them or worship them; for I, the LORD your God, am a jealous God, punishing the children for the sin of the fathers to the third and fourth generation of those who hate me, ¹⁰but showing love to a thousand generations of those who love me and keep my commandments.

¹¹"You shall not misuse the name of the LORD your God, for the LORD will not hold anyone guiltless who misuses his name.

¹²"Observe the Sabbath day by keeping it holy, as the LORD your God has commanded you. ¹³Six days you shall labor and do all your work, ¹⁴but the seventh day is a Sabbath to the LORD your God. On it you shall not do any work, neither you, nor your son or daughter, nor your manservant or maidservant, nor your ox, your donkey or any of your animals, nor the alien within your gates, so that your manservant and maidservant may rest, as you do. ¹⁵Remember that you were slaves in Egypt and that the LORD your God brought you out of there with a mighty hand and an outstretched arm. Therefore the LORD your God has commanded you to observe the Sabbath day.

¹⁶"Honor your father and your mother, as the LORD your God has commanded you, so that you may live long and that it may go well with you in the land the LORD your God is giving you.

¹⁷"You shall not murder.

¹⁸"You shall not commit adultery.

¹⁹"You shall not steal.

²⁰"You shall not give false testimony against your neighbor.

²¹"You shall not covet your neighbor's wife. You shall not set your desire on your neighbor's house or land, his manservant or maidservant, his ox or donkey, or anything that belongs to your neighbor."

Now follow the ten fundamental commandments (together with the prologue in v. 6), known to us as the Ten Commandments and called "the Ten Words" in the Old Testament (4:13; 10:4; Exod. 34:28); the Greek name Decalogue, which we use as well, also means "Ten Words" (although it should be pointed out that the Greek term stresses the oneness of the commandments, something like "the law of the Ten Words"). We will limit our discussion to the following, since the Ten

Commandments have been explained in the commentary on Exodus in this series.[2]

The Scriptures speak explicitly of *ten* "words" (Exod. 34:28; Deut. 4:13; 10:4), and also of two stone tablets on which they were written (Exod. 31:18; 32:15–16; 34:1, 29; Deut. 10:3–5). But they do not give us any further indication as to their division; as a result, opinion differs on this point.

The most important question concerning the numbering of the commandments is whether the commandment concerning the worship of ("other gods") and that concerning images should be counted as one or as two commandments. They are counted as two by Josephus, Philo, Origen, Tertullian and other church fathers, the Greek Orthodox church, the Reformed church, and most modern expositors.

Among those who count them as one there is further division of opinion. Since they have one less commandment here, they must compensate elsewhere in order to retain ten commandments. Some do this by taking the prologue (v. 6) as the first of the Ten Words (thus the Pseudo-Jonathan Targum, the Talmud, the Septuagint, and rabbinic Judaism up to the present). Others divide the commandment concerning coveting (thus Augustine, the Roman Catholic church, and the Lutheran church).

Among more recent exegetes the view that the commandments concerning "other gods" and "idols" should be counted as two is predominant. We consider this the correct view, if for no other reason than that the attempts of the older view to retain the number ten appear to be unsuccessful. The Jewish solution, which considers the prologue to be the first commandment, places dissimilar elements side by side. The splitting up of the commandment concerning covetousness cannot be maintained either. This is especially clear when "you shall not covet your neighbor's house" is placed first, as it is in Exodus, and is thus considered a separate commandment. It would be easier to defend Augustine's approach: he followed the wording of Deuteronomy and placed "you shall not covet your neighbor's wife" first, making it a separate commandment. But again it can be said that such a separate commandment makes little sense in view of the separate commandment against adultery. There is also no reason to prefer the version of Deuteronomy over that of Exodus.

The view that takes the prohibitions against "other gods" and

---

[2]W. H. Gispen, *The Bible Student's Commentary—Exodus* (Grand Rapids: Zondervan, 1982), 185–99.

against "idols" as two commandments, on the other hand, is entirely plausible. Israel's history shows that both these commandments were necessary. To Israel, "You shall have no other gods before me" did not necessarily mean that any and all bowing down to images was prohibited: Israel did make images and did bow down to them with the purpose of worshiping the Lord through them—the golden calf at Horeb and those at Dan and Bethel are examples.

This does not alter the fact that there is a close connection between these two commandments. Even if no idolatry is *intended* in the worship of an image, it can nevertheless *be* or *become* idolatry. Ahijah reproaches Jeroboam for making "other gods, idols made of metal" (1 Kings 14:9); the NIV rendering, which is entirely possible, equates "other gods" and "idols" (it is also possible to translate "other gods and idols made of metal," cf. KJV). In the background of this equation stands the fact that this image was not merely seen as symbolic of the deity, but that the deity was thought to be actually present in the image, and hence the image as such was given divine honor. Thus the image, even though the name Jahweh was connected with it, became in fact an idol. Thus Hosea says, "Throw out your calf-idol, O Samaria . . . a craftsman has made it; it is not God" (Hos. 8:5–6; cf. 13:2), implying that the calf was considered to be God, or at least was worshiped as God.[3]

This view, which makes the prohibition of images essentially a variation on the prohibition of "other gods," is not foreign to the Decalogue, as would appear from the sanction that follows the image commandment. Apparently this sanction belongs not only with the latter, but also with the prohibition against "other gods," as indicated by the words "I . . . am a jealous God,"[4] i.e., a God who does not tolerate any other beside Him to share the honor and love that are due Him. "Jealous" therefore appears to refer both to the "other gods" and to the images that are looked upon as "other gods," i.e., to both commandments that are seen here in terms of their inner unity. Only thus is it understandable why the sanction is found only here and why we do not find a similar sanction also after the prohibition against "other gods."

---

[3]Cf. my *Israel en de Baals*, 2nd ed. (Kampen: J. H. Kok, 1928), n. 137; also J. Köberle, *Sünde und Gnade.* . .(Munich, 1908), 102.

[4]The root *qana* can mean "to be zealous" as well as "to be jealous"; the former would give the sense that God is zealous against sin; in the context "jealous" is preferable.

But all this does not detract from what was said earlier about the fact that these two prohibitions should be considered two commandments, nor does it prove (as some claim) that the sanction is a later addition that is not in the spirit of the original text. There is nothing incongruous in the Lord's giving on the one hand a separate commandment to oppose Israel's erroneous idea that it could worship the Lord in the form of an image while on the other hand wanting to make it clear to Israel that such a bowing down was in fact nothing but idolatry.

There is also difference of opinion as to the distribution of the Ten Commandments among the two tablets: some have thought of five and five, others of four and six or even three and seven. The Scriptures do not provide any clues on this point, and guessing has little value.

What can be said is that the law of the Ten Commandments can be divided into two parts on the basis of its contents: the first four commandments are religious in nature (i.e., directly concerned with the relationship with God), while the other six are ethical (concerned with human relationships). We do not object to speaking of the commandments of "the first tablet" and "the second tablet," as long as it is done in a figurative sense, since it is not certain whether this division coincided with the division found on the two stone tablets.

The law of Israel contains also other collections of commands or prohibitions; thus, with varying degrees of justification, terms are used like the *cultic Decalogue* of Exodus 34:11–26, the *Shechemite Dodecalogue* (twelve commandments) of Deuteronomy 27:11–26, the *Canaanite Decalogue* of Exodus 23, and also of a *cultic decalogue* in Exodus 20:23–26 and 23:13–19 combined.

The Scriptures, however, give the name "the Ten Words" only to the group of laws under discussion and assign to it (and this is the main point) a very special significance. These commandments were proclaimed by the Lord on Horeb in the hearing of the people and were written by the Lord Himself on two stone tablets, which he gave to Moses to be placed in the ark (Exod. 24:12; Deut. 4:13; et al.). These commandments are the foundation of the entire law and also of the covenant made at Horeb, which is why they are also called "the tablets of the covenant" (Deut. 9:9, 11, 15) and the ark in which they are placed is called "the ark of the covenant" (Num. 10:33; et al.).

The Mosaic law is usually considered to contain three aspects: the *moral,* the *civil,* and the *ceremonial* law. It is in our opinion better to speak of the "religio-moral" or "religio-ethical" law, rather than of the "moral" law, because it encompasses both the religious and the ethical aspects of life. Of these three, the moral or religio-ethical law (whose essence is summarized in the Ten Commandments although it is not identical with them) is still valid for us, the other two are not. The civil law was intended specifically for Israel, while the ceremonial law has found its fulfillment in Christ.

This does not alter the fact that the Ten Commandments, as part of the Old Testament, must be read in the light of the New Testament. The Old Testament imprint is clearly discernible in the opening words, which remind of the Exodus from Egypt, while also the Sabbath law has a specifically Old Testament flavor.

Calvin (*Institutes* 2.8.1) and others observe that the same things we are to learn from the two tablets of the law are also taught us to some extent by the inner law, written on the hearts of all people; but, because of the darkening of man's heart, the Lord has given us a written law, that it might witness with more clarity to those things that were not sufficiently clear in the law of nature and that it might the more vividly impress our mind and memory.

But in this we must not lose sight of the fact that when the revelation of Scripture makes known anew to man the originally inculcated law, it does this in a manner different from the general revelation given originally to man. The special revelation is always and everywhere revelation from God vis-à-vis Jesus Christ, and it therefore always links the demand of the law with Christ.

Thus also the law of the Ten Commandments is related to Christ. Today, the demand to serve the one true God includes the demand to approach Him through the only Mediator between God and man, Jesus Christ.

The covenant, of which the Ten Commandments are the Magna Carta, is ultimately nothing else than the covenant of grace, anchored in Christ. The superscription therefore reads, "I am the LORD your God, who brought you out of Egypt, out of the land of slavery"; this bringing out is the redemptive work of God, which foreshadows the redemptive work of Christ and in which its essence is already present. The name Jahweh (LORD) says the same, because it is the covenant name of God under the old dispensation. The law of the Ten Commandments thus contains the demand to know the only true God *in Christ* and to serve Him out of gratitude for *the redemption wrought by Christ*.

All this does not detract from the truth of Calvin's statement. The essential content of the religio-ethical law, of which the Ten Commandments are largely a summary, is without doubt the same as that which was implanted in man at the Creation, and of which man retains some awareness, no matter how vague and distorted it may be, especially with regard to the commandments of the "first tablet."

The religio-ethical law revealed in the Scriptures must not be equated with the Ten Commandments in an absolute sense. When we distinguish, as mentioned above, between moral, civil, and religious law, it should not be understood in the sense that these three laws are entirely separate and clearly demarcated, so that we could indicate in which chapter the one ends and the other begins. Rather, the three kinds of laws are frequently interwoven.

Thus, the moral law cannot simply be equated with the Ten Commandments. Especially the fourth commandment is significant in this respect in that it clearly has a ceremonial aspect. On the other hand, it is significant that the Mosaic law also contains laws of a purely religio-ethical nature outside the Ten Commandments. For example, there are the commands to love the Lord and to love the neighbor. Furthermore, Israel's civil and ceremonial laws contain (as is true of every part of the Scriptures) religio-ethical principles that as such belong to the moral law.

We can thus say only that the law of the Ten Commandments is *predominantly* (i.e., apart from the ceremonial element in the fourth commandment) a summary of the religio-ethical law. But it is *a* summary rather than the only possible summary. Another summary is given in the double commandment to love (Matt. 22:37–40); when we compare the law of the Ten Commandments with this double commandment, we find the following.

In the first place, the Ten Commandments are predominantly negative (only the fourth and fifth commandments are positive in form, and even in the fourth commandment the negative is in fact still dominant: "you shall not do any work"). In general they thus speak not directly of obligations that must be fulfilled but of sins that must be avoided.

Furthermore, the Ten Commandments are concerned primarily with deed and word; only in the tenth commandment is the disposition expressly mentioned (the first commandment is formulated so broadly that we cannot say that either the external or the inward is prominent).

Finally, the Ten Commandments are much more concrete and worked out in detail than the commandment of Matthew 22. It should be noted that when the Ten Commandments speak of sins against the neighbor, only very crass sins are mentioned. No mention is made at all of the sins so forcefully condemned by the prophets: the unjust administration of justice, the oppression of widows and orphans, and failing to show justice and mercy (cf. Mic. 6:8).

This character of the law of the Ten Commandments is related to the special purpose for which it was given and the place it occupies in the history of revelation.

The negative form and the emphasis on the external are connected on the one hand with the fact that the summary of the law is intended not for unfallen man but for man as a sinner and on the other hand with the fact that it has the character of a foundational law, of instruction in the first principles. Finally, this law serves not only as a guide for the life of the individual, but also as the foundation for Israel's national existence.[5]

The content and meaning of the Ten Commandments were clarified for Israel by further revelation. This happened on the one hand through the rest of the Mosaic law, not only by the elaboration of the principles given here in a multitude of specific laws, but also (and not least in the Book of Deuteronomy) by a further, and also positive, unfolding of those principles: the love for the Lord, the God of the covenant, and love for the neighbor are explicitly inculcated (Deut. 6:5; Lev. 19:18), as well as the demands of justice and mercy, specifically with regard to the socially weak.

On the other hand, the prophets proclaimed the content of the law to Israel in their own way. With respect to the "first tablet," they are zealous for the Lord the God of Israel and declaim idolatry and worldliness. With respect to the "second tablet," there are some direct and concrete reminders of the Ten Commandments (Jer. 7:9ff.; Hos. 4:2), but the prophets also strongly emphasized what is said in the rest of the law concerning administration of justice and respect and support for the socially weak.

In the New Testament, the content of God's demands and especially

---

[5]It is worth noting that the Mosaic penal code can be organized almost entirely around the Ten Commandments (if the penal provisions for infractions of ceremonial laws are subsumed under the fourth commandment). Conversely, almost all of the Ten Commandments are supported by provisions of the penal code. The theocratic character of the Mosaic law brings with it that offenses against God and crimes against morality occupy an important place in the penal code, which assumes that the entire law of God in its external aspects must be maintained by the government. (Of course, the more inward aspect of the religio-ethical law as expressed especially in Deuteronomy in the law of love falls outside the scope of the penal code.)

the meaning of the Ten Commandments are further clarified by our Savior's words (especially in the Sermon on the Mount) and later by the apostles.

Seen in the light of the Scriptures as a whole, the Ten Commandments are also for the New Testament believer a summary of what God asks of His people (on the basis of the special claim He has to them because of Christ's redemption) and of man in general (on the basis of His claim as Creator). The special, negative, concrete, and more external form in which the Ten Commandments express these demands has not lost its value with the end of the old dispensation, but has been shown through the ages to have immense power to bind God's demand on man's conscience.

The fact that the Ten Commandments as stated in Deuteronomy differ from the text of Exodus 20 indicates that at least one of the two is not a verbatim presentation of the Ten Commandments as they were pronounced at Sinai and written on stone tablets by God Himself. The most logical assumption, which is also supported by the nature of several of the changes, is that the text of Exodus is the original one and that Moses' restatement in Deuteronomy is somewhat free. We believe that he was led in this by the Spirit of God, who caused him to present these commandments with some modifications, some of which are entirely insignificant, while others reflect something of the specific spirit of God's revelation in Deuteronomy. There is no need to elaborate on the fact that both versions of the Ten Commandments have divine authority. Besides, the fact that the Ten Words—like the prophecy of Isaiah 2:2–4 (cf. Mic. 4:1–3) and the Lord's Prayer—have been given to us in more than one form is entirely in keeping with the character of the Scriptures. Even though we are bound by the words of Scripture, it nevertheless teaches us in many ways to guard against an idolatrous worship of the letter.

The differences between the Ten Commandments in Exodus and Deuteronomy are all of secondary importance and minimal. The most important differences are the following.

The *second commandment* in Exodus 20:4 reads, "You shall not make for yourself an idol in the form of anything . . ."; in Deuteronomy 5:8 we read, "You shall not make for yourself an idol in the form of anything. . . ." [6] The motive for this variation is uncertain; we might say that the statement in Exodus is more concrete and vivid because it

---

[6]The difference consists in the absence of the *waw* before *kal*, "any," in Deuteronomy 5:8; the English versions do not attach much significance to this

Deuteronomy 5:6-21

presents that which is "in heaven above," etc., as distinct entities in their own right.

In the *fourth commandment,* "Remember the Sabbath day" of Exodus 20:8 is replaced by "Observe the Sabbath day" in Deuteronomy 5:12. This change may be intended to clarify, indicating that the Sabbath must be remembered in a way that includes its observance. Furthermore, Deuteronomy adds, "as the LORD your God has commanded you"; this is entirely in keeping with the exhorting character of the Deuteronomic revelation (cf. also v. 16).

Also, in verse 14 "nor your animals" has been expanded: "nor your ox, your donkey or any of your animals." This elaboration again agrees with the character of Deuteronomy.

More important is that verse 14 adds, "so that your manservant and maidservant may rest, as you do." This is connected with the change made in verse 15. The grounding of the Sabbath commandment in creation, given in Exodus 20:11, is absent here; rather, Deuteronomy refers the Sabbath to Israel's deliverance from slavery in Egypt. This serves first of all to expand the Sabbath commandment to include servants but also to provide a basis for the commandment itself. All this is clearly connected with the social tenor that is part of the entire Deuteronomic revelation.

In the *fifth commandment,* Deuteronomy adds again "as the LORD your God has commanded you" (see above, v. 12). Furthermore, "and that it may go well with you" is added to "so that you may live long," again in keeping with the more expansive style of Deuteronomy.

In the *ninth commandment* (v. 20), Deuteronomy reads *shaw',* "false," instead of *shaqer,* "mendacious" (Exod. 20:16). The former concept is broader, indicating perhaps that more than the outright and explicit lie in giving testimony is condemned.

In the *tenth commandment* (v. 21), "your neighbor's wife" is mentioned first, rather than "your neighbor's house" (Exod. 20:17). The Deuteronomic redaction gives special attention to the woman (cf. the emphasis on the servants in the fourth commandment). While in Exodus the house comes first and the woman is mentioned as part (albeit the most important part) of the household, in Deuteronomy her special position is intentionally emphasized by being mentioned first.

omission and generally render both versions of the second commandment identically (although some, such as the KJV, indicate the omission by italicizing "or" in Deut. 5:8). —TRANS.

(This does, of course, not mean that Exodus negates the special position of the woman in the household; it merely does not emphasize it.) Furthermore, the word "covet," which occurs twice in Exodus 20:17, is replaced the second time by a different verb in Deuteronomy, "set your desire on." It is possible that this change is merely stylistic, but it is likely that the use of the different verb also serves to underline the exceptional position of the woman.

Also in keeping with the more elaborate style of Deuteronomy is the addition of "or land" in the tenth commandment. (This addition shows clearly that the law is intended primarily for life in Canaan; this is also indicated by the mention of "ox" and "donkey," both here and in the fourth commandment, since these are the work animals of the farmer; "house" should therefore also be understood in its customary sense, even though it could also refer to "tent.") [7]

For a further explanation of the individual commandments we refer to the reader to Dr. Gispen's commentary on Exodus 20:1–17 in the *Bible Student's Commentary*. We will limit ourselves to the following observations:

For verse 6, see comments on verse 2. Concerning "love" (*hesed*) in 5:10, see comments on 7:9.

Concerning verse 17 ("You shall not murder") we note that this verb, which occurs forty-six or forty-seven times in the Old Testament, is never used of God's slaying someone nor of killing in battle; it is used only once in connection with the killing of a murderer demanded by the law (Num. 35:30).[8] Apart from this single exception the verb is used only for wrongful killing, i.e., murder. However, it is not limited to killing "with malice aforethought" (Num. 35:16–21, 31; Deut. 22:26), but also of unintentional manslaughter (Num. 35:11, 24–28; Deut. 4:42; 19:3, 4, 6; Josh. 20:3, 5, 6; cf. also Num. 35:12). "Murder" is therefore strictly speaking too strong a word, since it would exclude unintentional manslaughter; "kill" (KJV) would be too weak, since it would exclude the legitimate taking of a person's life. "Slay" would probably come

---

[7]The following differences are merely a matter of form. In verse 9, Deuteronomy adds a *waw* before "third and fourth generation": "and [or, 'even'] to the third. . . ." Similarly, a *waw* is inserted in verses 17–21 at the beginning of each of the last five commandments. Also, the *kethib* of verse 10 reads "his commandments" instead of "my commandments; this is probably a textual corruption. A few differences of a purely orthographic nature (*matres lectionis*) may be ignored here.

[8]These observations are based on an article by J. J. Stamm in *Theologische Zeitschrift*, Basel, I 2, 81ff.

closer to the meaning of the word. There can be no doubt that this word is used in the Decalogue intentionally. The Old Testament clearly teaches that (apart from God's taking someone's life) there is a taking of human life that is permitted or even commanded. In the case of (intentional) murder the murderer must be put to death (Exod. 21:12), and death is also the punishment for abusing or cursing one's parents, for certain sexual sins, and for idolatry (Exod. 21:14–17; Lev. 20; Deut. 13; 21:18–23). Killing in battle is also generally permitted, and even commanded in the case of the slaying with the ban (Deut. 7). In case of self-defense, killing is allowed but restricted (Exod. 22:2–3).

5:22 *These are the commandments the LORD proclaimed in a loud voice to your whole assembly there on the mountain from out of the fire, the cloud and the deep darkness; and he added nothing more. Then he wrote them on two stone tablets and gave them to me.*

This is a concluding statement. "To your whole assembly": see comments on verses 4–5. "And he added nothing more": Moses proclaimed here only the Ten Words that the Lord spoke in the hearing of all the people. This emphasizes that these Ten Words occupy a unique position among all the laws that were given to Israel; they might be called the constitution of the covenant. This uniqueness is also reflected in the fact that this law was written on stone tablets—a reminder that runs ahead of the sequence of events and to which Moses will return in its historical context in 9:10–11.

2. Moses the mediator of the laws that follow; concluding exhortation (5:23–33)

In verses 23–31 Moses describes (in more detail than in Exod. 20:18–21) how he, at the people's request and with the Lord's approval, acted as mediator in receiving the rest of the commandments.

5:23–27 *When you heard the voice out of the darkness, while the mountain was ablaze with fire, all the leading men of your tribes and your elders came to me.* ²⁴*And you said, "The LORD our God has shown us his glory and his majesty, and we have heard his voice from the fire. Today we have seen that a man can live even if God speaks with him.* ²⁵*But now, why should we die? This great fire will consume us, and we will die if we hear the voice of the LORD our God any longer.* ²⁶*For what mortal man has ever heard the voice of the living God speaking out of fire, as we have, and survived?* ²⁷*Go near and listen to all that* *the LORD our God says. Then tell us whatever the LORD our God tells you. We will listen and obey.''*

These verses describe the request made by the leading men and the elders on behalf of the people. "While the mountain was ablaze with fire," cf. 4:11. The "glory" of the Lord (v. 24) is the radiant light that surrounds Him, but also in a more general sense the revelation of His deity; the latter is intensified by the addition "his majesty." The people acknowledge to have experienced that man can live even if God speaks with (or to) him; they indicate that this is a miracle of grace they have received from God (see comments on 4:33). But they feel that this fact has been made sufficiently clear to them, and they ask (v. 25) to be spared further exposure to God's voice; both the fire and the voice filled them with fear. They are deeply convinced that what they have experienced is something unique, something that "mortal man" (lit., "flesh," i.e., the creature in all his fragility, the sharpest possible antithesis to "the living God") has never before experienced. They therefore ask (v. 27) to be spared a continuation of this experience. Moses can be their mediator, he can go up alone (without the people observing even from afar—cf. v. 30) to hear what else the Lord has to say, and he can relay this to them. They promise beforehand, not only to listen to what Moses will report to them, but also to obey.

5:28-31 The LORD heard you when you spoke to me and the LORD said to me, "I have heard what this people said to you. Everything they said was good. ²⁹Oh, that their hearts would be inclined to fear me and keep all my commands always, so that it might go well with them and their children forever!

³⁰"Go, tell them to return to their tents. ³¹But you stay here with me so that I may give you all the commands, decrees and laws you are to teach them to follow in the land I am giving them to possess."

God decided the matter, since granting or denying this request exceeded Moses' authority. But as it turned out, he did not have to present the people's request to the Lord; the Lord, without being asked, declares that the people have spoken well (v. 28). The fear of the Lord that spoke through their words was to their credit; in fact, this fear was indeed the purpose of the divine manifestation (cf. Exod. 20:20).

In verse 29 the wish "Oh that they had such a mind as this always" (RSV), i.e., "that their hearts would be inclined to fear me and keep all my commandments always," are added to the Lord's decision. While approving of their words, the Lord also indicates that a momentary

111

emotion is not sufficient. The Lord does not speak of this generation only, but also of the generations to come ("always," "their children"). Moses must go and tell the people to return to their tents (v. 30); they no longer have to witness God's proclamation. Moses, on the other hand, must again take his place in the immediate presence of God's manifestation, so that he may hear the rest of what God wants to say to Israel. "All the commandments" (Hebrew singular, cf. ASV, RSV) looks at the unity of of the law, the Lord's further proclamation, "decrees and laws" (see comments on 4:1) at its pluriformity.

5:32–33 *So be careful to do what the Lord your God has commanded you; do not turn aside to the right or to the left. ³³Walk in all the way that the Lord your God has commanded you, so that you may live and prosper and prolong your days in the land that you will possess.*

Moses' exhortation to the people to do all that the Lord has commanded them is closely tied in with the immediately preceding. "What the Lord your God has commanded you" includes both the Ten Words and that which is still to come. "Do not turn aside to the right or to the left" anticipates the image of "the way" in verse 33. "The way" encompasses Israel's lifestyle and religio-ethical orientation as determined by God's laws, which Israel must keep in every respect.

C. GENERAL EXHORTATIONS AND COMMANDS (6:1–8:20)

1. New introduction (6:1–3)

In 5:1–5 Moses gave a general introduction; here he gives a new introduction to what is to follow. Since 12:1 contains another, very brief, introduction, verses 1–3 relate to what precedes 12:1, more specifically to 6:4–9:6 (9:7–11:32 is of a more historical nature).

6:1 *These are the commands, decrees and laws the Lord your God directed me to teach you to observe in the land that you are crossing the Jordan to possess, . . .*

"These are the commands" (lit., "This is the commandment") summarizes all that is commanded as a unit (cf. "the law" in 4:44); "decrees and laws" (see comments on 4:1) points to the separate commandments. "Directed me to teach you," cf. 5:31. Again (cf. 4:14) it is said that these commandments are to be kept in Canaan, which Israel is about to enter; some of these laws are indeed intended specifically for life in the Promised Land.

6:2-3 *. . . so that you, your children and their children after them may fear the* LORD *your God as long as you live by keeping all his decrees and commands that I give you, and so that you may enjoy long life. ³Hear, O Israel, and be careful to obey so that it may go well with you and that you may increase greatly in a land flowing with milk and honey, just as the* LORD, *the God of your fathers, promised you.*

"So that you. . .may fear the Lord": this is the reason why Moses must teach them all this; the fear of the Lord will show itself in the keeping of His commandments, as Moses adds. This also applies to "your children and their children after them," i.e., to all coming generations. And this is again linked to the blessing: first, "that you may enjoy long life," whereby we should think in the first place of the individual Israelite, who is addressed here (cf. lit., "you and your son and your son's son," v. 2a), but also of Israel as a nation and of its being settled in the land for a long time. Verse 3 then adds prosperity and increase ("that it may go well with you and that you may increase greatly"), as the Lord had promised Israel (cf. 1:11) through the patriarchs (Gen. 12:1; et al.) as well as directly (Lev. 26:9). Israel will receive these blessings in Canaan, "a land flowing with milk and honey." This is a stereotyped expression, indicating the fertility and wealth of the land (cf. Exod. 3:8); milk is reminiscent of animal husbandry and the honey is mentioned as a product eminently desirable because of its sweetness; there is insufficient basis for the opinion that this expression has its origin in mythology and referred originally to the food and drink of the gods.

2. Israel must love and obey only the Lord (6:4-9)

Now begins the statement of "the commands, decrees and laws," announced in verses 1-3. Verses 4-9 are closely related to what was said in the prologue to the Ten Commandments; the negative "no other gods" is here complemented with a more positive statement. Jewish religious law requires that these verses, together with 11:13-21 and Numbers 15:37-41, must be recited by every adult male in the morning and in the evening; this confession of Judaism is named after the first word of verse 4, *Shema*. Because of the importance of verse 4, Jewish tradition requires that the last letter of both the first and the last words of the verse be written extra large.

6:4 *Hear, O Israel: The Lord our God, the Lord is one.*

"Hear, O Israel": cf. 4:1; 5:1. The rendering "the Lord [Jahweh], our God, is one [or, the only] Lord [Jahweh]" is not acceptable, since it would mean that there is only one Jahweh, in contrast to, e.g., the baals, of which there are several. But what follows (e.g., v. 14, but also v. 5) indicates that the contrast is not between one Jahweh or more Jahwehs, but rather between one God or more than one god. This is why we would render the verse, "The Lord [Jahweh] is our God, the Lord [Jahweh] alone" (cf. Zech. 14:9; cf. also RSV mg.). The last word of verse 4 is "one," but it is used in a similar manner in Genesis 42:19. Thus, only the Lord (Jahweh) is Israel's God; it is not stated that He is also the only God. The purpose here is simply to impress upon Israel that they are to love and serve only the Lord (and not to worship other gods beside Him).

6:5 *Love the Lord your God with all your heart and with all your soul and with all your strength.*

From the fundamental truth of verse 4 follows the fundamental commandment of verse 5 that Israel must love the Lord. This does not contradict what was said in verse 2, that Israel must "fear" the Lord, a more common Old Testament way of describing the relationship between Israel and the Lord; rather, "Love the Lord" shows another aspect of this relationship. It is significant that the demand to love the Lord is placed at the beginning of the proclamation of the law announced in verses 1–3 (see below). This demand flows from the fact that the Lord is "your God" ("our God," v. 4), while the added words "with all your heart and with all your soul and with all your strength" have their foundation in the fact, stated in verse 4, that the Lord *alone* is Israel's God—there is no room for dividing this love between the Lord and another. In connection with the preceding (cf. 5:2), it is possible to relate the words "your God" to the covenant, but the expression has a very broad meaning and significance (cf. Introduction). It reminds one especially of the Lord's fatherhood and of the relationship of husband to wife (Israel; Exod. 34:15–16; Hos. 1–3). "Heart" and "soul" are here synonymous terms for the inner being, the seat of love; "with all your strength" indicates that their full

114

capacity to love must be brought into play; we can refer this to the powers of heart and soul, but also to those of the body—it goes without saying that love must express itself in deeds. In Matthew 22:37 (Mark 12:30; Luke 10:27) our Lord quoted this verse. [9] So Jesus did not give a new commandment; indeed, we might say that Deuteronomy, by placing this commandment first, indicates that this is the "first and great commandment," from which everything else stems. Nevertheless, the fundamental significance is clarified by Christ's explicit qualification and also by His statement that on this commandment and the commandment to love one's neighbor hang all the Law and the Prophets. It is clear in general that the New Testament, in comparison with the old, places much greater emphasis on the commandment to love and unfolds its implications with much greater richness and depth as a consequence of the much richer revelation of God's love in the sending of His Son (cf. 11:18ff.).

6:6–9 *These commandments that I give you today are to be upon your hearts. ⁷Impress them on your children. Talk about them when you sit at home and when you walk along the road, when you lie down and when you get up. ⁸Tie them as symbols on your hands and bind them on your foreheads. ⁹Write them on the doorframes of your houses and on your gates.*

The love for the Lord must show itself in the zealous keeping of "these commandments that I give you today," i.e., the demands proclaimed by God and presented to the people by Moses, both before and after this statement. These commandments are to be "upon your hearts" (cf. "in your hearts" in 11:18, and "write it on their hearts" in Jer. 31:33). "*Upon* your hearts" appears to be essentially synonymous with "*in* your hearts"; the former expression would seem to describe the heart as a tablet upon which the words are written (cf. Jer. 31:33; Prov. 3:3; 7:3; also Jer. 17:1). "Heart" here again refers more specifically to the seat of thought and memory but also of love (cf. v. 5), and "thought and memory" should therefore not be understood here in a strictly intellectual sense.

Verse 7 tells the Israelites to teach these commandments to their children (cf. vv. 20ff.) and to talk about them everywhere and always (cf. "without ceasing" in 1 Thess. 5:17 KJV); this serves to instruct the children (but is not limited to this instruction; they do not always have

---

⁹The words "with all your mind," which are added in Mark and Luke and replace "with all your strength" in Matthew, derive from the LXX, which, however, is not quoted verbatim. For a detailed comparison, see Keil.

the children with them "along the road"). The point is rather that the Israelites are to keep these commandments alive in their everyday thoughts and to remind themselves and others of them. Verses 8–9 (cf. Exod. 13:9, 16) state that these commandments (in written form) must be tied to the hands "as symbols" (i.e., to remind the Israelites of these commandments); they are also to be "as frontlets between your eyes" (RSV), i.e., on the forehead (we must think here of a band around the head on which the words are written). And finally, the commandments are to be written "on the doorframes of your houses and on your gates." Later Judaism took all this literally and believed that they fulfilled verses 8–9 by attaching small parchment scrolls to straps around the arm and forehead (the tephillin or phylacteries; cf. Matt. 23:5), and to the frames of house and room doors (the mezuzoth). The tephillin contained Exodus 13:1–10, 11–16; Deuteronomy 6:4–9; 11:13–21, while the mezuzoth contained Deuteronomy 6:4–9; 11:13–21. It is possible to hold different opinions as to the intent of the Scriptures here and in Exodus 13:9, 16, but in our opinion the figurative understanding is to be preferred. The reason why this description is so concrete can be explained by the fact that in ancient times the wearing of such symbols was a custom with which Moses was familiar. In view of this, it would be entirely possible that Moses told Israel to do something similar. But it is also possible that Moses used this custom as the basis for a metaphor (cf. Prov. 3:3; 7:3); this view would appear to be preferable, because (1) the context does not lead us to think of anything of such a strictly external nature; (2) "These commandments" in verse 6 refers not only to 6:6–9 but to all that Moses teaches Israel in this discourse, which makes a literal application of verses 8–9 impossible. When taken metaphorically, the tying on the hands and the writing on the doorframes indicate that one must constantly remind oneself of these commandments, while the "frontlet between the eyes" shows that one stands up for them and proclaims them to others; the tying on the hands may further indicate that the commandments are not only to be upon the heart (v. 6) or to be expressed verbally (v. 7), but are also to be implemented in deed.

3. Prosperity in Canaan must not keep Israel from worshiping the Lord and keeping His commandments (6:10–19)

6:10–15 *When the LORD your God brings you into the land he swore to your fathers, to Abraham, Isaac and Jacob, to give you—a land with large,* *flourishing cities you did nòt build, ¹¹houses filled with all kinds of good things you did not provide, wells you did not dig, and vineyards and olive groves you did not plant–then when you eat and are satisfied, ¹²be careful that you do not forget the LORD, who brought you out of Egypt, out of the land of slavery. ¹³Fear the LORD your God, serve him only and take your oaths in his name. ¹⁴Do not follow other gods, the gods of the peoples around you; ¹⁵for the LORD your God, who is among you, is a jealous God and his anger will burn against you, and he will destroy you from the face of the land.*

Moses warns Israel not to forget the Lord once they have reached Canaan and enjoy the abundance of the Promised Land. This "forgetting" could mean that the people, proud because of their prosperity, would begin to think that they owed all this to their own strength (cf. 18:11ff.). But here something else is in the foreground: Israel would forget the Lord and begin to serve other gods (v. 14) and see their blessings as coming from these gods (especially the Baals, the gods of the land; cf. Hos. 2:4, 7).

The premise of verse 10 is that Israel enters Canaan because the Lord brings them there in accordance with the promise He made to the forefathers. Israel will find there "large, flourishing cities," "houses filled with all kinds of good things," etc. But they have not built the cities or the houses nor have they provided the good things; the Lord will bring them into this land and He will simply give them all these things. It would therefore be gross ingratitude if Israel, after enjoying the good things to the full, would forget the Lord their God who led them out of the land of slavery, Egypt (v. 12), and give their gratitude and praise for all this to other gods.

Israel must fear the Lord and serve Him only (this "serving" refers to the cultus, and thus especially to the offerings), and honor Him by taking their oaths in His name. "Fear" involves the heart, "serve" the hand, and "oaths" the mouth. Verse 14 states explicitly what is clearly in the background of verse 13: "Do not follow other gods." For the Lord "is among you" (v. 15) and He is a jealous God (see comments on 4:24): in His anger, aroused by their serving other gods, He would destroy them.

6:16 *Do not test the LORD your God as you did at Massah.*

At Massah Israel "tested" the Lord (Exod. 17:2, 7); the context in Exodus, which does not mention punishment, indicates that "testing" means that because of their unbelief and grumbling the Lord was, as it were, forced to give them a sign of His omnipotence. The name Massah ("testing," "place of testing"), which served as a permanent reminder of this "testing" of the Lord, became a proverbial expression (cf. Ps. 95:8; see also Deut. 9:22; 33:8) and is used as such in this verse. Interpretations differ. We would explain the text on the analogy of Exodus 17:2, 7 as a warning to Israel: When Israel has received all the proofs of the Lord's favor and power described in verses 10ff., they must not force the Lord, as it were, to provide still more miracles because of their attitude of unbelief. This is the sense in which Jesus quotes this verse in Matthew 4:7. Such a testing would be a forgetting of the Lord and the blessings He bestowed on Israel. This interpretation links this verse with what precedes it. Others relate this verse more directly to the announcement of God's anger in verse 15; verse 16 then intensifies the warning of the preceding verse, and "test" should be taken in the sense of "provoking in the extreme,"—to see if the Lord's anger will indeed be aroused and if He will be able to punish. In view of Exodus 17:2, 7 and Matthew 4:7, however, the former interpretation would appear to be correct.

6:17–19 *Be sure to keep the commands of the* Lord *your God and the stipulations and decrees he has given you.* ¹⁸*Do what is right and good in the* Lord's *sight, so that it may go well with you and you may go in and take over the good land that the* Lord *promised on oath to your forefathers,* ¹⁹*thrusting out all your enemies before you, as the* Lord *said.*

The exhortation not to forget the Lord in favor of other gods is now continued with an exhortation to keep His commandments. "Stipulations": see comments on 4:45. "He has given you": Israel had already received these stipulations at Horeb. "As the Lord said" (v. 19): cf. Exodus 23:27–28; 34:11.

4. The obligation to instruct the children in the Law (6:20–25).

6:20–25 *In the future, when your son asks you, "What is the meaning of the stipulations, decrees and laws the* Lord *our God has commanded you?"* ²¹*tell him: "We were slaves of Pharaoh in Egypt, but the* Lord *brought us out of Egypt with a mighty hand.* ²²*Before our eyes the* Lord *sent miraculous signs and wonders—great and terrible—upon Egypt and Pharaoh and his whole household.* ²³*But he brought us out from there to bring us in and give us the land that he promised on oath to our forefathers.* ²⁴*The* Lord *commanded us to obey all these decrees and to fear the* Lord *our God, so that we might always prosper and be kept alive, as is the case today.* ²⁵*And if we are careful to obey all this* *law before the LORD our God, as he has commanded us, that will be our righteousness."*

The obligation to instruct the children in Israel's sacred traditions is repeatedly brought before Israel in Deuteronomy (cf. v. 7). These verses assume that the son has first asked a question (v. 20; cf. Exod. 13:14)—which is not to deny that the obligation to provide instruction exists even if the son does not ask. "What is the meaning of the stipulations . . .": the answer given would indicate that the question concerns not so much the content of the laws as the manner in which they came into existence. The question thus opens up an avenue for explaining the motivations that should lead to the keeping of the laws. "Stipulations": see comments on 4:45. "Decrees and laws": see comments on 4:1.

The answer the father is to give describes first the deliverance from Egypt through the Lord's mighty hand (vv. 21–23) and then points out that the Lord has commanded all this "that we might always prosper and be kept alive, as is the case today." The fact that the Lord first delivered them and only then gave them His laws (cf. 5:6ff.) provides a strong motivation for keeping those laws out of gratitude. "So that we might always prosper" adds a second motivation: Israel's well-being, indeed, their very life depends on the keeping of the law. Also from this perspective the giving of the law is the continuation of the deliverance from Egypt. Not only did the Lord deliver Israel from slavery, He also showed them the way that leads to life. "Be kept alive" refers, like "that we might always prosper," both to individuals and to Israel as a whole.

Verse 25 adds that the careful obedience to the law "will be our righteousness," i.e., they will be righteous before God in this way, and thus they may hope for His favor and blessing. This must not be understood as a contrast to justification by grace through faith. The entire law and the Lord's covenant with Israel contained in it are based on grace; keeping the law is therefore essentially an act of faith, a holding fast to the covenant and the grace that is given in the covenant. The justification expressed in "that will be our righteousness" is thus to be understood in the sense of James 2:20ff.—it is in principle a justification by faith (cf. Introduction), although it is not presented here with New Testament clarity, but rather in a veiled, legalistic manner (cf. Introduction). "All this law": the various commands are here seen as a single entity, hence the singular. "To obey all this law before the LORD our God," i.e., to obey it in such a manner that it is acceptable to

Him who sees all and tests the heart. This is thus not the same as evaluating obedience to the law by human standards.

5. Warning against mixing with the Canaanites (7:1-8)

7:1-2 *When the LORD your God brings you into the land you are entering to possess and drives out before you many nations—the Hittites, Girgashites, Amorites, Canaanites, Perizzites, Hivites and Jebusites, seven nations larger and stronger than you—²and when the LORD your God has delivered them over to you and you have defeated them, then you must destroy them totally. Make no treaty with them, and show them no mercy.*

When by the Lord's help Israel will have conquered the Canaanite tribes, they must destroy them utterly (*cherem*, see comments on 2:34). No quarter must be given, which also means that no treaty must be made with them (cf. Exod. 23:32; 34:12), since this would mean that they would be allowed to live (albeit under certain conditions and possibly in a subservient position, but nevertheless as Israel's allies). The Canaanites must be exterminated, both as a punishment for their sins and to forestall their being a spiritual danger to Israel.

7:3-4 *Do not intermarry with them. Do not give your daughters to their sons or take their daughters for your sons, ⁴for they will turn your sons away from following me to serve other gods, and the LORD's anger will burn against you and will quickly destroy you.*

A separate prohibition against intermarriage between Israelites and Canaanites is added (cf. Exod. 34:16). Since the extermination of the Canaanites commanded in verse 1 would not take place all at once (cf. 7:22), there would be ample opportunity for such intermarriage. The lawgiver forbids such marriages because of the danger of idolatry they bring with them (cf. 5:7; 6:14). "From following me": although Moses speaks, "me" of course refers to the Lord, in whose name Moses speaks. For the added threat, cf. 6:15.

7:5 *This is what you are to do to them: Break down their altars, smash their sacred stones, cut down their Asherah poles and burn their idols in the fire.*

Israel is commanded to destroy the sacred places of the Canaanites (cf. Exod. 23:24; 34:13). In their simplest and most common form these consisted of an (outdoor) altar, with an upright stone and a sacred pole beside it; also mentioned are their idols. Temples or other sacred buildings are not included in this list; these were less common, but they did exist and served in the first place as a shelter for the idol or "carved image." "Sacred stones" (*massebot*): the *masseba* could serve a number of purposes (e.g., it could be simply a memorial), and was originally not prohibited as such (Gen. 28:18, 22; 31:51ff.; Exod. 24:4; Josh. 4:20ff.). However, here the *massebot* are "sacred stones," probably symbols of the Baal, and in any case dedicated to idolatrous worship. This is why Israel is forbidden to place them beside the altar of the Lord (16:22). The "Asherah poles" were dedicated to the goddess Asherah, who was closely related to Astarte, the most prominent female deity in the Canaanite religion. These Asherah poles are also expressly prohibited in 16:21 and they are never used in Israel's legitimate cultus, owing to their inherently pagan character. The stones must be smashed, the poles cut down. The idols were made of wood or stone; the wooden images were sometimes overlaid with gold or silver (see comments on v. 25), and idols were sometimes made of cast metal (Isa. 40:19). Since the idols are to be burned, Moses here speaks primarily of wooden images, but this would by extension also include the destruction of other images.

A reason behind the command to destroy the sacred places of the Canaanites was certainly that these could not be tolerated in the land that was in a special sense the Lord's. But the primary purpose was to keep Israel from participating in Canaanite idolatry. History shows how necessary this measure was—in spite of the prohibitions, Israel fell into this idolatry again and again.

7:6–8 *For you are a people holy to the LORD your God. The LORD your God has chosen you out of all the peoples on the face of the earth to be his people, his treasured possession.*

7The LORD did not set his affection on you and choose you because you were more numerous than other peoples, for you were the fewest of all peoples. 8But it was because the LORD loved you and kept the oath he swore to your forefathers that he brought you out with a mighty hand and redeemed you from the land of slavery, from the power of Pharaoh king of Egypt.

These verses present the underlying motivation of the preceding. Israel must not participate in any way in the Canaanite practices because Israel is a people "holy to the LORD," a people dedicated to Him, set apart for Him. He has chosen Israel out of all the nations to be His "treasured possession," which expresses the same idea as "holy." Israel is the Lord's own people and therefore is to serve and worship

Him. He chose Israel, rather than another nation, not because it was such a great nation (v. 7; cf. Exod. 19:5–6)—indeed, he says, "you were the fewest of all peoples." This is not to be understood literally, but as hyperbole; in comparison with peoples like the Egyptians, Babylonians, and Assyrians, Israel was indeed small. Verse 8 then states the reason for Israel's election: the Lord's sovereign love for this people (cf. 7:8, 13; 10:15; 23:5; Hos. 11:1) and His faithfulness to the oath He swore to the forefathers. But if this is the basis of Israel's election as "his people, his treasured possession," then Israel has double reason to dedicate themselves in humble gratitude to the service of this God. The reminder of the deliverance from Egypt serves to reinforce this argument.

6. Serve the Lord, the God of faithfulness and love (7:9–16)

In connection with the preceding, Israel is exhorted to keep the Lord's commandments and to be mindful of the faithfulness and love He shows to those who love Him and of the punishment He metes out to those who hate Him.

7:9–11 *Know therefore that the* LORD *your God is God; he is the faithful God, keeping his covenant of love to a thousand generations of those who love him and keep his commands.* [10]*But*

> *those who hate him he will repay to their face by destruction;*
> *he will not be slow to repay to their face those who hate him.*

[11]*Therefore, take care to follow the commands, decrees and laws I give you today.*

"Know therefore": be deeply convinced (the singular refers in the first place to Israel, but also to the individual Israelite). "The LORD your God is God": He is the true God whom alone you must serve (cf. vv. 1–8). And you have every reason to serve Him (cf. 5:9; Exod. 20:5–6): He is the faithful God, who keeps (lit.) "the covenant and the unfailing love [*chesed*] to those who love Him and to those who keep His commandments, to a thousand generations." The word *chesed* could also be translated "faithfulness"; it sometimes has the more general meaning "kindness," "mercy," but it can refer as well to the kind, benevolent, and favorable disposition and attitude that makes one loyal to one's obligations toward those to whom one is related with special ties. When used of God, it then refers to His covenant faithfulness, His loyalty based on the covenant relationship. The fact that "covenant" immediately precedes *chesed* would indicate that this is what is in view here. Verse 10 contraposes His attitude toward those who hate Him: He will destroy them without delay "to their face," i.e., not as in an ambush, but directly and openly, so that the haters will clearly know what is happening to them. This, like the words "he will not be slow," describes God's retribution in notional terms, since it will be realized fully only in the Last Judgment. Furthermore, verse 10 speaks only of retribution on the individual; the punishment on subsequent generations (5:9; Exod. 20:5) is not mentioned here, although it is not thereby denied (cf. also 24:16; Jer. 31:29–30; Ezek. 18). This emphasis on personal retribution and the absence of any mention of the punishment on following generations puts into clear relief the "thousand generations" of verse 9: the *chesed* far exceeds the retribution.

Verse 11 concludes by exhorting to keep, "therefore," the commandments, decrees, and laws (cf. 6:1).

7:12–16 *If you pay attention to these laws and are careful to follow them, then the* LORD *your God will keep his covenant of love with you, as he swore to your forefathers.* ¹³*He will love you and bless you and increase your numbers. He will bless the fruit of your womb, the crops of your land—your grain, new wine and oil—the calves of your herds and the lambs of your flocks in the land that he swore to your forefathers to give you.* ¹⁴*You will be blessed more than any other people; none of your men or women will be childless, nor any of your livestock without young.* ¹⁵*The* LORD *will keep you free from every disease. He will not inflict on you the horrible diseases you knew in Egypt, but he will inflict them on all who hate you.* ¹⁶*You must destroy all the peoples the* LORD *your God gives over to you. Do not look on them with pity and do not serve their gods, for that will be a snare to you.*

These verses contain a more detailed description of the blessings Israel will receive from the Lord if they keep the commandments. "If you pay attention . . ." (lit., "and it shall be because you hear"): there is a legalistic element in this phraseology; it is as if the Lord gives blessing in exchange for Israel's obedience to the law. Nevertheless, the Lord's sovereign love remains the foundation of the entire relationship (cf. v. 8 and Introduction). "Will keep his covenant of love with you": see comments on verse 9.

Verses 13–15 describe what this means in concrete terms (cf. Exod. 23:25–27). There are a few elements in this description that are reminiscent of the messianic era rather than of conditions as they exist or have ever existed on this earth under the curse (see v. 14 and esp.

v. 15). This does not mean that this promise is deceptive; because the keeping of the law demanded in verse 12 will always remain imperfect, Israel could never, even during its best periods, receive the full blessing that comes with the keeping of the law. The fullness of this blessing awaits the consummation of all things, when it will be given and received, not as a result of Israel's keeping of the law, but on the basis of God's forgiving grace (Isa. 33:24). Here also it became evident that the law was not able to give life (Gal. 3:21) and was "put in charge to lead us to Christ" (Gal. 3:24).

The first thing mentioned in the description of the blessing God will bestow on Israel when they are obedient to the law is that He will "love" them, from which flows His "blessing"; this is then further elaborated as a blessing of fertility of the people ("increase your numbers," "the fruit of your womb"), of the land, and of the cattle. Verse 14 underlines this again with respect to the people and the cattle (cf. Exod. 23:26).

Verse 15 (cf. Exod. 15:26; 23:25) promises that the Lord will keep Israel free from disease. The "horrible diseases" of Egypt are specially mentioned: not Israel, but Israel's enemies will be struck by them. Especially in this verse the description reminds us of the messianic era (Isa. 33:24, see above). "The horrible diseases of Egypt" (cf. 28:27, 35, 60; Exod. 15:26): the reference is to virulent diseases that are indigenous to Egypt, perhaps the most prominent of which is elephantiasis and perhaps also the plague (cf. 28:27).

Verse 16 speaks of Israel's complete victory over the peoples (the Canaanites) the Lord "gives over" to them. The second half of the verse again adds the exhortation not to spare them and not to serve their gods. If they failed to do this, Israel would be like an animal caught in a trap: their destruction would soon follow.

7. Do not fear the Canaanites; destroy their idols (7:17–26)

7:17–24 *You may say to yourselves, "These nations are stronger than we are. How can we drive them out?"* [18]*But do not be afraid of them; remember well what the LORD your God did to Pharaoh and to all Egypt.* [19]*You saw with your own eyes the great trials, the miraculous signs and wonders, the mighty hand and outstretched arm, with which the LORD your God brought you out. The LORD your God will do the same to all the peoples you now fear.* [20]*Moreover, the LORD your God will send the hornet among them until even the survivors who hide from you have perished.* [21]*Do not be terrified by them, for the LORD your God, who is among you, is a great and awesome God.* [22]*The LORD your God will* *drive out those nations before you, little by little. You will not be allowed to eliminate them all at once, or the wild animals will multiply around you. ²³But the LORD your God will deliver them over to you, throwing them into great confusion until they are destroyed. ²⁴He will give their kings into your hand, and you will wipe out their names from under heaven. No one will be able to stand up against you; you will destroy them.*

The Lord promises Israel that He will give the Canaanites over to them. When Israel fears that they will not be able to conquer them (v. 17; "you" and "yourselves" are singular), they must remember what the Lord did to Pharaoh and to all of Egypt (v. 18; cf. 4:34; 6:22). He brought the "great trials" (cf. 4:34) and the "miraculous signs and wonders" of the Exodus upon them. He will do the same to the Canaanites. Verse 20 adds that the Lord will also send "the hornet" (cf. Exod. 23:28), a vicious type of wasp, among them.[10] These will pursue any Canaanites that remain after Israel's victory and find them in their hiding places and destroy them. This is apparently intended figuratively; cf. Joshua 24:12, where Joshua says that the Lord drove out the two kings of the Amorites by means of hornets. The hornets are the symbol of the destructive power with which He will pursue the Canaanites even in their hiding places. There is therefore no reason for Israel to be terrified, since the Lord with all His might is in their midst (v. 21).

Verse 22 adds that this extermination will take place only gradually (concerning "he will not be slow" in v. 10, see comments on that verse). The reason for this was to prevent that as a result of the depopulation the wild animals would take over (Exod. 23:29–30), as did happen later after the deportation of the ten tribes (2 Kings 17:25–26. Another reason for the above was that the Lord wanted to test Israel (Judg. 3:1ff.). The extermination was also delayed because of Israel's unfaithfulness (Judg. 2:20ff.).

Verses 23–24 continue the promise of the destruction of the Canaanites. The Lord will throw them "into great confusion until they are destroyed" (as clearly happened in the case of Gibeon, Josh. 10:10). Their kings He will also give into their power (v. 26), and Israel will utterly destroy them, so that their names will not be remembered (cf. Josh. 10:22ff.; 11:12; 12:7–24).

---

[10]Some render this, "will send even the hornet," i.e., the Lord will send every power against the Canaanites, even the smallest ones, such as the hornet. But this would appear to be incorrect. The hornets are here depicted as symbolic, not of a minor, but of an extremely destructive power.

7:25–26 *The images of their gods you are to burn in the fire. Do not covet the silver and gold on them, and do not take it for yourselves, or you will be ensnared by it, for it is detestable to the LORD your God.* ²⁶*Do not bring a detestable thing into your house or you, like it, will be set apart for destruction. Utterly abhor and detest it, for it is set apart for destruction.*

The promise is followed by a restatement of the command to destroy the idols (cf. 7:5). Again, they are to be burned (once again, wooden idols are primarily in view). But a comment is added about the "silver and gold on them," the overlay that covered the wooden core (cf. Isa. 30:22). Israel must not fall prey to greed and take this silver and gold; it would be a snare to them and would lead to their destruction (cf. 7:16). This silver and gold is "detestable [KJV, an abomination] to the LORD." Anyone who brings such an abomination into his house will be struck with the ban (*cherem;* cf. 2:34) that should have been applied to the detestable thing (cf. the story of Achan, Josh. 7:19ff.). The silver and gold of the idols must therefore be pulverized and thrown away (cf. Exod. 32:20; 2 Kings 23:24–25; 2 Chron. 15:16; cf. Isa. 30:22).

8. Keep the commands of the Lord (8:1–6)

8:1–6 *Be careful to follow every command I am giving you today, so that you may live and increase and may enter and possess the land that the LORD promised on oath to your forefathers.* ²*Remember how the LORD your God led you all the way in the desert these forty years, to humble you and to test you in order to know what was in your heart, whether or not you would keep his commands.* ³*He humbled you, causing you to hunger and then feeding you with manna, which neither you nor your fathers had known, to teach you that man does not live on bread alone but on every word that comes from the mouth of the LORD.* ⁴*Your clothes did not wear out and your feet did not swell during these forty years.* ⁵*Know then in your heart that as a man disciplines his son, so the LORD your God disciplines you.*

⁶*Observe the commands of the LORD your God, walking in his ways and revering him.*

Again Moses exhorts Israel to keep the commandments (vv. 1, 6), this time reminding them especially of the wilderness journey.

The reason why Israel is to keep "every command" (or "the whole command") is, besides life and increase (cf. 4:1; 6:3), that by doing so they will take possession of Canaan (cf. 4:1). Moses refers thus again to the obedience that Israel already now, before the conquest, must exercise; Moses usually speaks of keeping the commandments in

Canaan, and in large part the commandments are designed for life in Canaan, but Israel is, of course, at this point already obligated to obedience (cf. v. 2).

The exhortation is reinforced by a reminder of the forty-year stay in the wilderness (1:31; 2:7), of "the way" in which the Lord led them. These forty years were important for pedagogic reasons (cf. v. 5). In contrast to Canaan, the wilderness was the place where the Lord "sent hardships"[11] designed to "test" them "in order to know what was in your heart," i.e., to see whether they would keep the commandments. Of course, this is an anthropomorphic statement. God knows the heart and His testing is not designed to find out something He does not know, but rather to bring out into the open that which is hidden, for His own glory and justification and for the *heil*[12] of those who are His.

Of those hardships, verse 3 mentions specifically the lack of bread, the common staple, so that they were hungry; the Lord gave them manna instead, something unknown to them. This is also part of the hardship (cf. v. 16). The addition, "which neither you nor your fathers had known" characterizes the manna as unfamiliar and therefore less desirable food (cf. Num. 21:5). Nevertheless, the "feeding" also expresses their experience of God's care (cf. v. 4). Through these hardships and His care in the midst of them, God wanted to teach them that "man does not live on bread alone but on every word that comes from the mouth of the LORD." The intent is apparently that in this instance it was the manna that came "from the mouth of the LORD," i.e., that came into being through His word of power. The essential meaning does not change when in Matthew 4:4 and Luke 4:4 the Savior refers that which comes "from the mouth of the LORD" directly to the divine word of power itself (i.e., the creating and sustaining power that emanates from God; cf. Gen. 1:3; Ps. 33:6; Heb. 1:3). The general import is, of course, that the Lord wanted to teach Israel to trust, not in anything created, but only in the Creator.

Verse 4 adds that during those forty years their clothes did not wear out and their feet did not swell (cf. 29:5, which speaks of the sandals rather than the feet). This undoubtedly is also to be understood as a miracle of God's power and care, and hence is mentioned with the

---

[11]The usual translation, "to humble you and to test you" is in our opinion incorrect, since there is then no logical connection between the humbling and the testing. We prefer the rendering "sent hardships to test you" (cf. TEV); see also v. 3)

[12]See note on p. 29.

manna. This does not preclude Israel's making use of the natural means of making clothing (and sandals) during the wilderness journey, even as the feeding with the manna does not exclude the use of natural sources of food insofar as these were available.

Verse 5 draws the conclusion: As a man disciplines his son, so the Lord has disciplined Israel in the wilderness, teaching Israel to trust in the Lord alone (vv. 3–4; cf. 4:36; 11:2; cf. Ps. 94:10; Hos. 11:1–4). Israel must know this in their heart, i.e., they must be deeply aware of this. And therefore they must keep the commandments of this God— this was the purpose of the discipline (v. 6).

9. **Do not forget the Lord in the midst of Canaan's blessings (8:7–20)**

After a reminder of the past and its lessons (8:1–6), Moses turns again to the future with its blessings, its calling, and its dangers.

8:7–10a *For the* Lord *your God is bringing you into a good land—a land with streams and pools of water, with springs flowing in the valleys and hills; ⁸a land with wheat and barley, vines and fig trees, pomegranates, olive oil and honey; ⁹a land where bread will not be scarce and you will lack nothing; a land where the rocks are iron and you can dig copper out of the hills.*

¹⁰When you have eaten and are satisfied,

First he describes the "good land" where the Lord will bring Israel. We must keep in mind that Moses describes the riches of the land in contrast to the desert or steppe region where Israel has spent the last forty years. He describes it therefore in the first place as "a land with streams and pools of water, with springs flowing in the valleys and hills," i.e., a fertile land. This is why it is rich in produce (even more important than agriculture in Canaan was arboriculture, and the most important "trees" were the grapevine, the figtree, and the olive tree). Consequently (v. 9), "bread will not be scarce," a litotes for "abundant." Furthermore, the land contains iron and copper (the "rocks are iron," i.e., are ferriferous). Job 28:1–11 speaks of mining, but it is not known whether the Israelites ever mined iron or copper in their land. In Canaan proper, the rock contains little iron or copper (this is also true of the basalt rock, cf. comments on 3:11), and few places are known where these ores can be found. Iron is found only in Wadi Adshlun, which enters the Jordan from the east; copper mining is known from the region between the Dead Sea and Petra. In the Lebanon mountains, on the other hand, cupriferous and ferriferous rock is not rare (cf. Ezek. 27:19); perhaps Moses had this in mind (cf. 1:7). Verse 10a rounds out the picture by describing the people as they will be there in the land, fully satisfied.

8:10b *Praise the Lord your God for the good land he has given you.*

Finally, Moses states what all this must lead to: Israel must praise the Lord their God "for the good land he has given you."

8:11-20 *Be careful that you do not forget the Lord your God, failing to observe his commands, his laws and his decrees that I am giving you this day.* [12]*Otherwise, when you eat and are satisfied, when you build fine houses and settle down, [13]and when your herds and flocks grow large and your silver and gold increase and all you have is multiplied, [14]then your heart will become proud and you will forget the Lord your God, who brought you out of Egypt, out of the land of slavery. [15]He led you through the vast and dreadful desert, that thirsty and waterless land, with its venomous snakes and scorpions. He brought you water out of hard rock. [16]He gave you manna to eat in the desert, something your fathers had never known, to humble and to test you so that in the end it might go well with you. [17]You may say to yourself, "My power and the strength of my hands have produced this wealth for me." [18]But remember the Lord your God, for it is he who gives you the ability to produce wealth, and so confirms his covenant, which he swore to your forefathers, as it is today.*

[19]If you ever forget the Lord your God and follow other gods and worship and bow down to them, I testify against you today that you will surely be destroyed. [20]Like the nations the Lord destroyed before you, so you will be destroyed for not obeying the Lord your God.

On the other hand, Moses warns the people that in the midst of Canaan's abundance they must not forget the Lord their God—the God who led them out of Egypt and who in the wilderness protected them, cared for them, and tested them (vv. 14b–16). They must not let pride get the better of them and attribute their abundance to their own strength. Israel must remember the Lord; it was He who gave them the strength to acquire all this, and if they forget Him they will "surely be destroyed."

"Venomous snakes" (v. 15; KJV. "fiery serpents"): highly dangerous snakes (cf. Num. 21:6). On verse 16, cf. verses 2–3. The addition "so that in the end it may go well with you" characterizes the stay in the wilderness as a preparation for life in Canaan (cf. v. 5). In this, Israel is a type of the life of the church and of the individual believer (cf. James 1:12).

Verse 18 reminds once again of the covenant made with the forefathers. It, rather than any merit on Israel's part, is the reason why the Lord does all this. The words "as it is today" may be a later addition (cf. 2:30; 4:20), although we could also say that the Lord had already given an initial confirmation of the covenant by giving the land east of the Jordan into Israel's possession.

Verses 14 and 17 placed the cause of forgetting the Lord in pride; in verse 19 this forgetting is related to the following of other gods; there can, of course, be a close connection between the two. On verse 19b, cf. 4:26; 6:14.

D. THE NARRATIVE OF THE GIVING OF THE LAW CONTINUED TO ILLUSTRATE ISRAEL'S STUBBORNNESS (9:1–10:11)

The narrative of the giving of the law at Horeb, which begins in 5:6–33 and was interrupted by the exhortations of 6:1–8:20, is now continued, especially to remind Israel of the stubbornness they have displayed again and again.

1. Introduction: Not because of their righteousness will Israel enter Canaan (9:1–6)

9:1–3 *Hear, O Israel. You are now about to cross the Jordan to go in and dispossess nations greater and stronger than you, with large cities that have walls up to the sky. ²The people are strong and tall—Anakites! You know about them and have heard it said: "Who can stand up against the Anakites?" ³But be assured today that the LORD your God is the one who goes across ahead of you like a devouring fire. He will destroy them; he will subdue them before you. And you will drive them out and annihilate them quickly, as the LORD has promised you.*

The words "Hear, O Israel" indicate a new beginning. Moses reminds Israel first of all of the position in which they find themselves. They are about to enter Canaan to dispossess the nations living there, nations that are superior to them in strength and numbers, and to capture their cities that are fortified with "walls up to the sky" (cf. 1:28). Of those nations, the Anakites are mentioned by name, since they are supposed to be invincible (cf. 1:28). Israel must be assured (lit., "know") that the impending conquest is solely the Lord's work. It is He who will go ahead of them across the Jordan, i.e., as their leader and commander (cf. 1:30), and as a "devouring fire" (cf. 4:24) that destroys the enemy. *He* will destroy the Canaanites, *He* will subdue them "before you," i.e., wherever Israel goes. And thus Israel will be able to "annihilate them quickly," as the Lord has promised (cf. 2:24ff.; Exod. 23:23, 27ff.). Over against this "quickly" stand the words "little by little" and "not . . . all at once" of 7:22; this means that the "quickly" here must be understood in a relative sense. It points to the efficacy of God's help, which at times will make the conquest progress rapidly, even though the completion of the conquest would take time.

9:4-6 *After the* LORD *your God has driven them out before you, do not say to yourself, "The* LORD *has brought me here to take possession of this land because of my righteousness." No, it is on account of the wickedness of these nations that the* LORD *is going to drive them out before you.* ⁵*It is not because of your righteousness or your integrity that you are going in to take possession of their land; but on account of the wickedness of these nations, the* LORD *your God will drive them out before you, to accomplish what he swore to your fathers, to Abraham, Isaac and Jacob.* ⁶*Understand, then, that it is not because of your righteousness that the* LORD *your God is giving you this good land to possess, for you are a stiff-necked people.*

Then comes the main point. Israel must not only realize that the conquest is God's doing, they must be equally aware that God does not give them the land because of their righteousness. One reason for the annihilation of the other nations is their wickedness (vv. 4–5). But this in itself does not explain why it is *Israel* that receives the land. Verse 5b gives the positive reason: It is because of the promise the Lord made to the forefathers under oath (cf. 7:8). Verse 6 repeats "not because of your righteousness" and adds that, far from being righteous, Israel is a "stiff-necked people," a people that generally refuses to obey, like the ox that refuses to bow its neck under the yoke (cf. Exod. 32:9). And thus the foundation has been laid for what follows.

2. The first stone tablets; the golden calf; Moses' intercession (9:7–24)

To illustrate the statement that Israel is a stiffnecked people, Moses reminds his hearers of their sins in the wilderness, especially that of the making of the golden calf at Mount Horeb (for this story, see Exod. 32:1ff.; for Moses' stay on the mountain that preceded it, see Exod. 24:12–31:17).

9:7–8 *Remember this and never forget how you provoked the* LORD *your God to anger in the desert. From the day you left Egypt until you arrived here, you have been rebellious against the* LORD. *⁸At Horeb you aroused the* LORD'*s wrath so that he was angry enough to destroy you.*

Throughout the wilderness journey, from the Exodus to their arrival at this place, the Israelites rebelled against the Lord. "From the day you left Egypt" does not have to be taken in a strictly literal sense; the people grumbled even before they departed and also shortly after the departure, before the crossing of the Red Sea (Exod. 5:20ff.; 14:11). But especially at Horeb the people aroused the Lord's anger with the golden calf.

9:9–10 *When I went up on the mountain to receive the tablets of stone, the tablets of the covenant that the* LORD *had made with you, I stayed on the mountain forty days and forty nights; I ate no bread and drank no water. ¹⁰The* LORD *gave me two stone tablets inscribed by the finger of God. On them were all the commandments the* LORD *proclaimed to you on the mountain out of the fire, on the day of the assembly.*

But before going into detail, Moses first sketches the situation in order to show the people's sin in its full dimensions. He had climbed up Mount Horeb to receive the two stone tablets of the covenant. He remained on the mountain for forty days and forty nights without eating bread or drinking water; this was an indication of the extreme sanctity of what transpired there. Then the Lord gave Moses the two tablets inscribed by God's finger with the words He had spoken from the fire (5:4), i.e., the Ten Commandments (4:13; 5:5ff.; Exod. 34:28). "On the day of the assembly," i.e., when Moses had gathered the people before the Lord. How much reason the people had to feel a close tie of grateful love with the Lord!

9:11–14 *At the end of the forty days and forty nights, the* LORD *gave me the two stone tablets, the tablets of the covenant. ¹²Then the* LORD *told me, "Go down from here at once, because your people whom you brought out of Egypt have become corrupt. They have turned away quickly from what I commanded them and have made a cast idol for themselves."*

¹³And the LORD *said to me, "I have seen this people, and they are a stiff-necked people indeed! ¹⁴Let me alone, so that I may destroy them and blot out their name from under heaven. And I will make you into a nation stronger and more numerous than they."*

But how different was the reality! The Lord gave Moses the stone tablets after forty days but told him immediately afterward of the terrible corruption of the people. The contrast is reinforced by the reiteration of the "forty days and forty nights." The fact that the Lord gave the tablets to Moses in spite of what was happening down below finds an explanation in God's wanting to leave it to Moses to break the tablets to pieces before the eyes of the people (see v. 17). The words of the Lord recorded in verses 12–14 are virtually the same as those in Exodus 32:7–10. The Lord commands Moses (v. 12) to go down at once (in order to deal with the sin as soon as possible) and then says what Israel has done: they have made for themselves a cast idol. "Your people whom you brought out of Egypt": the Lord addresses Moses as the head and leader of the people, and in this role he is called upon to take action against the sin; the phrase also indicates that the Lord intends to negotiate the fate of the people with Moses and to put their fate in his hands (v. 14). But the "your" and "you" also imply something else; for the time being the Lord detaches Himself from this people. He no longer recognizes them as His people. He does not want to remember that He Himself led them out of Egypt (cf. by contrast Moses' statement in v. 26). "They have turned away quickly": the fact that they have broken the covenant so soon after it was made shows the immensity of their sin. The term "cast idol" apparently also was applied to a wooden idol with metal overlay (cf. v. 21).

In verse 13 the Lord, on the basis of what He has seen of this people, pronounces them to be "a stiff-necked people indeed" (cf. 9:6). Then the Lord speaks of destroying Israel and of making Moses "into a nation stronger and more numerous than they." This expresses the immensity of Israel's sin and of God's anger. God does not consider Israel's destruction too severe a punishment. But the Lord does not make a final decision; He asks for Moses' permission to destroy Israel and adds a promise for Moses. This is a strongly anthropomorphic statement—the Lord places the fate of the people in Moses' hands. In this, the Lord honors Moses as the head of the people and as the one who led Israel out of Egypt (v. 12). In that capacity—which he had received at God's command—the Lord grants His faithful servant the right to decide the fate of the people. He negotiates with Moses, as a master can discuss with his servant the abandoning of a task they had undertaken together. At the same time, the Lord gives Moses the opportunity to act as mediator and save the people. The promise to make Moses a great nation gives this episode the character of a test for

Moses, to see whether he will be true to his calling as mediator by subordinating his own name and greatness to the preservation of the people. Concerning Moses' attitude, see verses 18ff., 25ff.

9:15–17 *So I turned and went down from the mountain while it was ablaze with fire. And the two tablets of the covenant were in my hands. ¹⁶When I looked, I saw that you had sinned against the LORD your God; you had made for yourselves an idol cast in the shape of a calf. You had turned aside quickly from the way that the LORD had commanded you. ¹⁷So I took the two tablets and threw them out of my hands, breaking them to pieces before your eyes.*

Moses now describes how he descended just as God had told him, and how God's words were confirmed by what he saw. In violent indignation he threw the two tablets to the ground, breaking them to pieces, to show that Israel was not worthy of possessing these two tablets that contained the basis of the covenant. We can also say that the covenant made at Horeb was indeed nullified by this sin, as long as we remember that according to Moses' later statement to the Lord he still considered Israel the Lord's people (9:29).

9:18–20 *Then once again I fell prostrate before the LORD for forty days and forty nights; I ate no bread and drank no water, because of all the sin you had committed, doing what was evil in the LORD's sight and so provoking him to anger. ¹⁹I feared the anger and wrath of the LORD, for he was angry enough with you to destroy you. But again the LORD listened to me. ²⁰And the LORD was angry enough with Aaron to destroy him, but at that time I prayed for Aaron too.*

Then Moses narrates how he fell prostrate before the Lord for forty days and forty nights to pray for the people (cf. vv. 25ff.). To do this, he had once again climbed the mountain (cf. Exod. 34:28). In Exodus 32:11–14 this intercession is placed *before* Moses' descent; the solution of this apparent difficulty probably is that Moses' intercession began immediately, before his descent, and continued later. Moses, in response to the offer made him in verse 14, acts as intercessor and mediator, placing the well–being (*heil*[13]) of the people ahead of his own importance. "Once again" (v. 18), cf. v. 9. The abstaining from food and drink is in both cases a general expression of being filled with

---

[13]See note on p. 29.

reverence for God's holiness, but here it also points to the sorrow he felt at the sin of the people.

Verse 19 refers back to verse 14 and concludes with the Lord's answer to his prayers (cf. 10:1–2). "Again the LORD listened to me": on earlier occasions the Lord had answered Moses' prayers on behalf of the people (cf. e.g., Exod. 17:14ff.).

Verse 20 adds that Moses' intercession also included Aaron, with whom the Lord was especially angry because of his role in this sin. Even though Aaron was at that time not yet high priest, nevertheless he, together with Hur, had been given the leadership of the people as Moses' representative (Exod. 24:14) and had already been designated high priest by divine appointment (Exod. 28:1). The fact that Aaron was spared only as the result of Moses' intercession is clear proof that the Aaronic priesthood, like all of Israel's blessings, was a gift of the Lord's sovereign grace.

9:21 *Also I took that sinful thing of yours, the calf you had made, and burned it in the fire. Then I crushed it and ground it to powder as fine as dust and threw the dust into a stream that flowed down the mountain.*

Moses destroyed the cast idol. He "burned it in the fire," which indicates that its core was wood; the gold overlay was pulverized and thrown into the stream that ran down from Mount Horeb (for further details, see Exod. 32:20).

9:22–24 *You also made the LORD angry at Taberah, at Massah and at Kibroth Hattaavah.*
²³And when the LORD sent you out from Kadesh Barnea, he said, "Go up and take possession of the land I have given you." But you rebelled against the command of the LORD your God. You did not trust him or obey him. ²⁴You have been rebellious against the LORD ever since I have known you.

Since Moses' statement in verse 7 encompassed the entire wilderness journey, he now adds reminders of other incidents during that journey in which Israel showed themselves to be stiff-necked. Moses does not present these incidents in chronological order. First he mentions Taberah, where the people grumbled about God's guidance (Num. 11:1–3); next, Massah, where they rebelled because of lack of water (Exod. 17:1ff.); then Kibroth Hattaavah ("Graves of Desire"), where they wanted meat (Num. 11:4ff.); and finally Kadesh Barnea (cf. 1:26ff.). Moses only elaborates on the last of these four incidents, the sin at Kadesh Barnea, because it was the most drastic in its consequences: there Israel rejected outright the Lord's command and refused to believe His word.

Verse 24 draws the conclusion that Israel has been rebellious throughout the wilderness journey (cf. v. 7). Moses here expresses this with the words, "ever since I have known you" (cf. Exod. 5:20ff.)—a clear reminder of all the grief and sorrow he has suffered from this people.

3. Moses' intercession (continued); the new stone tablets (9:25–10:11)

After the excursus of verses 22–24, Moses continues the narrative of what took place at Mount Horeb, to give further proof that Israel will not enter Canaan because of its own righteousness (9:4–6) but solely because of the Lord's faithfulness to the covenant and His forgiving grace in answer to Moses' intercession.

9:25–29 *I lay prostrate before the LORD those forty days and forty nights because the LORD had said he would destroy you. ²⁶I prayed to the LORD and said, "O Sovereign LORD, do not destroy your people, your own inheritance that you redeemed by your great power and brought out of Egypt with a mighty hand. ²⁷Remember your servants Abraham, Isaac and Jacob. Overlook the stubbornness of this people, their wickedness and their sin. ²⁸Otherwise, the country from which you brought us will say, 'Because the LORD was not able to take them into the land he had promised them, and because he hated them, he brought them out to put them to death in the desert.' ²⁹But they are your people, your inheritance that you brought out by your great power and your outstretched arm."*

Moses first comes back to his intercession, mentioned in verse 18. In verses 26–29 Moses relates what he prayed; the words are essentially the same as in Exodus 32:11–13. The differences in detail are understandable, since in both cases we have a shortened (and hence not verbatim) statement of what Moses prayed during those forty days and forty nights.

Moses begins his plea by pointing out that Israel is the Lord's people and His inheritance. "Inheritance" is used here in the sense of "possession," and "your people, your inheritance" thus means "the people that belongs to you." Moses supports this statement by pointing out that the Lord brought Israel out of Egypt by His "great power" and "mighty hand." Thus the Lord has made Israel His own people, and the fact that He has done so much for them should make them all the more dear to Him.

The presupposition of Moses' argument is thus that the sin of the people has not destroyed this special relationship between the Lord and Israel. Note how Moses' statement makes use of the Lord's own words in verse 12, "*Your* people whom *you* brought out of Egypt"; Moses says in effect, "No Lord! You cannot shift the responsibility for this people onto my shoulders—they are ultimately your responsibility, not mine."

In verse 27 Moses also mentions the patriarchs: the Lord must remember them, i.e., the oath He swore to them (cf. 7:8), and He must therefore overlook their stubbornness and sin.

The third argument Moses presents (v. 28) is that, if Israel is destroyed, the Egyptians will revile the name of the Lord; they will say that the Lord brought Israel out of Egypt "to put them to death in the desert" (i.e., this was the Lord's intended purpose, or at least the result of His leading them out); and He did this, either because He lacked power or because He hated them.

Verse 29 places over against the allegation of the Lord's hate toward Israel the truth of His elective love ("your people, your inheritance"), and over against the thought of His powerlessness, His great power and His "outstretched arm," manifested in the deliverance from Egypt (cf. v. 26).

10:1–5 *At that time the LORD said to me, "Chisel out two stone tablets like the first ones and come up to me on the mountain. Also make a wooden chest. ²I will write on the tablets the words that were on the first tablets, which you broke. Then you are to put them in the chest."*

³So I made the ark out of acacia wood and chiseled out two stone tablets like the first ones, and I went up on the mountain with the two tablets in my hands. ⁴The LORD wrote on these tablets what he had written before, the Ten Commandments he had proclaimed to you on the mountain, out of the fire, on the day of the assembly. And the LORD gave them to me. ⁵Then I came back down the mountain and put the tablets in the ark I had made, as the LORD commanded me, and they are there now.

Concerning the result of Moses' intercession, cf. also 10:11. "At that time" leaves room for the possibility that Moses received the following command not immediately after his prayer but more generally around that time although, of course, as a result of his prayer. God's answer contains measures to replace the shattered stone tablets (cf. Exod. 34:1ff.)—which means that God intends to restore the broken covenant relationship. The Lord commands Moses to chisel out new stone tablets like the first ones and to bring them up the mountain (v. 1; cf. Exod. 34:1). He must also make a wooden chest or ark. The Lord will write on the new tablets the same words He had written on the first ones, and Moses must place these new tablets in the ark. Verses 3–5 recount the implementation of all this. As is true elsewhere in Moses' discourses, elements that belong logically together are placed together to the partial neglect of the chronological sequence. Exodus shows that the command to make the ark was given before the sin with the golden calf (Exod. 25:10ff.) and that the ark was made as part of the building of the tabernacle, while the tablets were not placed in the ark until the dedication of the tabernacle (Exod. 40:20).

The only thing said about the ark here (v. 2) is that it is to be the repository for the tablets, which is why it is called "the ark of the covenant" (v. 8). Elsewhere we read that the cover of the ark (the "atonement cover") with its cherubim is the place above which the Lord's presence is manifested, so that the ark can represent God Himself; thus it is also called "the ark of God" or "the ark of the Lord." "On the day of the assembly" refers to the day when Moses had gathered all Israel before the Lord (4:10).

10:6–7 *(The Israelites traveled from the wells of the Jaakanites to Moserah. There Aaron died and was buried, and Eleazar his son succeeded him as priest. 7From there they traveled to Gudgodah and on to Jotbathah, a land with streams of water.*

These verses contain a fragmentary report of Israel's travels through the wilderness and mention Aaron's death and his being succeeded by Eleazar. They interrupt the flow of Moses' discourse and differ in tone from what precedes and from what follows after verse 9 (many of the English versions therefore place vv. 6–9 in parentheses). The Israelites are not addressed here but are spoken about in the third person. The content of these verses also sets them apart from their context, since they deal not with the events at Horeb but with later events. We may assume that these words were inserted here from another source either as part of the discourse (i.e., by Moses himself) or later when the book was edited (whoever the redactor may have been). The reason for this interpolation may have been what is said in verse 6 concerning Aaron's death. According to 9:20, Moses interceded with the Lord specifically on Aaron's behalf, but the result of this intercession has not yet been mentioned. This report states that Aaron died at Moserah rather than at

Horeb; thus we learn by implication that the threat of 9:20 was averted by Moses' prayer. The succession by his son Eleazar also proves that Aaron had again found favor with the Lord.

We do not know the location of "the wells of the Jaakanites" (KJV, Beeroth Benejaakan), nor are we familiar with the other names, which are also found with minor variations in Numbers 33:30ff. (although the sequence differs). The reason for this is probably that different journeys are in view. Also, Numbers 33:38 (cf. Num. 20:22ff.) indicates that Aaron died on Mount Hor, while here he is said to have died at Moserah; this does not necessarily constitute a contradiction, since we can assume that Moserah lay near this mountain.

Verse 7 does not relate to Aaron's death and is thus apparently included for the sake of completeness. The addition "a land with streams of water" shows why Israel stopped here (cf. the "wells of the Jaakanites" in v. 6).

10:8–9 *At that time the LORD set apart the tribe of Levi to carry the ark of the covenant of the LORD, to stand before the LORD to minister and to pronounce blessings in his name, as they still do today. ⁹That is why the Levites have no share or inheritance among their brothers; the LORD is their inheritance, as the LORD your God told them.)*

"At that time" does not refer to verses 6–7 but goes back to verse 5. The expression refers to the time of the events at Horeb (also in 9:20; 10:11), to which we now return. Whether these verses are an integral part of Moses' discourse is another question (see comments on v. 9).

Verse 8 states that "at that time," i.e., at Horeb, the Lord set apart the·tribe of Levi for His service. The inclusion of this fact here is probably due to its connection with the ark, mentioned in verse 5, to the actions of the Levites relative to Israel's sin (cf. Exod. 32:26ff.), and finally to complete what was said in verse 6 concerning the priests. These verses, like the rest of Deuteronomy (cf. 18:1ff.), speak of the priests and Levites jointly, without entering into the distinction between the priestly service, which was specifically entrusted to the sons of Aaron (Exod. 28–29), and the service of the rest of the Levites, which consisted in assisting the priests (Num. 3:5).[14]

First is mentioned the carrying of the ark (cf. 31:9, 25), called here "the ark of the covenant of the LORD," since the tablets of the covenant

---

[14]Concerning the problem involved, cf. *Het Godswoord der Profeten* 4:336ff.

were placed inside it (v. 5). Carrying the ark was part of the supporting services performed by the nonpriestly Levites; this task was assigned specifically to the Kohathites (Num. 3:30–31; 4:15). The following statement, "to stand before the Lord to minister," refers to the task of the Aaronic priests (cf. Exod. 29), which includes all priestly functions carried out at the sanctuary—the bringing of offerings, the care for the lampstand, etc. Finally, "to pronounce blessings in his name" was also the task and privilege of the Aaronic priests (cf. Num. 6:23ff.).

Because of this special calling, the tribe of Levi received "no share or inheritance among their brothers," i.e., unlike the other tribes they did not own land in Canaan.

Since these things are stated here as fact, not as a future matter (as in 18:2), this verse (and perhaps v. 8) is apparently an addition by a later (inspired) author. "The Lord is their inheritance": Levi's share is that this tribe has a special claim to the Lord Himself, in whose special service they stand. One of their privileges is therefore that they receive a portion of anything that is given to the Lord (cf. 18:1ff.). The Levites did receive forty-eight cities with some land around them, but this is quite different from the "inheritance," the territories allotted to the other tribes. On "As the Lord your God told them," cf. Numbers 18:20, 24. If this verse is indeed a later addition, the second person ("*your* God") is somewhat curious; it is possible that the author used it to adapt the verse to Moses' style.

10:10–11 *Now I had stayed on the mountain forty days and nights, as I did the first time, and the Lord listened to me at this time also. It was not his will to destroy you.* 11*"Go," the Lord said to me, "and lead the people on their way, so that they may enter and possess the land that I swore to their fathers to give them."*

Once again Moses comes back to his intercession, this time to relate, more directly than in verses 1–5, the result: "The Lord listened to me at this time also" (cf. 9:19). Instead of destroying Israel the Lord commanded Moses to "lead the people on their way" toward Canaan, the land He had sworn to the forefathers to give them. This promise will be fulfilled, in spite of the unfaithfulness of the people, thanks to the intercession of the mediator (cf. Exod. 32:34ff.).

E. A NEW SERIES OF EXHORTATIONS (10:12–11:32)

1. Fear the Lord and love Him (10:12–22)

10:12–13 *And now, O Israel, what does the LORD your God ask of you but to fear the LORD your God, to walk in all his ways, to love him, to serve the LORD your God with all your heart and with all your soul, ¹³and to observe the LORD's commands and decrees that I am giving you today for your own good?*

Moses, on the basis of the Lord's grace of which he has just reminded his hearers, exhorts Israel again to fear the Lord their God, to love Him, and to keep His commandments. "What does the LORD your God ask of you?" Nothing more, but also nothing less, than what follows here. Israel does not have to be uncertain as to what they must do to please their God (cf. Mic. 6:8).

Fearing and loving the Lord are mentioned here together; where only one of the two is mentioned (fearing in 5:26; 6:24; loving in 6:5), the other is not excluded but is rather implied. "His ways": the conduct He has prescribed in the law; "to walk in all his ways" is thus keeping all His commandments, which is stated explicitly in verse 13. "Serve" refers to the cultic worship. "With all your heart and with all your soul" (cf. 4:29; 6:5) means that Israel must worship only Him, and must and can do this therefore with their whole being. "For your own good" reinforces the exhortation by pointing to the result of obedience (cf. 5:33; 6:24).

10:14–15 *To the LORD your God belong the heavens, even the highest heavens, the earth and everything in it. ¹⁵Yet the LORD set his affection on your forefathers and loved them, and he chose you, their descendants, above all the nations, as it is today.*

Israel must feel impelled to obedience by the favor that has been bestowed on them. He to whom belong heaven and earth (the addition "even the highest heavens" indicates that heaven in its fullest extent is in view here; cf. "God of gods and Lord of lords" in v. 17), this great God who could have called any nation or all nations into His service set His affection only on Israel's forefathers and has chosen their descendants above all nations. On "as it is today," cf. 2:30; 8:18.

10:16 *Circumcise your hearts, therefore, and do not be stiff-necked any longer.*

"Circumcise your hearts" (lit., "circumcise the foreskin of your heart"): the foreskin can symbolize uncleanness, but signifies primarily

141

the profane, that which has not been devoted to God. The foreskin of the heart is thus the worldly disposition that turns away from God and does not reckon with Him; circumcision is then the putting aside of that disposition, in other words, the turning to God to pay attention to Him and to listen to Him (cf. 30:6, where the Lord Himself will perform the circumcision; Lev. 26:41; Jer. 4:4; Ezek. 44:9). "Do not be stiff-necked any longer": they must set aside the disobedience and rebelliousness that has characterized them thus far (9:6, 13, 22–24).

10:17–19 *For the* LORD *your God is God of gods and Lord of lords, the great God, mighty and awesome, who shows no partiality and accepts no bribes. ¹⁸He defends the cause of the fatherless and the widow, and loves the alien, giving him food and clothing. ¹⁹And you are to love those who are aliens, for you yourselves were aliens in Egypt.*

As in verse 14, Moses again points to the greatness of God to underline the demand of obedience. He is the "God of gods" (cf. Ps. 136:2), i.e., the greatest God; this does not imply that there are other gods (according to v. 14 *all* things belong to Him), but simply that they are presented as if they exist in order to give concrete expression to the greatness of Israel's God. The same applies to the expression "Lord of lords" (= "the greatest Lord") to the extent that we can think here of "lords" in the sense of other gods who are worshiped (note that "Lord" here is *adonai*, not *Jahweh*); but "lords" undoubtedly also refers to human rulers. (Cf. also Ps. 95:3; 1 Tim. 6:15; Rev. 17:14; 19:16.) The following words describe God as "great, . . . mighty and awesome": this is how He has revealed Himself in the great and mighty things He has done for Israel (v. 21). These attributes must, like the fact that he is "God of gods and Lord of lords," bring Israel to fear and also to love this God.

Moses then praises the Lord's justice and mercy: He is an uncorruptible Judge and takes to heart the fate of the socially weak, the widow and orphan, whose cause He defends, and the alien (1:16), whom He shows love by providing food and clothing (cf. Ps. 146:7–9). All this must be understood as speaking of God's guidance of man's lot, in which this justice and mercy becomes evident. But it can also speak of His law, in which He prescribes similar actions on man's part: the judges must be impartial, uncorruptible, and just (cf. 16:19; 27:26; Lev. 19:15; et al.), and must defend the cause of the oppressed, while all are enjoined to show mercy to the wretched, to those in distress.

Moses exhorts his hearers explicitly to do the latter, especially with

regard to the alien. The motivation for this is (as the context shows)
that in this way they will be "imitators of God" (Eph. 5:1). A second
motivation is added: they themselves were strangers in Egypt (cf. 5:15;
Exod. 22:21; Lev. 19:34). Strictly speaking, this was not true of Moses'
audience, but the distinction between the generations is ignored here in
favor of the concept of the unity of Israel (cf. 1:30).

10:20 *Fear the* Lord *your God and serve him. Hold fast to him and take your
oaths in his name.*

Once again Moses gives the general exhortation to fear the Lord, this
time specified in a threefold demand that can be related to the hand
("serve," cf. v. 12), the heart ("Hold fast"), and the mouth ("take
your oaths"). Cf. 6:13.

10:21–22 *He is your praise; he is your God, who performed for you those great
and awesome wonders you saw with your own eyes.* [22] *Your forefathers who
went down into Egypt were seventy in all, and now the* Lord *your God has made
you as numerous as the stars in the sky.*

"He is your praise": He is the one you must praise but also the one
in whom you glory (cf. Jer. 17:14). The phrase (taken in either sense) is
clarified by what follows: "He is your God. . . ." "Awesome": these
things are to be remembered with fear and trembling, not only by their
enemies, the Egyptians, but also by Israel (cf. also v. 17). The wonders
are those Israel saw during the Exodus and the wilderness journey with
their "own eyes"—again the distinction between the generations is
ignored (cf. v. 19).

Verse 22 illustrates these "great and awesome wonders" by pointing
to their outcome: the seventy people who went down to Egypt (Gen.
46:27; Exod. 1:5) have become a people "as numerous as the stars in
the sky" (cf. 1:10; Gen. 15:5).

2. Keep the commandments, remembering the Lord's mighty deeds (11:1–7)

11:1–7 *Love the* Lord *your God and keep his requirements, his decrees, his
laws and his commands always.* [2] *Remember today that your children were not
the ones who saw and experienced the discipline of the* Lord *your God: his
majesty, his mighty hand, his outstretched arm;* [3] *the signs he performed and the
things he did in the heart of Egypt, both to Pharaoh king of Egypt and to his
whole country;* [4] *what he did to the Egyptian army, to its horses and chariots,*

how he overwhelmed them with the waters of the Red Sea as they were pursuing you, and how the LORD brought lasting ruin on them. ⁵It was not your children who saw what he did for you in the desert until you arrived at this place, ⁶and what he did to Dathan and Abiram, sons of Eliab the Reubenite, when the earth opened its mouth right in the middle of all Israel and swallowed them up with their households, their tents and every living thing that belonged to them. ⁷But it was your own eyes that saw all these great things the LORD has done.

Once again the demand, "Love the LORD your God [cf. 10:12] and keep his requirements" is repeated; Israel must do this "always" (cf. 4:10).

Added to this is the exhortation to remember all that the Lord has done for them in the past. The intent is of course that the remembrance of these things will kindle the love demanded in verse 1. "Remember": keep them before your consciousness, consider them (cf. RSV). "Your children were not the ones . . .": the Hebrew sentence is incomplete (the verse reads lit., "And know today not for [or, to] your children who have not known . . ."; see comments on v. 7). In a manner reminiscent of 5:3, Moses emphasizes here the responsibility of the generation he is addressing. This statement must not be taken in a strict sense because most of those standing before Moses had not witnessed the Exodus—the Exodus generation (those who were twenty years of age or older) had died in the wilderness. Moses considers those who witnessed the Exodus and those who saw the miracles in the wilderness as one generation and contrasts them to those who will only hear about these things from their parents. These "children" are therefore not only the children that were alive at the time of Moses' discourse, who were too young to have a conscious recollection of the miracles of the wilderness journey, but also the generations after them (similarly, in 5:3 the "fathers" are the patriarchs).

"Who saw and experienced" is the beginning of a long parenthetical sentence that runs through verse 6. This sentence summarizes what these children and the coming generations do not or will not know through their own experience. At the same time, Moses' hearers (in the sense indicated above) *have* experienced and seen these things directly. "Discipline": the Hebrew word used here does not only mean "discipline" in the sense of "punishment," "chastisement," or "correction," but, as frequently elsewhere, religio-ethical instruction or education in a general sense (cf. 4:35; 8:5). The "discipline of the LORD" thus includes all lessons for Israel contained in the Lord's "majesty, his mighty hand," etc.; the general impact of these lessons is the awareness of how much reason there is to fear the Lord (cf. v. 6) and to love Him (cf. vv. 3–4). On "his majesty," cf. 3:24; 4:34. On "his mighty hand, his outstretched arm," cf. 4:34. In the verses that follow Moses lists concrete facts: the miracles of Egypt (v. 3; cf. 4:34; 6:22), the crossing of the Red Sea (v. 4; cf. Exod. 14), and all that the Lord had done for them during the wilderness journey (v. 5). An example of the latter is God's judgment on Dathan and Abiram (cf. Num. 16:31–33); this does not detract from the fact that verse 5, on the analogy of verse 3, encompasses both God's blessings and His judgments. The fact that only Dathan and Abiram are mentioned here and not Korah (who is elsewhere mentioned first; cf. Num. 16:1) may be because Korah's sons did not perish with him, so that his descendants were still one of the Levite families.

Verse 7 completes the thought. It is somewhat irregular in form. Verses 2b–6 constitute a parenthetical sentence, and the main clause that began in verse 2a should now be completed, which verse 7 does not formally do. The thought, however, is clear: not your children but *you* were witnesses of the great things the Lord has done; and therefore your responsibility is all the greater and you have all the more reason to fear and love that God.

3. Keep the commandments, that you may enjoy Canaan's blessings (11:8–25)

The exhortation to obedience is repeated and reinforced by a reminder of the benefits: The Israelites will be able to conquer Canaan (v. 8), to live long in the land (v. 9), and to experience God's blessing that gives rain and fertility. Verses 18–21 repeat the exhortation of 6:6–9, with the promise of a long possession of the land. Verses 22–25 promise that Israel's obedience will enable them to dispossess the nations of Canaan. Moses thus speaks of obedience both before entering Canaan (vv. 8, 22–25) and afterward (vv. 9, 10–17).

11:8–9 *Observe therefore all the commands I am giving you today, so that you may have the strength to go in and take over the land that you are crossing the Jordan to possess, ⁹and so that you may live long in the land that the LORD swore to your forefathers to give to them and their descendants, a land flowing with milk and honey.*

"All the commandments," lit., "the whole commandment," that is, the law viewed as a unit. "So that" introduces that which is promised as a reward for obedience. "Have the strength": if they keep the commandment now, before they cross the Jordan, the Lord will give them the inner strength (courage) to enable them to enter Canaan and to conquer it. Verse 9 then speaks of the obedience they must show in Canaan, which will ensure their continued possession of the land. "Flowing with milk and honey": see comments on 6:3.

11:10–17 *The land you are entering to take over is not like the land of Egypt, from which you have come, where you planted your seed and irrigated it by foot as in a vegetable garden. ¹¹But the land you are crossing the Jordan to take possession of is a land of mountains and valleys that drinks rain from heaven. ¹²It is a land the LORD your God cares for; the eyes of the LORD your God are continually on it from the beginning of the year to its end.*

¹³So if you faithfully obey the commands I am giving you today—to love the LORD your God and to serve him with all your heart and with all your soul— ¹⁴then I will send rain on your land in its season, both autumn and spring rains, so that you may gather in your grain, new wine and oil. ¹⁵I will provide grass in the fields for your cattle, and you will eat and be satisfied.

¹⁶Be careful, or you will be enticed to turn away and worship other gods and bow down to them. ¹⁷Then the LORD's anger will burn against you, and he will shut the heavens so that it will not rain and the ground will yield no produce, and you will soon perish from the good land the LORD is giving you.

Israel must keep the commandments—Canaan's fecundity is entirely dependent on the Lord's blessing. It is different from Egypt (v. 10), where there is also no rainfall. In the Nile Delta (where Goshen was) it rains more than elsewhere in Egypt, but even there rain is uncommon, and in the south of Egypt it almost never rains. The fertility of Egypt depends on the annual flooding of the Nile and on the degree to which the inhabitants can take advantage of this. The water of the Nile is diverted by means of canals and distributed over the fields as needed by means of the waterwheel, which in earliest times was apparently operated by foot (in more recent descriptions the waterwheels are powered by camels or other domestic animals). Thus, the irrigation of the land and therefore its fertility depends in large measure on man himself.

"As in a vegetable garden" indicates that also in Canaan irrigation was used but only on a small scale in the case of a vegetable garden (this was of course possible only if there was water nearby, e.g., a brook or stream).

But in general Canaan's soil receives water in a different manner (v. 11). The Egyptian method of irrigation could not be used, since Canaan, unlike Egypt, is a land of hills and valleys; nor was it necessary, because there is usually no lack of rain in Canaan. The land "drinks," not as a result of human effort, but directly "from heaven." And not only does "the LORD your God" provide rain, He cares for the land all year long. Thus Israel is reminded, on the basis of this characteristic difference between Egypt and Canaan, that in Canaan they will be dependent in an absolute sense on the Lord's good will.

Verses 13–15 begin to draw the conclusion: if they walk in the way of obedience, Israel "will eat and be satisfied" as a result of God's blessing. Verse 13, cf. 10:12. "Rain . . . in its season" (v. 14): the rainy season lasts from October until May. Although the winter rains are also necessary for a good harvest, the "autumn and spring rains" (lit., "the former rain and the latter rain") are mentioned as especially important. The "autumn rain" falls in October and November, the beginning of the agricultural year, and prepares the land for plowing and sowing. The "spring rain" falls in April and May and provides the grain with the moisture necessary to endure the heat of early summer. Thus there will be grain, new wine, and oil (the three chief products of Palestinian agriculture) for the people and grass for the cattle; and thus Israel will eat the products of agriculture and animal husbandry and be satisfied. (For more detailed comments, see 28:1–12; see also Lev. 26:3, 5.)

Verses 16 and 17 present the other side of the picture (in the form of a warning, "Be careful"). If Israel is disobedient, they will miss out on the blessing and be removed from the land. Moses mentions especially the worst form of disobedience (v. 16), turning away from the Lord and worshiping other gods. Verse 17, cf. 4:26; 28:23–24; Lev. 26:19–20. The punishment consists in the first place in the absence of rain. Then, they "will soon perish from the good land"—in the context, this could be the result of drought (which produces famine; cf. Hos. 2:2, 8ff.; 4:3), but the sense is broader and may include a perishing as the result of political events.

11:18–21 *Fix these words of mine in your hearts and minds; tie them as symbols on your hands and bind them on your foreheads. ¹⁹Teach them to your children, talking about them when you sit at home and when you walk along the road, when you lie down and when you get up. ²⁰Write them on the doorframes of your houses and on your gates, ²¹so that your days and the days of your children may be many in the land that the LORD swore to give your forefathers, as many as the days that the heavens are above the earth.*

If Israel keeps the commandments, they will continue to possess Canaan. Verses 18–21a are an almost verbatim repetition of 6:6–9 (q.v.). Verse 21b reinforces the exhortation with the promise of a long stay in Canaan. "As many as the days that the heavens are above the earth," i.e., as long as this earthly dispensation lasts (cf. Ps. 89:30; Job 14:12).

11:22–25 *If you carefully observe all these commands I am giving you to follow—to love the L*ORD* your God, to walk in all his ways and to hold fast to him—* *[23]then the L*ORD* will drive out all these nations before you, and you will dispossess nations larger and stronger than you.* *[24]Every place where you set your foot will be yours: Your territory will extend from the desert to Lebanon, and from the Euphrates River to the western sea.* *[25]No man will be able to stand against you. The L*ORD* your God, as he promised you, will put the terror and fear of you on the whole land, wherever you go.*

This continued possession presupposes that they first conquer the land; this is why, by way of completion and clarification, Moses adds that if they are obedient they will conquer the whole land (v. 22 begins with "for," not expressed in the NIV; cf. KJV).

Verse 23, cf. 1:28; 7:1–2; 9:1. "Before you," i.e., wherever you go. The southern border will be "the desert" (v. 24), i.e., south of the territory of Judah, the northern border of Lebanon, the eastern border the Euphrates (cf. 1:7; Gen. 15:18), the western border the "western sea," i.e., the Mediterranean Sea.

Verse 25, cf. 2:25; 7:24; Exodus 23:27. "As he promised you" may have these references in view, but also (if it is referred back to the entire promise of vv. 23ff.) places such as Genesis 15:18.

4. Curse or blessing (11:26–32)

The exhortation to keep the commandments is concluded and once again reinforced by a reminder of the consequent blessing and curse.

11:26–28 *See, I am setting before you today a blessing and a curse—* *[27]the blessing if you obey the commands of the L*ORD* your God that I am giving you today;* *[28]the curse if you disobey the commands of the L*ORD* your God and turn from the way that I command you today by following other gods, which you have not known.*

First, Moses states that today he is setting before Israel the choice between blessing and curse. They will receive one or the other, depending on whether or not they obey the Lord's commandments. Disobedience is once again described in its concrete manifestation of idolatry. "Which you have not known": from whom, in contrast to the Lord, you have not received help or blessing, and with whom you have therefore no relationship.

11:29–30 *When the LORD your God has brought you into the land you are entering to possess, you are to proclaim on Mount Gerizim the blessings, and on Mount Ebal the curses. ³⁰As you know, these mountains are across the Jordan, west of the road, toward the setting sun, near the great trees of Moreh, in the territory of those Canaanites living in the Arabah in the vicinity of Gilgal.*

When Israel will be in Canaan, blessing and curse must be proclaimed (cf. 27:11–13). Already here, Moses appoints the place where this is to happen. The usual rendering is "on Mount Gerizim" and "on Mount Ebal." But according to Joshua 8:33, the people (and the priests) stood between the two mountains when this proclamation was made; half the people faced Mount Gerizim, the other half Mount Ebal. The command and its execution are more in agreement when we render the words here, "against Mount Gerizim" and "against Mount Ebal," which is grammatically possible. Mount Gerizim and Mount Ebal face each other; in the fertile valley between them lay Shechem. The choice of location undoubtedly was connected with the fact (apart from the suitable topography) that Shechem was a place of great importance, centrally located in the land, a place to which for Israel a sacred tradition was attached (see comments on v. 30). The reason why the blessing is associated with Mount Gerizim and the curse with Mount Ebal may be that the Gerizim was the southernmost of the two; for someone facing east (cf. our expression "to orient oneself"), south will be to the right (and is so called in Hebrew). The righthand side is the place of honor, and the idea of happiness seems to have been associated with this (cf. Gen. 48:17).

Verse 30 describes the location of these mountains. "West of the road," or "the western road" probably refers to the north-south road that lay west of the Jordan; Ebal and Gerizim lie indeed relatively close to this road, to the west (Abraham came along this road to Shechem, Gen. 12:6). If the intended meaning is "the western road," it would distinguish this road from another north-south road that lay east of the Jordan. "In the territory of those Canaanites living in the Arabah": the Arabah is the Jordan Valley (see comments on 1:1), especially the western part of the valley, where part of the Canaanites (in the narrower sense of the word) lived. But Ebal and Gerizim do not lie in the Jordan Valley, although they are located in the territory of the Canaanites (in the broader sense of the word). But we would then expect "living in the land west of the Jordan" or "living across the Jordan." It is possible that the Arabah is mentioned because it was the part of Canaan proper closest to Israel. "Across from Gilgal": this is of course not the Gilgal near Jericho (Josh. 4:20; 5:9), but another Gilgal, near Shechem (cf. Josh. 9:6; 10:6ff.).

The addition "near the great trees of Moreh" (or, "Diviner's tree") reminds of the fact that Abraham settled here and built an altar on this spot (Gen. 12:6–7; cf. also Gen. 35:4).

11:31–32 *You are about to cross the Jordan to enter and take possession of the land the LORD your God is giving you. When you have taken it over and are living there, ³²be sure that you obey all the decrees and laws I am setting before you today.*

There is reason to face Israel with the choice between blessing and curse. The people are about to enter Canaan to live there, at which point the obligation to keep all the commandments they have received begins (cf. 4:5–6). And with this Moses has also made the transition to the presentation of the most important laws in the following chapters.

III. Specific Laws
(12:1–26:19)

The first part of Moses' second discourse, which was of a more general nature, is followed by a presentation of specific laws. Some of these are a repetition of laws that are also found in other books of the Pentateuch, but many are unique to Deuteronomy.

After the superscription (12:1), we can distinguish two parts: 12:2–16:17, which contains laws primarily of a cultic or ceremonial nature, and 16:18–25:19, which contains largely civil laws. It is possible that we should understand "decrees" in verse 1 to refer to the cultic laws, "laws" to the civil laws.

A. SUPERSCRIPTION (12:1)

12:1 *These are the decrees and laws you must be careful to follow in the land that the LORD, the God of your fathers, has given you to possess—as long as you live in the land.*

In this superscription (cf. 4:44–49), Israel is urged to keep the laws that are to follow, specifically when the people will have settled in Canaan. "Decrees and laws": cf. 4:45.

B. LAWS PRIMARILY OF A CULTIC AND CEREMONIAL NATURE (12:2–16:17)

1. One place of worship (12:2–28)

The main thought of this section is that in Canaan there will be only one place of worship to which the Israelites shall bring their offerings and gifts. Accordingly, any participation in the cultus of the Canaanites is forbidden (vv. 2ff.) as is the continuation of the practices Israel followed in the fields of Moab (v. 8) and the bringing of sacrifices anywhere they please (v. 13). The sacrificing on the so-called "high places" (i.e., places of sacrifice under the open sky[15]), a practice Israel followed for many centuries in imitation not only of the Canaanites but also of the patriarchs, is thus in principle forbidden, although room is left for deviation from the rule under exceptional circumstances (see below).

Apart from the concluding exhortation in verse 28, we can distinguish three parts (vv. 2–7; 8–12; 13–27). [16] Each section presents the law of the one cultus place in its own way. Some believe that these three sections were originally independent versions, and it is not inconceivable that either Moses or a later redactor had this law before him in three versions and combined them into our present chapter. The main point is, however, that verses 2–28 should be read as a unit, in which the one law is proclaimed three times with various additions. Concerning the major critical question relative to this chapter, see Introduction. The centralization of the cultus had begun in the desert with the building of the tabernacle. The law of Deuteronomy 12 explicitly demands this centralization for the time when Israel will be in Canaan. It was, however, not realized until much later (it was fully implemented only after the Captivity); nevertheless, this centralization

---

[15]The term "high place" refers to the artificial platform that made a given location into a place of sacrifice. The name thus does not refer to the evaluation of the places that were usually chosen for the erection of the platform or "high place," such as hills (cf. v. 2). It was possible to have a "high place" in a valley, e.g., in the Valley of Hinnom.

[16]Some English versions take verses 13–14 as the end of the second section, so that the third section begins with verse 15 (NIV, RSV, NASB, TEV); others follow our division (JB, NEB, LB)—TRANS.

is important in sacred history and in the history of revelation. It was of utmost significance for the unity of Israel when the tabernacle stood at Shiloh and especially after the building of the temple. After the Captivity, the temple of Zerubbabel was a focal point for the Jews of the Diaspora that did much to create a sense of solidarity. Furthermore, the abolition of the worship on the "high places" turned out to be, at least after the Captivity, an important element in the counteracting of paganizing influences.

But apart from these effects, the centralization of the cultus also had a drastic influence on the development of the cultus itself. On the one hand, the centralization of the cultus in tabernacle and temple allowed the cultus to achieve a splendor that would have been impossible without such a center. On the other hand, the centralization increased the distance between the offering cultus and every-day life and created the possibility that the cultus could be abolished by the destruction of the one temple. Thus the centralization was a preparation for the new covenant, which would be without external offerings and altar.

a. *Destroy the Canaanite cultus* (12:2–7)

12:2–3 *Destroy completely all the places on the high mountains and on the hills and under every spreading tree where the nations you are dispossessing worship their gods. ³Break down their altars, smash their sacred stones and burn their Asherah poles in the fire; cut down the idols of their gods and wipe out their names from those places.*

Here Israel is commanded to destroy completely the Canaanite places of sacrifice (the so-called high places: places of sacrifice under the open sky (cf. 7:5). These were usually located on higher elevations ("on the high mountains and on the hills") and near shade trees ("under every spreading tree"). The high elevations were chosen because it was believed that they were closer to the deity (who was thought to reside in the heavens), the trees in part for practical reasons (cf. Hos. 4:13), in part also because these green trees were seen as a manifestation of the divine power of nature, whose worship was the essence of Canaanite paganism.

"Every spreading tree" is hyperbole. Verse 3 lists the things that were usually found in the sacred places: the altar, the sacred stone, the Asherah pole, and the idol. All these must be destroyed (cf. 7:5, 25), which would effectively eradicate the cultus in those places. This would also mean that the name of the deity worshiped there would be eradicated, since the deity was tied to the cultus place (cf. v. 5).

12:4–7 *You must not worship the LORD your God in their way. ⁵But you are to seek the place the LORD your God will choose from among all your tribes to put his Name there for his dwelling. To that place you must go; ⁶there bring your burnt offerings and sacrifices, your tithes and special gifts, what you have vowed to give and your freewill offerings, and the firstborn of your herds and flocks. ⁷There, in the presence of the LORD your God, you and your families shall eat and shall rejoice in everything you have put your hand to, because the LORD your God has blessed you.*

The law of the one cultus place is now linked with the preceding. Israel must not worship the Lord "in their way" (v. 4). The contrast in verse 5 indicates that this refers not only to the items mentioned in verse 3 (sacred stones, etc.), but also, and indeed in the first place, to the many *places* of worship ("on the high mountains. . .") as such. The whole cultus of the "high places" is forbidden (cf. vv. 8, 13). On the other hand it is significant that it is especially the *pagan character* of the cultus on the "high places" that is emphasized (cf. v. 3). The danger that threatened Israel (and to which they later succumbed) was precisely that they would take over the sacred places of the Canaanites and along with the places (to one degree or another) the pagan cultus it represented (vv. 29–31). This is the danger against which Israel is specifically warned here. Thus, we can say that we find here in principle some allowance for the possibility of worship on the "high places," provided that this worship is free of pagan admixtures (e.g., Samuel).

Verse 5 presents the contrast. There will be one place, which the Lord will choose from among the tribes, where Israel must go to bring their offerings. Over against the choice of cultus places on the basis of natural characteristics (mountains, hills, trees) is placed God's choice and directive. This is also emphasized in Exodus 20:24. The difference with Exodus 20 is that here the one cultus place is emphasized in contrast to the multiplicity of the Canaanite places of worship: "the place the LORD your God will choose from among all your tribes."

"To put his Name there for his dwelling": we can also say that God Himself dwells there; the expression states this in a more indirect and veiled manner. The Name of God is God Himself as He associates with people, as He makes Himself known to them and gives them the opportunity to call on Him. When the Lord's Name dwells in a place, then that is *the* place to call on that Name (and in that Name, on God Himself).

This one chosen place was first Shiloh, where the tabernacle was placed after the conquest (Josh. 18:1), and later Jerusalem, where the temple was built. Both of these places were chosen by the Lord (Shiloh, see Jer. 7:12; Jerusalem, see 2 Sam. 24:18; 1 Chron. 21:18). "For his dwelling" has the tabernacle and temple in view, the dwelling place of God (or of His Name).

To that place the Israelites must bring their offerings and gifts. These are here assumed to be familiar concepts. First, the two most important kinds of offerings (if the offerings are categorized on the basis of the manner in which they are brought) are mentioned: the *burnt offerings,* which were placed on the altar in their entirety (Lev. 1), and the *sacrifices,* the fellowship offerings (traditionally called peace offerings), of which only the blood and fat were placed on the altar, while the meat (except for the priest's portion, 18:3) was eaten by the offerer and his guests in a communal meal in the sacred place (cf. vv. 7, 27; Lev. 3). To both the burnt offerings and the fellowship offerings were added food and drink offerings (Num. 15:4ff.).

Then follow various offerings and other gifts that were not intended for the altar, differentiated according to the reason why they were brought. The *tithes* (cf. 14:22–29; Lev. 27:30–33; Num. 28:21, 24) were taken from the produce of field and tree and from the offspring of herd and flock. Under certain circumstances (when the distance was too great to take them to the central sanctuary) the tithes could be sold and the proceeds taken to the sanctuary (14:24–25). Concerning the question of the allocation of the tithes, see comments on 14:22ff.

The *special gifts* (*terumah;* KJV. "heave offering"; RSV. "the offering that you present"; JB. "the offerings from your hands") were taken from the fruit of the land (Num. 15:19). Some think that the word in this context refers especially to the firstfruits (which are otherwise not mentioned here; cf. 18:4). But Ezekiel 20:40 distinguishes between the firstfruits and the *terumah,* which is why some think of gifts that were brought without obligation in addition to the firstfruits and tithes. *What you have vowed* is literally "your vows." The *freewill offerings* are offerings one was not obligated to bring either by law or by a vow (cf. Lev. 7:16; 22:21; 23–38; Num. 15:3; 29:39). Concerning the *firstborn,* cf. 15:19ff.; Exodus 13:2, 12ff.; Numbers 18:15ff. We are faced here with a problem as to the allocation of the firstborn (similar to the problem of the tithes, see 14:22ff.). According to Deuteronomy, the "firstborn of your herds and flocks," i.e., the firstborn of animals that could be sacrificed, are used for the offering meal. But Numbers 18:15ff. indicates that these firstborn are in general to be given to the priests for their subsistence, and that the firstborn ox, sheep, and goat must be offered in the manner of the fellowship offering, while the meat belongs to the priest. A possible solution is that the priest held an offering meal to which he also invited the offerer.

Verse 7 mentions separately the offering meal, which played a prominent role in most of the items listed in verse 6. The offering meal was an important part of the ritual of the "sacrifices" in the here intended sense of "fellowship offering." The offerings that were brought because of a vow, and the freewill offerings, also were fellowship offerings and thus also included an offering meal. Concerning the tithes and the firstborn, see comments on verse 6. Israel must enjoy all these festivities in the place chosen by the Lord, not in local "high places" with their pagan traditions. "In the presence of the LORD your God": in the one place where the Lord "put his Name. . .for his dwelling" (v. 5), the place where He is present in a special way and where "eating in His presence" is therefore a special way of having fellowship with Him.

"Rejoice": the joyful character of the cultus repeatedly comes to the fore in Deuteronomy, a corollary of the love and kindness expressed in God's blessing (cf. 7:12ff.). The fact that "your families" (including the women, vv. 12, 18) also participated in the offering meals is emphasized in Deuteronomy (cf. 14:26; 15:20; 16:11, 14). "Because the LORD your God has blessed you": also that which one has acquired by one's own hand has been received through the Lord's blessing; this is why gratitude must be the underlying motive in all this joyfulness and in the bringing of the offerings.

b. *Present practices to be discontinued (12:8–12)*

The law of the central sanctuary is restated, this time with a historical emphasis: the law will go into force when Israel shall live in safety.

12:8–12 *You are not to do as we do here today, everyone as he sees fit, ⁹since you have not yet reached the resting place and the inheritance the LORD your God is giving you. ¹⁰But you will cross the Jordan and settle in the land the LORD your God is giving you as an inheritance, and he will give you rest from all* *your enemies around you so that you will live in safety. ¹¹Then to the place the LORD your God will choose as a dwelling for his Name—there you are to bring everything I command you: your burnt offerings and sacrifices, your tithes and special gifts, and all the choice possessions you have vowed to the LORD. ¹²And there rejoice before the LORD your God, you, your sons and daughters, your menservants and maidservants, and the Levites from your towns, who have no allotment or inheritance of their own.*

Verse 8 contrasts the law as it is to be applied in the future with the practice of "today," when everyone does "as he sees fit." The context indicates that this is said of cultic activities, specifically those that found a measure of excuse in the conditions of that time. It is probable that "here today" (i.e., in the fields of Moab) there were, besides the cultus at the tabernacle, also cultic practices carried out by smaller groups in places that were considered suitable for the purpose. Moses does not explicitly approve of this, but neither does he clearly condemn these practices.[17]

Rather, Moses would appear to excuse the present practice by explaining it to be a corollary of the fact that Israel has not yet reached the promised "resting place," Canaan (v. 9). Although the tabernacle was Israel's central sanctuary, it did not have a permanent location as yet and therefore could not bind Israel to one place of worship chosen by the Lord. We may also suppose that under these temporary conditions the organization of the tabernacle and its service was not such that it could take care of all needs.

Moses' attitude toward the practice as it existed in the fields of Moab also points to the excusability of the worship on the "high places" in Canaan before the time indicated in verse 10, i.e., before the building of the temple (and after the decline of the sanctuary at Shiloh), cf. 1 Kings 3:2.

But what is valid today will not be acceptable in the future (vv. 10–11). Israel will enter Canaan, the Lord will give them rest from their enemies, and then He will choose a place "as a dwelling for his Name" (cf. v. 5). The addition "he will give you rest from all your enemies around you so that you will live in safety" definitely points (more clearly than v. 5) to the time of David and Solomon and thus to

---

[17]These practices were in fact against the law of Leviticus 17:3–6, which specified that the Israelites were not to kill any animal except in front of the tabernacle in the manner of a sacrifice. It is possible that this law (which was not maintained in Canaan, see comments on v. 15) had been suspended after Israel's transition from the wilderness to the fields of Moab.

Jerusalem as the place where God is to be worshiped. Nevertheless, we do not have to exclude Shiloh from the picture presented here; when Shiloh was appointed as the location of the tabernacle, the promise of verse 10 found its initial fulfillment under Joshua. This was followed by a period of decline (the capture of the ark) that ended under David. Concerning "burnt offerings," etc., see comments on verse 6. In verse 11, the KJV translates, "all your choice vows which ye vow unto the LORD," which might give the impression that "lesser vows" could be taken elsewhere. The NIV rendering correctly precludes this interpretation.

Verse 12 again completes the picture. Instead of "in the presence of the LORD your God, you. . .shall eat and shall rejoice" (v. 7), we read here simply, "rejoice before the LORD your God" (cf. 14:26; 16:11; 26:11; 27:7; Lev. 23:40), which brings out even more clearly that the presence of the Lord is the source of the rejoicing. The "families" of verse 7 are presented in more detail here: the female members are specifically mentioned (cf. v. 18; only the male members are mentioned in Exod. 23:17; 34:23); the menservants and maidservants must also participate, as well as the Levites, who are to be invited to the offering meal, since they have "no share among their brothers" (cf. v. 19; 10:9). The law allotted them the tithes for their subsistence (Num. 18:21), but places such as this indicate that the law also assumes that the Levites will frequently find themselves in an unfavorable social position because the law on the tithes will not always be implemented conscientiously. The cities they were given (which included some land, Num. 35:1–8; Josh. 21:1–40) were not intended to make up for the lack of an inheritance like that of the other tribes.

The addition "from your towns" (lit., "gates," cf. KJV; this can refer to both cities and villages, cf. Exod. 20:10) is used a number of times with reference to the Levites (12:18; 14:27; 16:11, 14; 18:6; 26:12) and also to aliens, widows, and orphans (14:21; 16:11, "living among you"). This does not necessarily contradict the fact that the Levites had their own cities, but is rather a general indication that Israel is to be concerned with their lot.

Deuteronomy 12:13-14

c. *Profane slaughtering of animals permitted anywhere* (12:13-
   27)

The law of the central cultus place is restated once more, this time
with an important addition concerning the permissibility of profane
slaughtering of animals.

12:13-14 *Be careful not to sacrifice your burnt offerings anywhere you please.*
¹⁴Offer them only at the place the LORD will choose in one of your tribes, and
there observe everything I command you.

Israel is first reminded that it must bring its burnt offerings only at
the place the Lord will choose (cf. vv. 5-6, 11). Only the burnt
offerings are mentioned here; the other offerings are dealt with in
verses 17-18. This is probably because the offering meal was a part of
these other offerings only and the emphasis here is on eating.
"Anywhere" (v. 13), literally, "at every place"; the Hebrew word
makom can mean simply "place," but it may also have the more
special sense of "offering place," which is undoubtedly intended here.
The Israelites would not think of offering in any arbitrary place but they
would be tempted to offer in places that were "offering places" by
Canaanite tradition (cf. vv. 2-3) or because of their use by the
patriarchs. "Observe everything I command you" (v. 14) points to
what follows in verses 17-18.

12:15-16 *Nevertheless, you may slaughter your animals in any of your towns*
and eat as much of the meat as you want, as if it were gazelle or deer,
according to the blessing the LORD your God gives you. Both the ceremonially
unclean and the clean may eat it. ¹⁶But you must not eat the blood; pour it out
on the ground like water.

Moses now begins to speak of slaughtering animals and eating meat.
In verse 17 he will speak about the offerings, but he precedes this with a
statement about profane slaughtering, i.e., slaughtering for the sole
purpose of eating the meat, without it being an offering. It may have
been an ancient custom to give any slaughtering of an animal suitable
for sacrifices the character of a sacrificial act. This was indeed true of
Israel during the wilderness journey (Lev. 17:3-6). But if the bringing
of offerings and the accompanying offering meal were permitted only at
the central sanctuary, (vv. 17-18), then those who lived far away from
the sanctuary would have few opportunities to eat meat. This would
cause objections, even though meat was usually eaten only on festive

158

occasions, and it would hinder the implementation of the law of the central sanctuary. Therefore the law stipulates that it is permissible to slaughter and eat meat without the slaughtering taking on the character of an offering; this may therefore be done anywhere.

"Both the ceremonially unclean and the clean may eat it," in contrast to the offering meal, in which only the ceremonially clean could participate (Lev. 7:20). This clearly indicates that the slaughtering and eating that are in view here have a profane character. "As if it were gazelle or deer": these animals could not be offered (wild animals were not to be brought to the altar, only domestic animals), but they could be eaten (they were clean animals), and they had thus from of old been eaten without any idea of offering (they could always be eaten, even by the ceremonially unclean; cf. Lev. 17:13).

The only limitation is that the blood must not be eaten, as is also true of the offering meal (v. 16; cf. Gen. 9:4; Lev. 17:10–14). Of course, in the case of a profane slaughtering the blood cannot be poured on or by the altar (cf. vv. 27–28); this is why it must simply be poured on the ground "like water," i.e., like a profane substance, and the ground will absorb and "cover" it (cf. Lev. 17:13).

12:17–19 *You must not eat in your own towns the tithe of your grain and new wine and oil, or the firstborn of your herds and flocks, or whatever you have vowed to give, or your freewill offerings or special gifts. [18]Instead, you are to eat them in the presence of the LORD your God at the place the LORD your God will choose—you, your sons and daughters, your menservants and maidservants, and the Levites from your towns—and you are to rejoice before the LORD your God in everything you put your hand to. [19]Be careful not to neglect the Levites as long as you live in your land.*

But while it is permissible to eat meat, the Israelites must not eat offering meals (and by implication must not bring burnt or fellowship offerings) "in your own towns" (cf. v. 12), i.e., anywhere except in the one place of worship. For verses 17–18, see also comments on verses 5–6 and 11–12. Verse 19 adds the general exhortation to take care of the Levites, expanding the thought implied in the inclusion of the Levites in the offering meal (v. 18). Prior to the implementation of this law, the Levites had many opportunities to serve in the cultus on the "high places," and would receive part of the offering for their services. These opportunities were eliminated by the command to sacrifice in one place only, and Moses, in proclaiming this law, thus had reason to make special provision for the Levites.

12:20–27 *When the* LORD *your God has enlarged your territory as he promised you, and you crave meat and say, "I would like some meat," then you may eat as much of it as you want.* ²¹*If the place where the* LORD *your God chooses to put his Name is too far away from you, you may slaughter animals from the herds and flocks the* LORD *has given you, as I have commanded you, and in your own towns you may eat as much of them as you want.* ²²*Eat them as you would gazelle or deer. Both the ceremonially unclean and the clean may eat.* ²³*But be sure you do not eat the blood because the blood is the life, and you must not eat the life with the meat.* ²⁴*You must not eat the blood; pour it out on the ground like water.* ²⁵*Do not eat it, so that it may go well with you and your children after you, because you will be doing what is right in the eyes of the* LORD.*

²⁶*But take your consecrated things and whatever you have vowed to give, and go to the place the* LORD *will choose.* ²⁷*Present your burnt offerings on the altar of the* LORD *your God, both the meat and the blood. The blood of your sacrifices must be poured beside the altar of the* LORD *your God, but you may eat the meat.*

These verses restate the content of verses 13–19 (on the one hand the permission to slaughter, on the other, the law of the one cultus place) with some variations, the most important being the limitation imposed in verse 21 (see also v. 20). The words "as I have commanded you" would appear to refer back to verse 15; we get the impression that this section is a later addition, whose primary purpose is the limitation imposed in verse 21.

Verses 20–25 repeat the permission to slaughter (cf. vv. 15–16). A new element is that this permission is somewhat restricted here. Verse 20 states that it will apply "when the LORD your God has enlarged your territory as he promised you." If Israel's territory remained small, there would be no need for this permission, since the central sanctuary would be easily accessible to all. The emphasis here thus falls on the fact that this permission is granted for purely practical reasons. Verse 21 carries this further by saying that the permission to slaughter applies "if the place where the LORD your God chooses to put his Name is too far away from you." It appears that we must draw the conclusion from this that the permission did not apply to those who lived near the sanctuary (especially not to those living in Jerusalem or, earlier, in Shiloh) who were still obligated to keep the old regulation that slaughtering was always a cultic act (to be performed at the one central sanctuary); cf. comments on verse 15.

On "as he promised you" (v. 20), cf. Exodus 23:27–33; see also Genesis 15:18. Verse 23 provides the motivation for the prohibition on the use of blood: "the blood is the life," literally, "the blood is the soul *[nepesh*]," the life bearer or life itself (cf. Gen. 2:7; cf. Lev. 17:11). He who eats blood therefore eats life itself, and this is not permitted. Man may eat the meat, but the soul or life belongs to God, and in the blood He gives this life to man on the altar "to make atonement. . .on the altar; it is the blood that makes atonement for one's life" (Lev. 17:11). Verse 25b: cf. verse 28.

Verses 26–27 repeat the law of the central cultus place (cf. vv. 17-18). "Your consecrated things": that which belongs to the Lord, such as the tithes and the firstborn (v. 17). "Whatever you have vowed to give" is mentioned separately, perhaps because these things are not consecrated per se, but become consecrated when they are vowed to the Lord; this is also true of the freewill offerings and the special gifts, and the entire category is represented here by that which has been vowed to be given.

Like verse 6 (but unlike v. 13), verse 27 specifically mentions the "sacrifices" (fellowship offerings) alongside the burnt offerings and indicates the main difference between them. The burnt offerings are placed on the altar in their entirety (the meat is burned, the blood is poured out, cf. Lev. 1), while the meat of the "sacrifices" may be eaten and only the blood is poured beside the altar (cf. Lev. 3:2, 8, 13); the fat, which was also placed on the altar is not mentioned here—the intent is not to give a detailed description of the ritual.

d. *Concluding exhortation* (12:28)

12:28 *Be careful to obey all these regulations I am giving you, so that it may always go well with you and your children after you, because you will be doing what is good and right in the eyes of the* Lord *your God.*

It is best to refer this concluding exhortation to the entire section from verse 2 through verse 28. We find a similar exhortation in verse 25b; here, at the end of the whole law, the exhortation is stated in more detail (cf. 6:18; 11:21).

2. Do not follow Canaanite practices (12:29–32)

12:29–32 *The* Lord *your God will cut off before you the nations you are about to invade and dispossess. But when you have driven them out and settled in their land,* ³⁰*and after they have been destroyed before you, be careful not to be ensnared by inquiring about their gods, saying, "How do these nations serve their gods? We will do the same."* ³¹*You must not worship the* Lord *your God in*

---

their way, because in worshiping their gods, they do all kinds of detestable things the LORD hates. They even burn their sons and daughters in the fire as sacrifices to their gods.
³²See that you do all I command you; do not add to it or take away from it.

These verses warn against following Canaanite practices and are continued in 13:1-8; they no longer deal with the one place of worship demanded in verses 2–28, yet their content is closely related to it. The primary purpose of the law was to combat the danger that Israel would follow the pagan Canaanite practices. This could happen in several ways. Israel could begin to worship the Canaanite gods directly; they could begin to "worship" the Lord in a pagan manner; or Israel could combine the worship of the Lord with that of idols. The one could easily lead to the other, and our verses do not make a sharp distinction between these various forms of pagan or paganized cultus; they speak in one breath of idolatry (v. 30) and of serving the Lord in a pagan manner (v. 31). "Ensnared": if Israel serves idols, it will face perdition as surely as the animal that is caught in a trap (cf. 7:16, 25).

"How do these nations serve their gods? We will do the same": the idea was common in the ancient Near East, and could also be adopted by Israel, that each land had its own gods and that Canaan's fields would not yield its produce and Israel could not live there in safety unless Israel gave these gods the homage they had received from of old.

It was possible to practice the Canaanite worship while attaching the Lord's name to it (cf. above). This is what verse 31 has in mind: You must not serve the Lord "your God" (emphatic, in contrast to the Baals with whom Israel has nothing to do) in a pagan, Canaanite manner. The reason for this prohibition is that much of what was part of the Canaanite way of worship was detestable to the Lord. The most terrible example, mentioned here, is the child sacrifices to Moloch, in which a child would first be sacrificed in an offering ritual and then burned. The view of some that in ancient times human sacrifices were permitted in Israel and that they are even prescribed in Exodus 22:29 is totally unfounded.[18] On the other hand, we do hear of human sacrifice in Israel's apostate cultus (2 Kings 16:3; 21:6; 23:10). The practice is forbidden in Deuteronomy 18:10; Leviticus 18:21; 20:2ff.

Verse 32 concludes the warning with an exhortation to keep with care "all I command you." This refers in the first place to the

---

[18]Even Ezekiel 20:25 cannot be used in support of this view. Cf. *Het Godswoord der profeten* 4:66–67.

preceding, but also includes "all" that Moses commands Israel. Nothing must be added to or taken away from it—it must be honored as the inviolable Word of God (cf. 4:2).

3. The prophet who seduces to idol worship (13:1-5)

In this chapter the punishment on those who seduce to idolatry is specified (a prophet or dreamer, 13:1-5; a relative or friend, 13:6-11; and a town that practices idolatry 13:12-18); later the punishment for idolatry in general will be given (17:2–7).

The punishment is severe; the seducers must be put to death and the idolatrous city must be destroyed completely (struck with the ban), because idolatry is the most direct and fundamental sin against the Lord Himself (cf. vv. 5, 10) and the most radical transgression of the Lord's covenant (cf. 17:2), the source of Israel's blessing (cf. v. 17). This severity is intended strictly as a safeguard, as is clear from the care with which the lawgiver seeks to prevent anyone from becoming the victim of a frivolous or malicious accusation (cf. 13:10, 14; 17:4, 6, 7; 19:15).

This section deals specifically with the seduction to idolatry by a prophet or dreamer.

13:1–2 *If a prophet, or one who foretells by dreams, appears among you and announces to you a miraculous sign or wonder, ²and if the sign or wonder of which he has spoken takes place, and he says, "Let us follow other gods" (gods you have not known) "and let us worship them,"*

In Israel, the term "prophet" did not only refer to the true representative of God but to anyone who claimed to speak God's Word on the basis of divine revelation. Thus, those who falsely claimed to speak on God's behalf, whom we would call "false prophets," would also be called "prophets." It is such a "false prophet" that is in view here. Besides the prophet is mentioned the "dreamer," i.e., the person who received or pretended to receive divine revelation in the form of dreams.

A prophet can also receive revelatory dreams (Num. 12:6). The reason why the "dreamer" is mentioned separately here (cf. also 1 Sam. 28:6) may be that individuals who were not prophets in the full sense of the word could also receive revelatory dreams (Gen. 20:3; 28:12; et al.) or could pretend to have received such dreams. The lawgiver now states the case where such a prophet or dreamer urges the people to worship other gods (gods Israel has not "known," i.e., with whom Israel has nothing to do; cf. 11:28), predicting "sign or wonder" (cf. 4:34) that does indeed occur. What is meant is apparently something unusual or marvelous (cf. Isa. 7:14; 38:7) that would serve to create faith in the prophet's or dreamer's divine mission and in the power of the gods in whose name he spoke and whose worship he urged upon Israel (18:20).

13:3–5 *you must not listen to the words of that prophet or dreamer. The* LORD *your God is testing you to find out whether you love him with all your heart and with all your soul. 4It is the* LORD *your God you must follow, and him you must revere. Keep his commands and obey him; serve him and hold fast to him. 5That prophet or dreamer must be put to death, because he preached rebellion against the* LORD *your God, who brought you out of Egypt and redeemed you from the land of slavery; he has tried to turn you from the way the* LORD *your God commanded you to follow. You must purge the evil from among you.*

Even if the announced sign or wonder does occur, Israel must not let themselves be seduced to listen to that prophet or dreamer, but must put him to death. The nonoccurrence of the announced sign would prove that the prophet in question has not been sent by God (18:22), but the occurrence does not prove the opposite. Only the revelation the Lord gives Israel is normative; at this point specifically Moses' words, to which nothing may be added and from which nothing must be taken away (12:32)—this is the norm by which also the words of the prophets must be tested.

When the sign announced by the false prophet does take place, it must be ascribed to the Lord's will rather than to the power of the false god (v. 3b). The Lord is testing Israel (cf. 8:2) to find out if Israel loves the Lord with heart and soul (cf. 6:5).[19: ks]

Israel must not follow idols but the Lord (again called emphatically "your God," v. 4); they must serve Him and hold fast to Him. Even the miracles of the false prophets must move Israel to do this, since they are His means of testing their love for Him (v. 3).

Instead of following the false prophet, Israel must put him to death

---

[19]This is all that is said here about the signs of such false prophets, and is indeed the main point. God's working does, of course, not exclude secondary causes. There is no reason to limit the cause of the occurrence of such announced signs to deceit or to what we would call "chance"; these may have played an important role in many such cases, but the Scriptures also speak of "counterfeit miracles, signs and wonders" (2 Thess. 2:9; cf. also Matt. 24:24).

(v. 5). It is not indicated how he is to be executed; in Israel stoning was the common manner of execution, and this would apply to the idolater (cf. v. 10; 17:5). On the other hand, the prophets of Baal were "slaughtered" by Elijah (1 Kings 18:40).

In order to motivate the punishment, the sin is described at some length. Such a false prophet has preached apostasy from the Lord, Israel's God and Deliverer from the land of slavery, Egypt.

The addition, "You must purge the evil from among you" (cf. 17:7, 12; 19:19; 21:21; et al.) serves to make it clear that Israel (because of its covenant with the Lord) is a holy nation in which evil cannot be tolerated. The expression is used in 1 Corinthians 5:13 in connection with the expulsion of willful sinners from the church. Its use here and in 1 Corinthians shows the distinction between the old and the new covenant. The once common view, based on this section of Deuteronomy, that the church has the right and the duty to put heretics to death, ignores this distinction (apart from the fact that the heretic and the idolater cannot be equated).

4. The relative or friend who secretly entices to idolatry (13:6–11)

The fact that the secret attempt to seduce to idolatry on the part of a relative or friend is singled out here does, of course, not imply that more overt attempts and attempts on the part of other persons would not be punished. But only secret attempts had to be made public, all the more so when kinship or friendship would make one inclined to want to spare the guilty party.

13:6–7 *If your very own brother, or your son or daughter, or the wife you love, or your closest friend secretly entices you, saying, "Let us go and worship other gods" (gods that neither you nor your fathers have known, *[7]*gods of the peoples around you, whether near or far, from one end of the land to the other),*

"If your very own brother" is literally "If your brother, the son of your mother" (cf. KJV). The NIV captures the force of the phrase, which indicates the closest of relationships. We could further paraphrase, "If someone, even your very own brother. . . ." Polygamy was common in Israel, and thus it was possible for someone to have many half brothers who had the same father but a different mother. But even if it is your full brother you must not spare him.

Similarly, the closeness of the relationships is reinforced in the expressions "the wife you love" (rather than simply "your wife") and "your closest friend" (lit., "the friend who is as your own life," rather than merely "your friend").

The individual Israelite, rather than Israel as a whole (as in v. 12), is addressed here, especially the male Israelite ("your husband" is not included in the list in v. 6). The case presented is that one of those mentioned has secretly tried to entice the person addressed in these verses to worship other gods. The words that follow are not those of the tempter, but are added by Moses and are appropriately placed in parentheses in the NIV. "Neither you nor your fathers have known" these gods. This means that there is no relationship between Israel and these gods, who are thus not only "other gods" but also "foreign gods." Verse 7 adds that *all* foreign gods are included, the gods of *all* peoples around them, "whether near or far, from one end of the land to the other" ("the peoples around you" is thus intended in the broadest sense).

13:8–11 *do not yield to him or listen to him. Show him no pity. Do not spare him or shield him.* ⁹*You must certainly put him to death. Your hand must be the first in putting him to death, and then the hands of all the people.* ¹⁰*Stone him to death, because he tried to turn you away from the LORD your God, who brought you out of Egypt, out of the land of slavery.* ¹¹*Then all Israel will hear and be afraid, and no one among you will do such an evil thing again.*

Moses then prescribes the attitude required in a case such as this. In the first place, the individual approached must not yield or listen. But this is not sufficient: the tempter must be put to death, and the one who has been approached must take the initiative. He must not spare the tempter or shield him from exposure. This is stated with three different words ("Show him no pity. Do not spare him or shield him"). What is asked here is extremely difficult because of the close ties with the tempter.

Verse 9 then states what the person must do: "You must certainly put him to death" (an emphatic statement); actually, the people as a whole must put him to death, not only the person who had been approached—although the latter must take the initiative (cf. 17:7) and cast the first stone (since death by stoning is indicated, v. 10). Before the guilty party is stoned, however, he must first be brought before the assembly (which was already implied in v. 8, "do not shield him"); the matter must be investigated and sentence pronounced (cf. 17:4).

Verse 10 indicates that the guilty party must be stoned to death, and

166

motivates the punishment by characterizing the sin: "He tried to turn you away from the LORD your God"—"your God" is again emphatic and is underlined by the reminder of His deliverance from Egypt.

Verse 11 shows the beneficial result intended by the lawgiver: "All Israel will hear and be afraid, and no one among you will do such an evil thing again."

5. The city that falls into idolatry (13:12-18)

Again, an attempt to seduce to idolatry is dealt with, this time an attempt directed at an entire city. The sequel shows that the case presented assumes that the attempt has been successful. The sanction in this case is not so much against the seduction as against the actual commitment of idolatry, specifically in the case of an entire city. The lawgiver begins by describing the rumor and then demands investigation and punishment. "You" refers to Israel as a whole.

13:12–13 *If you hear it said about one of the towns the LORD your God is giving you to live in* [13]*that wicked men have arisen among you and have led the people of their town astray, saying, "Let us go and worship other gods" (gods you have not known),*

The law thus begins by stating the case that Israel hears that the population of one of its cities has allowed itself to be drawn into idolatry and that it serves gods other than the Lord. "Gods you have not known" is again an editorial comment on Moses' part to indicate the reprehensible nature of the proposition.

13:14–18 *then you must inquire, probe and investigate it thoroughly. And if it is true and it has been proved that this detestable thing has been done among you,* [15]*you must certainly put to the sword all who live in that town. Destroy it completely, both its people and its livestock.* [16]*Gather all the plunder of the town into the middle of the public square and completely burn the town and all its plunder as a whole burnt offering to the LORD your God. It is to remain a ruin forever, never to be rebuilt.* [17]*None of those condemned things shall be found in your hands, so that the LORD will turn from his fierce anger; he will show you mercy, have compassion on you, and increase your numbers, as he promised on oath to your forefathers,* [18]*because you obey the LORD your God, keeping all his commands that I am giving you today and doing what is right in his eyes.*

Of course, Israel must not act on the basis of a mere rumor. The lawgiver demands emphatically that the matter be investigated thoroughly (cf. 17:4), i.e., by the judges competent to deal with these matters. But if the evidence is sufficient (at least two witnesses are required, 17:6) that one of Israel's cities has indeed done "this detestable thing," then the most severe punishment possible must be meted out (v. 15). The first and most important aspect is that all inhabitants of that city must be put to the sword. But this is only part of the *cherem,* the ban (see comments on 2:34) that is to be imposed on the city. The livestock must also be destroyed. And even the city itself and everything in it must be burned (v. 16). The "plunder," i.e., all the material possessions, must be brought to the public square and the entire city must be burned. The city itself is never to be rebuilt—it is to "remain a ruin forever" (cf. Josh. 6:26; 8:28). The city and its contents were to be burned, literally, "completely, before the LORD your God" (cf. KJV); the NIV and other versions render "completely" as "as a whole burnt offering," and the word can indeed mean this. But ban and offering are never equated in the Old Testament; rather, they are contrasted (1 Sam. 15:15).

Verse 17 adds the warning that nothing may be taken from the "plunder" of the city—nothing must escape destruction (cf. Josh. 7). Finally, the purpose of this action is indicated: that the Lord will turn from His fierce anger, which was aroused by this detestable sin, and may show Israel mercy and fulfill the promise of increase made to the forefathers (which means that Israel will receive restitution for the numbers it lost in the destruction of the city). And this will happen because Israel obeys the Lord and keeps His commands (and thus holds fast to the covenant that comprises all Israel's *heil;* see note on p. 29).

6. Certain mourning customs forbidden (14:1–2)

14:1–2 *You are the children of the LORD your God. Do not cut yourselves or shave the front of your heads for the dead, ²for you are a people holy to the LORD your God. Out of all the peoples on the face of the earth, the LORD has chosen you to be his treasured possession.*

Leviticus 19:28 forbids the cutting of the body when in mourning; here is added the shaving of the front of the head (lit., "between the eyes," cf. Lev. 19:27; 21:5). These customs were undoubtedly common among the pagan nations, especially the Canaanites (for similar customs, cf. 1 Kings 18:28; Isa. 15:2). Israel must not do this; it must distinguish itself from the other nations as a people that belongs to the

Lord. Verse 1 expresses this by calling Israel "the children of the LORD" (cf. 32:6). This should not simply be equated with the saving "sonship" of which the New Testament speaks but is a more general indication of the special relationship of each Israelite, as a member of the people of the covenant, to the Lord (even though for believers this relationship meant salvation; see further comments on Hos. 1:10 in this commentary series). This relationship of Father and children is incompatible with the practice of pagan mourning customs: anyone who has God as his Father must not bear the signs of paganism on his body.

Verse 2 states the same thing in different words. Israel belongs to the Lord as a "holy" people, i.e., a people the Lord has made His own and in whose midst He is with His presence. He has made Israel His "treasured possession" through His gracious election (the root of all Israel's blessings)—this is why Israel must not become like the nations.

The question whether there was a special reason why Israel was forbidden to adopt these customs (as well as similar customs, such as that of Lev. 19:27 or tattooing, Lev. 19:28b) cannot be answered with certainty. It is possible that this prohibition was designed to impress upon Israel that they, as the Lord's children, were not to mutilate or mar their bodies. But this is not explicitly stated, and apparently something else stands in the foreground, namely that Israel as the Lord's people must not bear the marks of paganism. A contributing element was probably the thought that these customs were based on idolatrous or superstitious ideas; but we do not know for certain what these may have been (some believe that these disfigurements were intended to make one unrecognizable to the spirit of the dead, who, it was feared, would take revenge upon the living for insults received in life). This prohibition was not always observed in Israel (cf. Jer. 16:6; Ezek. 7:18; cf. Isa. 3:24; Amos 8:10).

7. Clean and unclean animals (14:3-21)

This section consists largely of regulations as to which animals are clean and which are unclean; the former may be eaten, the latter may not.[20] Apart from the addition at the end concerning the cooking of a young goat in its mother's milk (v. 21; cf. Exod. 23:19), the content of

---

[20]Another classification is animals suitable for offerings and those that are not. None of the unclean animals could be offered (Gen. 8:20) or given as tithes (Lev. 27:32), nor could their firstborn be given to the Lord (Lev. 27:26; Num. 18:15). But

this section is essentially the same as Leviticus 11:2–23 (the rest of Lev. 11 contains a number of distinctions between clean and unclean animals that are not found in Deuteronomy: Lev. 11:27–28, 29–30, 41ff.).

The Old Testament distinction between "clean" and "unclean" (in the external, ceremonial sense) encompasses much more than what is said here about the distinction between animals that could or could not be eaten. This section also deals with the eating of animals found already dead (v. 21), while Leviticus 11:24–40 deals extensively with uncleanness caused by carcasses (the laws of purification then follow in chs. 12–15).

This entire distinction between ceremonial cleanness and uncleanness has a temporary character from the standpoint of revelation history and is intended to make way for the fuller revelation of the New Testament dispensation (cf. Matt. 15:11; Acts 10:12–13). This does not deny the fact that the distinction had importance in the history of God's revelation. It was a means of instilling in Israel by transference a deep aversion to moral uncleanness. And this distinction served, especially during the Dispersion, as a powerful factor in keeping Israel from mixing with other peoples.

The latter is especially true of our laws. It is clear that a law that denied so many kinds of meat to Israel (among them those that were much sought after elsewhere, such as the pig) would, if observed, significantly hinder close ties with other nations. This effect can clearly be seen in the time after the Captivity. All this applies even more strongly to the eating of blood (Gen. 9:4; Lev. 3:17) and the prohibition on eating the meat of animals found already dead (v. 21). The concern for keeping these commandments later led to the development of a special method of slaughtering (whereby the flesh was not to be torn, not even by a minor imperfection in the knife, and the blood was to be drained in a special manner) and to the concept that the least deviation from this method made the slaughtered animal into an animal "already found dead."

But if we assume that the lawgiver did indeed have in mind the purposes outlined above, questions remain as to many details and the historical background.

---

not all clean animals could be offered: only the ox, sheep, goat, turtle dove, and young doves were suitable, but not the deer and other nondomestic animals mentioned in verse 4 (cf. 12:15).

It is likely that the laws given by God tied in with many things that already existed in Israel as custom or tradition. We know that the distinction between clean and unclean animals (in a ceremonial sense) played an important role among many pagan nations; the Scriptures themselves indicate that this distinction goes back to earliest antiquity. Thus we may assume that Israel had a tradition concerning clean and unclean animals prior to Horeb, and that the lawgiver tied in to this tradition. But many questions remain as to the why and how, questions that cannot be answered with certainty.

In general, it is clear that Israel was to observe these commands for religious reasons, in order to live like a "holy" people, a people that belonged to the Lord. This is stated in verse 1 in connection with mourning customs and restated in verse 21 relative to the eating of carcasses, and it is undoubtedly also the motivation for not eating unclean animals. The people must keep these commandments for the sake of the Lord who had given them.

Another question is whether we can find a motive why these commands (and perhaps also the tradition with which they are linked) prohibit the eating of these animals in particular. We have no certainty on this point. The Scriptures themselves do not enlighten us (in contrast to the prohibitions on eating blood, Lev. 17:11, and on the tendon attached to the socket of the hip, Gen. 32:32). The split hoof and chewing the cud are not reasons but rather characteristics (which apply only to large land animals).[21] It is possible that a scheme such as this would result in the classification of some animals that would otherwise not have been unclean as unclean for the sake of consistency. Nevertheless, the reason for declaring certain animals unclean must generally be sought elsewhere.

It is possible that the Mosaic law or the tradition behind this law was influenced by Israel's environment, whether by adopting that which existed elsewhere or by consciously opposing it. We also find the prohibition against eating pork in Egypt and in India. Lucianus comments that in Syria some considered the pig sacred and offered it, while others considered it unclean. We know from other sources that among the Canaanites the pig must have occupied an important position both as a domestic animal and for offerings. The Scriptures indicate that the pig later played a role in the pagan cultus adopted by the Israelites (Isa. 65:4; 66:17; cf. also v. 3) and that pigs were kept in

---

[21]It is a curious fact that similar, and in part identical, laws are also found in the Manu tradition of India.

Palestine in Jesus' day, even in herds (Matt. 7:6; 8:30). Not only the pig, but also various other animals are known to have played an important role in the mythology and cultus of many pagan nations, and that they were frequently associated with a deity or with demons.

There is no reason at all to assume that the commandments given here to Israel were based on specifically pagan concepts (including totemism, to which some have related them). The belief in demons is not a specifically pagan notion; it is possible that some birds were declared unclean at least in part because they were in the popular mind closely associated with demons (see comments on vv. 11–18). It is also entirely feasible that Israel (already in pre-Mosaic times) adopted certain customs from its environment—which does not necessarily imply that it also adopted the pagan concepts associated with these customs.

But it is more likely that Israel was forbidden to eat certain animals out of opposition to pagan myths and rituals and to counteract the possibility of Israel's participation in these rituals. Some would explain, for example, the fact that the pig is declared unclean as a reaction against its prominence in the Canaanite cultus. Yet objections can be raised against this view. It is true that the prohibition on eating pigs would for the pious Israelite be reinforced by the contrast observed in the Canaanite cultus. But if we seek to explain the prohibition on the basis of this contrast, we are faced with the question why it is the pig in particular that is declared unclean, and not other animals that were also used in the Canaanite cultus. This seems to indicate that there was another reason for this prohibition; perhaps we must think simply of a natural aversion (perhaps also found among other peoples), connected also with a striving for physical cleanliness, which the lawgiver also impresses upon Israel for religious reasons (apparently with symbolic significance; cf. Exod. 19:10; et al.).

Such motives (i.e., natural aversion leading to a national custom that the law accommodated and a desire for bodily cleanliness inculcated by the law) would also apply to the creeping animals and to small winged animals (v. 20, lit., "every teeming thing that flies"), probably primarily insects. The reason why carnivores are considered unclean may be that they eat blood and carrion. The same motives behind the prohibition of the eating of blood and carrion on Israel's part may also lie behind this; in the case of the eating of blood the motivation was of a distinctly religious nature (Lev. 17:11). This does not exclude the possibility that the carnivorous animals also evoked a natural aversion that played a role in their being declared unclean. The suggestion that these laws are based on sanitary or health considerations is not likely, although such considerations could play a role in the keeping of these laws. Finally, it should be noted that some of the names of the animals in this section are uncertain, as a comparison of the various versions shows.

First the large land animals are dealt with (vv. 4–8), then the aquatic animals (vv. 9–10), and then the winged animals (vv. 11–20). Leviticus 11 also deals with the animals that "move about on the ground" (Lev. 11:29–30, 41–42).

14:3 *Do not eat any detestable thing.*

The opening statement summarizes all that follows and has the character of a *prohibition;* this is also true of what follows, although for the sake of clarification the latter section adds which animals may be eaten. "Any detestable thing" comprises that which must not be eaten (unclean animals and animals found dead); these things are detestable in God's sight and should also be to Israel. The word expresses how completely Israel must reject these foods—the holiness of God's people is at stake. This strong emphasis on the ceremonial laws is a characteristic of the old dispensation.

a. *Large land animals* (14:4–8)

14:4–8 *These are the animals you may eat: the ox, the sheep, the goat, ⁵the deer, the gazelle, the roe deer, the wild goat, the ibex, the antelope and the mountain sheep. ⁶You may eat any animal that has a split hoof divided in two and that chews the cud. ⁷However, of those that chew the cud or that have a split hoof completely divided you may not eat the camel, the rabbit or the coney. Although they chew the cud, they do not have a split hoof; they are ceremonially unclean for you. ⁸The pig is also unclean; although it has a split hoof, it does not chew the cud. You are not to eat their meat or touch their carcasses.*

Verses 4–6 list those animals that may be eaten, i.e., clean animals. First they are listed individually (vv. 4b–5; in contrast to Lev. 11, which lists only the unclean animals). Verse 6 gives the common characteristics of these clean land animals: they have "a split hoof divided in two" and chew the cud. These are characteristics, rather than reasons why they are clean (cf. above). Of the most prominent ruminant families (as classified in modern zoology), the camel is explicitly excluded in verse 7, while the giraffe is not mentioned at all.

In verses 7–8 several larger land animals that may *not* be eaten are mentioned; they are explicitly called "unclean." The list is not complete; horses, donkeys, cats, and dogs are not mentioned. These verses list only those animals that have one of the characteristics given in verse 6 but lack the other. Verse 7 mentions three animals that chew the cud but do not have split hooves (camel, rabbit, and coney), while verse 8 speaks of an animal that does have split hooves but does not ruminate, the pig (cf. above).[22]

The conclusion of verse 8 states again explicitly that the meat of these animals must not be eaten and adds that their carcasses must not be touched. The latter is thus a separate command, which underlines the uncleanness of these animals (according to Lev. 11:39 one could not touch the carcass of a clean animal either without becoming unclean; the same is true of touching a living unclean animal, Lev. 11:26).

b. *Aquatic animals* (14:9–10)

14:9–10 *Of all the creatures living in the water, you may eat any that has fins and scales. ¹⁰But anything that does not have fins and scales you may not eat; for you it is unclean.*

Any aquatic animal without fins or scales is unclean (e.g., the eel and shrimp).

c. *Winged animals* (14:11–20)

14:11–20 *You may eat any clean bird. ¹²But these you may not eat: the eagle, the vulture, the black vulture, ¹³the red kite, the black kite, any kind of falcon, ¹⁴any kind of raven, ¹⁵the horned owl, the screech owl, the gull, any kind of hawk, ¹⁶the little owl, the great owl, the white owl, ¹⁷the desert owl, the osprey, the cormorant, ¹⁸the stork, any kind of heron, the hoopoe and the bat.*

¹⁹All flying insects that swarm are unclean to you; do not eat them. ²⁰But any winged creature that is clean you may eat.

---

[22]The words "although they chew the cud, they do not have a split hoof " in verse 7 is not a scientific statement but is based on appearance, since what is important are the external characteristics. The rabbit is not a ruminant but moves its jaws like one. The camel, on the other hand, does have a split hoof but underneath the two parts of the hoof is a thick sole, so that it can be considered an animal that does not have a split hoof and is thus declared unclean, in keeping with the scheme.

Verses 12–19 list the larger birds that may not be eaten. The word "unclean" is not used here, and the reason why they must not be eaten is not mentioned. The meaning of the Hebrew names is not always certain. Many of the birds listed are birds of prey that eat carrion and garbage; it may also be significant that they generally live in ruins and desolate places and are in the popular imagination associated with demons (cf. Isa. 34:13ff.). Verse 19 adds, literally, "and every teeming thing that flies," indicating small animals, most likely insects, as the NIV translates.

Verse 20 repeats the permission of verse 11 regarding the clean animals in this group; only here it says "winged creature" instead of "bird," since the lawgiver here undoubtedly includes the four kinds of grasshopper that were the exception to the rule of verse 19 (see Lev. 11:21–22; grasshoppers were commonly used for food).

14:21a *Do not eat anything you find already dead. You may give it to an alien living in any of your towns, and he may eat it, or you may sell it to a foreigner. But you are a people holy to the LORD your God.*

Besides the eating of unclean animals, the eating of "anything you find already dead" is also prohibited (cf. Lev. 17:15), i.e., the carcass of an animal, whether it has been killed by a wild animal or has died of natural causes (Exod. 22:31; Lev. 17:15). The reason for this prohibition is probably that the blood had not completely drained out of such animals and the eating of blood was forbidden (12:16, 23ff.; in Lev. 17:15 the prohibition on the eating of blood immediately precedes the prohibition on eating carcasses).

Exodus 22:31 commanded that an animal torn by wild beasts was to be given to the dogs. In our text it is permitted to give it to the "alien living in any of your towns," or to sell it to a foreigner. It could of course be thrown to the dogs, but the objection that the meat would thus be lost is answered here, and it is therefore more likely that the commandment will be kept (Lev. 17:15 indicates that the alien who eats anything found dead will become unclean). The "alien" is someone who lives in Israel and has obtained the status of "semi-citizen" there; the "foreigner" is an outsider without any ties of citizenship (e.g., a traveling merchant); this is why the animal is *sold* to the foreigner, but *given* to the alien. The conclusion again states why Israel must not eat it (cf. v. 2).

14:21b *Do not cook a young goat in its mother's milk.*

Finally, a prohibition of a different nature: a young goat must not be boiled in its mother's milk (cf. Exod. 23:19b; 34:26b).[23] Young goats were a delicacy (Gen. 27:9, 14; Judg. 6:19; 13:15); apparently they were sometimes cooked in milk to make the meat tastier. But this must not be its own mother's milk. The reason for this prohibition is not clear. It is possible that it combats a superstitious pagan custom, but it is equally possible that it is based on and sanctions an awareness that there is something unnatural in cooking a young goat in the milk that was to nourish it, a violation of the divine order of creation.

8. The tithes (14:22–29)

Here regulations are given for the tithes (cf. 12:6), first for the annual tithes (vv. 22–27) and then for the triennial tithes (vv. 28–29).

The main point concerning the annual tithes is that these (together with the firstborn of the livestock) must be eaten at the central sanctuary in a festive offering meal, and instructions are given as to how this must be done.

We are faced with a difficulty here. In Numbers 18:21–24 (cf. Lev. 27:30) the tithes are to be given to the Levites, who in turn must give a tithe to the priests; we can say that this is based on the concept that the Lord is the actual owner of the land and that the user of the land therefore owes Him tribute money (cf. Gen. 47:23ff.; Lev. 25:24). But in these verses and elsewhere in Deuteronomy (12:6–7, 17; 26:12ff.) the tithes are to be used for offering meals (in 12:6–7 this is not stated as something new but is assumed to be known); in Deuteronomy, therefore, the tithes, like the meat of the fellowship offerings, are considered means for having fellowship with God.

The problem of the difference in definition and purpose reminds us of a similar difficulty with respect to the firstborn of the livestock (see comments on 12:6). In the case of the firstborn, it is possible to see the divergent regulations (they are to be given to the priests, and they are also to be eaten at offering meals) as complementing each other. This kind of solution is difficult to accept in the case of the tithes; Numbers 18:21 states explicitly that *all* tithes (i.e., those mentioned there) are for the Levites. And if we were to assume that part of these tithes could

---

[23]This cannot be explained as "in goat's milk"; the text speaks clearly of the milk of its own mother. The explanation "as long as it is still drinking its mother's milk" is arbitrary; we would then rather expect to find that a goat at such a young age should not be slaughtered at all.

still be used for the offering meal (Deut. 14:22 then speaks of this part), this assumption would be refuted by Deuteronomy 14:28–29, which specifies that the *triennial* tithes, in contrast to the annual tithes, must be given to the Levites and others.

The rabbis (at least as early as Josephus's time) solved the problem in a different manner; they saw in Deuteronomy 14 a second tithe, taken from the nine-tenths that remained after the tithe for the Levites had been taken out.[24]

Christian theologians also adopted the view that the Deuteronomic tithe was a second tithe (thus Keil and Oehler), and it is difficult to find a better explanation.

The critical school holds that the regulations of Numbers 18 and of Deuteronomy cannot be harmonized. Some believe the Deuteronomic regulation to be the older one, which was later changed by the priests in their favor; others (in our opinion with better reason) believe that Numbers 18 is older and that Deuteronomy modified the regulation in view of the centralization of the cultus.

On the basis of the scriptural data we cannot but conclude that all the laws in question date from Mosaic times (cf. Num. 18:1; Deut. 1:1; 5:1). It is conceivable that some laws were later modified or supplemented in view of changed conditions;[25] but from a Bible-believing perspective it is most natural, here and in similar cases, to take the Mosaic origin of the various laws as our starting point.

And it cannot be argued that this is impossible in the case in question. We must not forget that what is unclear to us may well have been clear to Israel due to oral explanation and tradition. The rabbinic view may have been based on such an ancient tradition.

The absence of any mention of the annual tithes for the Levites in Deuteronomy may be explained by the fact that Deuteronomy gives regulations for offering meals to be celebrated by the people, and thus has a different purpose than the regulation of the income of the Levites (although it is curious that also in 18:4, where the firstfruits are to be given to the priests, the tithes are not mentioned; but 18:4 may be a

---

[24]Josephus even considered the triennial tithe, called the "tithe for the poor" by the rabbis, a *third* tithe. It is possible that those who took the law seriously did indeed give all these tithes (cf. Tobit 1:7–8). It is, on the other hand, curious that where Josephus speaks, not as interpreter of the law, but as a witness to the customs of his time, he assumes that the tithes were for the priests, even to the exclusion of the Levites.

[25]Cf. the astute arguments of A. v. Hoonacker in *Le sacerdoce lévitique* (Louvain, 1899), pp. 383ff.

summary rather than a complete listing, and the tithes may be included in the firstfruits).

The rabbinic view of the Deuteronomic tithe as a second tithe becomes more plausible when it is assumed that we do not have a "tithe" in the strict sense of the word here. It would be somewhat strange if each year one-tenth of the grain, new wine, and oil (to which were added the firstfruits and the meat of the fellowship offerings and of the firstborn of the livestock) had to be consumed in offering meals. The possibility (vv. 23–24) that these "tithes" could be brought to the sanctuary if the distance was not too great also raises the question whether we should think here of tithes in the strict sense or (perhaps based on a less technical and more popular usage of the term) of tithes in a broader sense: "portions that were to be set aside for sacred use." The "tithes" in question then would be similar in nature to the firstfruits (i.e., votive offerings), which, because they were largely used by the offerer himself, were not subject to regulations as strict as those that applied to the "true" tithes. The objection (not conclusive in itself) that a double tithe would impose a heavy burden on the people would then also lose much of its force.

Finally, it is not necessary to consider the triennial tithe of verses 28–29 as a *third* "tithe." It is more likely that it is the same tithe as that mentioned in the preceding verses, which every third year was to have a different purpose. In Deuteronomy 26:12 this third year is called "the year of the tithe"; the reason for this is probably that these tithes then were not for one's own use, and consequently tithes were more like tithes in the stricter sense of the word (cf. 26:13–15). But they must have been distinguished from the tithes of Numbers 18:21, since the latter were strictly for the Levites and apparently had to be given every year. (Concerning the firstfruits, see comments on 18:4 and 26:1ff.)

a. *The annual tithe* (14:22–27)

The main point of this section is that the annual tithe is to be used to hold an offering feast at the central sanctuary (cf. 12:6–7, 11, 17–18).

14:22–23 *Be sure to set aside a tenth of all that your fields produce each year.* *23Eat the tithe of your grain, new wine and oil, and the firstborn of your herds and flocks in the presence of the* LORD *your God at the place he will choose as a dwelling for his Name, so that you may learn to revere the* LORD *your God always.*

First, there is the obligation to set aside one tenth "of all that your fields produce each year." This is further specified in verse 23 as "grain, new wine and oil." It is to be used to hold an offering meal. For the sake of completeness, the firstborn of herd and flock are also mentioned (cf. 12:17; 15:19–20), since these were to provide the meat for this meal. "Each year," literally, "year by year": the time appointed was when the Israelites visited the sanctuary on the occasion of the harvest festivals (cf. Exod. 23:16), especially the Feast of Tabernacles in the fall (cf. v. 27). On "as a dwelling for his Name" (v. 23), cf. 12:5. "So that you may . . .": the motivation behind these offering meals was of course the fear of the Lord, but they also served to evoke this fear, since they reminded Israel that it owed all these gifts not to its own labors or to the Baals (8:11ff.; 26:1ff.; Hos. 2:4, 7) but to the Lord, whom Israel must therefore worship, serve, and love with a holy fear.

14:24–26a *But if that place is too distant and you have been blessed by the* LORD *your God and cannot carry your tithe (because the place where the* LORD *will choose to put his Name is so far away),* ²⁵*then exchange your tithe for silver, and take the silver with you and go to the place the* LORD *your God will choose.* ²⁶*Use the silver to buy whatever you like: cattle, sheep, wine or other fermented drink, or anything you wish.*

But unless one lived near the sanctuary it was not feasible to carry one's tithe there. For this reason it was permissible to sell the tithes (and the firstborn) and to buy at the sanctuary whatever was needed for the offering meal.

"And you have been blessed by the LORD your God" (v. 24): the reason the sanctuary is too far away is that the Lord has given Israel a large territory (cf. 12:20–21; we could also think of the blessing of a large harvest, but the distance would make the bringing of the actual tithe impossible in any case).

14:26b–27 *Then you and your household shall eat there in the presence of the* LORD *your God and rejoice.* ²⁷*And do not neglect the Levites living in your towns, for they have no allotment or inheritance of their own.*

The purpose is for the Israelite to have fellowship with the Lord in this offering meal and to rejoice—not only the Israelite, but also his family. Verse 27 adds that the Levite must not be neglected. He must also be invited to the meal. For the entire section, cf. 12:7, 12, 18–19.

b. *The triennial tithe* (14:28–29)

14:28–29 *At the end of every three years, bring all the tithes of that year's produce and store it in your towns, ²⁹so that the Levites (who have no allotment or inheritance of their own) and the aliens, the fatherless and the widows who live in your towns may come and eat and be satisfied, and so that the LORD your God may bless you in all the work of your hands.*

We assume that the triennial tithe is the same as the annual tithe of verses 22–27 (cf. also 26:12–15). Every third year this tithe was then to be given to the Levites, the aliens, the widows, and the orphans. "At the end of every three years," i.e., at the end of the agricultural year that ends in the fall with the completion of the harvest (Exod. 23:16). This tithe must be stored "in your towns" rather than be taken to the sanctuary; it is intended for the groups mentioned in verse 29 who live in these towns, i.e., for the socially underprivileged. These people were to "eat and be satisfied." This tithe was for their subsistence, not for an offering meal for them that would have to be held at the sanctuary because of the sacred nature of these tithes (cf. 26:13–15). The conclusion, by way of encouragement, reminds of God's blessing that will follow the keeping of this commandment.

9. The year for canceling debts (15:1–11)

This section (even as 14:28–29 and vv. 12–18) contains regulations of a social nature.

15:1–3 *At the end of every seven years you must cancel debts. ²This is how it is to be done: Every creditor shall cancel the loan he has made to his fellow Israelite. He shall not require payment from his fellow Israelite or brother, because the LORD's time for canceling debts has been proclaimed. ³You may require payment from a foreigner, but you must cancel any debt your brother owes you.*

These verses contain the actual institution of the year for canceling debts. The time is "at the end of every seven years." Here, as in 14:28, we must think of the agricultural year, which ended in the fall (cf. also 31:10); the normal time to pay debts was probably after the harvest. But every seventh year debts were to be remitted. A number of older and also more recent exegetes have interpreted this as a full cancellation of all debts. What is in view here, however, is rather a postponement, a not-calling-in of outstanding debts. In favor of this view is the Hebrew word that is rendered "cancel debts" in the NIV (KJV, RSV, "release"; NASB, JB, NEB, "remission"; the same word is used in Exod. 23:11 of letting land lie unplowed, which is not the same as giving up the land) as well as the entire description in verse 2, which forbids only the calling in or collecting of an outstanding debt.

We must also keep in mind that the law envisions the lending to the poor in need (cf. vv. 7ff.), which includes the lending of seed grain to the poor farmer. Business debts did not play a role in ancient Israel.[26] This law is apparently closely connected with those of Exodus 23:10 and Leviticus 25:2–7, 20ff., which required that the land was to lie fallow every seventh year, while anything the land might produce that year, any volunteer crop, was to be left for the poor and the wild animals (the so-called Sabbath year; in the law it is called only "the year for canceling debts," KJV and "the year of release"; Deut. 15:9; 31:10). The law in this section is in a sense a necessary corollary of the law of Exodus 23:10, since the farmer who had no harvest could not pay his debts. But also (and not in the last place), the debtors in view here include the poor who did not own any land, and who could therefore only benefit from the Sabbath year. It is therefore better to say in general that this law serves to reinforce the character of the Sabbath year (as well as the Sabbath) as a social provision.

"His fellow Israelite or brother," literally, "his neighbor and his brother": the second word explains the first; only the "brother" (i.e., fellow-Israelite) was considered a "neighbor." This regulation applies only to the fellow-Israelite, not to the "foreigner," the man who lived among Israel only temporarily, such as a merchant, without being a full citizen or a "semi-citizen" or "alien" (although not stated explicitly, we may assume that this law did apply to the latter). The foreigner has nothing to do with this law or with Israel's law in general; he does not observe the Sabbath year either, and can thus continue to transact business as usual. "Has been proclaimed": the Sabbath year, like the Year of Jubilee, was apparently proclaimed publicly (Lev. 25:9). "The LORD's time for canceling debts has been proclaimed" can also be rendered "The time for canceling debts has been proclaimed in honor of the Lord"; the Lord has instituted the release and it is to be observed in His honor.

---

[26]Later, when conditions changed, business debts were also considered to fall under the law, but they were exempted from this particular regulation by means of the so-called *prosbole*, a clause that reserved to the creditor the right to call in the debt at any time.

15:4–6 *However, there should be no poor among you, for in the land the LORD your God is giving you to possess as your inheritance, he will richly bless you, ⁵if only you fully obey the LORD your God and are careful to follow all these commands I am giving you today. ⁶For the LORD your God will bless you as he has promised, and you will lend to many nations but will borrow from none. You will rule over many nations but none will rule over you.*

"However" introduces a correction of or limitation on the preceding. This cancellation of debts should hardly be necessary, since "there should be no poor among you"; the blessing of the Lord in accordance with His promise (cf. 1:11) would mean that none of them would be poor. This statement, taken in isolation, would be in direct contradiction to verse 11: "There will always be poor people in the land." But verse 5 states the condition on which verse 4 is based: Israel must "fully obey" the Lord and be "careful to follow all these commandments" (i.e., the entire law Moses proclaims). Because the condition will always be met imperfectly, verse 11 can say that there will always be poor people in the land. But verse 4 indicates that their presence is proof of Israel's unfaithfulness and reason to keep the commandments of verses 1–3.

Verse 6 repeats (still contingent upon the condition of verse 5) the promise of the Lord's blessing, and draws from this a conclusion concerning lending in relation to the nations: the Israelites will not be debtors to the nations, but creditors. It has been said that this verse has been fulfilled frequently since the Middle Ages; but the position of the Jews as creditors during the past centuries is not a fulfillment of this promise (which is conditional upon verse 5), but rather its caricature. Israel will "rule over many nations" as a result of its position as creditor (cf. 28:1).

15:7–11 *If there is a poor man among your brothers in any of the towns of the land that the LORD your God is giving you, do not be hardhearted or tightfisted toward your poor brother. ⁸Rather be openhanded and freely lend him whatever he needs. ⁹Be careful not to harbor this wicked thought: "The seventh year, the year for canceling debts, is near," so that you do not show ill will toward your needy brother and give him nothing. He may then appeal to the LORD against you, and you will be found guilty of sin. ¹⁰Give generously to him and do so without a grudging heart; then because of this the LORD your God will bless you in all your work and in everything you put your hand to. ¹¹There will always be poor people in the land. Therefore I command you to be openhanded toward your brothers and toward the poor and needy in your land.*

Here the lawgiver returns to the situation that can be expected as a result of Israel's sin, and imposes, returning to the perspective of verses 1–3, the obligation to lend to the poor brother. If there is a poor brother in Israel (in spite of verses 4–6, which will not be fully realized because of the sin of the people), the Israelite must willingly lend him whatever he needs. Even the approach of the Sabbath year must not deter the Israelite from fulfilling this obligation, because the poor brother "may then appeal to the LORD against you, and you will be found guilty of sin." Rather, the Israelite must lend what is needed, even if the Sabbath year is near, "without a grudging heart," i.e., not because he does not dare do otherwise, but cheerfully (2 Cor. 9:7). In this manner the Israelite may expect the Lord's blessing. Verse 11, see comments on verse 4.

10. Hebrew servants to be freed after six years' service (15:12–18)

This is largely a restatement of Exodus 21:2–6 (cf. Jer. 34:8ff. and Lev. 25:39ff.).

15:12–15 *If a fellow Hebrew, a man or a woman, sells himself to you and serves you six years, in the seventh year you must let him go free. ¹³And when you release him, do not send him away empty-handed. ¹⁴Supply him liberally from your flock, your threshing floor and your winepress. Give to him as the LORD your God has blessed you. ¹⁵Remember that you were slaves in Egypt and the LORD your God redeemed you. That is why I give you this command today.*

If a Hebrew man or woman has become a servant[27] (cf. Exod. 21:7–17), he or she must be set free in the seventh year (i.e., the seventh year of service, not the Sabbath year of v. 1). Verses 13–14 add an element that was not included in Exodus 21:2–6: the freed servant must be given liberally "from your flock, your threshing floor and your winepress," lest he be immediately in need. Verse 15 reminds Israel of their own servitude in Egypt and of the fact that the Lord set them free;

[27]Here (and in Lev. 25:44) it is assumed that the individual has sold himself into servitude, either because of debts or due to poverty, which was the most common situation. This does not mean that in other cases (e.g., an Israelite who was captured in battle and bought from his captors by another Israelite) this regulation would not apply. Exodus 21:2 says, "If you buy a Hebrew servant," which includes purchase for any reason. It should be noted that according to Leviticus 25:39 an Israelite should not be treated as a slave in the strict sense of the word.

this is a repeated motive in the law (and especially in Deuteronomy) for dealing kindly with servants and orphans (cf. 5:15; 10:19; 16:12; 24:18, 22; also Exod. 22:21; 23:9; Lev. 19:34).

15:16–17 *But if your servant says to you, "I do not want to leave you," because he loves you and your family and is well off with you, ¹⁷then take an awl and push it through his ear lobe into the door, and he will become your servant for life. Do the same for your maidservant.*

But the servant must not be sent away against his will; if he would rather stay he should be allowed to do so.²⁸

If the servant chooses to remain, he loses forever the right to be free. He becomes a servant in perpetuity (this does not take into consideration that in the Year of Jubilee all Hebrew servants were to be set free, Lev. 25:39ff.). His master must "nail" him to the door of the house by pushing an awl through is earlobe, symbolizing that the servant belongs to this house forever. The earlobe may have been chosen for purely practical reasons or because the ear represents hearing and thus obedience.

15:18 *Do not consider it a hardship to set your servant free, because his service to you these six years has been worth twice as much as that of a hired hand. And the LORD your God will bless you in everything you do.*

The lawgiver comes back to the subject of setting servants free and says that this is not an unreasonable demand. The servant has earned for his master twice as much as a hired hand, i.e., he has done twice as much as a hired hand. We might also think of the fact that the servant was at the disposal of his master day and night ("has been worth" can refer to wages, but also to the result of the servant's labor; cf. Zech. 8:10).

---

²⁸One reason for the refusal to leave might be the desire to stay with one's wife (who, if she had been given to the servant by his master, belonged to the latter) and children (Exod. 21:4–5). The fact that our text does not mention this reason merely indicates that the statement of the law here is not intended to be complete; it does not prove that this reason no longer existed. The addition in verse 17, "Do the same for your maidservant," does not mean that the maidservant was to be set free at the same time as her husband, but rather that she also was to be set free after six years' service.

11. Offering firstborn male animals (15:19–23)

15:19–23 *Set apart for the LORD your God every firstborn male of your herds and flocks. Do not put the firstborn of your oxen to work, and do not shear the firstborn of your sheep. ²⁰Each year you and your family are to eat them in the presence of the LORD your God at the place he will choose. ²¹If an animal has a defect, is lame or blind, or has any serious flaw, you must not sacrifice it to the LORD your God. ²²You are to eat it in your own towns. Both the ceremonially unclean and the clean may eat it, as if it were gazelle or deer. ²³But you must not eat the blood; pour it out on the ground like water.*

In Exodus Israel had been told that all male firstborn of men and animals belonged to the Lord and were to be consecrated to Him (Exod. 13:2, 12; 22:29b–30); the firstborn male child was to be redeemed, but the firstborn male animal was to be offered (to the extent that it was suitable for offering; the firstborn donkey, however, was to be redeemed, Exod. 13:2, 13–15). Exodus bases this law on the historical fact that the Lord slew the firstborn of Egypt; this does not, of course, exclude the possibility that this law was also connected with an existing custom and thus had a more general significance as well (similar to the law on the firstfruits).

Our text restates the law with respect to animals (herds and flocks, i.e., the animals suitable for offering; the donkey of Exod. 13:13 is not mentioned here) and provides further detail (cf. also Num. 18:15ff.).

First, the general conclusion is drawn from the statement "set apart for the LORD" (KJV, "sanctify unto the Lord") that these animals are to be withdrawn from common (profane) use. The oxen must not be used for work (pulling carts, plowing, or threshing), and the sheep and goats must not be shorn. Verse 20 then states that the animals must be eaten in the presence of the Lord at the central sanctuary each year (cf. 12:6–7),[29] i.e., as an offering meal, which means that they are to be offered to the Lord as a fellowship offering (cf. v. 21). Concerning Numbers 18:15ff., which states that the meat was to be given to the priests, see comments on 12:6.

It could happen, of course, that the animal had a defect or serious

---

[29]Probably especially during the Passover (described in 16:1–8), which was a special reminder of the Exodus and with which the offering of the firstborn was also connected (Exod. 13:15). The stipulation of Exodus 22:30, "give them to me on the eighth day," could no longer be carried out when the law of the central sanctuary went into force in Canaan. The stipulation retained significance, however, as an indication that the animal had to be at least eight days old if it was to be offered (cf. Lev. 22:27).

flaw (v. 21). In that case it still could not be used for profane purposes (v. 19b), but it could not be offered either (cf. 17:1; Lev. 22:19ff.). It could be eaten, not as an offering meal and not at the central sanctuary, but "in your own towns," wherever one lived, and partaking of this meal did not require ceremonial cleanness; thus it could be eaten "as if it were gazelle or deer." But the blood could not be eaten (v. 23; cf. 12:14–15, 22–23).

12. The feasts (16:1–17)

This chapter contains regulations concerning the three great annual feasts (cf. Exod. 12; Lev. 23; Num. 28–29). The emphasis lies (as in the case of the tithes and the firstborn) on the fact that these must be celebrated at the central sanctuary, and what is stated about the feasts is largely limited to what is connected with this fact. This is probably also the reason why only the three feasts are mentioned here during which Israel was required to visit the sanctuary (Exod. 23:14–17; 34:18, 24–25) and not the Feast of Trumpets or the Day of Atonement, for which this was not a requirement.

a. *The Passover* (16:1–8)

16:1–4a *Observe the month of Abib and celebrate the Passover of the* LORD *your God, because in the month of Abib he brought you out of Egypt by night.* ²*Sacrifice as the Passover to the* LORD *your God an animal from your flock or herd at the place the* LORD *will choose as a dwelling for his Name.* ³*Do not eat it with bread made with yeast, but for seven days eat unleavened bread, the bread of affliction, because you left Egypt in haste—so that all the days of your life you may remember the time of your departure from Egypt.* ⁴*Let no yeast be found in your possession in all your land for seven days.*

The Passover, in remembrance of the Exodus, must be celebrated in the month of Abib (called Nisan after the Captivity), which corresponds approximately with our April. The date is assumed to be known (cf. Exod. 12:6). The name "Passover" is derived from the Lord's "passing over" the houses of the Israelites (Exod. 12:27ff.). It is strictly speaking the name of the feast (v. 1), but is also applied to the Passover offering (v. 2). According to Exodus 12:6–7, this offering consists of a lamb that is slaughtered and eaten on the evening of the fourteenth of Abib. In verse 1 "Passover" may refer to this offering; in verse 2 it is clearly used in this sense, as the words "an animal from your flock or herd" indicate, and is applied also to offerings that were slaughtered during the seven-day Feast of Unleavened Bread that followed the Passover (Exod. 23:15). These are not the burnt and sin offerings brought on behalf of the whole congregation (Num. 28:19–26), but, as verse 3 indicates, fellowship offerings (perhaps consisting especially of the firstfruits, cf. 15:19ff.). These animals must be sacrificed and the following offering meal held "at the place the LORD will choose as a dwelling for his Name" (cf. 12:5, 11), i.e., at the central sanctuary (cf. vv. 5–6). Verse 3 adds that the Passover must not be eaten with anything made with yeast—only with unleavened bread. The addition "for seven days" further clarifies that the eating of the "Passover" occupies a full week, and that the term is thus used here in a broader sense than in Exodus 12:6. "Unleavened bread" is bread made without yeast, so that the dough does not rise and the loaves are flat. In order to ensure the strict implementation of the law of verse 3, verse 4a stipulates that during that time no yeast must be seen at all in Israel (cf. Exod. 12:19; 13:7).

The prohibition on yeast during the Passover is historically motivated in verse 3. It is a reminder of the haste with which the Israelites left Egypt (Exod. 12:11), which necessitated the eating of unleavened bread (Exod. 12:39). This is why Moses also calls it "the bread of affliction," which refers directly to the difficulties of the Exodus, as is clarified by the addition that Israel must remember the departure from Egypt. But indirectly it refers back to the misery of life in Egypt, of which the problems of the Exodus were merely the final chapter. And the memory of all this affliction must serve to fill Israel with gratitude toward their Redeemer.

This historical motivation of the unleavened bread does of course not exclude the possibility that it also had another significance. Thus it has been said (with an appeal to Luke 12:1; Mark 8:15; Matt. 16:6; 1 Cor. 5:6–8; Gal. 5:9) that the yeast was symbolic of spiritual and moral decay because it promotes fermentation. But it cannot be proven that this is also the view implied in the law. It is true that yeast was not to be used in the grain offering (Lev. 2:11), but Leviticus 7:13 shows that as such it was not considered incompatible with the sacredness of the cultus. But verse 4a gives the prohibition on yeast a character that transcends its historical motivation and definitely considers yeast to be in conflict with the sacredness of the Passover (cf. Exod. 12:19, where the death penalty is imposed on the eating of yeast during the

Passover); it is clear that the New Testament interpretation of yeast could easily be derived from this view.

16:4b *Do not let any of the meat you sacrifice on the evening of the first day remain until morning.*

This verse refers specifically to the feast of the animal sacrificed on the evening of the first day, i.e., the Passover lamb, sacrificed on the evening of the fourteenth (this in contrast to verses 2–3). Moses reminds the Israelites that none of this meat may remain until morning (cf. Exod. 12:10; 23:18; 34:25; Num 9:12).

16:5–7 *You must not sacrifice the Passover in any town the LORD your God gives you ⁶except in the place he will choose as a dwelling for his Name. There you must sacrifice the Passover in the evening, when the sun goes down, on the anniversary of your departure from Egypt. ⁷Roast it and eat it at the place the LORD your God will choose. Then in the morning return to your tents.*

Again (cf. v. 2) and more emphatically is stated that the Passover must be sacrificed at the central sanctuary and thus not "in any town," i.e., wherever the Israelites lived. On the occasion of the first Passover, in Egypt, the Passover lamb was slaughtered and eaten in the houses and the blood was put on the doorframes (Exod. 12:1ff.). This practice was perhaps also followed in Canaan, after the tabernacle had fallen into decline and before the building of the temple. This law prescribes that when there will be a central sanctuary in Canaan, the Passover must be celebrated there (cf. 2 Chron. 30:16; 35:5–6). This meant that the application of the blood to the doorframes was no longer required and that the blood was to be poured out at the altar as the blood of an offering (2 Chron. 30:17; 35:11), and certainly also that, as in the case of the other fellowship offerings, the fat was to be burned on the altar. We may assume that such a practice was already followed when the Passover was celebrated at Sinai (Num. 9:1–5). The time of the sacrifice is specified as "when the sun goes down"—the time of day when Israel left Egypt (elsewhere it is specified as "at twilight," lit., "between the two evenings," Exod. 12:6).

The Passover is to be prepared with fire—it is to be roasted (cf. 2 Chron. 35:13), not boiled (cf. RSV; see Exod. 12:8)—and eaten at the central sanctuary. The following words have been interpreted in different ways. "Return to your tents" is literally, "turn [depart; cf. 1:7, "break camp"] and go into your tents." This phrase gives the impression that the Israelites are told to return home, which is strange in view of the "assembly" that is to be held on the seventh day (v. 8), which assumes the presence of the people at the sanctuary, and also in view of verses 2–3, which speak of a seven-day celebration at the sanctuary. Some have tried to resolve this by referring the phrase to a return to the tents where the Israelites stayed while at the sanctuary, rather than to a returning home. But this solution is not without problems. The expression "to your tents" elsewhere always means "home" (1 Sam. 13:2; et al.), and the words "turn and go" would seem to indicate a longer journey. Another solution would therefore appear more plausible to us, namely, that these words merely constitute a *permission* to go home for those who had come only to celebrate the Passover in the narrower sense of verse 5.

16:8 *For six days eat unleavened bread and on the seventh day hold an assembly to the LORD your God and do no work.*

The Passover in the narrower sense is followed by the Feast of Unleavened Bread, which lasts seven days (v. 3). It is a six-day feast, to which is added a seventh, special day. This seventh day is celebrated with a festive "assembly," and no work must be done on this day (the same was true of the first day, Exod. 12:16; Lev. 23:7).

b. *The Feast of Weeks* (16:9–12)

16:9–12 *Count off seven weeks from the time you begin to put the sickle to the standing grain. [10]Then celebrate the Feast of Weeks to the LORD your God by giving a freewill offering in proportion to the blessings the LORD your God has given you. [11]And rejoice before the LORD your God at the place he will choose as a dwelling for his Name—you, your sons and daughters, your menservants and maidservants, the Levites in your towns, and the aliens, the fatherless and the widows living among you. [12]Remember that you were slaves in Egypt, and follow carefully these decrees.*

This feast is called the Feast of Weeks because it is to be celebrated after seven weeks (hence also its later name, Pentecost, i.e., the feast of the fiftieth day). The seven weeks must be counted from the day the grain harvest begins (i.e., the barley harvest, which was the first grain crop to be harvested). This does not set a fixed date; but Leviticus 23:15 fixes the day as that on which the sheaf of the first grain is brought to the priest—the second day of the Feast of Unleavened Bread (the second day of the Passover; cf. Lev. 23:11). The reason for the *seven* weeks is thus that it is a feast of thanksgiving for the completed grain harvest (in Exod. 23:16 it is therefore called the Feast of Harvest; the offerings mentioned are the firstfruits of the wheat harvest [Exod. 23:16; 34:22] and the loaves made of the firstfruits [Lev. 23:17; cf. Num. 28:26, "the day of firstfruits"]).

The offerings are called "freewill offerings" here; they are to be in proportion to the blessing received from the Lord and would include the firstfruits of the grain harvest (Exod. 23:16ff.) but also animal offerings. Besides these offerings brought by individuals, there were also communal offerings (Lev. 23:17-20; Num. 28:26ff.).

The freewill offerings are to be used in offering meals (v. 11). Here, as frequently in Deuteronomy, the emphasis falls on the festive aspect: "Rejoice before the LORD your God." The sources of this rejoicing are the fellowship with the Lord, the thought of Him, and the riches that Israel possesses in such a God. Again, these festivities are to take place at the central sanctuary "at the place he will choose as a dwelling for his Name." Not only the offerer and his family, including the servants, must participate in this festive occasion, but also the Levites and those who are socially underprivileged (cf. 12:7, 12, 18; 14:23; 15:20).

Verse 12 concludes with a reminder of Israel's servitude in Egypt (cf. 5:15; 15:15; 24:22) as a stimulus both to social consideration and to that gratitude that will lead Israel to a careful obedience to the laws Moses proclaims here.

c. *The Feast of Tabernacles* (16:13-15)

16:13-15 *Celebrate the Feast of Tabernacles for seven days after you have gathered the produce of your threshing floor and your winepress. ¹⁴Be joyful at your Feast—you, your sons and daughters, your menservants and maidservants, and the Levites, the aliens, the fatherless and the widows who live in your towns. ¹⁵For seven days celebrate the Feast to the LORD your God at the place the LORD will choose. For the LORD your God will bless you in all your harvest and in all the work of your hands, and your joy will be complete.*

Concerning this feast, cf. Leviticus 23:34-36, 39-43; Numbers 29:12-38. In Exodus 23:16 and 34:22 it is called the Feast of Ingathering. The name Feast of Tabernacles is derived from the booths made of branches of palms and other trees (Lev. 23:40). This must be a reminder of the "booths" (i.e., tents) in which Israel lived during the wilderness journey (Lev. 23:43-44). This is not to deny the possibility that there was also a natural reason for this making of a living in booths. In the wine-producing regions of Israel booths are still built in the vineyards. It is also well possible that the Canaanites had this custom and that the law concerning this feast is related to that custom. Since this feast was to be celebrated at the central sanctuary, the booths were to be built in its vicinity and acquired (especially in Jerusalem[30]) the character of temporary pilgrim dwellings.

Here Moses says first that the feast must last seven days (to which is added an eighth day with a sacred assembly, Lev. 23:36, 39). The time is the end of the harvest of the grain ("threshing floor"), wine, and oil ("winepress"), i.e., at the end of the agricultural year (Exod. 23:16; 34:22). The grape harvest and the ingathering of the fruit from the trees marked the end of the harvest; but the grain harvest (which had already been celebrated in part in the Feast of Weeks and the Passover) was also celebrated during the Feast of Tabernacles.

"Your Feast" would seem to indicate that this feast was to be considered the feast par excellence (cf. Judg. 21:19; Lev. 23:39, "the festival to the Lord"). Verse 14 again emphasizes the festive nature of the feast, in which also the poor must participate (cf. v. 11); the festivities would, of course, again involve the joyful offering meals.

Verse 15 indicates that this feast must be celebrated at the central sanctuary (v. 15). The joyful nature of the feast is once again accentuated, and the motivation is stated: the Lord's blessing.

d. *Summary* (16:16–17)

16:16–17 *Three times a year all your men must appear before the* Lord *your God at the place he will choose: at the Feast of Unleavened Bread, the Feast of Weeks and the Feast of Tabernacles. No man should appear before the* Lord *empty-handed:* [17]*Each of you must bring a gift in proportion to the way the* Lord *your God has blessed you.*

By way of summary, Moses states that all male Israelites must "see the face of the Lord" three times per year. The traditional reading is, "must appear before the Lord," but in our opinion the reading "see" (*yir'eh*) is more likely: the Israelites must go and see the Lord, i.e., visit Him there where His Name dwells. There is no essential difference between the two readings, except that "see" speaks of God in more anthropomorphic terms.

---

[30]During the time when the tabernacle still stood at Shiloh, the Israelites danced among the vineyards on the occasion of this feast (Judg. 21:21), and the booths were probably built there.

This same demand is made of Israel in Exodus 23:17; 34:23. "All your men": the preceding (16:11, 14) indicates that the women were also expected to attend the feasts. But the obligation rests especially on the men, who, if they have families, should bring their families, including the female members, whenever possible (cf. 1 Sam. 1:4). No age limit is indicated. "No man should appear before the LORD empty-handed": each one must bring offerings and gifts (cf. Exod. 23:15 with reference to the Feast of Unleavened Bread; 34:20). Verse 17 adds that the gift must be in proportion to the blessing received from the Lord (cf. v. 10; also 2 Cor. 8:12; 9:7).

C. LAWS PRIMARILY OF A CIVIL NATURE (16:18–26:19)

After the group of laws that began in 12:2, which were primarily cultic or ceremonial in nature, now follows a collection of primarily civil laws. The first part (16:18–18:22) contains mainly laws concerning officials: judges (16:18–20; 17:8–13), the king (17:14–20), priests (18:1–8), and prophets (18:9–22).

1. The judges (16:18–20)

In 1:13–17 Moses reminded Israel how he appointed judges at Horeb (cf. Exod. 18:13ff.). He now gives further instructions concerning the judges for the time when Israel shall live in Canaan. When the people have settled throughout the land, there must be judges in every town. In 17:8–13 the stipulation is added that difficult cases must be referred to the higher court that sits in the place where the central sanctuary will be located. All this was not implemented immediately and the purpose—a just administration of justice—was never fully realized. The higher court mentioned in 17:8–13 could not be established until there was a central sanctuary (see also comments on 17:8–13). The local administration of justice was generally far from perfect, due in part to the absence of a sufficiently powerful authority so that "everyone did as he saw fit" (Judg. 17:6), and in part to the untrustworthiness of the judges (as the writings of the prophets from the time of the kings show). The function of local judges was assumed in the first place by the elders (the elders of the city took the place formerly occupied by the family elders). Although this law would appear to speak of judges in a more special sense (21:2 mentions elders *and* judges), these judges would naturally be chosen also from among the elders; and Deuteronomy involves the elders in general in the administration of justice (19:12; 21:6, 19-20; 22:18; 25:7ff.). We also hear of "the people" administering justice (1 Kings 21:13) as well as Judges such as Deborah (Judg. 4:4-5) and Samuel (1 Sam. 7:6, 15ff.). When Israel became a kingdom, the king became the supreme judge, who administered justice through personal decisions in specific cases and also through his officials. Furthermore, the priests were from of old the jurists and interpreters of the law (cf. Isa. 28:7; Deut. 21:5; 1 Chron. 23:4; 26:29). We do not know exactly what the spheres of authority of these various functionaries were or how they were related to one another. We are told of a regulation of the administration of justice by David and by Jehoshaphat. David appointed six thousand Levites as "officials and judges" east and west of the Jordan (1 Chron. 23:4; cf. 26:29); these were probably added to the elders to assist the latter with their knowledge of the law so that in larger towns justice was henceforth administered by the elders and Levites. Jehoshaphat appointed judges in each of the "fortified cities" of Judah (2 Chron. 19:5ff.) and also installed a supreme court in Jerusalem (see comments on 17:8-13). The organization of this supreme court may indicate that the local courts also consisted of Levites, priests, and elders.

16:18 *Appoint judges and officials for each of your tribes in every town the* LORD *your God is giving you, and they shall judge the people fairly.*

The appointment of officials and judges (see comments on 1:15) must be (lit.) "according to your tribes" (cf. 1:13). To this extent the ancient genealogical division will thus retain some importance. Nothing is specified as to the number of judges. Moses merely states the principle and emphasizes that the administration of justice must be fair.

16:19-20 *Do not pervert justice or show partiality. Do not accept a bribe, for a bribe blinds the eyes of the wise and twists the words of the righteous.* ²⁰*Follow justice and justice alone, so that you may live and possess the land the* LORD *your God is giving you.*

This great principle of fairness is further elaborated. The verbs are singular and are thus addressed to the people as a whole (although the implementation rests specifically with the judges—but see also the example of the people as judges, 1 Kings 21:13). Justice must not be "perverted" (cf. Exod. 23:6) and it must not be "partial" (lit., "you shall not regard faces"; 1:17); nor must the judges accept bribes (cf. Exod. 23:8). But Israel (through its judges) must "follow" (in the sense of "actively pursue") justice, in order that it "may live" and possess the land ("may live" thus means here in the first place "that you will not perish before you take possession"). Here again life and the enjoyment of Canaan's blessings are tied to the keeping of God's commands. The fact that the taking possession of Canaan is promised as the fruit of obedience indicates that, although verse 18 speaks clearly of the time after the settlement in Canaan, the demand in verse 20 of fair justice applies equally to the period preceding the conquest.

2. Against desecration of the altar and against idolatry (16:21–17:7)

These regulations are of a different character than the immediately preceding and in content are more closely related to chapters 12–13.

16:21–22 *Do not set up any wooden Asherah pole beside the altar you build to the LORD your God, [22]and do not erect a sacred stone, for these the LORD your God hates.*

Beside a Canaanite altar usually stood a wooden pillar or pole (Asherah pole) and a stone pillar ("sacred stone"; see comments on 7:5; cf. also Judg. 3:7; 6:25). The pole was dedicated to Astarte (Asherah), the stone to Baal. The setting up of sacred stones was also known in Israel (Gen. 28:18, Jacob at Bethel; Exod. 24:4, beside the altar!), but in view of the stay in Canaan, the setting up both of a stone pillar and of a wooden pillar beside the altar of the Lord is forbidden; the reason is of course to prevent intermingling with Canaanite paganism. The sacred pole is mentioned a number of times in connection with Israel's apostate cultus (2 Kings 17:10; 18:4; Mic. 5:13; et al.) as characteristic of the mixing with paganism.

17:1 *Do not sacrifice to the LORD your God an ox or a sheep that has any defect or flaw in it, for that would be detestable to him.*

Cf. 15:21; Lev. 22:20ff.

17:2–7 *If a man or woman living among you in one of the towns the LORD gives you is found doing evil in the eyes of the LORD your God in violation of his covenant, [3]and contrary to my command has worshiped other gods, bowing down to them or to the sun or the moon or the stars of the sky, [4]and this has been brought to your attention, then you must investigate it thoroughly. If it is true and it has been proved that this detestable thing has been done in Israel, [5]take the man or woman who has done this evil deed to your city gate and stone* *that person to death. ⁶On the testimony of two or three witnesses a man shall be put to death, but no one shall be put to death on the testimony of only one witness. ⁷The hands of the witnesses must be the first in putting him to death, and then the hands of all the people. You must purge the evil from among you.*

These verses deal with the punishment of idolatry (cf. 13:1–19). While chapter 13 dealt first with the enticement to idolatry (by a prophet or relative) and then with the idolatry of an entire city (13:13–19), here the issue is idolatry on the part of individuals, whether man or woman. "In violation of his covenant": "covenant" is here virtually synonymous with "law," especially the Ten Words (cf. 4:13), of which the first is in view here. "Contrary to my command": the context speaks about the Lord in the third person, but here the Lord Himself speaks. This is possible because Moses is the Lord's mouthpiece, and this brings to the fore the fact that this is *God's* prohibition. "The sun or the moon or the stars of the sky," cf. 4:19. "Investigate it thoroughly," cf. 13:14; since the sin is serious and the punishment severe, great care must be taken not to condemn an innocent person (cf. vv. 6–7). "To your city gate" (v. 5): the citizens came to the open area by the city gate for various functions, e.g., to hold court (21:19) and to carry out the death penalty (21:21; 22:24; Acts 7:58; Heb. 13:12). The latter took place *outside* the gate, both to symbolize the expulsion of the condemned from the community and to prevent the contamination of the city by the dead body (cf. "outside the camp," Lev. 24:14; Num. 15:36; an exception is found in 22:21).

"The man or woman" (v. 5): these words appear to be superfluous and are thought by some to be an erroneous interpolation of a copyist. If they are correct they emphasize that not only a man but also a woman must be punished in this manner.

Verse 6 demands two or three witnesses; this is a general rule of law (19:15; Num. 35:30), which is included here as a reminder because of the seriousness of the matter (cf. v. 4). In order to set up an additional safeguard against false witness, verse 7 stipulates that the witnesses must begin the execution. But then "all the people" (i.e., all the citizens of the city) must participate to demonstrate that they collectively turn against the sinner and his or her sin and absolve themselves of all responsibility. Thus Israel "must purge the evil from among [them]" (cf. 13:5) for the sake of God's honor and the people's welfare (*heil*).

3. The high court at the central sanctuary (17:8–13)

This regulation is a continuation of 6:18–20 (q.v.), which dealt with the judges. Difficult cases must be referred to the supreme court, which will sit there where the central sanctuary will be located. The existence of such a body is not prescribed but is rather assumed (we can say that it is prescribed by implication). The example of such a supreme court was Moses himself, to whom the judges appointed at Sinai were to refer difficult cases (1:18; Exod. 18:26). After the settlement in Canaan, cases could be referred to, e.g., Judges like Deborah and Samuel and later to the king. It is not until King Jehoshaphat that we hear of the appointment of a supreme court (2 Chron. 19:6ff.) that had jurisdiction "in any matter concerning the LORD" and "in any matter concerning the king" (v. 11; i.e., in matters of the cultus and in civil matters). Jehoshaphat charged this court especially with deciding difficult cases that were referred to it from the various towns. It consisted of Levites, priests, and family heads (v. 8). The high priest had supreme authority in matters relating to the cultus, the "leader of the tribe of Judah" in civil matters (v. 11). The Levites served as court officials (v. 11).

17:8–9a *If cases come before your courts that are too difficult for you to judge—whether bloodshed, lawsuits or assaults—take them to the place the LORD your God will choose. ⁹Go to the priests, who are Levites, and to the judge who is in office at that time.*

Israel is addressed—what is demanded here must be implemented by Israel as a nation even though in each court case only a few persons are directly involved: the local judges and the parties to the lawsuit. It is not entirely clear whom Moses has in mind here. It is not his intention to regulate the matter in detail, which is why he addresses Israel as a whole. In any case, it is clear that in difficult cases the parties (and their witnesses) must go to the central sanctuary. We may assume, that, in accord with Moses' intent, the parties have first brought their case before the local judge, who then had to declare himself incompetent to deal with this case. It is also possible that the local judges (or a delegation sent by them), together with the parties to the suit, had to go to the central sanctuary to present the case they had initially investigated. Furthermore, the requirement of verses 10–11 that the decision of the supreme court be accepted as final (with the threat of punishment in v. 12) probably relates in the first instance to the parties to the lawsuit (especially the injured party); but the local judges and authorities were naturally also obligated to abide by the ruling.

"Too difficult for you to judge": there is no question of an appeal of a lower-court decision to the higher court, but only of referral of cases that are too difficult for the local courts. "Whether bloodshed, lawsuits or assaults" (lit., "between blood and blood, between cause and cause, and between stroke and stroke"): in order to render a just verdict the judge must be able to distinguish between the various kinds of manslaughter (whether with malice aforethought or not; cf. 19:4ff.; Exod. 21:12ff.), of disputes, and of assault.

"To the place the LORD your God will choose": the idea that the supreme juridical authority will sit in the place where the central sanctuary is located apparently assumes that the priests will have an important role in this court.

Verse 9 therefore assumes that to this court belong in the first place "the priests, who are Levites," besides whom Moses mentions "the judge who is in office at that time." Even as in 16:18, Moses only gives general guidelines, leaving the specifics to later development. The term "the priests, who are Levites," which is common in Deuteronomy (18:1; 24:8; et al.), apparently includes not only the priests proper, the sons of Aaron, but also the rest of the Levites who were given to the priests as assistants. The term "priest" is thus used in a broader sense.[31] The addition "who are Levites" emphasizes that only the tribe of Levi is called to this "priesthood" (i.e., to the service at the sanctuary in general).

"The judge who is in office at that time" is thus a nonpriestly individual; the singular does not mean that there can only be one secular judge (cf. the plural in 19:17). We can think of the president of a college of judges. The relationship between the priests and the secular judges is not clarified. Moses does not make a distinction between cultic and secular matters as does 2 Chronicles 19:11 (see above); verse 8 mentions only secular cases. But we can also render "or to the judge," which would indicate that in some cases the matter was to be decided by the priests and in others by the secular judge. In general, instruction in and explanation of the law was especially the work of the priests (*torah*, vv. 10–11; cf. Lev. 10:11).

---

[31]Cf. A. v. Hoonacker, *Le sacerdoce lévitique* . . . , (Louvain, 1899), pp. 17–75.

17:9b-13 *Inquire of them and they will give you the verdict. ¹⁰You must act according to the decisions they give you at the place the LORD will choose. Be careful to do everything they direct you to do. ¹¹Act according to the law they teach you and the decisions they give you. Do not turn aside from what they tell you, to the right or to the left. ¹²The man who shows contempt for the judge or for the priest who stands ministering there to the LORD your God must be put to death. You must purge the evil from Israel. ¹³All the people will hear and be afraid, and will not be contemptuous again.*

The court's decision was binding on all. This is stated with the emphatic reminder (v. 10) that the verdict is rendered "at the place the LORD will choose" (lit., "from the place . . ."). The fact that this court sits in the place where God dwells symbolizes in an especially emphatic manner that this court dispenses justice in God's name (cf. 1:17). "They direct you" (v. 10) and "they teach you" (v. 11) are both the same verb (*yarah*, from which is derived *torah*, "law," "instruction"); it refers to the binding exposition and application of the law by the priests.

Verse 12 again indicates the sacrilegious nature of rebellion against the instructions of the priest; the priest "stands ministering there to the LORD your God." The punishment for this contempt of the priest (and equally, of the judge), which is sinful presumption, is nothing less than death. Thus "you must purge the evil from Israel" (cf. 13:5; 17:7) and present a warning to all the people (cf. 13:12).

4. The king (17:14-20)

This regulation concerns the kingship. First, the appointment of a king is mentioned (vv. 14-15), and then the king is given three prohibitions and one all-encompassing command (vv. 16-20). We do not find specifics concerning the king's rights and duties with regard to his subjects, although verse 20 indicates a principle that should govern his conduct toward them. These verses thus do not present anything like a complete law concerning the kingship.

17:14-15 *When you enter the land the LORD your God is giving you and have taken possession of it and settled in it, and you say, "Let us set a king over us like all the nations around us," ¹⁵be sure to appoint over you the king the LORD your God chooses. He must be from among your own brothers. Do not place a foreigner over you, one who is not a brother Israelite.*

It is assumed that Israel, once they have settled in Canaan, might want to have a king. This is *permitted,* which is different from the appointment of judges, which was *commanded* (16:18). "Like all the nations around us": when Israel sees the advantages of having a king, they may want to have one themselves; this is not wrong in itself, but Israel must not lose sight of the distinction between themselves and the other nations. Because the Lord is Israel's King only a theocratic king must reign in Israel, i.e., a king through whom the Lord Himself rules His people. Thus verse 15 stipulates in the first place that the king must be appointed by God Himself. This is indeed what happened in the history of Saul (1 Sam. 9), David (1 Sam. 16), and David's descendants, at least in general (2 Sam. 7:11ff.). Furthermore, the king must be an Israelite (a brother among brothers, cf. v. 20), not a foreigner; the latter would be in conflict with the demands of the theocracy (in which a foreigner would have no part) and thus unworthy of God's people. This "foreigner" does not refer to foreign domination (Israel would not willingly choose this), but rather to someone living in Israel who has managed to gain influence (an example of such a person, albeit not as a candidate for the kingship, would be Shebna, Isa. 22:15). The prohibition on a foreign king appears to assume that human choice can play a role (cf. David's appointment of Solomon, 1 Kings 1); this human element nevertheless always required the well-founded conviction that the king thus appointed was also the one chosen by the Lord (cf. Nathan's actions in 1 Kings 1). The kings of the northern kingdom, in contrast to those of Judah, generally did not fulfill the requirement of verse 15 (Hos. 8:4).

17:16–17 *The king, moreover, must not acquire great numbers of horses for himself or make the people return to Egypt to get more of them, for the* LORD *has told you, "You are not to go back that way again." [17]He must not take many wives, or his heart will be led astray. He must not accumulate large amounts of silver and gold.*

Three things the king must not do: he must not acquire many horses, many wives, or much silver and gold—all this is based on the general principle that the king must guard against "the pride of life" (1 John 2:16 RSV). Cf. Isaiah 2:7, where horses are also mentioned along with silver and gold. "Horses" refers by implication to excessive military preparations, since the horse was used especially in war. Israel and its kings must trust in the Lord, rather than in horses and chariots (cf. Pss. 20:7; 33:16–17; 147:10); this does not exclude military measures per se, and the military use of horses (which was unknown in Israel before Solomon's time) is not forbidden here. But Israel's king must always be aware of Israel's unique position as the Lord's people, and this awareness should also dominate his foreign policy and his military measures, under the special guidance of God through the word of the prophets. Thus Isaiah warned against the alliance with Egypt and the trust in Egypt's horses (30:16; 31:1–2).

The prohibition concerning the acquisition of many horses gains a special flavor by the addition that the king, in order to get more horses, must not send the people back to Egypt, since this would be in direct conflict with the Lord's command. The Scriptures do not record this command but it is apparently known to Moses and to the people (cf. also 28:68). The purport of this verse is not entirely clear to us. Egypt is mentioned several times as a land of many horses and war chariots (Exod. 14:9 et al.; 1 Kings 10:28–29; Isa. 30:16; 31:1–2). This verse may refer to marching against Egypt with an army to bring back many horses after the victory, or (and more probably so, cf. Isa. 30:16; 31:1–2) to an alliance with Egypt, which would obligate Israel's king to supply the Pharaoh with auxiliary troops or soldiers in exchange for horses.

The king must not take many wives, "or his heart will be led astray." The import of this statement is sufficiently exemplified by Solomon (1 Kings 11:1ff.). The prohibition of silver and gold (cf. Isa. 2:7) encompasses the desire for luxury in general. The question may arise whether this law does not in part reflect a different spirit than the story of Solomon's wealth and power in 1 Kings; it is clear that not all that is said about Solomon in 1 Kings is given approval. Specifically, Solomon's having many wives is condemned (1 Kings 11:1ff.). But no opprobrium is attached to his having much silver and gold and many horses and chariots (1 Kings 4:26; 10:26ff.; cf. 2 Chron. 1:14ff.), and 1 Kings 3:13 specifically attributes Solomon's wealth to the Lord. The only solution seems to be that what is stated here is the general rule and that Solomon was an exception based on God's special dispensation, which is then implicit in the revelation of 1 Kings 3:13.

17:18–20 *When he takes the throne of his kingdom, he is to write for himself on a scroll a copy of this law, taken from that of the priests, who are Levites. ¹⁹It is to be with him, and he is to read it all the days of his life so that he may learn to revere the Lord his God and follow carefully all the words of this law and these decrees ²⁰and not consider himself better than his brothers and turn from the* *law to the right or to the left. Then he and his descendants will reign a long time over his kingdom in Israel.*

A command is added to the prohibitions: the king is bound to keep the law. He must have a copy of the law written on a scroll. "This law" encompasses the totality of the laws Moses is presenting to the people, i.e., the main contents of Deuteronomy. Moses thus assumes that "this law" will then have been written down (cf. 31:9). "Taken from that of the priests, who are Levites": the priests are the keepers of the written Law, which was placed next to the ark of the covenant (31:26). "It [the copy of the law] is to be with him," i.e., it is to be at his disposal continuously and he must read in it "all the days of his life"; thus he will "learn to revere the LORD" (an inner disposition) and "follow carefully all the words of this law and these decrees" (the practical application). Both the personal and the official life of the king must be pervaded by God's law. Verse 20 gives as purpose and result of this study of the law that the king will "not consider himself better than his brothers." Without the fear of the Lord, the ruler will fall into pride (cf. also vv. 16–17) and presumption, forgetting that his subject is his brother, and thus, in the spirit of paganism, disdain him and trample his rights (cf. 1 Kings 21:7). The conclusion urges the command upon the king by pointing to the reward: his kingship will be confirmed, not only during his own reign, but also afterward, when his descendants will continue to reign. The final words, "in Israel," in the midst of the Lord's people, summarize the riches of the privilege.

5. The priests (18:1–8)

These verses do not contain a complete law concerning the priesthood, but only regulations regarding the income of the priests (vv. 1–5) and the rights of priests who live elsewhere in the land to serve at the central sanctuary (vv. 6–8).

18:1–2 The priests, who are Levites—indeed the whole tribe of Levi—are to have no allotment or inheritance with Israel. They shall live on the offerings made to the LORD by fire, for that is their inheritance. ²They shall have no inheritance among their brothers; the LORD is their inheritance, as he promised them.

"The priests, who are Levites": this expression, common in Deuteronomy (see comments on 17:9), uses "priests" in a broader sense to include not only the priests who are authorized to bring offerings but also their "helpers," who are elsewhere called Levites. None of these (for the sake of clarification is added "the whole tribe of Levi") shall own any land in Canaan (cf. 10:9; 12:12; see also below, comments on v. 8). They must live on the portion of the offerings allotted to them. "For that is their inheritance," literally, "and his inheritance." The literal sense of the Hebrew expression would appear to refer to "the Lord's inheritance," which usually designates Israel (4:20; 9:26, 29). Some versions take "inheritance" in a somewhat different sense: "his [the Lord's] rightful dues" (RSV), "his dues" (JB), "and other sacrifices" (TEV). The NIV rendering is more free but is in agreement with the idea expressed in verse 2: "The LORD is their inheritance" (cf. Num. 18:20).[32] What land ownership is to the other tribes, the Lord is to the tribe of Levi: the source of their income.

18:3–5 *This is the share due the priests from the people who sacrifice a bull or a sheep: the shoulder, the jowls and the inner parts. 4You are to give them the firstfruits of your grain, new wine and oil, and the first wool from the shearing of your sheep, 5for the LORD your God has chosen them and their descendants out of all your tribes to stand and minister in the LORD's name always.*

Verse 3 states that those who sacrifice a bull or a sheep must give to the priests the shoulder, the jowls, and the inner parts (the stomach, specifically the rennet–stomach, the fourth stomach of ruminants, apparently chosen because of its fattiness). Elsewhere the priests' portion of the fellowship offerings is defined as "the breast that is waved and the thigh that is presented" (Lev. 7:34; cf. Exod. 29:27; Lev. 10:14; Num. 6:20; 18:18), which is considerably more than what is prescribed here (due to the inclusion of "the breast that is waved"). If the "sacrifice" of verse 3 is the same as the fellowship offerings of Leviticus 7:34, then we would have to assume (unless we accept a contradiction) either that the earlier regulation of Leviticus 7 is modified here, or that the two regulations are complementary. But it is questionable whether both regulations refer to the same thing. Rabbinic Judaism referred verse 3 not to the offerings but to the livestock that was slaughtered for profane use; in more recent times the solution has

---

[32]The LXX reading also merits consideration; it omits "and," so that we can translate, "the offerings made to the Lord by fire are his inheritance, which they shall eat."

also been sought in this direction. [33] The word "sacrifice" then would be rendered "slaughtered" (cf. Deut. 12:15, 21). Verse 4 adds the firstfruits (cf. Num. 18:12-13); the proportion is not specified but according to the Talmud it had to be at least one-sixtieth of the yield; the "first wool" is mentioned only here. Concerning the manner in which they were to be presented at the sanctuary, see 26:1-10.

Verse 5 gives the reason: the Lord has chosen them (lit., "him") and their descendants from all the tribes of Israel to minister at the sanctuary (cf. 10:8).

18:6-8 *If a Levite moves from one of your towns anywhere in Israel where he is living, and comes in all earnestness to the place the LORD will choose, 7he may minister in the name of the LORD his God like all his fellow Levites who serve there in the presence of the LORD. 8He is to share equally in their benefits, even though he has received money from the sale of family possessions.*

These verses assume a situation where the Levites live throughout the land and only some of them live in the place where the central sanctuary stands or near it and minister there (in rotation). The issue here is the rights of the Levites who live farther away from the sanctuary. The term "Levite," like "priests" in verse 1, is to be understood in a broad sense and is not limited to those who performed "helping" tasks. The reason that "Levite" rather than "priest" is used here is that those who lived far from the sanctuary and could thus not participate in the central cultus are in view. They are given the right to change their status; the Levite could come to "the place the LORD will choose," where the central sanctuary is, and has the same right to minister there as his brothers who live there; he must share in their benefits. We must keep in mind that only a general principle is given here, not a detailed regulation. The intent is not that all those who came to the sanctuary were to be involved immediately in the work at the sanctuary, but rather that they were to be included in the list from which the various groups of Levites were called, in turn, to do duty.

Nor do these verses say that all Levites had the same rights, since this would eliminate the distinction made elsewhere between priests and Levites in the narrower sense of the terms. All that is stated here is that the Levites (of whatever rank) who came to the central sanctuary

---

[33]A. v. Hoonacker, *La sacerdoce lévitique*, pp. 416ff.; for yet another view, see Keil.

have the same rights as those who live near the sanctuary. We may assume that this would mean that each was given rights in accordance with his appropriate position or status—the one as priest, authorized to bring offerings, the other as helper. The general terms "minister" and "serve in the presence of the LORD" (v. 7) apply to both groups.

"Where he is living" (v. 6): the verb implies "sojourning," "living as a stranger," indicating that the Levites do not own land (cf. vv. 1–2). "Even though he has received money from the sale of family possessions": the meaning of this phrase is not entirely clear, but the NIV rendering makes sense. Even though the Levites were not given land in Canaan, they could own property. The towns that were assigned to the Levites and the land around them cannot be in view here, since these could not be sold (see comments on 12:12; cf. Lev. 25:34). But this was not true of their houses (v. 33) and other possessions. Furthermore, it was not impossible nor forbidden for a Levite to acquire land that could be sold (cf. Jer. 32:7; Jeremiah belonged to a priestly family).[34]

6. Against pagan practices; the prophet (18:9–22)

This section is closely related to what was said earlier about the judges, the king, and the priests, since it deals with the prophet (vv. 15ff.; vv. 9–14 may be considered an introduction).

18:9–14 *When you enter the land the LORD your God is giving you, do not learn to imitate the detestable ways of the nations there. [10]Let no one be found among you who sacrifices his son or daughter in the fire, who practices divination or*

---

[34]The critical approach generally connects these verses with the statement in 2 Kings 23:8–9 that King Josiah, when he destroyed the high places in Judah, allowed the priests of these high places, whose work and source of income had been taken away, to come to Jerusalem. These priests were not allowed to serve at the altar and received only the right to eat unleavened bread with their brothers. These verses then are thought to refer to the same event but would allow the priests of the high places to serve at the altar. Second Kings 23:8–9 then would show that these broader rights were not put into practice (probably because of opposition on the part of the priests of Jerusalem). However, these verses make no reference to the priests of the high places; it would indeed be strange if the lawgiver would give them the same rights as the priests of Jerusalem. Furthermore, these verses speak of the Levites from all of Israel, while 2 Kings 23:8–9 speaks only of the priests of the high places from Judah (the priests of the high places in Israel were slaughtered on their own altars by Josiah, 2 Kings 23:20; cf. 13:2). Furthermore, our verses refer to a voluntary move, while 2 Kings 23:8–9 speaks of a forced move. (Cf. Van Hoonacker, *Le sacerdoce lévitique,* pp. 184ff.)

sorcery, interprets omens, engages in witchcraft, ¹¹or casts spells, or who is a medium or spiritist or who consults the dead. ¹²Anyone who does these things is detestable to the LORD, and because of these detestable practices the LORD your God will drive out those nations before you. ¹³You must be blameless before the LORD your God.

¹⁴The nations you will dispossess listen to those who practice sorcery or divination. But as for you, the LORD your God has not permitted you to do so.

By way of introduction to what will be said later about the true prophet, these verses deal with pagan surrogates: divination, sorcery, etc. Moses adds a prohibition on human sacrifice, which is directly related to verses 15–22, and is also elsewhere mentioned as the ultimate pagan abomination (2 Kings 17:17; 2 Chron. 33:6).

"When you enter the land": the lawgiver again speaks specifically of the time after the conquest (cf. 17:14; 12:29). "The nations there" refers to the Canaanites. This is a more detailed statement of the earlier warning against following the detestable practices of the Canaanites, including human sacrifices in 12:30–31 (q.v.). Various forms of divination and sorcery are listed (cf. Exod. 22:18; Lev. 19:26, 31; 20:6, 27; Isa. 8:19; et al.).

"Who practices divination": the Hebrew stem is used in Ezekiel 21:21–22 for divination by means of casting lots (specifically by means of throwing down arrows), but it is also used for divination in a broader sense (e.g., consulting spirits, 1 Sam. 28:8; cf. also Num. 23:23; 1 Sam. 6:2; 2 Kings 17:17; Isa. 3:2; Mic. 3:7). "Sorcery": we prefer the sense "cloud reader," i.e., one who makes predictions on the basis of the shape and direction of the clouds. "Engages in witchcraft" refers to someone who is supposed to have access to supernatural powers to influence the course of events. "Casts spells": the word is used in Psalm 58:5 of snake charming; in this context it may be preferable to think of someone who drives out evil spirits. "Who is a medium or a spiritist": the Old Testament mentions several times the calling up of the spirit of a deceased person in order to ask about the future (1 Sam. 28:3ff.; 2 Kings 21:6; Isa. 8:19). But other spirits (demons) could also be consulted. "Who consults the dead": this refers to a different method of establishing contact with the dead, perhaps by visiting their graves (Isa. 65:4).

"Anyone who does these things" (v. 12) is detestable to the Lord. And the Lord will drive out the Canaanites before Israel because they practice these detestable things. Therefore, how foolish and irresponsible it would be for Israel to imitate these practices! Israel is called to better things (v. 13); they must be blameless before the Lord their God. They must keep His commandments and live as their relationship with Him demands. This is further elaborated in verse 14. The nations listen to the practitioners of sorcery and divination (see v. 10), but the Lord (*"your* God," emphatic) does not allow Israel to do this. This does not mean that the Lord has given the other nations permission to do so but rather that He has allowed them to go their own way (Acts 14:16). Israel, on the other hand, must realize that it has the Lord as its God and that it is a people holy to Him. The sequel indicates that Israel has been given something much better.

18:15 *The LORD your God will raise up for you a prophet like me from among your own brothers. You must listen to him.*

Over against the practices through which the nations seek to gain supernatural knowledge, Moses places the Lord's gift to Israel: the light of prophecy (cf. Isa. 8:19–20). The Lord will raise up "a prophet" in Israel. According to Peter (Acts 3:22–23) and Stephen (Acts 7:37) this was fulfilled in Christ (cf. also John 4:25).[35] But this does not eliminate the possibility that this verse refers in the first instance to "common" human prophets. Three considerations argue in favor of this view. First, the contrast between verse 15 and verses 9:14: Israel must not seek help from diviners, etc., for the Lord will make sure that there will be a prophet when needed; second, the larger context of this section deals with other functionaries (judges, king, priests); and third, what is said in verses 20–22 about the false prophet and the way in which Israel may discern between the true and the false prophet.

We are therefore of the opinion that this section refers in the first place to the prophets the Lord will raise up in Israel in the course of the centuries. The singular "a prophet" must then be taken in a collective sense, or better yet, in a distributive sense: in each given situation there will be a prophet to whom you must listen. Like the king (17:15), the prophet must be "from among your own brothers," here in special contrast to the foreign diviners and sorcerers. "The LORD your God will raise up for you": the true prophet is called by the Lord and is a manifestation of the Lord's care for His people. To such a prophet Israel must listen—not to the diviners. See also comments on verse 18.

---

[35]Jesus' statement that Moses wrote of Him (John 5:46; cf. John 1:45) may refer to this verse (among others); but this is not necessarily the case, since the statement may also refer to Genesis 3:15 and other passages.

18:16–20 *For this is what you asked of the* LORD *your God at Horeb on the day of the assembly when you said, "Let us not hear the voice of the* LORD *our God nor see this great fire anymore, or we will die."*
¹⁷The LORD *said to me: "What they say is good. ¹⁸I will raise up for them a prophet like you from among their brothers; I will put my words in his mouth, and he will tell them everything I command him. ¹⁹If anyone does not listen to my words that the prophet speaks in my name, I myself will call him to account. ²⁰But a prophet who presumes to speak in my name anything I have not commanded him to say, or a prophet who speaks in the name of other gods, must be put to death."*

In verse 17 Moses points to what happened at Mount Horeb "on the day of the assembly" (cf. 9:10; 10:4; cf. Deut. 5:23ff.; Exod. 20:15ff.). Israel asked that the Lord no longer speak to them directly, but only through Moses, and the Lord approved (v. 19).

What follows presents a problem (vv. 18–20). The *form* would indicate that this is a continuation of what according to verse 17 the Lord said at Horeb (the Lord is still the speaker and speaks about Israel in the third person and to Moses in the second, which is in agreement with v. 17, but differs from v. 15). But the words of verses 18–20 are not found in the narrative of Deuteronomy 5:23ff. nor in Exodus 20:15ff. Nor would we expect them there, since in those sections the Lord did not speak of what He would do later in Canaan but rather of the manner in which He would further reveal Himself at Horeb.

On the other hand, the *content* of verses 18–20 constitutes a logical continuation of verse 15. It is possible that Moses presents the revelation given here (concerning the prophets as mediators of revelation) as already given at Horeb, because it was implicit in the revelation (concerning Moses as the mediator of revelation) given there. If it is felt that this explanation is too free and that the words should be taken in an entirely literal sense, then we must understand verses 18–20 to be a revelation presented here by Moses for the first time, which he received at Horeb in connection with what is recorded in Deuteronomy 5:23ff., which certainly is not possible.

In any case, the meaning of "like me" of verse 15, which is restated here as "like you," becomes clear in this context. Even as the Lord at Horeb used Moses as the mediator of His revelation, so He will in the future raise up prophets as mediators of His revelation. This is also stated explicitly in the words, "I will put my words in his mouth [cf. Num. 22:38; 2 Sam. 23:2; Jer. 1:9; 5:14] and he will tell them everything I command him"—the classical description of a prophet. If this is the purport of "like you," then it is also clear that this does not preclude the differences in degree between Moses and the later prophets, and that there is thus no conflict with Numbers 12:6–8 (cf. Heb. 3:2) and Deuteronomy 34:10. The characterization of the prophet as a mediator, like Moses, of God's revelation also implies that the prophet's task does not only involve foretelling the future (even though this is of importance; cf. v. 22 and the contrast with the diviners, etc. of vv. 10–11), but also includes giving voice to the will and commandments of the Lord.

These verses thus speak in the first place of merely human prophets. But we should keep in mind that they point in the final analysis to the supreme Prophet and Teacher, Jesus Christ. This is warranted by Acts 3:22–23; 7:37 and also follows from the fact that all of the Old Testament prophetism points to Him in whom it finds its fulfillment and completion. In Him the words "like you" are fulfilled in a higher sense (cf. Heb. 3:2) and even surpassed (Heb 3:5–6). Finally, the fact that the word "prophet" is used in the singular here is not accidental; we may see in this a Spirit-given pointer to the One in whom this statement finds its complete fulfillment.

Verse 19 adds that he who does not listen to the words of the prophet (which are thus the Lord's words) will be "called to account" by the Lord (lit., "I will require it of him"). By the same token the false prophet, whether he has falsely spoken in the Lord's name or in the name of other gods (cf. 13:1ff.), must die.

18:21–22 *You may say to yourselves, "How can we know when a message has not been spoken by the* LORD*?" ²²If what a prophet proclaims in the name of the* LORD *does not take place or come true, that is a message the* LORD *has not spoken. That prophet has spoken presumptuously. Do not be afraid of him.*

Here Moses himself speaks again. These verses are closely related to the immediately preceding, however; what was stated in verse 19 raises the question how the word of the prophet who speaks falsely in the name of the Lord may be discerned (of course, this question would not come up in connection with those prophets who speak in the name of other gods). The criterion given is that the words of the false prophets will not be fulfilled. Note that no general characteristic is given here that can always be used to distinguish false from true prophecy. In the first place, verse 22 only deals with predictions (and then only with predictions whose fulfillment can be verified), whereas the words of the prophets were not limited to predicting the future (cf. v. 18). Furthermore, the *non*fulfillment of the prophecy is proof that it is false, but the fulfillment of a prophecy is not therefore guarantee of its genuineness. The possibility that the announcements of false prophets will be fulfilled is explicitly assumed in 13:1ff. While those verses refer to the prophets of other gods, and specifically to the announcement of miraculous signs, there is no reason why this would not also be true of false prophets and of predictions in a more general sense. The idea that fulfillment or nonfulfillment of prophecy is the criterion par excellence for distinguishing true from false prophecy is not found elsewhere in the Scriptures.[36] Our text only gives a criterion that applies in certain cases but that, because it is easily applied and the cases in question would not be rare, is nevertheless of great practical value. "Do not be afraid of him": do not be intimidated by his speaking in the Lord's name and his further pretense of importance—do your duty and kill him (cf. v. 20).

7. The cities of refuge (19:1–13)

For this section, cf. 4:41–43; Exodus 21:12–14; Numbers 35:9–34; for its implementation, cf. Joshua 20. The practice of blood revenge, which was also known in Israel, is not abolished by this law but restricted (cf. comments on 4:41ff.).

According to Numbers 35:14 there were to be three cities of refuge east of the Jordan and three west of the Jordan. Moses had already set aside the three cities east of the Jordan (Deut. 4:41–43); here the command of Numbers 35:14 is repeated for Canaan proper (cf. v. 1) and a command is added to set aside three more cities if territory expands (vv. 8–9).

19:1–3 *When the LORD your God has destroyed the nations whose land he is giving you, and when you have driven them out and settled in their towns and houses, ²then set aside for yourselves three cities centrally located in the land the LORD your God is giving you to possess. ³Build roads to them and divide into three parts the land the LORD your God is giving you as an inheritance, so that anyone who kills a man may flee there.*

Verse 1 indicates that the command to set aside three cities concerns Canaan proper, the land west of the Jordan (cf. 12:29), since the destruction of the nations is described as still future, while the enemies

---

[36]Concerning this entire question, cf. G. Ch. Aalders, *De Profeten des Ouden Verbonds* (Kampen, 1918), pp. 224–235 and my *Het Godswoord der Profeten* 3:179-88.

east of the Jordan had already been defeated (ch. 2–3). "Build roads to them": the cities of refuge must be easily accessible (the objection that a good road would help the pursuer as much as the pursued is not valid, since a poor road and a consequently longer journey would certainly increase the possibility of the pursuer overtaking the pursued). The land must be divided into three regions, each with a city of refuge.

19:4–7 *This is the rule concerning the man who kills another and flees there to save his life—one who kills his neighbor unintentionally, without malice aforethought. ⁵For instance, a man may go into the forest with his neighbor to cut wood, and as he swings his ax to fell a tree, the head may fly off and hit his neighbor and kill him. That man may flee to one of these cities and save his life. ⁶Otherwise, the avenger of blood might pursue him in a rage, overtake him if the distance is too great, and kill him even though he is not deserving of death, since he did it to his neighbor without malice aforethought. ⁷This is why I command you to set aside for yourselves three cities.*

Concerning the purpose of the cities of refuge, see comments on 4:42 and Numbers 35:11ff. "Pursue him in a rage": the avenger's zeal and desire for revenge could lead to injustice. "If the distance is too great": if there was not a city of refuge in each part of the land, there might not be a city of refuge close enough for the killer to reach in time.

19:8–9 *If the LORD your God enlarges your territory, as he promised on oath to your forefathers, and gives you the whole land he promised them, ⁹because you carefully follow all these laws I command you today—to love the LORD your God and to walk always in his ways—then you are to set aside three more cities.*

Three further cities must be added to the three cities of refuge west of the Jordan if Israel's territory expands (bringing the total to nine, since the three cities set aside east of the Jordan are left out of consideration here). The expansion of the territory would involve the Lord's giving Israel "the whole land" so that it would stretch to the farthest borders mentioned in the promise (from the river of Egypt to the Euphrates, Gen. 15:18; cf. 1:7; 11:24). But Moses makes it clear that this part of the promise will be fulfilled only if Israel carefully follows "these laws" and loves the Lord (cf. 11:22ff.). This is thus also the reason why this part of the promise was never fulfilled and these last three cities of refuge were never needed. Under David and Solomon Israel's sphere of influence did extend to the Euphrates, but this did not mean that the cities in the territory farther east were inhabited by Israelites; there was thus no reason to set aside cities of refuge there.

19:10 *Do this so that innocent blood will not be shed in your land, which the LORD your God is giving you as your inheritance, and so that you will not be guilty of bloodshed.*

This verse states the purpose not only of the two preceding verses but of the entire institution of the cities of refuge. They must prevent innocent blood from being shed (i.e., the blood of the person who killed unintentionally), since that would bring blood-guilt on the people.

19:11–13 *But if a man hates his neighbor and lies in wait for him, assaults and kills him, and then flees to one of these cities, ¹²the elders of his town shall send for him, bring him back from the city, and hand him over to the avenger of blood to die. ¹³Show him no pity. You must purge from Israel the guilt of shedding innocent blood, so that it may go well with you.*

A man who kills with malice aforethought, on the other hand, is not allowed to seek refuge in one of these cities (cf. Exod. 21:14). The "elders" (the local authorities) of his own town must bring him back from the city of refuge and make sure that he receives his punishment. This assumes that he has first been tried and sentenced (by the entire assembly, Num. 35:24). The sentence must be carried out by the avenger of blood, who in case of intentional murder had to do what in other situations was the responsibility of the people (13:9; 21:21; 22:21; et al.) or of the authorities (22:18–19; 25:2–3). Thus the guilt of shedding innocent blood will be purged from Israel, "so that it may go well with you"—the promise of well-being (*heil*) and blessing is here again used as a means of encouraging the implementation of the command; thus, by implication, Israel's well-being is the purpose behind the giving of the command.

8. Moving boundary stones; witnesses (19:14–21)

19:14 *Do not move your neighbor's boundary stone set up by your predecessors in the inheritance you receive in the land the LORD your God is giving you to possess.*

This regulation makes it clear that Moses proclaims laws not only for the immediate but also for the distant future. He speaks of boundaries established by those in the past and thus addresses generations in the future. Moses prohibits the moving of "boundary stones," markers that defined the boundaries of a field (many such markers have been found in Babylonia and other areas). The moving of such stones is classified in 27:17 as one of the crimes that falls under the curse and is also elsewhere characterized as a serious sin (Job 24:2; Prov. 22:28; 23:10; Isa. 5:8). "Set up by your predecessors": what has been established in the distant past gives rights that must be honored as holy.

19:15–21 *One witness is not enough to convict a man accused of any crime or offense he may have committed. A matter must be established by the testimony of two or three witnesses.*

¹⁶If a malicious witness takes the stand to accuse a man of a crime, ¹⁷the two men involved in the dispute must stand in the presence of the LORD before the priests and the judges who are in office at the time. ¹⁸The judges must make a thorough investigation, and if the witness proves to be a liar, giving false testimony against his brother, ¹⁹then do to him as he intended to do to his brother. You must purge the evil from among you. ²⁰The rest of the people will hear of this and be afraid, and never again will such an evil thing be done among you. ²¹Show no pity: life for life, eye for eye, tooth for tooth, hand for hand, foot for foot.

Verses 15–21 deal with witnesses, not only witnesses who provide proof but also those who accuse (cf. v. 16). Verse 15 states the rule that one witness is not sufficient to prove guilt;[37] two or three are required (cf. John 8:17; 2 Cor. 13:1; Heb. 10:28). A similar rule is also found in 17:6 and in Numbers 35:30, where it relates specifically to the death penalty. Here the rule covers any kind of crime where witnesses are involved.

In verses 16–17 it is clear that the "witness" is not only one who gives testimony in a case, but also the accuser himself. "If a malicious witness takes the stand": this is a somewhat elliptic statement, since it could generally not be known that a witness was "malicious" until the case had been investigated: the idea is that the procedure described here must be followed in order to establish whether a witness was giving false testimony. "The two men involved in the dispute," i.e., the accused and the "witness" (in this case the one witness who is the accuser). "In the presence of the LORD before the priests and the judges": before the supreme court in the place where the central sanctuary stands (17:8–9). If the accusation turns out to be false the

---

[37]"One witness is not enough to convict a man" does not mean that a case brought by one accuser should not be investigated (cf. v. 17; but cf. also 1 Tim. 5:19).

accuser is to receive the punishment the accused would have received if the accusation had been true (there is a similar rule in the Code of Hammurabi, 3-4). Thus Israel must "purge the evil" from among them (cf. 13:55 17:7), with the secondary purpose of deterring others (cf. 13:11). Israel must guard against weakness and apply the *jus talionis* (the law of equal retribution, already implied in v. 19) in all its strictness (Exod. 21:24-25; Lev. 24:20).

9. Military laws: before the battle (20:1-9)

The regulations in these verses, as well as in verses 10-20, relate in part to the wars that Israel would have to wage later, after they settled in Canaan (cf. v. 6, "vineyard," vv. 10, 15; but cf. v. 16).

20:1-4 *When you go to war against your enemies and see horses and chariots and an army greater than yours, do not be afraid of them, because the LORD your God, who brought you up out of Egypt, will be with you.* ²*When you are about to go into battle, the priest shall come forward and address the army.* ³*He shall say: "Hear, O Israel, today you are going into battle against your enemies. Do not be fainthearted or afraid; do not be terrified or give way to panic before them.* ⁴*For the LORD your God is the one who goes with you to fight for you against your enemies to give you victory."*

By way of introduction verse 1 states the general thought that Israel must not be afraid of their enemies. Horses and chariots were important in the armies of the nations around Israel and inspired fear in Israel when they began the conquest (Josh. 11:4-6). But Israel must trust in the Lord (cf. Isa. 31:3).

Verses 2-4 establish that before the battle the priest must speak to the army and encourage them not to fear (cf. 1:29-30). "When you are about to go into battle": after the army has gathered and before they are arranged in battle formation (cf. v. 9). "The priest": there must always be a priest with the army (cf. Phinehas in the battle against the Amalekites, Num 31:6; Hophni and Phinehas with the ark, 1 Sam. 4:4, 11; Saul's unauthorized offering before the battle, 1 Sam. 13:9ff.; the priestly oracle, 2 Sam. 5:19, 23; the priests with the trumpets, 2 Chron. 13:12, cf. Num. 10:8-9).

20:5-8 *The officers shall say to the army:* "*Has anyone built a new house and not dedicated it? Let him go home, or he may die in battle and someone else may dedicate it.* ⁶*Has anyone planted a vineyard and not begun to enjoy it? Let him go home, or he may die in battle and someone else enjoy it.* ⁷*Has anyone* *become pledged to a woman and not married her? Let him go home, or he may die in battle and someone else marry her." ⁸Then the officers shall add, "Is any man afraid or fainthearted? Let him go home so that his brothers will not become disheartened too."*

Then follow several grounds for exemption from military duty and the dismissal of the fearful. This has been taken by some as reflecting impractical idealism that would make it impossible to wage war. But the modern military also allows exemptions, and the armies of antiquity were generally much smaller. Also, in Israel's case the victory belonged to the Lord (v. 1). An example of the implementation of these regulations is found in 1 Maccabees 3:55ff.

Verses 5–7 list the grounds for exemption, which must be presented by the officers (cf. 1:15) to the army before further preparations are made for the battle. Anyone who has recently built a house or planted a vineyard and anyone who is "engaged to be married" is exempt from battle, to prevent that he would not be able to enjoy the benefits if he were to fall in battle. These exemptions are not based on an abstract concept of human dignity and the correlative notion of human rights, but rather on something else. In Deuteronomy the promise of earthly blessing stands in the foreground, a blessing Israel would receive on the basis of election and of the covenant, if they are obedient to God's will. These regulations seek to prevent that anyone would miss out on his share in the blessing by falling in battle.[38] In the case of the man pledged to a woman, the lawgiver also has the woman in mind (cf. 24:5). Furthermore, this exemption was important for the continuation of the family (cf. also 25:5ff.).

"Dedicated" (v. 5): the emphasis falls on his having lived in the house for a period of time (according to Josephus one year; see below v. 7) rather than on the dedication. "Vineyard" (v. 6): the Hebrew word can refer to both oliveyards and vineyards. "Begun to enjoy it," literally, "has not enjoyed the fruit of it": this was the fruit of the fifth year, since the fruit of the first three years was not to be used and the fruit of the fourth year was to be given to the Lord (Lev. 19:23ff.). "Become pledged to a woman" (v. 7): the pledge or "engagement," established by the giving of the *mohar,* the wedding money or bride price, by the prospective groom to the father of the bride and accepted

---

[38]Cf. G. von Rad, *Das Gottesvolk im Deuteronomium* (Stuttgart, 1929), pp. 37ff., 48.

by the latter. In 24:5 this exemption is extended to one year after the marriage.

Also, those who are "afraid or fainthearted" (v. 8; cf. Judg. 7:3) are exempt; the regulation is almost an exhortation to leave, since they would be a danger to the spirit of the army—fear is infectious. Anyone who is afraid in spite of the exhortation of verse 3 does not belong in an army that must derive its strength from trust in the Lord.

20:9 *When the officers have finished speaking to the army, they shall appoint commanders over it.*

Only after all this has been taken care of can the army be organized and officers (cf. 1:15) be appointed.

10. Military laws: treatment of enemies and of fruit trees (20:10–20)

20:10–18 *When you march up to attack a city, make its people an offer of peace. ¹¹If they accept and open their gates, all the people in it shall be subject to forced labor and shall work for you. ¹²If they refuse to make peace and they engage you in battle, lay siege to that city. ¹³When the LORD your God delivers it into your hand, put to the sword all the men in it. ¹⁴As for the women, the children, the livestock and everything else in the city, you may take these as plunder for yourselves. And you may use the plunder the LORD your God gives you from your enemies. ¹⁵This is how you are to treat all the cities that are at a distance from you and do not belong to the nations nearby.*

¹⁶However, in the cities of the nations the LORD your God is giving you as an inheritance, do not leave alive anything that breathes. ¹⁷Completely destroy them—the Hittites, Amorites, Canaanites, Perizzites, Hivites and Jebusites— as the LORD your God has commanded you. ¹⁸Otherwise, they will teach you to follow all the detestable things they do in worshiping their gods, and you will sin against the LORD your God.

The treatment of enemies is regulated, first of enemies that live far away (vv. 10–14) and then of the Canaanites (vv. 16–20).

Verses 10–11 stipulate that before a city is attacked it must first be offered "peace," i.e., must be given the opportunity to surrender voluntarily (v. 11; cf. the Assyrian commander and Jerusalem, 2 Kings 18:31–32). If the city accepts the offer, the inhabitants shall be subject to forced labor for Israel (cf. Exod. 1:11; Josh. 9:21, 27; 1 Kings 9:20–21), but their lives will be spared.

Verses 12–14 then state what must be done if the city rejects the offer and is captured by Israel after a siege: all the men of the city must be put to death with the sword and the women, children, livestock, and everything else is to become Israel's property. Verse 15 notes that the preceding applies to cities "that are at a distance from you" but not to those of the nations nearby, of the Canaanites; verses 16–20 indicate how these must be dealt with. The Israelites must kill "anything that breathes," which refers in the first place to the people of the city (cf. Josh. 11–14) and includes the women and children. "Completely destroy" (strike with the ban, *cherem*), cf. 2:34; 3:6; 13:16. "The Hittites. . .": cf. 7:1, where the Girgashites are also mentioned, bringing the list to seven nations. On "as the Lord your God has commanded you," see 7:2. Verse 18 states the reason for the more severe treatment: the danger that Israel will participate in their idolatry (cf. 7:1ff.; 12:31).

20:19–20 *When you lay siege to a city for a long time, fighting against it to capture it, do not destroy its trees by putting an ax to them, because you can eat their fruit. Do not cut them down. Are the trees of the field people, that you should besiege them? 20However, you may cut down trees that you know are not fruit trees and use them to build siege works until the city at war with you falls.*

When siege is laid to a city, the fruit trees must not be destroyed. The phrase "for a long time" is added because this would be more likely to happen after a long siege, especially because of increasing embitterment. A practical reason for the prohibition is that the fruit must be available as food for the besieger. The added remark that trees are not people that can be fought indicates that the lawgiver also condemns senseless destruction and the coarsening that often accompanies war. Verse 20 then allows trees other than fruit trees to be cut down and used in the siege effort.

11. Atonement for an unsolved murder (21:1–9)

Blood that is shed by a murderer calls for retribution (Gen. 4:10), and the murderer must therefore be put to death (cf. comments on 19:11ff.). If the murderer is unknown, then the unavenged blood guilt rests on the people (cf. 19:10) unless they seek atonement.

21:1–2 *If a man is found slain, lying in a field in the land the Lord your God is giving you to possess, and it is not known who killed him, 2your elders and judges shall go out and measure the distance from the body to the neighboring towns.*

The case is presented that a body is found in the field and it is not known who committed the murder (if the body was found in a city, the first part of what follows would of course not be applicable). In this case, it must first be determined which city is nearest to the scene of the murder; this must be done by the elders and judges of the nearest cities. The elders are the official representatives of the people and the judges represent the law. Together they determine (by measurement if necessary) which city is nearest. This city becomes responsible and must therefore seek atonement.

21:3–4 *Then the elders of the town nearest the body shall take a heifer that has never been worked and has never worn a yoke ⁴and lead her down to a valley that has not been plowed or planted and where there is a flowing stream. There in the valley they are to break the heifer's neck.*

To make atonement, the elders of the nearest city must take a heifer to a place that fulfills certain requirements, and there break its neck. This is not an offering (in which case it would have been a sin offering), since that required sacrifice and the pouring out of blood and would have to be done on an altar and in a sacred place. The intent here is apparently that the animal (symbolically) takes the place of the murderer. It must be a heifer that has never worked (v. 3), i.e., has never been used for any other purpose, which emphasizes the special nature and importance of the ceremony (cf. 15:19; Num. 19:2). Its neck must be broken in a place that has not been plowed or planted (v. 4), which also emphasizes the importance of the ceremony. Furthermore, this place must be in a valley with running water in connection with the washing of hands in verse 6, a symbolic act by which the elders remove any guilt or suspicion that may rest on them; the flowing stream must provide the water for this act but it must also carry away the blood guilt that was washed off in the water.

21:5 *The priests, the sons of Levi, shall step forward, for the Lᴏʀᴅ your God has chosen them to minister and to pronounce blessings in the name of the Lᴏʀᴅ and to decide all cases of dispute and assault.*

The "priests, the sons of Levi" are also involved; the expression refers to members of the tribe of Levi in general (cf. 18:1). They have no special function but must be present because the Lord has chosen them to minister (to carry out the cultus) and to bless in His name (cf. 10:8; 18:5). In legal disputes, especially in cases of assault, mistreatment, etc., their decision as to the manner in which atonement must be made for the perpetrated evil is final. They are God's representatives and represent (in a different sense than the judges of v. 2) justice. Their presence is thus required to give validity to the ceremony.

21:6–9 *Then all the elders of the town nearest the body shall wash their hands over the heifer whose neck was broken in the valley, ⁷and they shall declare: "Our hands did not shed this blood, nor did our eyes see it done. ⁸Accept this atonement for your people Israel, whom you have redeemed, O LORD, and do not hold your people guilty of the blood of an innocent man." And the bloodshed will be atoned for. ⁹So you will purge from yourselves the guilt of shedding innocent blood, since you have done what is right in the eyes of the LORD.*

The elders then must wash their hands (cf. Pss. 26:6; 73:13; Matt. 27:24) to remove symbolically anything that may attach to them (perhaps the appearance or suspicion of blood guilt, although it is better to think of the blood guilt itself, v. 8, since this guilt rests in a ceremonial sense on the land as a result of the murder and especially on the nearest city represented by the elders). They must wash their hands over the heifer whose neck was broken because they cannot rid themselves of the blood guilt arbitrarily but only in the framework of God's provision, in which the symbolic substitution of the murderer by the heifer plays an important role. They must declare their innocence while doing this by saying that their hands did not shed "this blood" (the blood of the murder victim) and that their eyes did not see the murder take place (since they would have had to come to the aid of the victim or provide information that would have led to the conviction of the murderer). This declaration of innocence does not contradict the washing off of the guilt but indicates that the guilt that rests on them is not moral guilt—which is the reason why it can be washed away in this manner.

Verse 8 states the main point—the prayer to the Lord to accept the atonement for the innocent blood. Here it becomes clear that the ceremony does not bring atonement in an actual (i.e., magical) sense but is entirely symbolic. The removal of the guilt (which is considered to be present, but only in a ceremonial sense, see v. 7) can be accomplished only by an act of divine grace. "For your people Israel, whom you have redeemed": the prayer reminds the Lord of the love He has shown His own people, Israel, in the past and appeals to that same love for the present.

Verse 9 concludes that in this manner Israel will purge the guilt of shedding innocent blood from themselves by doing what is right in the Lord's eyes (in this case by carrying out the required ceremony). By doing this Israel expresses that they do not take the shedding of innocent blood lightly and that the only reason the murderer is not punished is that Israel cannot do so.

12. Marrying a captured woman (21:10-14)

21:10-14 *When you go to war against your enemies and the* LORD *your God delivers them into your hands and you take captives, ¹¹if you notice among the captives a beautiful woman and are attracted to her, you may take her as your wife. ¹²Bring her into your home and have her shave her head, trim her nails ¹³and put aside the clothes she was wearing when captured. After she has lived in your house and mourned her father and mother for a full month, then you may go to her and be her husband and she shall be your wife. ¹⁴If you are not pleased with her, let her go wherever she wishes. You must not sell her or treat her as a slave, since you have dishonored her.*

Verses 10-11 state the case that Israel has taken captives in battle and that an Israelite sees among them a woman to whom he is attracted. He may take this woman as his wife, but only under certain conditions. This law clearly does not extend to Canaanite women (cf. 7:3; 20:16-17;) and thus applies to wars that Israel would wage later.

Verses 12-14 then state the conditions. In the foreground is the desire to protect the woman from any rough treatment. This is already clear from the fact that the man must take her into his home first and allow her to mourn for a full month. The shaving of the head and the trimming of the nails (v. 12) was apparently a purification ceremony (for the shaving, cf. Lev. 14:8; Num. 8:7); this, plus the putting aside of the clothes she had worn as a captive, indicate the transition from non-Israelite status to that of belonging to the community of the Lord's people. She then must be given a month to mourn her father and mother (who may have perished in the war, but from whom she is in any case separated), and only after that may the Israelite take her as his wife.

Verse 14 adds that if the man is no longer pleased with her, he must not sell her (cf. also Exod. 21:8) but must let her go free. The marriage safeguards her from the lot to which she would have been exposed as a captive. This does not mean, of course, that she, as long as she is in the man's home, has the same position as a free woman. Her husband can send her away without a certificate of divorce (24:1).

Deuteronomy 21:15–17

The treatment prescribed here shows the woman the goodness of Israel's God, who defends those who have no rights. If she becomes a part of Israel permanently, this treatment will help to tie her to this nation and its God.

13. The right of the firstborn of an unloved woman (21:15–17)

21:15–17 *If a man has two wives, and he loves one but not the other, and both bear him sons but the firstborn is the son of the wife he does not love, ¹⁶when he wills his property to his sons, he must not give the rights of the firstborn to the son of the wife he loves in preference to his actual firstborn, the son of the wife he does not love. ¹⁷He must acknowledge the son of his unloved wife as the firstborn by giving him a double share of all he has. That son is the first sign of his father's strength. The right of the firstborn belongs to him.*

Polygamy was not uncommon in Israel. The law does not prohibit it, but does seek to protect the rights of those involved (cf. also Exod. 21:10). The case presented here concerns two wives, the one loved by her husband, the other not (cf. Rachel and Leah, Gen. 29:30; Hannah and Peninnah, 1 Sam. 1:2). This could lead to a situation where the husband, when making a will, would want to give the rights of the firstborn to the son of the wife he loved rather than to the son of the unloved wife, even though by rights it belonged to the latter. This is prohibited, and this law thus defends not only the son but also his mother, the unloved wife, whose rights would be violated if her firstborn son would be denied his rights. "A double share" (v. 17) was apparently what the firstborn should receive by rights. But this was not the only thing. As firstborn he also had the right and the duty to act as head of the family and to provide for the widows and unmarried daughters of his deceased father. On "the first sign of his father's strength," cf. Gen. 49:3.

14. Punishing a rebellious son (21:18–21)

21:18–21 *If a man has a stubborn and rebellious son who does not obey his father and mother and will not listen to them when they discipline him, ¹⁹his father and mother shall take hold of him and bring him to the elders at the gate of his town. ²⁰They shall say to the elders, "This son of ours is stubborn and rebellious. He will not obey us. He is a profligate and a drunkard." ²¹Then all the men of his town shall stone him to death. You must purge the evil from among you. All Israel will hear of it and be afraid.*

The son described here is "stubborn and rebellious" and "a profligate and a drunkard" (cf. Prov. 23:21; Luke 15:13, 30). The issue is thus not so much the commission of public misdemeanors (which would fall under the normal penal code), but rather a general attitude. When exhortation and even discipline fail (cf. Prov. 19:18; 23:13–14; et al.), the parents must take him to the elders (cf. 19:12) who sit "at the gate," the place where public matters were dealt with (cf. 17:5; 25:7). Upon the accusation of his parents all the men of the town must stone the son until he dies. Again, Israel must purge the evil from among them so that all Israel will hear of it and be afraid (cf. 13:5, 11).

This law, when taken literally, speaks of an obligation on the part of the parents to take the son before the elders rather than of a right. Nothing is said about the case where the parents fail to fulfill their obligation. By giving so much power to the parents, this law strengthens parental authority (cf. 27:16; Exod. 21:17; Lev. 20:9). From the fact that no juridical decision was required, one could conclude that the word of the parents determined the fate of the son; nevertheless, since the law generally does not regulate all details, we may assume that the elders could exert some control. It is in any case significant that the father is not given the absolute right over life and death (like the Roman paterfamilias; cf. also Gen. 38:24). This law also serves to keep the father from assuming this right on his own initiative (cf. also Prov. 19:18).

15. Various laws (21:22–22:12)

21:22-23 *If a man guilty of a capital offense is put to death and his body is hung on a tree, ²³you must not leave his body on the tree overnight. Be sure to bury him that same day, because anyone who is hung on a tree is under God's curse. You must not desecrate the land the LORD your God is giving you as an inheritance.*

When a man was executed for a capital offense and his body had been hung from a tree or a pole to hold it up to public shame (cf. Josh. 10:26; 2 Sam. 4:12), it was to be taken down and buried the same day (i.e., before sunset, Josh. 8:29; 10:26–27). The reason given is that "anyone who is hung on a tree is under God's curse" (this is applied to Christ in Gal. 3:13). Such a person had made himself deserving of the death penalty in its most severe form. If the body were left hanging it would desecrate the land, and this must not happen to "the land the LORD your God is giving you as an inheritance" (which is therefore a holy land). We may ask whether the land was not desecrated during the time the body was permitted to hang there. The answer is probably that the desecration should not be understood in an excessively external sense; putting the body on the tree and letting it hang there for a short time was part of the penalty and thus part of the purging of evil from Israel. But allowing the body to *stay* there would desecrate the land.

22:1-4 *If you see your brother's ox or sheep straying, do not ignore it but be sure to take it back to him. ²If the brother does not live near you or if you do not know who he is, take it home with you and keep it until he comes looking for it. Then give it back to him. ³Do the same if you find your brother's donkey or his cloak or anything he loses. Do not ignore it.*

⁴If you see your brother's donkey or his ox fallen on the road, do not ignore it. Help him get it to its feet.

The Israelites must be ready and willing to help out their fellow Israelites with respect to livestock and other possessions. We find a similar stipulation in Exodus 23:4-5, where it concerns an enemy's rather than a brother's possessions. The emphasis here lies on the help one owes to a "brother" (fellow-Israelite). But to the extent that the law deals with livestock it also expresses concern for animals.

Verses 1-3 deal with the required attitude toward anything a brother may have lost: livestock that has strayed (ox, sheep, donkey) or a cloak or anything else that has been lost. "Do not ignore it" as if it were none of your concern. That which has strayed or has been lost must be returned to the owner. If the owner lives too far away or is not known, the finder must take the thing or animal home until the owner comes looking for it; if the owner did not come looking for it, the finder could probably keep it.

Verse 4 speaks of seeing a brother's donkey or ox that has fallen on the road (according to Exod. 23:5 "fallen down under its load," which is probably also the intent here); one must help the owner get the animal to its feet.

22:5 *A woman must not wear men's clothing, nor a man wear women's clothing, for the LORD your God detests anyone who does this.*

The wearing of clothes of the opposite sex is forbidden. The reason is not stated. This stipulation appears to be related to the prohibition in verses 9-11 on bringing together that which is heterogeneous. Some assume that these prohibitions are directed against certain pagan customs or ideas related to the cultus in which such intermingling would have played a role, but no historical data have been found to back up this assumption. We would therefore rather side with the view that these prohibitions are designed to instill respect for the God-given order of creation and for the distinction between sexes and kinds it presents. But, if this is correct, it does not mean that these prohibitions therefore follow immediately from the order of creation—if this were the case, they would still be binding in their literal form even after the passing of the Old Testament dispensation. Rather, this instilling of respect for the order of creation is achieved here by means of prohibitions of such an external nature that they clearly reflect the imprint of the old dispensation. "Men's clothing": the Hebrew word does not refer only to clothing, but also to weapons and other objects (cf. rsv. "anything that pertains to a man").

22:6-7 *If you come across a bird's nest beside the road, either in a tree or on the ground, and the mother is sitting on the young or on the eggs, do not take the mother with the young.* ⁷*You may take the young, but be sure to let the mother go, so that it may go well with you and you may have a long life.*

If one finds a bird's nest, it is permitted to take the eggs or the young, but the mother must be let go. Pity on the mother certainly is not the motivation here, since her young may be taken away. However, a limitation is imposed on interference with nature, and extermination, like wanton destruction (cf. 20:19–20), is prohibited. There may also be a practical consideration behind this law, but it serves in general to instill respect for nature as created by God (cf. 14:21b; Lev. 22:28). The addition "so that it may go well with you and you may have a long life" provides, as frequently in Deuteronomy, a stimulus to keep the command. We do not know why these words are placed here; they apply to all the commandments. It is difficult to accept the suggestion that this addition relates this command to the command to honor one's parents (5:16; Exod. 20:12), which has the same addition, since it is also found repeatedly in other contexts (4:40; 5:29; 6:2, 3, 24; 12:28).

22:8 *When you build a new house, make a parapet around your roof so that you may not bring the guilt of bloodshed on your house if someone falls from the roof.*

When building a new house, a parapet must be installed around the roof (which was flat so that people often spent time there, Josh. 2:6; Matt. 10:27), lest someone fall off. This would make the owner guilty of bloodshed through negligence, and blood guilt would rest on his house (and thus on the owner). Cf. Exodus 21:33ff.

22:9–11 *Do not plant two kinds of seed in your vineyard; if you do, not only the crops you plant but also the fruit of the vineyard will be defiled.*
¹⁰Do not plow with an ox and a donkey yoked together.
¹¹Do not wear clothes of wool and linen woven together.

These are prohibitions against mixing heterogeneous things (cf. Lev. 19:19). Concerning the motivation, see comments on verse 5.

Two kinds of seed must not be planted in the same vineyard (v. 9). It was probably customary to grow vegetables between the vines; these vegetables could not be of two different kinds (in Lev. 19:19 the prohibition applies to the "field" and is thus not limited to the vineyard). If two kinds of seeds are planted, the crops (both those sown and the grapes) will (lit.) "become holy," i.e., they can no longer be used for common (profane) purposes. This does not necessarily mean that the produce was "forfeited to the sanctuary" (cf. NIV mg.), since this would be difficult to implement. The main point is that the effective loss of the crops would keep the Israelites from disobeying this rule.

Verse 10 prohibits plowing with an ox and a donkey together (Lev. 19:19 speaks of mating different kinds of animals), and verse 11 forbids the wearing of clothing made of wool and linen woven together.

22:12 *Make tassels on the four corners of the cloak you wear.*

Concerning the tassels, see Numbers 15:37ff., where these tassels (which must contain a blue cord) are explained as reminders of God's commandments.

16. Marriage violations (22:13–30)

Marriage is firmly protected by the imposition of the death penalty on adultery. Yet the position of the man and that of the woman are not identical. The lawgiver accepts the common law that allowed a man to have more than one wife, while the woman could belong to only one man. For the married woman, therefore, any sexual relations outside of marriage constituted adultery, and she was also guilty of prostitution if she had had sexual relations before marriage. The man, on the other hand, was considered guilty of adultery only if he slept with the wife of his neighbor or with "a virgin pledged to be married," but not if he had sexual relations with an unpledged girl; even if he were already married, he could take the unpledged girl as his wife. But while the law is stricter with respect to the woman, it also protects her, first, against slander on the part of her husband and second, by allowing the pledged woman who is raped in the field to go free because her guilt has not been established.

22:13–21 *If a man takes a wife and, after lying with her, dislikes her* [14]*and slanders her and gives her a bad name, saying, "I married this woman, but when I approached her, I did not find proof of her virginity,"* [15]*then the girl's father and mother shall bring proof that she was a virgin to the town elders at the gate.* [16]*The girl's father will say to the elders, "I gave my daughter in marriage to this man, but he dislikes her.* [17]*Now he has slandered her and said, 'I did not find your daughter to be a virgin.' But here is the proof of my daughter's virginity." Then her parents shall display the cloth before the elders of the town,* [18]*and the elders shall take the man and punish him.* [19]*They shall fine him a hundred shekels of silver and give them to the girl's father, because this man has given an Israelite virgin a bad name. She shall continue to be his wife; he must not divorce her as long as he lives.*

[20]*If, however, the charge is true and no proof of the girl's virginity can be found,* [21]*she shall be brought to the door of her father's house and there the men of her town shall stone her to death. She has done a disgraceful thing in Israel by being promiscuous while still in her father's house. You must purge the evil from among you.*

This section, especially verse 21, shows how sharply the law condemns the surrender of chastity before marriage on the part of a woman.

Verse 13 poses the case that a man marries a woman, has relations with her, and afterward claims that she was not a virgin, that she had had sexual relations with someone else before marriage. "Dislikes her": cf. 2 Samuel 13:15; the dislike expresses itself in what the husband says about her.

Verses 14–20 deal with the case that the accusation is false. The girl's parents must then prove the falseness of the accusation by bringing proof of her virginity to the elders who sit at the gate, where public matters were dealt with (21:19). The proof consists of the cloth or sheet with the drops of blood of her first intercourse. The man will then be punished (cf. 25:1ff.) for slandering an Israelite virgin (the accusation concerned her actions prior to marriage) and pay the father a hundred shekels of silver (almost twice as much as the fine in v. 29) as reparation for the shame he has brought on that house.

Furthermore, the man must keep the accused woman as wife and he loses forever the right to divorce her. This gave the wife compensation by strengthening her position, but is also for the man (given his disposition, v. 13) severe punishment, especially when, as was probably usually the case, his social position would not allow him to take a second wife.

But if the accusation proves to be true (v. 20), the woman must be stoned to death like an adulteress (vv. 22–24), in front of her father's house. This place of execution dishonors her father's house, which is held jointly responsible, but it is also for the woman herself an aggravation of the punishment, since it reminds her of the extremely ignominious nature of her sin—"playing the harlot in her father's house" (RSV). "A disgraceful thing," means literally "folly," the opposite of "wisdom," of which the fear of the Lord is the beginning (Prov. 1:7); "folly" has therefore the connotation of "wickedness," "godlessness." The addition "in Israel" (cf. Gen. 34:7) further characterizes the deed as contrary to Israel's moral standards, which are holy because they are based on God's will. Thus Israel will purge the evil from among them (cf. 13:5).

22:22 *If a man is found sleeping with another man's wife, both the man who slept with her and the woman must die. You must purge the evil from Israel.*

If a man has sexual relations with a married woman, both parties must die (cf. Lev. 18:20; 20:10), probably by being stoned to death (cf. v. 24).

22:23–27 *If a man happens to meet in a town a virgin pledged to be married and he sleeps with her, ²⁴you shall take both of them to the gate of that town and stone them to death—the girl because she was in a town and did not scream for help, and the man because he violated another man's wife. You must purge the evil from among you.*

²⁵But if out in the country a man happens to meet a girl pledged to be married and rapes her, only the man who has done this shall die. ²⁶Do nothing to the girl; she has committed no sin deserving death. This case is like that of someone who attacks and murders his neighbor, ²⁷for the man found the girl out in the country, and though the betrothed girl screamed, there was no one to rescue her.

Since being engaged was considered as binding as being married (cf. v. 24, "another man's wife"), this case is essentially the same as that in verse 22; both involve adultery. The penalty is also the same, but the law here is more explicit. It states the manner of execution and considers the possibility that she may not be guilty.

Verse 23 states that the woman must be held guilty if it happened in town, since she could have cried for help if the act took place against her will.

The situation is different if it happened in the field (verses 25–27); only the man must be put to death, since it is presumed that the woman did cry for help, but that no one came to help her.

22:28–29 *If a man happens to meet a virgin who is not pledged to be married and rapes her and they are discovered, ²⁹he shall pay the girl's father fifty shekels of silver. He must marry the girl, for he has violated her. He can never divorce her as long as he lives.*

If a man rapes an unpledged girl, he does not commit adultery even if he is married, since a man may have more than one wife (cf. Exod. 22:16). There is therefore no question of capital punishment in this case. The man must give the father of the girl fifty shekels of silver (half the amount of v. 19) as bride price (cf. Exod. 22:16) and he must marry the girl, with the stipulation that he can never divorce her. Exodus 22:17 also states that the father may refuse to give the girl to the man in marriage (although the man must still pay the bride price).³⁹

22:30 *A man is not to marry his father's wife; he must not dishonor his father's bed.*

On this verse, cf. 27:20; Leviticus 18:8. A man must not marry his stepmother. "His father's wife" is a woman other than his mother (cf. Lev. 18:7 with 18:8). "Marry" (lit., "take"): it is apparently assumed that the father is deceased. We may take for granted that a case such as that of Reuben and Bilhah (Gen. 35:22) is forbidden; the law does not seek to be complete. For other cases, see Leviticus 18:6ff. The addition "he must not dishonor his father's bed" characterizes such a marriage as incest (cf. Lev. 18:6ff.).

---

³⁹The NIV obscures the distinction between the Hebrew construction for "rape" in verse 25 ("seize, overpower" + "lie with" = "rape") and that for "seduction" in verse 28 ("grab, capture" + "lie with" = "seduce"). The context also shows the distinction by adding "and they are discovered" in verse 28. —ED.

17. Exclusion from the assembly of the Lord (23:1–8)

These verses regulate exclusion from and inclusion in the "assembly of the LORD," a term that describes Israel as a community that is holy and grounded in fellowship with the Lord. Admission to that community is thus essentially the same as acquiring Israelite citizenship, but it is also very clearly considered a sacred matter. But we must remember that exclusion from Israel's national community and exclusion from fellowship with Israel's God, although they frequently went together, were nevertheless not the same thing (see comments on v. 1).

Concerning the foreign nations mentioned in verses 3–7, we should note that they could in principle be admitted to Israel's citizenship (through circumcision; Exod. 12:48; Num. 9:14; 15:14–16). This law gives regulations concerning a few specific nations.

23:1–2 *No one who has been emasculated by crushing or cutting may enter the assembly of the LORD.*

²No one born of a forbidden marriage nor any of his descendants may enter the assembly of the LORD, even down to the tenth generation.

Excluded is first of all anyone who has been "emasculated by crushing or cutting"; according to Leviticus 22:24 the offering of emasculated animals was also forbidden. The reason for this exclusion may be in part a condemnation of pagan cultic practices, which involved emasculation in honor of the deity (e.g., in the cultus of the goddess Cybele of Asia Minor). But emasculation also occurred frequently (and especially) outside the cultus, specifically in connection with service in the harem. The Scriptures mention "eunuchs," also in Israel; these were usually, but apparently not always, emasculated individuals. The basis for this prohibition was therefore probably more general; such a mutilation of man's God–created nature was incompatible with the holiness of God's people. This is then to be understood in an external, ceremonial sense; in another sense, participation in the blessing (*heil*) of God's people is not denied the emasculated individual (cf. Isa. 56:3–4).

Verse 2 adds to the emasculated "one born of a forbidden marriage" (KJV, "bastard"). The rabbis referred the Hebrew word to those who were born out of wedlock or from incest (cf. 22:30). Whether children born out of wedlock as such are meant is not certain (cf. Judg. 11:1).

The purpose of the regulation is to guard the holiness of Israel as the "assembly of the LORD," which is again to be understood in an external, ceremonial sense.

"Even down to the tenth generation" means "not even their remotest descendants" (cf. v. 3); "ten" is the number of totality or all-inclusiveness.

23:3–6 *No Ammonite or Moabite or any of his descendants may enter the assembly of the LORD, even down to the tenth generation. ⁴For they did not come to meet you with bread and water on your way when you came out of Egypt, and they hired Balaam son of Beor from Pethor in Aram Naharaim to pronounce a curse on you. ⁵However, the LORD your God would not listen to Balaam but turned the curse into a blessing for you, because the LORD your God loves you. ⁶Do not seek a treaty of friendship with them as long as you live.*

Also excluded are the Ammonites and the Moabites, again "down to the tenth generation," to which here is added "forever" (KJV; omitted in NIV). The reason for this exclusion is that the Ammonites and Moabites did not show friendship to Israel on the wilderness journey (see also comments on 2:29); they (i.e., Balak, the king of the Moabites) hired Balaam to pronounce a curse on Israel (to them applies therefore the dictum, "Whoever curses you I will curse," Gen. 12:3). The fact that the Lord in His love turned the curse into blessing does not diminish Balak's sin. In the light of this, Israel must never seek "peace or good relations with them" (lit., "their peace nor their prosperity," cf. KJV). See also comments on verse 8.

23:7–8 *Do not abhor an Edomite, for he is your brother. Do not abhor an Egyptian, because you lived as an alien in his country. ⁸The third generation of children born to them may enter the assembly of the LORD.*

In contrast to the preceding, the Edomites and the Egyptians must not be "abhorred." The third generation born to them (i.e., the great-grandchildren of those who lived among Israel as strangers) could enter the assembly of the Lord (by circumcision). The reason for this milder treatment is in Edom's case that Edom is Israel's "brother" (blood relation), and in the case of the Egyptians that Israel "lived as an alien in [their] country." Edom's hostile attitude on the wilderness journey (Num. 20:18ff.) is not taken into consideration, nor even the oppression Israel suffered in Egypt. It may be that the evil these nations have done to Israel is not counted against them because of the positive things that counterbalance them. It is also possible that the lawgiver had a different reason that is not stated here.

18. The purity of the camp (23:9–14)

23:9 *When you are encamped against your enemies, keep away from everything impure.*

When Israel goes to war, the army camp must be kept pure: the Lord Himself is present in the camp (see v. 14). This entire law is a typical example of the manner in which the lawgiver, by means of regulations of an external nature, wants to impress upon Israel the fact that the Lord is in their midst. This law envisions Israel's future battles; entirely different regulations concerning purity applied to Israel's camp in the wilderness, which required only that those who were unclean for a longer period of time be removed (Num. 5:1–4).

23:10–11 *If one of your men is unclean because of a nocturnal emission, he is to go outside the camp and stay there. ¹¹But as evening approaches he is to wash himself, and at sunset he may return to the camp.*

In case of a noctural emission, the individual must leave the camp and must not return until sunset. Then, after washing himself, he may return to the camp (cf. Lev. 15:16, which stipulates that such an individual is unclean until evening).

23:12–13 *Designate a place outside the camp where you can go to relieve yourself. ¹³As part of your equipment have something to dig with, and when you relieve yourself, dig a hole and cover up your excrement.*

Nor must the camp be defiled by human excrement; the men must relieve themselves outside the camp in a designated place, where a hole is dug, and the excrement must be covered with dirt. A digging tool must be carried along specifically for this purpose.

23:14 *For the LORD your God moves about in your camp to protect you and to deliver your enemies to you. Your camp must be holy, so that he will not see among you anything indecent and turn away from you.*

The reason for both these regulations is that the Lord goes with Israel to protect them and to give them the victory; He is therefore present in the camp (cf. Num. 5:3, and the carrying of the ark into battle, Num. 10:35–36; 1 Sam. 4:3ff.; 2 Sam. 11:11). The camp must therefore be kept "holy," i.e., in accordance with the reverence owed to God's presence; anything "indecent," anything that would be contrary to that reverence, must be kept out, lest the Lord leave the place and thus also the army.

19. Various laws (23:15–24:5)

23:15–16 *If a slave has taken refuge with you, do not hand him over to his master.* ¹⁶*Let him live among you wherever he likes and in whatever town he chooses. Do not oppress him.*

A slave who "has taken refuge with you" (lit., "who has escaped from his master to you") must not be turned over to his master. Verse 16 shows that "to you" refers not to an individual but to Israel as a whole. The slave in question thus has not fled from one Israelite to another but rather from a foreign owner to Israelite territory. This slave must be allowed to live wherever he wants and must be treated well.

23:17–18 *No Israelite man or woman is to become a shrine prostitute.* ¹⁸*You must not bring the earnings of a female prostitute or of a male prostitute into the house of the Lord your God to pay any vow, because the Lord your God detests them both.*

Verse 17 reflects the institution of the "temple slaves" or hierodules that existed in the cultus of the Canaanites and of other ancient Near-Eastern peoples; these were women or also men who gave themselves to prostitution in the service of a deity who was believed to grant fertility and to control the sexual life (the men then in the sense of Lev. 18:22; cf. Rom. 1:27). The payment they received belonged to the temple. No Israelite man or woman may commit such a detestable thing (nevertheless, it was found frequently in later years in Israel, cf. 1 Kings 14:24; 15:12; 22:46; 2 Kings 23:7; Hos. 4:14; Amos 2:7; et al.). This verse does not imply that non-Israelite (Canaanite) hierodules were permitted; these were to be exterminated by the Israelites, and there was therefore no reason to mention them here.

Verse 18 forbids the bringing of the earnings derived from such detestable practices to the house of the Lord (cf. Hos. 9:1; Mic. 1:7). "To pay any vow": the prohibition is thus not limited to the sacred prostitution of verse 17, but can also include a case where someone prostitutes himself or herself in order to pay a vow with the money thus acquired. "The earnings . . . of a male prostitute," lit., "price of a dog" (cf. KJV, NIV mg.): the male prostitute is called a "dog," since the dog was considered the ultimate in uncleanness (cf. Rev. 22:15).

231

23:19-20 *Do not charge your brother interest, whether on money or food or anything else that may earn interest. ²⁰You may charge a foreigner interest, but not a brother Israelite, so that the LORD your God may bless you in everything you put your hand to in the land you are entering to possess.*

A foreigner may be charged interest, but not a fellow-Israelite, whether on a loan of money, of food, or of other things such as seed-grain (cf. Exod. 22:5; Lev. 25:5ff., where it is clear that this regulation concerns helping the poor; cf. also *Bible Student's Commentary* on Amos 5:11). The foreigner could be charged interest for two reasons: First, as a non-Israelite he was not owed the same kind of brotherly assistance as the Israelite; and second, loaning to a foreigner (e.g., a traveling merchant) was entirely different from helping a fellow-Israelite in need.

23:21-23 *If you make a vow to the LORD your God, do not be slow to pay it, for the LORD your God will certainly demand it of you and you will be guilty of sin. ²²But if you refrain from making a vow, you will not be guilty. ²³Whatever your lips utter you must be sure to do, because you made your vow freely to the LORD your God with your own mouth.*

A vow must be paid without delay; but not making a vow is not a sin. Both of these stipulations seek to counteract the rash making of vows, as well as to promote practicing truth in relation to the Lord (cf. Num. 30:2).

23:24-25 *If you enter your neighbor's vineyard, you may eat all the grapes you want, but do not put any in your basket. ²⁵If you enter your neighbor's grainfield, you may pick kernels with your hands, but you must not put a sickle to his standing grain.*

Both in the neighbor's vineyard and in his field one may eat of the produce, but it is unlawful to harvest it (cf. Matt. 12:1; Luke 6:1).

24:1-4 *If a man marries a woman who becomes displeasing to him because he finds something indecent about her, and he writes her a certificate of divorce, gives it to her and sends her from his house, ²and if after she leaves his house she becomes the wife of another man, ³and her second husband dislikes her and writes her a certificate of divorce, gives it to her and sends her from his house, or if he dies, ⁴then her first husband, who divorced her, is not allowed to marry her again after she has been defiled. That would be detestable in the eyes of the LORD. Do not bring sin upon the land the LORD your God is giving you as an inheritance.*

A man is not allowed to remarry a woman after he has divorced her if she has since been married to another. The main sentence and the actual prohibition are found in verse 4; the first three verses state the case. It is assumed first of all that a man marries a woman and the marriage is consummated (v. 1; cf. 21:13). The man then sends the woman away with a certificate of divorce. This is not something the law prescribes but assumes (see also 22:19, 29; Lev. 22:13; Num. 30:10). This apparently reflects common law, and we can say that by accepting this Moses sanctions the common law to a degree (cf. "Moses permitted you" in Matt. 19:8). It is also possible that the law further defines and corrects the common law by the manner in which it describes the latter, namely, by mentioning the grounds for divorce and the certificate of divorce. The grounds for divorce, however, are rather vague: "something indecent." The rabbis held vastly differing opinions on the meaning of this phrase; according to Rabbi Hillel, the phrase refers to something repulsive, e.g., a physical defect, but according to his school the wife's ruining a meal was sufficient grounds for divorce, and according to Rabbi Akiba a man could divorce his wife if he found another woman more attractive (cf. "for any and every reason," Matt. 19:3). The stricter school of Shammai, on the other hand, limited the expression to licentiousness and unchastity. But if the latter was thought of in terms of adultery, it would be in conflict with the intent of the law, since the adulteress was to be put to death. Most likely we must think of illness (e.g., skin disease) or physical defect; both the expression "something indecent" (or, "repulsive," "offensive"; cf. 23:14) and the phrase "finds . . . about her" would appear to point in this direction. But it was perhaps not contrary to the intent of the law when the expression was also applied to repulsive qualities or acts. In any case, it refers to more serious grounds for divorce than those allowed by the school of Hillel. On the other hand, it is clear that where the common law was normative the man was allowed considerable latitude, although practical considerations (loss of his bride price, hostility on the part of his wife's family) would tend to limit his actions somewhat (in some cases the man lost the right to divorce his wife, see 22:19, 29). The Old Testament does not mention the woman's right to divorce her husband; for later times, cf. Mark 10:12; 1 Corinthians 7:10, 13. The obligation to give a certificate of divorce could prevent a hasty sending away in a moment of anger; furthermore, the certificate of divorce was proof for the woman that she was free. The certificate is also mentioned in Isaiah 50:1 and Jeremiah 3:8.

We know that what is said here about divorce is not God's final word; in Malachi 2:16 divorce in general is condemned; for the New Testament, cf. Matthew 5:31–32; 19:7–9; Mark 10:4–12; Luke 16:18; 1 Corinthians 7:10–11.

Verse 2 states the further assumption that the woman, after the divorce, marries another man, and verse 3 adds that her second husband dies or also divorces her.

The actual prohibition is given in verse 4: in the case presented, the man must not remarry the woman (cf. Jer. 3:1). Evidently he could remarry her if she had not married after her divorce, but if she had done so, for her first husband to remarry her would be "detestable in the eyes of the LORD"—indeed, it would "bring sin upon the land" (cf. 21:23; Jer. 3:1).

How are we to understand this? We might be inclined to think in ceremonial terms, since we read that the woman must not remarry the first husband "after she has been defiled," which refers to sexual relations with the second husband. The law states that sexual intercourse makes unclean; but this uncleanness lasted only until evening (Lev. 15:18; cf. 1 Sam. 21:5), and the woman was thus not permanently unclean, and someone else could marry her. The reason why the first husband could not remarry her should perhaps be understood in an ethical rather than ceremonial sense. This remarrying of the first husband is "detestable in the eyes of the LORD," apparently because it is a violation of the holiness of marriage.

24:5 *If a man has recently married, he must not be sent to war or have any other duty laid on him. For one year he is to be free to stay at home and bring happiness to the wife he has married.*

A recently married man is exempt from military service (cf. 20:7). The phrase reads literally, "When a man has taken a new wife" (cf. KJV), which has led to the interpretation "When a man has taken another wife, in addition to the one he already has." But there is no basis for this interpretation, since there is no reason why a person marrying a second time would enjoy more privileges than he who married for the first time. The newly-wed man is simply exempt from military service and other duties (forced service, taxes) to allow him to devote himself to his family and to "bring happiness to the wife he has married." Concerning the motive behind this law, see comments on 20:5–8.

20. Justice and fairness (24:6–25:19)

Most of the laws that follow either belong in the area of criminal law or deal with fairness, mercy, or humanitarian concerns.

24:6 *Do not take a pair of millstones—not even the upper one—as security for a debt, because that would be taking a man's livelihood as security.*

It was permitted to ask for security to guarantee the repayment of a debt (cf. vv. 10ff.), but one could not take "a pair of millstones" (i.e., a handmill) or "even the upper one" (which could be removed separately, thus rendering the mill inoperative). By taking away something that is essential for the preparation of the daily bread, one takes away "a man's livelihood" (lit., a man's life"). Cf. also verse 13.

24:7 *If a man is caught kidnapping one of his brother Israelites and treats him as a slave or sells him, the kidnapper must die. You must purge the evil from among you.*

Kidnapping an Israelite and treating or selling him as a slave must be punished with death. "You must purge the evil from among you," cf. 13:5; et al. Cf. also Exodus 21:16, where the law is stated in more general terms ("another") and is thus not limited to kidnapping a fellow Israelite.

24:8–9 *In cases of leprous diseases be very careful to do exactly as the priests, who are Levites, instruct you. You must follow carefully what I have commanded them. ⁹Remember what the* LORD *your God did to Miriam along the way after you came out of Egypt.*

If anyone has a skin disease ("leprosy," cf. NIV mg.) he must follow exactly the instructions of the "levitical priests," which Moses has commanded (cf. Lev. 13–14). The command is underlined by reminding Israel of what the Lord did to Miriam—not the fact that she was punished with leprosy because of her actions against Moses (this would not be appropriate here), but rather that even she was at God's command sent outside the camp while she was leprous (Num. 12:14–15; cf. Lev. 13:46).

24:10–11 *When you make a loan of any kind to your neighbor, do not go into his house to get what he is offering as a pledge. ¹¹Stay outside and let the man to whom you are making the loan bring the pledge out to you. ¹²If the man is poor, do not go to sleep with his pledge in your possession. ¹³Return his cloak to*

235

him by sunset so that he may sleep in it. Then he will thank you, and it will be regarded as a righteous act in the sight of the LORD your God.

Further regulations concerning liens (cf. v. 6). Verse 10 stipulates that if someone makes a loan (cf. 23:19) and asks for a pledge or security, he must not go into the house of the borrower to take the security, but must wait outside for the borrower to bring the security to him. This would protect as much as possible the freedom of the borrower. If the man is poor (v. 12) and has given his cloak as security, it must be returned before sunset, since he needs it for use as a blanket (cf. Exod. 22:25–26; Job. 22:6; Prov. 22:7; Amos 2:8). Returning the cloak will be a righteous act in the sight of God (cf. 6:25).

24:14–15 *Do not take advantage of a hired man who is poor and needy, whether he is a brother Israelite or an alien living in one of your towns. ¹⁵Pay him his wages each day before sunset, because he is poor and is counting on it. Otherwise he may cry to the LORD against you, and you will be guilty of sin.*

A hired hand must be paid promptly (cf. Lev. 19:13). The hired hand is by definition poor and needy. He may be an Israelite or an "alien" who has settled in Israel and is protected by Israel's laws (cf. 1:16; Lev. 24:22). The hired hand must not be taken advantage of (lit., "do not oppress"), specifically by withholding his wages, which would be the most obvious way. He must be paid on the day he earned the wages, "because he is poor and is counting on it"; "it" is emphatic—this is the reason he came and worked, and this is what he needs. For the conclusion, cf. 15:9 and James 5:4.

24:16 *Fathers shall not be put to death for their children, nor children put to death for their fathers; each is to die for his own sin.*

Only the guilty party may be put to death. The Old Testament teaches on the one hand that the Lord "punishes the children for the sin of the fathers" (5:9; Exod. 20:5); this can be seen, apart from the continuing workings of His providence, in the application of the *cherem,* the ban, and in other punitive measures decreed by Him (13:3–17; Josh. 7:24; 2 Sam. 21:6, 8ff.). But the normal criminal law explicitly forbids applications of this principle: if the son deserves the death penalty, the father must not be put to death for or with him, or vice versa (cf. 2 Kings 14:6; 2 Chron. 25:4; see also Jer. 31:30; Ezek. 18:20).

24:17–18 *Do not deprive the alien or the fatherless of justice, or take the cloak of the widow as a pledge.* [18]*Remember that you were slaves in Egypt and the* LORD *your God redeemed you from there. That is why I command you to do this.*

The law protects especially widows, orphans, and aliens (cf. Exod. 22:21–22; 23:9), those whose social position was weak and who had no defender so that they were an easy target for oppression (cf. Isa. 1:17, 23). The law here forbids depriving aliens and orphans of justice; we can also include widows in this (cf. Exod. 22:21–22; 23:9). The reason widows are not mentioned with the aliens and orphans is that an additional protective measure is given for them. A widow's cloak may not be taken as pledge (this thus goes beyond what v. 12 stipulates concerning the cloak of the poor). Verse 18 underlines the command by pointing to the slavery in Egypt from which the Lord delivered Israel. Both the memory of their condition there, and their gratitude for the Lord's deliverance must lead Israel to abhor any oppression of the weak (cf. 15:15).

24:19–22 *When you are harvesting in your field and you overlook a sheaf, do not go back to get it. Leave it for the alien, the fatherless and the widow, so that the* LORD *your God may bless you in all the work of your hands.* [20]*When you beat the olives from your trees, do not go over the branches a second time. Leave what remains for the alien, the fatherless and the widow.* [21]*When you harvest the grapes in your vineyard, do not go over the vines again. Leave what remains for the alien, the fatherless and the widow.* [22]*Remember that you were slaves in Egypt. That is why I command you to do this.*

Allow the poor to glean. The Israelites must not try to harvest the very last of the grain, olives, and grapes. Some must be left for the alien, the orphan, and the widow (cf. Lev. 19:9–10; 23:22). Even today olives are harvested by beating the branches with sticks until the fruit falls. Verse 22, cf. verse 18.

25:1–3 *When men have a dispute, they are to take it to court and the judges will decide the case, acquitting the innocent and condemning the guilty.* [2]*If the guilty man deserves to be beaten, the judge shall make him lie down and have him flogged in his presence with the number of lashes his crime deserves,* [3]*but he must not give him more than forty lashes. If he is flogged more than that, your brother will be degraded in your eyes.*

It is assumed that a judge has sentenced someone to receive lashes because he was the guilty party in a dispute. This punishment was apparently not unusual (cf. 22:18) and was administered by striking the person's back with a stick (Prov. 10:13; 19:29; et al.). Egyptian pictures have been discovered that show the guilty party lying on the ground while his hands and feet are held. The punishment must be administered in the presence and thus under the supervision of the aged (v. 2). Furthermore, the judge must specify the number of lashes the person is to receive in proportion to his guilt. The maximum number of lashes is set at forty (this was in practice later reduced to thirty-nine, to prevent the possibility that miscounting would result in more than forty lashes, cf. 2 Cor. 11:24; this was, however, more due to respect for the letter of the law than to mercy, since the punishment had been made more severe by replacing the stick with a lash made of woven strips of leather). The reason for this limitation is that excessive punishment would degrade the "brother," which must not happen because he is a brother and belongs to the Lord's people.

25:4 *Do not muzzle an ox while it is treading out the grain.*

We can think here of the method, still in use in more recent times in the East, whereby the oxen are made to walk on the grain so that their hooves stamp the grain out of the ears, or also of the pulling of the threshing sledge. The stipulation that the ox must not be made to wear a muzzle while threshing is undoubtedly intended literally: the animal deserves sympathy and fair treatment (cf. 22:1–4; Prov. 12:10). But it is equally true that such a demand of fair treatment applies even more to the human laborer (1 Cor. 9:9; 1 Tim. 5:18).

25:5–10 *If brothers are living together and one of them dies without a son, his widow must not marry outside the family. Her husband's brother shall take her and marry her and fulfill the duty of a brother-in-law to her. ⁶The first son she bears shall carry on the name of the dead brother so that his name will not be blotted out from Israel.*

⁷However, if a man does not want to marry his brother's wife, she shall go to the elders at the town gate and say, "My husband's brother refuses to carry on his brother's name in Israel. He will not fulfill the duty of a brother-in-law to me." ⁸Then the elders of his town shall summon him and talk to him. If he persists in saying, "I do not want to marry her," ⁹his brother's widow shall go up to him in the presence of the elders, take off one of his sandals, spit in his face and say, "This is what is done to the man who will not build up his brother's family line." ¹⁰That man's line shall be known in Israel as The Family of the Unsandaled.

The term "levirate" derives from the Latin *levir,* "brother-in-law" (specifically the brother of the husband). This law deals with a special case of a widow's marriage to her deceased husband's brother.[40] When a married man dies without a son, his brother must marry his widow to raise up a son and heir for him. Similar institutions have been found in India, Persia, Afghanistan, among the Greeks, and fairly generally among the inhabitants of Africa. According to the Old Testament, the levirate was already known in the time of the patriarchs (Gen. 38). In the story of Ruth, the nearest kinsman has to marry the widow; this was probably a remnant of the ancient common law.

The basis for this institution is probably the desire to continue the name, and thus the family, of the deceased, a desire that also finds expression in the law governing the inheriting of daughters (Num. 27:4; cf. also Isa. 56:5). This was sanctioned by God's revelation and was supported in Israel by the promise concerning the seed of the woman (Gen. 3:15) and the promise to Abraham that his descendants would be numerous (at the heart of both of which lies the promise of the Redeemer). Thus, being blessed with children and the continuation of the family stood in the light of the great promise of blessing (*heil*). Another aspect of the desire to continue the family name was to keep the land owned by a family from passing to another (cf. Ruth 4:5).[41]

The levirate clearly bears the stamp of the time in which it originated. Especially the duty imposed on the woman (which she could not shirk, v. 5) indicates how dominant the family interests are. She must submit to these interests without questioning or reference to her personal preference. While this could entail a rich blessing for her (Ruth, who also exemplifies the loyalty a widow owed to her deceased husband), the concept as a whole has a typically Old Testament character. This is shown by the fact that the levirate (except for a limited number of cases) could be implemented only as long as polygamy was permitted. It is therefore important to note that this law on the one hand sanctions common law, while on the other hand limiting it significantly. Accord-

---

[40]The law forbade marrying the wife of a deceased brother (Lev. 18:16); it was permitted, however, after the death of the woman, to marry her sister.

[41]Against this view, Keil argues that the story of Ruth speaks of both levirate marriage and the institution of the *go'el,* the kinsman-redeemer. But although this is true (cf. 4:3), what is stated in 4:5 concerning the "raising up of the name of the dead over his inheritance" (cf. KJV) does not follow from the *go'el* concept, but from the levirate. We get the impression from the Book of Ruth that if the person for whom one became *go'el* was a childless widow, the *go'el* had to marry her, in order that their firstborn son might become owner of the land.

ing to Genesis 38 Judah feels *obligated* to give Tamar his next son each time one of her husbands dies, but this law allows for refusal on the part of the brother-in-law, albeit not without disgrace. Furthermore, this law (in contrast to Ruth, which reflects customary law) imposes the duty only on the *brother,* and then only if this brother and the deceased had lived together (see below). For the continuation of the levirate in later times, cf. Matthew 22:24ff.

"Are living together" (v. 5) could mean living in the same place (cf. Gen. 13:6; 36:7); a brother who lived elsewhere could not be asked to work the land of his deceased brother. The rabbis understood the expression to mean that the brothers still had the inheritance in common; this view (in the strictest sense of living in one house and having a shared household) is in our opinion the most likely one in view of the later words "outside the family." Thus the law greatly limited the levirate, which does of course not necessarily prevent that the customary law retained the levirate in a broader sense (Boaz). The Jews took the phrase "a son" to mean "a child" in general (cf. Matt. 22:25). This is incorrect; the law speaks of a son because it was the son who continued the family line. In favor of the Jewish view it has been pointed out that in the absence of a son the property would go to the daughters, and if the deceased had neither sons nor daughters, to his brother (Num. 27:8–9). But this argument is not valid, since we could then also conclude that there was reason for a levirate marriage only if the deceased had no brother, which is a contradiction in terms. Numbers 27:8–9 must apparently be understood to mean that the daughters or brother inherit only if there is no son and no son can be expected from a levirate marriage—for example, when the widow is past childbearing age. "Outside the family . . .": the widow has an obligation to the name and inheritance of her deceased husband (Ruth); this is why she must stay at home and be prepared for the levirate marriage. (The Hebrew reads, "Shall not go outside to a stranger," cf. KJV; the "stranger" is anyone outside the family.)

Verses 7–10 describe what happens if the brother-in-law refuses to marry the widow. The ceremony must take place in the gate in the presence of the elders (i.e., the local authorities); this serves to make the disgrace public and also to make the renunciation of his rights official. The disgrace lies primarily in the widow's spitting in her brother-in-law's face and in the words spoken by her. According to Ruth 4:7, the taking off of the shoe was a ceremony that was customary in transactions of purchase or exchange. The seller took off his shoe and gave it to the buyer as proof that he renounced any rights to his property; this is based on the idea that one takes possession of land by setting foot on it (according to some, Ps. 60:8 should be interpreted in this sense as well; the tossing of the sandal is symbolic of taking possession).

The taking off of the shoe in this text thus symbolizes that the brother-in-law is deprived of his right to the widow and the property of his brother. The widow is now free to marry someone outside the family (cf. v. 5), and we must assume that this "stranger" could then demand her portion of the family property. Verse 10 underlines the element of disgrace: the brother-in-law (and his family line after him) is punished for his refusal to build the house of his brother by being called "The Family of the Unsandaled."

25:11–12 *If two men are fighting and the wife of one of them comes to rescue her husband from his assailant, and she reaches out and seizes him by his private parts, ¹²you shall cut off her hand. Show her no pity.*

This stipulation, by its specific nature, has the imprint of being derived from life. Exodus 21:22 also assumes that men are fighting and that a woman takes part. The sentence required for the offense in these verses is, apart from the *lex talionis,* "an eye for an eye," the only instance of punishment by physical mutilation, which shows how serious the lawgiver considers this shamelessness to be.

25:13–16 *Do not have two differing weights in your bag—one heavy, one light. ¹⁴Do not have two differing measures in your house—one large, one small. ¹⁵You must have accurate and honest weights and measures, so that you may live long in the land the LORD your God is giving you. ¹⁶For the LORD your God detests anyone who does these things, anyone who deals dishonestly.*

Honest weights and measures must be used (cf. Lev. 19:35–36; Amos 8:5). The cheater has a larger weightstone (or measure) for buying, a smaller one for use in selling. Both weights and measures must be honest (v. 15). By doing this, Israel will live long in Canaan (cf. 4:26; 5:16). But the Lord detests anyone who uses double standards (cf. 18:12; 22:5; et al.). With these words ends the collection of laws; what follows is of a different nature.

25:17–19 *Remember what the Amalekites did to you along the way when you came out of Egypt. ¹⁸When you were weary and worn out, they met you on your journey and cut off all who were lagging behind; they had no fear of God.*

241

¹⁹When the LORD your God gives you rest from all the enemies around you in the land he is giving you to possess as an inheritance, you shall blot out the memory of Amalek from under heaven. Do not forget!

On the command to exterminate the Amalekites, cf. Exodus 17:9–14. The Amalekites had attacked Israel at Rephidim near Horeb; they had attacked from the rear and killed those who were lagging behind—an especially godless feat ("they had no fear of God" is used in a general sense). Therefore Israel must, when they have settled in Canaan, destroy the Amalekites. Concerning the execution of this command, see 1 Samuel 15; 27:8–9; 30:17; 2 Samuel 8:12.

21. Firstfruits and tithes (26:1–15)

This section, like 25:17–19, is an appendix to the law code. It outlines two liturgies, one for the bringing of the firstfruits, the other for the triennial tithe.

26:1–11 *When you have entered the land the LORD your God is giving you as an inheritance and have taken possession of it and settled in it, ²take some of the firstfruits of all that you produce from the soil of the land the LORD your God is giving you and put them in a basket. Then go to the place the LORD your God will choose as a dwelling for his Name ³and say to the priest in office at the time, "I declare today to the LORD your God that I have come to the land the LORD swore to our forefathers to give us." ⁴The priest shall take the basket from your hands and set it down in front of the altar of the LORD your God. ⁵Then you shall declare before the LORD your God: "My father was a wandering Aramean, and he went down into Egypt with a few people and lived there and became a great nation, powerful and numerous. ⁶But the Egyptians mistreated us and made us suffer, putting us to hard labor. ⁷Then we cried out to the LORD, the God of our fathers, and the LORD heard our voice and saw our misery, toil and oppression. ⁸So the LORD brought us out of Egypt with a mighty hand and an outstretched arm, with great terror and with miraculous signs and wonders. ⁹He brought us to this place and gave us this land, a land flowing with milk and honey; ¹⁰and now I bring the firstfruits of the soil that you, O LORD, have given me." Place the basket before the LORD your God and bow down before him. ¹¹And you and the Levites and the aliens among you shall rejoice in all the good things the LORD your God has given to you and your household.*

Concerning the firstfruits, see 18:4 (where they are said to belong to the priests).

When Israel has settled in Canaan (v. 1), anyone who is involved in agriculture must "take some of the firstfruits" of all that is produced and offer them to the Lord (v. 2). These firstfruits were apparently to be brought each year (cf. the stipulation in 14:22 concerning the tithes and the firstborn). The firstfruits were to be brought during the great feasts that were in part also feasts of thanksgiving for the harvest. The portion set aside was be put in a basket and taken to the place where the central sanctuary stood (cf. 12:5ff.). The offering was to be given to "the priest in office at the time" (v. 3; lit., "the priest who is in those days"). The expression would appear to refer to the high priest, but this does not preclude the possibility that the regular priests, functioning as the helpers and representatives of the high priest, could receive the baskets and place them before the Lord, although the entire procedure would be under the supervision of the high priest. A formula must be used when the basket is presented, which expresses that the individual recognizes that he has reached the land the Lord had promised to the forefathers. It is thus a confession that one owes everything to the Lord (and not, e.g., to the Baals, Hos. 2:8), to His favor bestowed on the forefathers, and to His faithfulness to His promises. "The LORD your God": "your" refers to the priest, who is the mediator between the Lord and the people, and who stands therefore closer to the Lord than the people; the Lord is *his* God in a special sense, although He is of course also the God of Israel (cf. vv. 2, 4).

The priest must take the basket (v. 4) and place it in front of the altar on behalf of the giver (cf. v. 10b). This symbolizes the giving of the basket to the Lord, who in turn gives it to the priest (18:4; cf. the waving before the Lord of the portion of the offering that falls to the priest, Exod. 29:26).

Verses 5–10a then prescribe another formula that must be pronounced "before the LORD your God"; it also has the character of praise in recognition of the blessings bestowed by the Lord.

First, Israel's humble beginnings are acknowledged. The patriarch Jacob was "a wandering Aramean" or, more literally, "a perishing Aramean" ("ready to perish," KJV). This alludes to the fact that Jacob spent many years in Aram, as had Abraham (Gen. 24:4), and that his mother, Rebekah, also came from there (Gen. 24:10), as did his wives. Jacob was "ready to perish" because he first had to flee from Esau, was later pursued by Laban, and finally had to go to Egypt because of famine. When Jacob went to Egypt he was the head of a small tribe; the Lord's blessing made him a large nation there. But new hardships came when the Egyptians began to oppress the Israelites (v. 6). But the

Lord, "the God of our fathers," heard their prayers, "saw" (paid attention to) their misery (v. 7), and brought them out of Egypt "by a mighty hand and an outstretched arm" (v. 8; cf. 4:34). He brought them to Canaan, a land "flowing with milk and honey" (cf. 6:3). The confession ends with the declaration that the worshiper here brings the firstfruits of the soil the Lord has given him. This is the conclusion drawn from all that precedes, and the bringing of the firstfruits is the acknowledgement that the bringer owes all to the free grace of the Lord Himself, before whom these words are spoken (v. 5).

"Place the basket before the LORD your God" (v. 10b) is a summary of the preceding (v. 4 indicated that the priest placed the basket before the Lord, but he was the mediator who did this on behalf of the bringer). Then he shall bow down before the Lord in worship. The ceremony ends with a joyful offering meal (cf. 12:7, 12); the (annual) tithes (14:22ff.), rather than the firstfruits, were used for this meal, since the latter belonged to the priest.

26:12–15 *When you have finished setting aside a tenth of all your produce in the third year, the year of the tithe, you shall give it to the Levite, the alien, the fatherless and the widow, so that they may eat in your towns and be satisfied. 13Then say to the LORD your God: "I have removed from my house the sacred portion and have given it to the Levite, the alien, the fatherless and the widow, according to all you commanded. I have not turned aside from your commands nor have I forgotten any of them. 14I have not eaten any of the sacred portion while I was in mourning, nor have I removed any of it while I was unclean, nor have I offered any of it to the dead. I have obeyed the LORD my God; I have done everything you commanded me. 15Look down from heaven, your holy dwelling place, and bless your people Israel and the land you have given us as you promised on oath to our forefathers, a land flowing with milk and honey."*

No liturgy is prescribed for the bringing of the annual tithes, probably because Deuteronomy speaks of these tithes only in connection with the offering meals (14:22ff.). To the extent that these annual tithes were for the priests and Levites (Num. 18:21–24), we may assume that they were to be brought in a manner similar to the firstfruits; it is possible that they were even included in the firstfruits, based on Deuteronomy's terminology. (See comments on 14:22–29.) There is a special reason why there is a separate liturgy for the triennial tithes. According to 14:28–29, this tithe (which was probably the same as the annual tithe, which every third year had a different purpose), was to be deposited in the nearest town for use by the Levites, aliens, etc. who lived there, that they might "come and eat and be satisfied." The bringing of these tithes thus did not involve the central sanctuary. In order to maintain the sacred character of these tithes, a liturgy is prescribed that was to be performed after these tithes were brought. Concerning verse 12, cf. 14:28–29. "When you have finished setting aside a tenth..." refers to the tithe of the entire harvest, including those crops that were harvested last. "The third year, the year of the tithe": the third year is called "the year of the tithe," not because in other years no tithes were brought, but because in the third year the tithe had a special purpose and thus special significance (cf. vv. 13–15; see comments on 14:22–29).

"Say to the LORD your God" (lit., "say before the LORD your God," v. 13a) could refer to the central sanctuary, but this is not explicitly stated (as in v. 2), and it was also possible to speak "before the LORD" at home (Gen. 27:7). But it would be more natural to assume that these words were spoken at the sanctuary on one of the occasions on which the Israelites were required to appear there in connection with the harvest (e.g., after completion of the harvest, 16:13). The prescribed declaration then begins in verse 13b. It is, however, not something that is merely pronounced before the Lord, it is also addressed directly to Him (the Lord spoken of only once in the third person, v. 14). First, the speaker declares that he has given the tithe of everything to the Levites, etc. "The sacred portion" indicates that the triennial tithes, although they were not taken to the sanctuary, nevertheless belonged to the Lord. "I have not turned aside from your commands nor have I forgotten any of them": this does not refer so much to the delivering of tithes as to what follows in verse 14. The tithes, before being turned over, were kept at home for some time, and this created the possibility that the tithe had been dealt with improperly, thus desecrating the sacred. The speaker must declare that he has not done this. "Eating while in mourning" (cf. Jer. 16:7; Ezek. 24:17): the "bread of mourners" was unclean (Hos. 9:4), since a dead body made the house and all that came in contact with it unclean for seven days (Num. 19:14). "Eaten any of the sacred portion" is literally "eaten of it." This probably does not refer to the tithe (since it should not be eaten at all), but rather to the supply from which the tithe was taken; this entire supply is thus declared to be clean. The tithe would also be desecrated if it were removed by an unclean person. "Offered any of it to the dead" may refer to the taking of food to the family of a deceased person, or perhaps to the custom of giving food to the dead by placing it in the grave. But we do not know if this custom, which is found in later

Judaism, was also known in ancient Israel. "I have done everything you commanded" refers to the keeping ceremonially clean of the tithe described above.

In verse 15 the declaration goes over into a prayer for God's blessing on Israel and on the land He has given, probably especially with the new agricultural year, which would soon begin, in mind. The prayer thus differs from the preceding declaration in that it is general rather than personal, although this does not mean that there is no connection: the one who prays also thinks of himself in his prayer, and his boldness in praying for Israel (and thus also for himself) is closely related to his obedience declared in the preceding verse.

22. Conclusion of the collection of laws (26:16–19)

These verses conclude the book of the law that began in 12:1.

26:16 *The Lord your God commands you this day to follow these decrees and laws; carefully observe them with all your heart and with all your soul.*

First, there is a general exhortation to keep the "decrees and laws" (cf. 4:5) "with all your heart and all your soul" (cf. 6:5; 10:12ff.). "This day" comes first in the Hebrew sentence and is emphatic—Israel must be deeply impressed by the importance of the proclamation they have heard today (cf. below).

26:17–19 *You have declared this day that the Lord is your God and that you will walk in his ways, that you will keep his decrees, commands and laws, and that you will obey him.* [18]*And the Lord has declared this day that you are his people, his treasured possession as he promised, and that you are to keep all his commands.* [19]*He has declared that he will set you in praise, fame and honor high above all the nations he has made and that you will be a people holy to the Lord your God, as he promised.*

The significance of the proclamation is now stated yet more emphatically and fully. The meaning of these verses is not clear in all details. According to the view that appears to us most probably correct, Moses describes what has happened as the making of a covenant, which is understood in terms of a contract. At the making of this covenant there is a declaration, first by God and then by Israel, of what is promised to and expected of the other party. The expressions "you have declared . . . the Lord has declared" must be understood to mean that (as may have been customary in making contracts) each party asks a declaration of the other.

Verse 17 then states the declaration that Israel, so to speak, has asked the Lord to make and which the Lord, as the first party to the covenant, makes. It concerns in the first place what He has promised (that He will be their God) and then what he asks of Israel (that they must walk in His ways, etc.).

Verses 18–19 state the declaration Israel has made to the Lord. Verse 18 then contains what Israel has promised. The words "that you are his people, his treasured possession as he promised" mean that Israel has accepted the Lord's promise that they will be His people (Exod. 19:5; cf. Deut. 7:6; 14:2). They promise to act accordingly, which is why the words "that you are to keep all his commands" follow.

Verse 19 then states what Israel has declared to expect from the Lord, namely, that He will set Israel high above the other nations (cf. 28:1)—an object of praise, fame, and honor (cf. Zeph. 3:19–20). The words can also be taken in the sense "to the praise, fame, and honor of the Lord" (cf. Jer. 13:11; 33:9; Isa. 62:3), but this does not appear to be the intent. Finally, the blessing (*heil*) that Israel expects to receive from the Lord is summarized in the words, "and that you will be a people holy to the LORD your God, as he promised." As a people that is holy to Him and belongs to Him, Israel has the Lord in their midst and stands under His protection. "As he has promised": Exodus 19:5 (cf. Deut. 7:6).

IV. Concluding Words
(Chapters 27–30)

These regulations concern the setting up of stones on which are written "the words of this law" and the establishing of an altar on Mount Ebal (27:1–8) as well as the proclamation of blessing and curse on Mount Gerizim and Mount Ebal (27:11–26). These two sections are separated by a general exhortation to keep the law (27:9–10). The actions mentioned above were designed to express that Israel would make the Lord's law the guideline for life and action in the land the Lord gave them. Concerning the implementation, see Joshua 8:30–35.

247

A. REGULATIONS CONCERNING THE PROMULGATION OF THIS LAW IN CANAAN (CHAPTER 27)

1. The altar on Mount Ebal (27:1–8)

27:1 *Moses and the elders of Israel commanded the people: "Keep all these commands that I give you today.*

This verse is an introduction, in which Israel is exhorted to keep the whole law; it indicates the purpose behind the stipulation concerning the setting up of stones on Mount Ebal. It is curious that both Moses and "the elders of Israel" are identified as speakers, although the "I" in the next sentence indicates that Moses does the actual speaking; the elders probably indicated their agreement in some way. "All the commands" (cf. 1:5; 4:8) refers to the body of laws that has been proclaimed in the preceding chapters; "I give you today" can also be rendered "I have given you today."

27:2–4 *When you have crossed the Jordan into the land the LORD your God is giving you, set up some large stones and coat them with plaster. ³Write on them all the words of this law when you have crossed over to enter the land the LORD your God is giving you, a land flowing with milk and honey, just as the LORD, the God of your fathers, promised you. ⁴And when you have crossed the Jordan, set up these stones on Mount Ebal, as I command you today, and coat them with plaster.*

As proof of their willingness to keep the law, Israel must set up on Mount Ebal large stones on which the law is written. "When you have crossed the Jordan" is literally "On the day you cross the Jordan" (cf. KJV); the NIV correctly renders the intent of the words. Israel then must write the laws on large stones, not by chiseling but by writing on the plaster with which the stones had been coated; this was a procedure that was common in Egypt. It was an easier process than chiseling the words into the stone, but was also less durable in the climate of Palestine (in contrast to Egypt's climate). This indicates that the intent was not to preserve the stones with the law for posterity, but rather to express symbolically that Israel intended to live by this law in Canaan.

"All the words of this law" (v. 3) certainly refers to the laws of Deuteronomy rather than to the entire Pentateuch (cf. "all these commands that I give you today," v. 1). The question whether only the laws of chapters 12–26 are meant or also the discourses (whether from 1:6 or from 5:1 on; see Introduction) is less easy to answer. We are inclined to take the latter view. Finally, was the "law" (whether with or without the discourses) to be written down verbatim or in summary form? The latter would undoubtedly be sufficient for a symbolic act, although it would not have been impossible to write down the entire law verbatim, since they are called "large stones" and their number is not specified. We may assume that Moses gave further oral instructions concerning the execution of this command. The last part of the verse states again when this must be done: "when you have crossed over." Verse 4 names the place where the stones must be set up: Mount Ebal (cf. 11:29). It is curious that it is this mountain, on which according to verse 13 the curse was to be proclaimed, that is chosen to set up the stones, rather than Mount Gerizim, the mountain of blessing. This may be connected with the fact that in verses 14ff. only the curses are given but not the blessings. All this may then be an indication that in Israel's history the curse of the law will be more prominent than the blessing (cf. 31:16–17), because the law, insofar as it was an expression of the principle "do this and you shall live," was not able to bring blessing (*heil*) to a sinful people (cf. Gal. 3:21); rather, it "was put in charge to lead us to Christ" (Gal. 3:24), who would redeem us from the curse of the law (Gal. 3:13) (but see below on v. 7).[42] Verse 4 repeats the command to coat the stones with plaster, while the command to write in verse 3 is repeated again in verse 8. But the discussion is interrupted by something else.

27:5–7 *Build there an altar to the LORD your God, an altar of stones. Do not use any iron tool upon them.* *6Build the altar of the LORD your God with fieldstones and offer burnt offerings on it to the LORD your God.* *7Sacrifice fellowship offerings there, eating them and rejoicing in the presence of the LORD your God.*

Israel must build an altar to the Lord on the same mountain and bring burnt offerings and fellowship offerings there. The setting up of the stones with the law written on them is a renewal of the covenant that must be celebrated with offerings (cf. Exod. 24:11). The altar must be made of unhewn stones in accordance with the stipulation of Exodus 20:25. Burnt offerings are offerings that are burnt entirely on the altar; they symbolize Israel's total self-surrender to the Lord. An important aspect of the fellowship offerings is the offering meal, during which Israel may "rejoice in the presence of the LORD" because of the blessings of the covenant relationship with Him—what was said above

---

[42]The Samaritan Pentateuch mentions Gerizim here rather than Ebal; this should probably be considered a tendentious emendation designed to increase the importance of the sanctuary built by the Samaritans on Mount Gerizim.

about the *curse* of the law being in the foreground is true only insofar as the law is an expression of the principle "do this and you shall live." In its deeper sense the law is part of the covenant of grace (cf. 5:6), and its restatement is thus a renewal of the covenant and cause for celebration and joy.

27:8 *And you shall write very clearly all the words of this law on these stones you have set up."*

Finally Moses comes back to the stones. "And you shall write on it very clearly all the words of this law" completes the command concerning the stones. The fact that the conclusion comes here, after the command concerning the altar, indicates that these stones are the main thing, while the interpolated command concerning the altar and the offerings is subsidiary.

2. New exhortation to keep the Law (27:9–10)

27:9–10 *Then Moses and the priests, who are Levites, said to all Israel, "Be silent, O Israel, and listen! You have now become the people of the* LORD *your God. ¹⁰Obey the* LORD *your God and follow his commands and decrees that I give you today."*

These verses contain another general exhortation to keep the law; they are closely related to 26:16–19. It is by no means strange that Moses places this general exhortation between two specific commands concerning the proclamation of the law in Canaan. The purpose of these commands is to help ensure Israel's keeping of the law. In verse 1 the elders were mentioned alongside Moses, but here it is "the priests, who are Levites" (the common designation in Deuteronomy for the members of the tribe of Levi, both priests and Levites) who stand with Moses. The "I" in verse 10 shows that Moses is the actual speaker, while the priests express their agreement. The priests were the logical persons to support a general exhortation such as this, since it was primarily they who were concerned with Israel's keeping of the law (cf. v. 14).

"Be silent . . . and listen!" places a strong emphasis on the importance of what is to follow. Moses first states that Israel has "now" (lit., "today") become the Lord's people (cf. 26:17–19). The conclusion drawn from this is that Israel must keep the commands and decrees they have received. The following command serves to promote this.

3. The proclamation of blessing and curse on Mount Gerizim and Mount Ebal (27:11–26)

The command, already given in 11:29, to proclaim blessing and curse on Mount Gerizim and Mount Ebal is elaborated here. The command is executed in Joshua 8:33–35.

27:11–13 *On the same day Moses commanded the people:*
[12]When you have crossed the Jordan, these tribes shall stand on Mount Gerizim to bless the people: Simeon, Levi, Judah, Issachar, Joseph and Benjamin. [13]And these tribes shall stand on Mount Ebal to pronounce curses: Reuben, Gad, Asher, Zebulun, Dan and Naphtali.

The time when these things must be done is again the period after the crossing of the Jordan (cf. v. 2). The people themselves must pronounce the blessings and curses. Six tribes are appointed to proclaim the blessing, and six to proclaim the curse. We cannot determine with certainty whether there was a special reason for the assignment of the tribes. The tribes who were to live in the southern part of Canaan were to pronounce the blessing, those who would live in the north and to the east of the Jordan were to pronounce the curse. But it may be more significant that only sons of Leah and Rachel are chosen for the blessing, and for the curse only sons of Jacob's other wives, to which are added Reuben and Zebulun in order to make the total six. The latter two may have been added because Zebulun was Leah's youngest son, while Reuben had been guilty of incest, the reason why he lost his birthright (Gen. 49:4).

27:14–26 *The Levites shall recite to all the people of Israel in a loud voice:*
[15]"Cursed is the man who carves an image or casts an idol—a thing detestable to the LORD, the work of the craftsman's hands—and sets it up in secret."
                         Then all the people shall say, "Amen!"
[16]"Cursed is the man who dishonors his father or his mother."
                         Then all the people shall say, "Amen!"
[17]"Cursed is the man who moves his neighbor's boundary stone."
                         Then all the people shall say, "Amen!"
[18]"Cursed is the man who leads the blind astray on the road."
                         Then all the people shall say, "Amen!"

¹⁹*"Cursed is the man who withholds justice from the alien, the fatherless or the widow."*

> *Then all the people shall say, "Amen!"*

²⁰*"Cursed is the man who sleeps with his father's wife, for he dishonors his father's bed."*

> *Then all the people shall say, "Amen!"*

²¹*"Cursed is the man who has sexual relations with any animal."*

> *Then all the people shall say, "Amen!"*

²²*"Cursed is the man who sleeps with his sister, the daughter of his father or the daughter of his mother."*

> *Then all the people shall say, "Amen!"*

²³*"Cursed is the man who sleeps with his mother-in-law."*

> *Then all the people shall say, "Amen!"*

²⁴*"Cursed is the man who kills his neighbor secretly."*

> *Then all the people shall say, "Amen!"*

²⁵*"Cursed is the man who accepts a bribe to kill an innocent person."*

> *Then all the people shall say, "Amen!"*

²⁶*"Cursed is the man who does not uphold the words of this law by carrying them out."*

> *Then all the people shall say, "Amen!"*

What follows is an elaboration of the command given in verses 11–13. At first glance it does not quite correspond to what precedes it, but the intent is apparently that the one must complement and clarify the other, specifically on two points. One is that the preceding speaks of both blessing and curse, while here only curse formulas are given. This is probably to be understood in the sense that the blessing formulas were to be proclaimed in a similar manner (concerning the fact that only curses are given here, see comments on v. 4); another consideration is that also in the Ten Words the negative element ("you shall not") is prominent.

The other point is that according to the preceding, blessing and curse must be pronounced by the *people* (including the tribe of Levi), while it is said here that the *Levites* must pronounce the curse formulas, while the people are to say only "Amen!" The intent is apparently that the people, by expressing their agreement with what the Levites have said, are considered to have spoken themselves. Furthermore, "all the people" must refer to the six tribes who were appointed to pronounce the curse, while the other six tribes would say "Amen!" to the blessings. Also, the fact that the tribe of Levi is among the tribes who are to pronounce the blessing indicates that "the Levites" of verse 14 are not the whole tribe, but a number of them selected for this purpose (according to Josh. 8:33 the Levites who carried the ark). The repeated "all the people" clearly indicates that here the elders do not act on behalf of the people, but that the people themselves (i.e., the men twenty years of age and older) say "Amen!"

Twelve curses are given, apparently intentionally corresponding to the number of Israel's tribes. Except for the last one, they are directly against the most serious sins. The one in verse 15 is religious in nature, the others are ethical. Verse 15 speaks against the man who makes a carved image (4:16) or a cast idol (9:12) and sets it up in secret, contrary to the second commandment (5:8; Exod. 20:4). "A thing detestable to the LORD," cf. 17:1; 18:12; 22:5; et al. "The work of the craftsman's hand," cf. 4:28.

Verse 16, cf. Exodus 21:17; verse 17, cf. 19:14; verse 18, cf. Lev. 19:14; verse 19, cf. 24:17; Exodus 22:21–22; verse 20, cf. 22:30; Leviticus 18:8; 20:11; verse 21, cf. Exodus 22:19; Leviticus 18:23; 20:15; verses 22–23, cf. Leviticus 18:9; 20:17 and Leviticus 18:17; 20:14; verse 24, cf. 19:11; 5:17. Verse 25 apparently refers to a judge; cf. 16:19; Exodus 23:8. Because the list of sins is of course not complete, verse 26 pronounces a general curse on those who do not uphold "the words of this law" (cf. 1:5) by carrying them out (cf. Gal. 3:10).

B. BLESSING AND CURSE (CHAPTER 28)

The command of 27:11–26 emphatically presented blessing and curse to the present generation; in a lengthy speech Moses now does this again more directly. First he speaks of blessing (vv. 1–14), then of curse (vv. 15–68). Cf. 7:12–16; Exodus 23:20–33; Leviticus 26.

1. Blessing for obedience (28:1–14)

28:1–2 *If you fully obey the LORD your God and carefully follow all his commands I give you today, the LORD your God will set you high above all the nations on earth. ²All these blessings will come upon you and accompany you if you obey the LORD your God:*

The unfolding of the blessing is prefaced by the major condition, "if you fully obey the LORD your God. . ." (cf. the contrast in v. 15). In order to show its decisive importance, Moses repeats the condition in verses 2 and 9, and again at the end in both positive and negative form (vv. 13–14). The content of all promised blessing (*heil*) is summarized in the promise that the Lord will set Israel high above all the nations of the earth (cf. 26:19). Verse 2 then introduces the blessings that will come on the basis of what was said in verse 1. "Come upon you and accompany you": the same applies to the curse (vv. 15, 45); blessing and curse are presented as living beings who (at the Lord's command, vv. 8, 20) follow Israel until they overtake it and do their work.

28:3-6

You will be blessed in the city and blessed in the country.

⁴The fruit of your womb will be blessed, and the crops of your land and the young of your livestock—the calves of your herds and the lambs of your flocks.

⁵Your basket and your kneading trough will be blessed.

⁶You will be blessed when you come in and blessed when you go out.

The fullness of God's blessing, which Israel will receive when it walks in the way of obedience, is now described with a sixfold "blessed." Israel will be blessed in all spheres and relationships of life. They will be blessed in the city and in the country (i.e., everywhere; v. 3); the fruit of the womb of man and animal will be blessed, as well as the fruit of the land (v. 4; cf. 7:13); the basket in which the fruit is stored will be blessed (v. 5; cf. 26:2) and the kneading trough in which the daily bread is prepared (cf. Exod. 12:34; the blessing will be that the basket and the trough will always be filled at the appropriate time); and Israel will be blessed when they come in and go out (i.e., always; cf. Num. 27:17; Ps. 121:8).

28:7-10 *The LORD will grant that the enemies who rise up against you will be defeated before you. They will come at you from one direction but flee from you in seven.*

⁸The LORD will send a blessing on your barns and on everything you put your hand to. The LORD your God will bless you in the land he is giving you.

⁹The LORD will establish you as his holy people, as he promised you on oath, if you keep the commands of the LORD your God and walk in his ways. ¹⁰Then all the peoples on earth will see that you are called by the name of the LORD, and they will fear you.

Moses then further details the content of the blessing. Israel's enemies will be defeated (v. 7); they will march against Israel along one road, as a well-organized army, but they will flee along seven, dispersed and scattered. Verse 8 speaks again of the blessing, this time adding "on your barns and on everything you put your hand to" (cf. vv. 3, 5). Verse 9 states that the Lord will establish Israel as His holy people, i.e., people who belong to Him (cf. v. 10; 7:6; 14:2; 26:19; Exod. 19:5). The Lord already *had* made Israel His holy people, but here the promise is given that this will be established in the future (if Israel keeps His commandments) and will be made manifest to all (cf. v. 10) in the prosperity Israel will receive from the Lord. "As he promised you on oath": cf. Exodus 19:5–6. Thus all nations will see that they "are called by the name of the LORD." The Lord, by calling Israel His people, has openly attached His name to them (cf. Jer. 14:9). Because of their fear of Israel they will do Israel no harm.

28:11-14 *The LORD will grant you abundant prosperity—in the fruit of your womb, the young of your livestock and the crops of your ground—in the land he swore to your forefathers to give you.*

¹²The LORD will open the heavens, the storehouse of his bounty, to send rain on your land in season and to bless all the work of your hands. You will lend to many nations but will borrow from none. ¹³The LORD will make you the head, not the tail. If you pay attention to the commands of the LORD your God that I give you this day and carefully follow them, you will always be at the top, never at the bottom. ¹⁴Do not turn aside from any of the commands I give you today, to the right or to the left, following other gods and serving them.

First, the blessing is again summarized, this time as "abundant prosperity," and is then detailed. Verse 11, cf. verse 4. Verse 12 mentions the rain, on which the fertility of the soil was so dependent (cf. 11:14); "the storehouse of his bounty" depicts the heavens as the place where God stores the rain (cf. Gen. 1:7; 7:11; Job 38:22). Israel will become so prosperous that it will lend to many nations but will not have to borrow from anyone (cf. 15:6). Thus Israel will become "the head, not the tail," it will occupy the place of honor among the nations, not that of dishonor (cf. Isa. 9:13). Israel will move ever upward, never downward (cf. RSV)—if they keep the Lord's commands (v. 13) and not deviate from them (v. 14). The most cardinal sin of all is given as an example: the following and serving of other gods (cf. 11:28). Cf. also verses 1, 2, 9; 5:29; et al.

2. Curse for disobedience (28:15–68)

28:15 *However, if you do not obey the LORD your God and do not carefully follow all his commands and decrees I am giving you today, all these curses will come upon you and overtake you:*

Over against the blessing is now set the curse, in case the people will not obey the Lord (vv. 15–68). Concerning the fact that the curses are presented at greater length, see comments on 27:4, 14. "Will come upon you and overtake you," see comments on verse 2.

28:16–19
You will be cursed in the city and cursed in the country.
[17] Your basket and your kneading trough will be cursed.
[18] The fruit of your womb will be cursed, and the crops of your land, and the calves of your herds and the lambs of your flocks.
[19] You will be cursed when you come in and cursed when you go out.

These verses run parallel with verses 3–6 (except that the basket and the kneading trough are mentioned before the fruit of the womb, etc.). The sixfold "cursed" announces the curse as it will spread throughout Israel's life.

28:20–26 The Lord will send on you curses, confusion and rebuke in everything you put your hand to, until you are destroyed and come to sudden ruin because of the evil you have done in forsaking him. [21] The Lord will plague you with diseases until he has destroyed you from the land you are entering to possess. [22] The Lord will strike you with wasting disease, with fever and inflammation, with scorching heat and drought, with blight and mildew, which will plague you until you perish. [23] The sky over your head will be bronze, the ground beneath you iron. [24] The Lord will turn the rain of your country into dust and powder; it will come down from the skies until you are destroyed.

[25] The Lord will cause you to be defeated before your enemies. You will come at them from one direction but flee from them in seven, and you will become a thing of horror to all the kingdoms on earth. [26] Your carcasses will be food for all the birds of the air and the beasts of the earth, and there will be no one to frighten them away.

The sixfold curse, like the sixfold blessing, is worked out in more detail (cf. v. 7). Verse 20 is still general in nature; the Lord will send "curses, confusion and rebuke," three synonyms that reinforce each other. "Confusion" may refer especially to a panic sent into the army by God (cf. 7:23), and "rebuke" to the curse spoken by God in His anger. Beginning with verse 21, Moses goes into detail. First he mentions separately the plague (the phrase reads literally, "will make the plague cling to you," cf. KJV), because of its dreadful character. Then follow seven afflictions (the number of fullness). On "wasting disease, with fever," cf. Leviticus 26:16. "Inflammation" and "scorching heat" are translations of Hebrew words that are found only here;

they indicate something burning and hot, but their precise meaning cannot be determined. These four afflictions thus threaten human life. The following word in the Masoretic Text is "sword" (cf. NASB), which would refer to murder and war. But the context makes the reading "drought" more probable, which is then the first of three plagues that will destroy the harvest. "Blight" (or "blasting," cf. RSV) is a disease of the grain common in Palestine and the surrounding region, a result of the scorching east wind. The Hebrew word rendered "mildew" may also refer to damage caused by November winds, which turn the ears of grain yellow without kernels developing in the ears (cf. Amos 4:9). Verses 23–24 then detail the drought already mentioned in verse 22. The sky will be bronze and the ground iron—both will be hard as metal, so that not a drop of rain falls from the sky and nothing sprouts from the ground (cf. Lev. 26:19). Instead of rain, sand and dust will fall upon them (v. 24; in Palestine the air can indeed be full of dust and sand when it is very hot). Israel will be defeated by their enemies (v. 25; cf. v. 7) so completely that they will be an object of horror to all the nations of the earth and the battlefield will be strewn with corpses that become food for the wild animals (the greatest indignity that could befall a dead body, cf. 1 Kings 14:11; Jer. 7:33; 16:4; et al.). Burial of the dead, and even the frightening away of the wild animals, is impossible because the survivors have fled.

28:27–34 *The LORD will afflict you with the boils of Egypt and with tumors, festering sores and the itch, from which you cannot be cured. ²⁸The LORD will afflict you with madness, blindness and confusion of mind. ²⁹At midday you will grope about like a blind man in the dark. You will be unsuccessful in everything you do; day after day you will be oppressed and robbed, with no one to rescue you.*

³⁰You will be pledged to be married to a woman, but another will take her and ravish her. You will build a house, but you will not live in it. You will plant a vineyard, but you will not even begin to enjoy its fruit. ³¹Your ox will be slaughtered before your eyes, but you will eat none of it. Your donkey will be forcibly taken from you and will not be returned. Your sheep will be given to your enemies, and no one will rescue them. ³²Your sons and daughters will be given to another nation, and you will wear out your eyes watching for them day after day, powerless to lift a hand. ³³A people that you do not know will eat what your land and labor produce, and you will have nothing but cruel oppression all your days. ³⁴The sights you see will drive you mad.

Moses further details the curse. Verse 27 lists four kinds of incurable illness: "the boils of Egypt," an especially terrible form of leprosy found in Egypt (elephantiasis); "tumors," cf. 1 Samuel 5:6, 9, 12; "festering sores"; and "the itch." Verse 28 then speaks of psychological suffering; "blindness" could refer to a physical defect, but its placement between "madness" and "confusion of mind" indicates a blindness based on a mental disorder. Verse 29 describes the result: at midday they will grope like a blind man in the dark (the simile indicates that verse 28 does not refer to literal blindness; cf. Isa. 59:10). Israel will be unsuccessful in all their undertakings (cf. Ps. 37:7) and will be oppressed and robbed "day after day." The latter is elaborated in verses 30ff., which contain a number of indications that the capture of the land by the enemy is in view here. Someone else (the enemy) will enjoy whatever Israel possesses (cf. Amos 5:11; Mic. 6:15; Zeph. 1:13; Deut. 20:5–7). Sons and daughters will be taken away into slavery (v. 32, cf. v. 41) and their parents will wait for them with powerless longing; their crops will be eaten by strangers (v. 33, cf. Isa. 1:7). Thus Israel will be an oppressed and mistreated people (cf. v. 29), driven mad by all they see (cf. "before your eyes," v. 31, and "you will wear out your eyes," v. 32).

28:35–37 *The LORD will afflict your knees and legs with painful boils that cannot be cured, spreading from the soles of your feet to the top of your head.*

36The LORD will drive you and the king you set over you to a nation unknown to you or your fathers. There you will worship other gods, gods of wood and stone. 37You will become a thing of horror and an object of scorn and ridicule to all the nations where the LORD will drive you.

Verse 35 announces another incurable illness (cf. v. 27): "painful boils" (a type of leprosy) on knees and legs, which make both walking and standing impossible; they will spread and affect the entire body. Verse 36 speaks of the deportation of not only the sons and daughters but of the entire nation (cf. vv. 32, 64), including the king, who will thus also be unable to save this people. In the captivity Israel will serve other gods (cf. 4:28), and will become an object of scorn and ridicule to all nations (v. 37).

28:38–44 *You will sow much seed in the field but you will harvest little, because locusts will devour it. 39You will plant vineyards and cultivate them but you will not drink the wine or gather the grapes, because worms will eat them. 40You will have olive trees throughout your country but you will not use the oil, because the olives will drop off. 41You will have sons and daughters but you will not keep them, because they will go into captivity. 42Swarms of locusts will take over all your trees and the crops of your land.*

⁴³The alien who lives among you will rise above you higher and higher, but you will sink lower and lower. ⁴⁴He will lend to you, but you will not lend to him. He will be the head, but you will be the tail.

In these verses, Moses sees Israel as still living in Canaan. A curse rests on all their labor: the locusts will destroy the field crops, the worms the grapes, and the (still unripe) olives will fall off the trees because of a disease. The Israelites will raise sons and daughters (v. 41) but they will not enjoy them because the children will be taken into captivity (cf. v. 32). Trees and field crops will be destroyed by "swarms of locusts." (The word rendered "swarms of locusts" is found only here; it is also rendered "whirring locust," but its exact meaning is unknown.) Thus Israel will become ever poorer (v. 43), and the alien will become master—lender rather than borrower (cf. vv. 12–13). The relative prosperity of the alien, while of course providentially arranged by God, may also have natural causes. Since the alien does not own land, he is not affected by the curse that rests on it; and with his other sources of income he will be able to enrich himself at the expense of the impoverished Israelites by becoming a moneylender.

28:45–57 *All these curses will come upon you. They will pursue you and overtake you until you are destroyed, because you did not obey the LORD your God and observe the commands and decrees he gave you. ⁴⁶They will be a sign and a wonder to you and your descendants forever. ⁴⁷Because you did not serve the LORD your God joyfully and gladly in the time of prosperity, ⁴⁸therefore in hunger and thirst, in nakedness and dire poverty, you will serve the enemies the LORD sends against you. He will put an iron yoke on your neck until he has destroyed you.*

⁴⁹The LORD will bring a nation against you from far away, from the ends of the earth, like an eagle swooping down, a nation whose language you will not understand, ⁵⁰a fierce-looking nation without respect for the old or pity for the young. ⁵¹They will devour the young of your livestock and the crops of your land until you are destroyed. They will leave you no grain, new wine or oil, nor any calves of your herds or lambs of your flocks until you are ruined. ⁵²They will lay siege to all the cities throughout your land until the high fortified walls in which you trust fall down. They will besiege all the cities throughout the land the LORD your God is giving you.

⁵³Because of the suffering that your enemy will inflict on you during the siege, you will eat the fruit of the womb, the flesh of the sons and daughters the LORD your God has given you. ⁵⁴Even the most gentle and sensitive man among you will have no compassion on his own brother or the wife he loves or his surviving children, ⁵⁵and he will not give to one of them any of the flesh of his children that he is eating. It will be all he has left because of the suffering your enemy will inflict on you during the siege of all your cities. ⁵⁶*The most gentle and sensitive woman among you—so sensitive and gentle that she would not venture to touch the ground with the sole of her foot—will begrudge the husband she loves and her own son or daughter* ⁵⁷*the afterbirth from her womb and the children she bears. For she intends to eat them secretly during the siege and in the distress that your enemy will inflict on you in your cities.*

Verses 45–46 summarize the preceding. Because of Israel's disobedience these curses will come upon them (cf. v. 15) and they will be "a sign and a wonder" to them and their descendants, a visible proof of the Lord's punishment (cf. 29:23ff.). "Forever" (*ᶜad–ᶜolam*) does not have to be taken in an absolute sense; over against this threat stands the promise of restoration, of being accepted again by the Lord (ch. 30). In the light of the revelation as a whole we know that both the threat and the promise in their deepest essence do find an absolute fulfillment, albeit not in the same persons.

In verses 47ff. a concrete threat of punishment is again added. First, the cause restated: Israel's sin, which is here defined as Israel's failure to serve the Lord joyfully in response to the abundance He has bestowed on them in Canaan. Therefore, the enemy that the Lord will send will bring hunger, thirst, nakedness, and want; he will put an iron yoke on Israel (i.e., Israel will be in harsh servitude to the enemy) until the enemy has destroyed Israel.

Verses 49ff. further describe this enemy. It is a nation "from far away, from the ends of the earth" (cf. Isa. 5:26, the Assyrians; Hab. 1:8, the Chaldeans); they are foreign and unknown to Israel, as is emphasized by the words, "whose language you will not understand (cf. Isa. 28:11; 33:19). "Like an eagle swooping down": with great swiftness descending on its prey; the same image is used in Jeremia 48:40; 49:22 (the Chaldeans; concerning the swiftness, see also Isa. 5:26; Hab. 1:6ff.). "Fierce-looking" is literally "fierce of face" (cf. Isa. 13:18). This nation will devour the produce and the herds until it has destroyed Israel (v. 51; "calves of your herds. . . ," cf. 7:13; et al.). It will besiege Israel in all their cities, until the high walls in which they put their trust fall down (v. 52). So great will be the suffering that the Israelites will eat their own children (this happened when Samaria was besieged by the Arameans, 2 Kings 6:28–29, and when Jerusalem was besieged by the Chaldeans, Lam. 2:20; 4:10, and by the Romans).

Verses 54–57 further elaborate the thought of verse 53. Even the most "gentle and sensitive"[43] man will value the flesh of his own children so much that he will refuse to share it with others. And the woman who has never let her foot touch the ground, who always was carried in a chair, acts even more despicably: she eats in secret, even the afterbirth and the newborn child, without sharing with anyone.

28:58–68 *If you do not carefully follow all the words of this law, which are written in this book, and do not revere this glorious and awesome name—the* LORD *your God—* [59]*the* LORD *will send fearful plagues on you and your descendants, harsh and prolonged disasters, and severe and lingering illnesses.* [60]*He will bring upon you all the diseases of Egypt that you dreaded, and they will cling to you.* [61]*The* LORD *will also bring on you every kind of sickness and disaster not recorded in this Book of the Law, until you are destroyed.* [62]*You who were as numerous as the stars in the sky will be left but few in number, because you did not obey the* LORD *your God.* [63]*Just as it pleased the* LORD *to make you prosper and increase in number, so it will please him to ruin and destroy you. You will be uprooted from the land you are entering to possess.*

[64]*Then the* LORD *will scatter you among all nations, from one end of the earth to the other. There you will worship other gods—gods of wood and stone, which neither you nor your fathers have known.* [65]*Among those nations you will find no repose, no resting place for the sole of your foot. There the* LORD *will give you an anxious mind, eyes weary with longing, and a despairing heart.* [66]*You will live in constant suspense, filled with dread both night and day, never sure of your life.* [67]*In the morning you will say, "If only it were evening!" and in the evening, "If only it were morning!"—because of the terror that will fill your hearts and the sights that your eyes will see.* [68]*The* LORD *will send you back in ships to Egypt on a journey I said you should never make again. There you will offer yourselves for sale to your enemies as male and female slaves, but no one will buy you.*

Once again the speaker makes a fresh start and pronounces the most terrible curses on Israel in case they are disobedient. Israel is told to "carefully follow all the words of this law, which are written in this book." "This law" refers to the content of Deuteronomy, and "this book" is thus Deuteronomy in its more or less final form. If Moses himself spoke these exact words, we must assume that he had written "this law" down beforehand, which means that he had the Book of Deuteronomy before him, albeit not in its final form. But it appears to us that we can with more probability assume that the phrase "which are

---

[43]Ridderbos renders this "spoilt and pampered" (also in v. 56).

written in this book" was added later, when Deuteronomy was written down, for the benefit of the reader.

The final words of the verse, "and do not revere this glorious and awesome name—the LORD your God" contain a further description of "carefully following"; it is the result and manifestation of the fear of the Lord. The object of this fear, or reverence, is twofold: the "name" and "the LORD your God." Both expressions have the same purport: the "name" is the name "LORD" (Yahweh, cf. Lev. 24:11); he who fears that name fears the Lord Himself, who made Himself known to Israel by that name (cf. also 12:5).

In verse 59 begins another list of punishments. First, disasters and illnesses, and especially the diseases of Egypt (cf. v. 27), but also every kind of disaster and illness *not* "recorded in this Book of the Law" (see comments on v. 58). Even though they cannot all be listed, they will all befall Israel if they are disobedient. As a result, the people who were once as numerous as the stars in the sky will become few in number (cf. 4:27). And the Lord, who at first took pleasure in blessing Israel and making it numerous, will now be pleased to do the opposite—an anthropomorphic statement that indicates that the Lord's love will, because of the people's sin, turn into holy anger and zeal to punish.

What is left of Israel will be taken away from Canaan and scattered among the nations (cf. 4:27), where they will serve foreign gods, gods made of wood and stone (cf. v. 36). But Israel will find no rest there; the hostile environment will keep them on the run, and Israel will find no place to settle. They will be filled with fear and anxiety (cf. Lev. 26:36ff.). They will be in "constant suspense" (lit., "your life will be in doubt before you," as something that hangs from a thread that may snap at any moment). The inner terror will make them long for the morning when it is evening and vice versa. And the description culminates in the Lord's threat that He will take Israel back to Egypt, the greatest disaster imaginable, since the deliverance from Egypt was the fundamental act of salvation (cf. also 17:16). "In ships": a cargo of slaves, without any chance of escape en route. "On a journey [lit., "by the way"] I said you should never make again": this refers of course not to the sea route in a literal sense, but rather to the journey back to Egypt in general (concerning the expression, see comments on 17:16). Their captors intend to sell them as slaves in Egypt, but what awaits them is the ultimate indignity and misery: no one will think them worth the slave price.

C. DISCOURSE AT THE RENEWAL OF THE COVENANT IN MOAB (CHAPTERS 29-30)

1. Renewal of the covenant (ch. 29)

29:1 *These are the terms of the covenant the* Lord *commanded Moses to make with the Israelites in Moab, in addition to the covenant he had made with them at Horeb.*

The view, held by some in the past, that this verse is a subscript to the preceding is untenable, since nothing has been said in the previous chapters of a renewal of the covenant in Moab. Rather, this verse is the superscription of what follows, where there is indeed mention of a covenant (vv. 9ff.). "The terms of the covenant," literally "the words of the covenant," refers to the discourse with which Moses made Israel enter into this covenant. "In Moab" is where Moses gave all these discourses (cf. 1:5). The renewal of the covenant, performed at the Lord's command through Moses' mediation, is a confirmation of the more fundamental covenant made at Horeb with offerings and the sprinkling of the people with blood (Exod. 24). Israel had transgressed this covenant in many ways (in the first place with the golden calf), but the Lord had nevertheless not annulled the covenant. This is why the ceremony of Exodus 24 is not repeated, even though there is reason to reaffirm the existing covenant (cf. also 6:17ff.; 27:9). *Moses* makes this covenant (even as the covenant at Horeb) with Israel in the sense that he is the Lord's representative (in v. 12 the Lord makes the covenant; in v. 14 it is again Moses).

29:2-8 *Moses summoned all the Israelites and said to them:*
Your eyes have seen all that the Lord *did in Egypt to Pharaoh, to all his officials and to all his land.* *³With your own eyes you saw those great trials, those miraculous signs and great wonders.* *⁴But to this day the* Lord *has not given you a mind that understands or eyes that see or ears that hear.* *⁵During the forty years that I led you through the desert, your clothes did not wear out, nor did the sandals on your feet.* *⁶You ate no bread and drank no wine or other fermented drink. I did this so that you might know that I am the* Lord *your God.*
⁷When you reached this place, Sihon king of Heshbon and Og king of Bashan came out to fight against us, but we defeated them. *⁸We took their land and gave it as an inheritance to the Reubenites, the Gadites and the half-tribe of Manasseh.*

Verse 2a, cf. 5:1; the covenant is thus renewed in an assembly called for this purpose. In verses 2b-8 Moses gives a historical survey, in which he mentions the most important acts of deliverance that not only Moses but also the people (albeit the previous generation) had witnessed (cf. 1:30; 4:34; 7:19; 11:2ff.). First, Moses states what happened in Egypt ("those great trials," cf. 4:34). In verse 4, a complaint is inserted about Israel's obduracy, which caused them not to understand or even see the manifestations of God's grace. This complaint is prompted by the words, "with your own eyes you saw" (v. 3); they saw, yet did *not* see nor understand in the deeper sense of the words (cf. Isa. 6:9; Jer. 5:21). The statement "the Lord has not given you a mind . . . or eyes" (cf. Isa. 6:10) is not intended to excuse them but shows that their obduracy is so deep-seated that no human power can remedy it. The only remedy lies in humble prayer (cf. Jer. 31:18). "A mind that understands" is literally "a heart to know"; the heart represents the inner man, and as such is the seat of understanding and knowledge, here not in a strictly intellectual sense, but an understanding that comprises the fear of the Lord (cf. 5:29).

Verse 5 then continues verse 3 and speaks of the wilderness journey. "I" is the Lord (as also in v. 6), who speaks through Moses. On "your clothes," see 8:4. On "you ate no bread" (v. 6), cf. 8:3. This time there is also mention of wine and fermented drink. "So that you might know that I am the Lord your God." He showed them that it is only He who sustains them, even in the absence of the normal sources of sustenance. Verse 7 summarizes what happened to Sihon and Og and their land (cf. 2:26ff.; 3:1ff., 12ff.).

29:9–15 *Carefully follow the terms of this covenant, so that you may prosper in everything you do. ¹⁰All of you are standing today in the presence of the Lord your God—your leaders and chief men, your elders and officials, and all the other men of Israel, ¹¹together with your children and your wives, and the aliens living in your camps who chop your wood and carry your water. ¹²You are standing here in order to enter into a covenant with the Lord your God, a covenant the Lord is making with you this day and sealing with an oath, ¹³to confirm you this day as his people, that he may be your God as he promised you and as he swore to your fathers, Abraham, Isaac and Jacob. ¹⁴I am making this covenant, with its oath, not only with you ¹⁵who are standing here with us today in the presence of the Lord our God but also with those who are not here today.*

From this, Moses now draws a conclusion with respect to the covenant. Verse 9 contains the general exhortation to keep "the terms [lit., 'words'] of this covenant," i.e., the covenant that is about to be made. "The terms of the covenant" are here, in contrast to verse 1, the preceding laws, which determine the content of the covenant (cf. 4:13).

This covenant is of course in essence the same as that made at Horeb (see comments on v. 1).

The actual making of the covenant begins in verse 10. Moses first states that they are standing here "in the presence of the LORD": He with whom they will make the covenant is present in His representative Moses. To make this even more emphatic, the leaders and the various groups of the people are mentioned separately. First the "leaders and chief men" and the "elders and officials" (cf. comments on 1:15ff.). Then all the men of Israel, as well as the women and small children and even the aliens who are in the camp (who are included in the covenant; among them are the Egyptians who came with Israel, Exod. 12:38; Num. 11:4, and the Midianites who joined Israel with Hobab, Num. 10:29). These aliens performed the work of servants, such as woodcutting and carrying water (cf. Josh. 9:21, 27).

Verse 12 completes the sentence begun in verse 10 ("You are standing here" is not in the Hebrew but has been added for the sake of clarity). They are standing here to enter into the covenant, and the Lord makes the covenant with them (cf. v. 14). The Lord thus initiates the covenant, and Israel's involvement is that they silently accept what Moses states. The covenant is confirmed with an oath (RSV, "sworn covenant")⁴⁴ : it is certain. Verse 13 states the content of the covenant. Israel is the Lord's people, the Lord is their God (cf. 26:17ff.; 28:9) in accordance with what He swore to the forefathers. Moses makes this covenant not only with those present but also with those who are not, i.e., their descendants. This does not directly refer to the expansion of the covenant to include the non-Israelite world, although it is true that this covenant is essentially one with the new covenant, which includes Jews and non-Jews alike.

29:16–29 *You yourselves know how we lived in Egypt and how we passed through the countries on the way here. ¹⁷You saw among them their detestable images and idols of wood and stone, of silver and gold. ¹⁸Make sure there is no man or woman, clan or tribe among you today whose heart turns away from the LORD our God to go and worship the gods of those nations; make sure there is no root among you that produces such bitter poison.*

---

⁴⁴The actual meaning of "oath" is "curse," which refers to the hypothetical curse one invokes on oneself if a contract or covenant is broken. Hence the word is used of the contract or covenant itself and characterizes it as something confirmed by the invoking of a curse on oneself in case of failure to live up to the terms. But in this case, since the Lord is the one making the covenant, this literal sense must not be emphasized.

¹⁹When such a person hears the words of this oath, he invokes a blessing on himself and therefore thinks, "I will be safe, even though I persist in going my own way." This will bring disaster on the watered land as well as the dry. ²⁰The LORD will never be willing to forgive him; his wrath and zeal will burn against that man. All the curses written in this book will fall upon him, and the LORD will blot out his name from under heaven. ²¹The LORD will single him out from all the tribes of Israel for disaster, according to all the curses of the covenant written in this Book of the Law.

²²Your children who follow you in later generations and foreigners who come from distant lands will see the calamities that have fallen on the land and the diseases with which the LORD has afflicted it. ²³The whole land will be a burning waste of salt and sulfur—nothing planted, nothing sprouting, no vegetation growing on it. It will be like the destruction of Sodom and Gomorrah, Admah and Zeboiim, which the LORD overthrew in fierce anger. ²⁴All the nations will ask: "Why has the LORD done this to this land? Why this fierce, burning anger?"

²⁵And the answer will be: "It is because this people abandoned the covenant of the LORD, the God of their fathers, the covenant he made with them when he brought them out of Egypt. ²⁶They went off and worshiped other gods and bowed down to them, gods they did not know, gods he had not given them. ²⁷Therefore the LORD's anger burned against this land, so that he brought on it all the curses written in this book. ²⁸In furious anger and in great wrath the LORD uprooted them from their land and thrust them into another land, as it is now."

²⁹The secret things belong to the LORD our God, but the things revealed belong to us and to our children forever, that we may follow all the words of this law.

These verses contain a warning against falling away and a threat of punishment in case the covenant is broken. Verse 16 begins with "for" (omitted in the NIV; cf. KJV), indicating that Israel has every reason to enter into and keep the covenant in the light of their past experience ("You yourselves," cf. comments on v. 2). Both in Egypt and during the wilderness journey Israel saw the detestable images of wood, stone (cf. 4:28), silver, and gold that the nations worshiped; how privileged Israel must feel in having this covenant with the Lord! Verse 18 draws the conclusion that no one must turn away from the Lord to worship the gods of those other nations. Such an individual (or clan or tribe) would be (lit.) "a root that bears poison and wormwood" (cf. Heb. 12:15), i.e., a poisonous plant (cf. 32:32; Hos. 10:4; Amos 5:7; 6:12), a source of ruin and destruction for himself and others (cf. 19:10; 21:1ff.). "Wormwood" is a shrub with an unpleasant smell and a very bitter flavor; it is not poisonous, but in the Scriptures it is usually associated with death and ruin (cf. Rev. 8:11). Verse 19 further details the deliberations of an individual who falls away. In his arrogance he thinks that things will go well with him even if he persists in his obduracy (i.e., even though he transgresses the covenant). What follows shows the end result of this kind of thinking. "This will bring disaster"—the Hebrew indicates that this is, as it were, the conscious *purpose* of his efforts (cf. NIV mg., "in order to"). The phrase literally reads, "to sweep away the watered with the dry," perhaps a proverbial expression; we can think of a raging stream that sweeps away everything in its path. Thus, such a reckless and abandoned breaker of the covenant will, if allowed to continue unchecked, drag his whole environment with him into perdition.

Furthermore (v. 20), the Lord's wrath will turn against him so that "all the curses written in this book" (cf. 28:58) will fall upon him; his name will be blotted out and he is singled out to perish from Israel.

Verses 22ff. are not a direct continuation of the preceding, where Moses spoke of an individual apostate. Here Moses foresees a future in which the whole nation has become apostate and is punished accordingly (these verses are related, however, to v. 18, which already spoke of "clan or tribe"). When this happens, a later generation will see the consequences and express its amazement.

The subject of the last part of the sentence (which runs from v. 22 through v. 24) is not exactly the same as that of the first part. "Your children who follow you in later generations" (lit., "the generation to come of your sons") is changed in verse 24 to "all the nations"; there is no major difference in sense, however, since verse 22 mentions "foreigners" along with "your children." The later generations will see the scars of the calamities that have befallen the land. Like Sodom, Gomorrah, Admah, and Zeboiim (Gen. 14:2; Hos. 11:8), the land will be covered with salt and sulphur and therefore entirely barren and infertile. When they see this, all the nations will ask what caused it. The answer (v. 25) will be that the inhabitants forsook the covenant of the Lord and worshiped other gods whom they did not know (cf. 11:28) and whom He had not given them (4:19), so that He brought on them all the curses (cf. 28:15-68) "written in this book" (cf. 28:58; the answer corresponds to "all the curses written in this book," even though we do not have to understand this expression to mean that the speaker will use these exact words with a copy of Deuteronomy in hand). Verse 28 concludes the answer and mentions specifically Israel's being taken away in captivity.

267

The concluding words in verse 29 are taken by some as part of the answer that began in verse 25. We consider them rather to be a concluding observation added by Moses. This view is supported by the words "to us and to our children" and by the exhortation at the end to keep the law; the rest of the verse is also most naturally explained in this way. "The things revealed" refers to all that is contained in "the words of this law"—the commandments as well as the blessings and curses connected with them. All this is for "us" and for "our children": they were revealed to Israel that Israel might live in accordance with them. Then there are the "secret things," all that God has not revealed. We should not limit this to God's plan and counsel (which have been revealed in part), although much of it does belong to the "secret things." The meaning is more general, and the intent here is to emphasize how valuable is that which has been revealed. Whatever "secret things" may be hidden in God, that which has been revealed is for us and for our children. We do not have to go up and get it from heaven (cf. 30:12–13). We have it with us, and let us therefore live and walk accordingly.

2. Restoration after repentance (30:1–10)

But Israel's rejection is not the end (cf. 4:29–31; Lev. 26:40ff.); when they return to the Lord after being dispersed among the nations, the Lord will take them back, return them to the land, and bless them again. And the Lord will circumcise their hearts so that they love Him.

The promise of blessing (*heil*[45]) is here, as frequently in the Old Testament, thus presented as contingent upon the conversion of the people. But the Old Testament also teaches that this is not an absolute contingency. In spite of sin, the covenant with Israel will be in force as long as necessary for the people to fulfill their task in sacred history (*heilshistorie*) in accordance with God's plan, especially by bringing forth the Messiah, according to the flesh. And this covenant in its deepest essence, i.e., as a covenant with the *church* embedded in Israel, will *never* be abrogated (cf. Isa. 54:10). The fulfillment of the promises that follow here can therefore not be dependent in an absolute sense on Israel's attitude; granted, the *heil* described here cannot be received by anyone apart from conversion—but that conversion itself

---

[45]See footnote p. 29.

is a gift of the covenant (Jer. 31:33); see also below, comments on verses 6, 10.

The fulfillment of this and similar predictions had its *beginning* when Israel returned from the Captivity, but not its consummation. External blessings like those described here were always received by Israel in limited measure, and the same is true of the inner *heil*, the circumcision of the heart. This does not mean that the rest will one day still be received in fullness by Israel as a nation. The promise of *heil* was indeed given to a nation, but embedded in this nation was the church, the heir of the promise in the full sense of the word. It is therefore clear that the promise of the circumcision of the heart finds its complete fulfillment only in the church of the new covenant (cf. Jer. 31:31ff. with Heb. 8:8ff.), in principle at Christ's first coming, and in fullness at His second coming. And also the promise of external blessing finds, in a higher sense, its complete fulfillment in the new heaven and earth, which will be inherited by the redeemed of Christ. This is preceded, however, by an initial fulfillment in all external blessings that are already now given to the church, i.e., in the increase in their numbers (cf. v. 6).

30:1–5 *When all these blessings and curses I have set before you come upon you and you take them to heart wherever the LORD your God disperses you among the nations, ²and when you and your children return to the LORD your God and obey him with all your heart and with all your soul according to everything I command you today, ³then the LORD your God will restore your fortunes and have compassion on you and gather you again from all the nations where he scattered you. ⁴Even if you have been banished to the most distant land under the heavens, from there the LORD your God will gather you and bring you back. ⁵He will bring you to the land that belonged to your fathers, and you will take possession of it. He will make you more prosperous and numerous than your fathers.*

Moses speaks of a time when (lit.) "all these things have come upon you, the blessing and the curse." What follows (even as what preceded in ch. 29) focuses primarily on the curse. But Moses also mentions the blessing. When "all these things" are fulfilled, the curse may finally predominate, but nevertheless, the people as a whole and the individual members (the latter even in times when the curse comes over the people as a whole) will have enjoyed blessing.

"[When you] take them to heart [cf. 4:39] wherever the LORD your God disperses you among the nations": when Israel in captivity is forced by circumstances to meditate on "all these things" and to learn from them, they will turn to the Lord and obey His voice as it speaks to them through the laws given by Moses. Even the children are included in this turning back to God.

When this happens (v. 3) the Lord will restore their fortunes and bring them back from captivity, even from the most distant land (v. 4), to the land of the forefathers, where He will bless and multiply them even more than He did the forefathers (concerning the fulfillment, see above).

30:6 *The LORD your God will circumcise your hearts and the hearts of your descendants, so that you may love him with all your heart and with all your soul, and live.*

This verse adds an inward blessing: the circumcision of the heart, i.e., the removal of the wrong disposition that turned away from God (cf. 10:16); the result will be that they love the Lord with all their heart and with all their soul, and thus they will live (cf. RSV). This promise of the renewal of the heart as a gift of God's grace is repeated frequently in the Prophets (cf. Jer. 31:33–34; 32:39–40; Ezek. 11:19; 36:26). In this text, the change of heart wrought by God has been preceded by the conversion mentioned in verse 2; here in verse 6 we have therefore not the once-for-all renewal, but rather a continuing renewal; the fact that the *entire* inner renewal (including the conversion of v. 2) is the result of a work of God's grace thus does not find expression here (but cf. v. 10; also 29:4).

30:7–10 *The LORD your God will put all these curses on your enemies who hate and persecute you. ⁸You will again obey the LORD and follow all his commands I am giving you today. ⁹Then the LORD your God will make you most prosperous in all the work of your hands and in the fruit of your womb, the young of your livestock and the crops of your land. The LORD will again delight in you and make you prosperous, just as he delighted in your fathers, ¹⁰if you obey the LORD your God and keep his commands and decrees that are written in this Book of the Law and turn to the LORD your God with all your heart and with all your soul.*

Part of the blessing is that "all these curses" (cf. 29:21) will now be put on Israel's enemies, so that they are rendered powerless. Verse 8 speaks again of the fruit of the inward renewal (cf. v. 6). Verse 9 returns to the external blessing with the words of 28:11 (concerning v. 9b, see 28:63; "your fathers" are all believing forefathers). Verse 10 again adds that Israel will receive these blessings only through obedience and turning to the Lord (cf. v. 8). This turning, the condition for what follows (cf. v. 2), is here itself the content of God's promise.

3. Concluding exhortation (30:11–20)

30:11-14 *Now what I am commanding you today is not too difficult for you or beyond your reach. ¹²It is not up in heaven, so that you have to ask, "Who will ascend into heaven to get it and proclaim it to us so we may obey it?" ¹³Nor is it beyond the sea, so that you have to ask, "Who will cross the sea to get it and proclaim it to us so we may obey it?" ¹⁴No, the word is very near you; it is in your mouth and in your heart so you may obey it.*

Moses concludes with an exhortation to keep the law. "Now" (lit., "for") refers back to the preceding, where Moses spoke of obeying the commands of the Lord. Here he adds that this is possible because the people know the commandments (cf. 29:29; Mic. 6:8). The law Moses gives Israel is not "too difficult," nor is it "beyond your reach." Verse 12 further explains these two expressions. The Hebrew word rendered "difficult" means literally "wonderful"; it is frequently used of God's miraculous deeds, and the first part of verse 12 parallels "not too difficult": the law "is not up in heaven," it is not beyond man's reach, not too wonderful to be grasped or understood (hence, not "hidden," KJV) and it is thus not part of the "secret things" (29:29). It does not have to be brought down from heaven—which would be impossible—because God has revealed it. This is the main point, to which is added in verse 11 "or beyond your reach," so that it would have to be retrieved from across the sea (v. 13). Verse 14 states the same thing positively: It is very near you, not because it has been written down for you, but because it is "in your mouth and in your heart"; "heart" here refers to the memory, as in our expression, "you know it by heart." (Moses apparently thinks of a future situation where the people will have been instructed in the law to the extent that they can recite its main contents from memory.) "So you may obey it": this is the purpose of the revelation of the law; God has done everything to enable you to keep His law. (In Rom. 10:6–10 the apostle uses these words in a somewhat different sense.)

30:15-20 *See, I set before you today life and prosperity, death and destruction. ¹⁶For I command you today to love the LORD your God, to walk in his ways, and to keep his commands, decrees and laws; then you will live and increase, and the LORD your God will bless you in the land you are entering to possess.*

---

[17]But if your heart turns away and you are not obedient, and if you are drawn away to bow down to other gods and worship them, [18]I declare to you this day that you will certainly be destroyed. You will not live long in the land you are crossing the Jordan to enter and possess.

[19]This day I call heaven and earth as witnesses against you that I have set before you life and death, blessings and curses. Now choose life, so that you and your children may live [20]and that you may love the Lord your God, listen to his voice, and hold fast to him. For the Lord is your life, and he will give you many years in the land he swore to give to your fathers, Abraham, Isaac and Jacob.

Finally, Moses gives a brief summary of the law he has presented. In verse 15, he characterizes the law on the basis of the blessing and curse associated with it: "life and prosperity, death and destruction" (cf. 11:26; Jer. 21:8). "Life" and "death" are primarily intended in a national sense (cf. v. 16), although we must not forget that the personal is contained in the national and the eternal in the temporal. In verse 16a Moses once again names the great principle that underlies the keeping of the law: love for "the Lord your God," love that will express itself in obedience to His commands. Verse 16b points to the blessing that obedience brings. Verse 17 then poses the alternative and mentions the most fundamental sin—the worship of other gods, for which the punishment is announced in verse 18. In verses 19–20 Moses concludes with the call to the people to choose life for themselves and their descendants by walking in the path he has shown them.

Part Three

Moses' Final Arrangements,
His Farewell Address, and His Death
(Chapters 31–34)

Moses' exposition of the law in the territory of Moab, introduced in
1:5, has been concluded. In chapters 31–32, Moses appoints Joshua his
successor and writes down the law and gives it to the priests and elders
to be read every seven years. Moses also writes a song at the Lord's
command and teaches it to the Israelites. In chapter 33 follows the
blessing that is Moses' farewell to the tribes of Israel, while chapter 34
contains the report of his death.

I. Moses' Final Arrangements
(31:1–13)

Moses, in view of his impending death, encourages the people and
appoints Joshua as his successor (vv. 1–8) and he writes down the law
and gives it to the priests and the elders (vv. 9–13).

31:1–2 *Then Moses went out and spoke these words to all Israel: ²"I am now a*
hundred and twenty years old and I am no longer able to lead you. The Lord
has said to me, 'You shall not cross the Jordan.'

Moses announces his impending death to the people. The words "then Moses went out and spoke these words to all Israel" are not a direct continuation of the preceding, but assume that Moses withdrew from the people and here again goes out to address them. He reminds them first of all that he is 120 years old (cf. 34:7; Exod. 7:7) and then states, "I am no longer able to lead you." The phrase reads literally, "I am no longer able to go out and come in" (RSV; cf. Num. 27:17), an expression that refers to all human activity (cf. 28:6). The intent is rendered accurately in the NIV. This does not mean that Moses feels his strength ebbing (which would contradict 34:7), but rather that he simply notes that soon he will no longer be with them, as Moses knows through a revelation from God (cf. 3:27).

31:3–6 *The LORD your God himself will cross over ahead of you. He will destroy these nations before you, and you will take possession of their land. Joshua also will cross over ahead of you, as the LORD said. ⁴And the LORD will do to them what he did to Sihon and Og, the kings of the Amorites, whom he destroyed along with their land. ⁵The LORD will deliver them to you, and you must do to them all that I have commanded you. ⁶Be strong and courageous. Do not be afraid or terrified because of them, for the LORD your God goes with you; he will never leave you nor forsake you."*

In view of their imminent separation, Moses encourages the people. He does this by means of a double contrast. First, he says that not he but the Lord will cross over ahead of them (vv. 2b–3a), and then he tells them that not he but Joshua will cross over ahead of them (v. 3b). On "as the LORD said," cf. 3:28. However, Joshua is only the instrument; all emphasis falls on the fact that it is the Lord who destroys the Canaanites (vv. 3a, 4—with a reminder of Sihon and Og, 2:24–3:11—and v. 5). "All that I have commanded you" (v. 5) refers to the total destruction of Canaanites (cf. 7:1–5). Because of all this, Israel must be strong and courageous (cf. 1:21; 20:3)—the Lord goes with them and He will not forsake them (cf. 4:31).

31:7–8 *Then Moses summoned Joshua and said to him in the presence of all Israel, "Be strong and courageous, for you must go with this people into the land that the LORD swore to their forefathers to give them, and you must divide it among them as their inheritance. ⁸The LORD himself goes before you and will be with you; he will never leave you nor forsake you. Do not be afraid; do not be discouraged."*

Moses then summons Joshua and publicly encourages him, in accord with the charge of 1:38 and 3:28. See also Numbers 27:22–23.

31:9–13 *So Moses wrote down this law and gave it to the priests, the sons of Levi, who carried the ark of the covenant of the LORD, and to all the elders of Israel. ¹⁰Then Moses commanded them: "At the end of every seven years, in the year for canceling debts, during the Feast of Tabernacles, ¹¹when all Israel comes to appear before the LORD your God at the place he will choose, you shall read this law before them in their hearing. ¹²Assemble the people—men, women and children, and the aliens living in your towns—so they can listen and learn to fear the LORD your God and follow carefully all the words of this law. ¹³Their children who do not know this law, must hear it and learn to fear the LORD your God as long as you live in the land you are crossing the Jordan to possess."*

These verses relate how Moses turns the law he wrote down over to the priests and the elders, with the charge that it be read to the people every seven years. There is no reason to assume that this took place immediately after the preceding. On the other hand, it is not necessary to make the interval between verses 8 and 9 so long that Moses could have written down the entire law during this period. It is much more probable that he had already written down most of the law beforehand. However, the emphasis here lies on the giving of the law to the priests and elders and the charge that it be read (it is also possible to translate, "And after Moses had written down this law he gave it . . . ; cf. 31:24). "This law" refers to the laws contained in Deuteronomy (cf. 1:5; 4:44; et al.). The priests and elders (the religious and secular authorities) are both mentioned; together they receive the command to make sure that the law is read to the people every seven years (v. 10). It must be read "in the year for canceling debts" (cf. 15:1ff.) during the Feast of Tabernacles (16:13). The reading thus must take place at the central sanctuary (v. 11), where Israel is to appear before the Lord during this feast to have fellowship with the Lord (cf. 16:16). The reason why the Feast of Tabernacles was chosen may be that it drew the most people, or that the living in booths was a reminder of the wilderness journey during which the law was given, or perhaps that it was an especially joyous feast and the reading of the law on that occasion would serve to teach Israel to rejoice in the riches of God's law (cf. Ps. 19:8–14). It is curious that "you" in "you shall read this law" is singular and is the equivalent of the impersonal "one" ("one shall read" is more idiomatically rendered "the law is to be read"); nothing is said about who must perform the public reading. "This law" (cf. v. 9): it is undoubtedly permissible to read selections (cf. "from the Law" in Neh. 8:18).

The whole nation must be assembled, men, women, children, and aliens. All these must thus learn to fear the Lord and to keep this law. Verse 13 states the same thing specifically with regard to the children (who were also included in v. 12; cf. 4:9; 11:19); it is especially necessary for them because they, unlike their parents, have not yet been instructed in the law. "Their" refers to the people of verse 12.

It has been said that the purpose of the public reading of the law must have been something else than promulgation of knowledge of the law, since one reading every seven years would be insufficient for this purpose. But, apart from the fact that this is clearly stated to be the purpose, there is nothing that says that this was the only way in which knowledge of the law was spread.

We do not know to what extent this law was implemented. We hear of a public reading of the law after the Captivity (Neh. 8; this took place in the seventh month); cf. also the public reading of the entire Pentateuch section by section on successive Sabbaths in later Judaism, in a cycle that began and ended with the Simhath Torah, the feast of the "joy of the law," the concluding celebration of the Feast of Tabernacles.

II. Introduction to the Song of Moses (31:14–30)

31:14–15 *The Lord said to Moses, "Now the day of your death is near. Call Joshua and present yourselves at the Tent of Meeting, where I will commission him." So Moses and Joshua came and presented themselves at the Tent of Meeting.*
15Then the Lord appeared at the Tent in a pillar of cloud, and the cloud stood over the entrance to the Tent.

In view of Moses' impending death, the Lord commands him to present himself with Joshua at the Tent of Meeting. "I will commission him" is God's confirmation of what Moses had done in 31:7. Moses and Joshua obey, and the Lord appears at the entrance to the Tent in a "pillar of cloud" (v. 15; cf. Num. 12:5).

31:16–22 *And the Lord said to Moses: "You are going to rest with your fathers, and these people will soon prostitute themselves to the foreign gods of the land they are entering. They will forsake me and break the covenant I made with* *them. [17]On that day I will become angry with them and forsake them; I will hide my face from them, and they will be destroyed. Many disasters and difficulties will come upon them, and on that day they will ask, 'Have not these disasters come upon us because our God is not with us?' [18]And I will certainly hide my face on that day because of all their wickedness in turning to other gods.*

[19]"Now write down for yourselves this song and teach it to the Israelites and have them sing it, so that it may be a witness for me against them. [20]When I have brought them into the land flowing with milk and honey, the land I promised on oath to their forefathers, and when they eat their fill and thrive, they will turn to other gods and worship them, rejecting me and breaking my covenant. [21]And when many disasters and difficulties come upon them, this song will testify against them, because it will not be forgotten by their descendants. I know what they are disposed to do, even before I bring them into the land I promised them on oath." [22]So Moses wrote down this song that day and taught it to the Israelites.

The carrying out of the Lord's intent to commission Joshua is not related until verse 23.[1] First, the Lord foretells Moses that in the future Israel will turn away from Him and that they will be severely punished for this. He also instructs Moses to write down a song and to teach it to the Israelites. In this song, the punishment and the restoration that follows are announced. The fact that this is inserted between verses 15 and 23 indicates that this prediction and this command are also intended for Joshua (cf. v. 19). This concerns life in Canaan, where Joshua will be the first leader of the nation; one of his tasks will be to warn the people against the apostasy of which the Lord speaks here (cf. Josh. 23–24).

In verse 16 the Lord predicts that after Moses' death Israel will serve the gods of Canaan. "To rest with one's fathers" originally referred to the family grave; here it is simply an idiomatic expression meaning "to die." "Prostitute themselves": they will serve these gods and thus breach the faithfulness they owe to the Lord; the concept behind this image is that the covenant between the Lord and Israel is like a marriage (cf. Hos. 1, 3). Israel is like a woman who follows an illicit lover. In verse 17 follows the announcement of punishment, which corresponds closely to the description of the sin in verse 16. Because the Israelites prostitute themselves with foreign gods, the Lord's anger will burn against them. Because they left Him, He will leave them;

---

[1]Some surmise that an error was made in the transmission of the text, and that verse 23 should follow immediately after verse 15. But see comments on these verses.

because they break His covenant, He will hide His face from them (withdraw His favor from them). Consequently, the people will be "destroyed" (lit., "devoured"); the enemies will take their income and possessions and thus destroy them (cf. 7:16). They will be struck by many disasters, so that they cannot but acknowledge that all this happens because they turned away from the Lord. But the Lord will continue to hide His face from them (v. 18), which indicates that the realization of verse 17 is not yet a true conversion.

In verse 19, the Lord instructs Moses (and Joshua) to write down the song that follows in chapter 32, a song that speaks of the disasters referred to in the preceding section, and to teach it to Israel. The plural "for yourselves" indicates that the command also applies to Joshua, while the singular forms "teach" and "have them sing" (lit., "put it in their mouths") indicate that Moses is still the prominent figure. This song is to be a witness for the Lord against the Israelites; this is clarified in what follows. First, their sin of turning to other gods is mentioned again (v. 20), a sin into which they will fall when they enjoy the abundance of good things in Canaan ("eat their fill and thrive," cf. 6:11–12; 8:12–14; 32:15). But this song will testify against them when disasters befall them, i.e., it will tell them that these disasters are punishment for their sin and also (as the content indicates) that their turning away is gross ingratitude in the face of the Lord's blessings. The song can serve as witness because "it will not be forgotten by their descendants," it will be transmitted from one generation to the next.

The Lord deems all this necessary because He knows Israel's disposition even now, before they have entered Canaan (cf. v. 27; also Gen. 6:5; 8:21). Verse 22 adds that Moses wrote down this song and taught it to the Israelites, which of course runs ahead of the actual events.

31:23 *The LORD gave this command to Joshua son of Nun: "Be strong and courageous, for you will bring the Israelites into the land I promised them on oath, and I myself will be with you."*

Only now comes the direct continuation of verses 14–15: the Lord's command to Joshua. The Lord (the Hebrew reads "he," but it is clear that the Lord is the speaker here) gives Joshua a "command" that is essentially a word of encouragement: Joshua will lead Israel into Canaan and God says, "I myself will be with you."

31:24–30 *After Moses finished writing in a book the words of this law from beginning to end, ²⁵he gave this command to the Levites who carried the ark of the covenant of the* LORD: ²⁶*"Take this Book of the Law and place it beside the ark of the covenant of the* LORD *your God. There it will remain as a witness against you. ²⁷For I know how rebellious and stiff-necked you are. If you have been rebellious against the* LORD *while I am still alive and with you, how much more will you rebel after I die!* ²⁸*Assemble before me all the elders of your tribes and all your officials, so that I can speak these words in their hearing and call heaven and earth to testify against them. ²⁹For I know that after my death you are sure to become utterly corrupt and to turn from the way I have commanded you. In days to come, disaster will fall upon you because you will do evil in the sight of the* LORD *and provoke him to anger by what your hands have made."*

³⁰*And Moses recited the words of this song from beginning to end in the hearing of the whole assembly of Israel:*

Before returning to the song in verse 28, the author reports the turning over of the Book of the Law to the Levites.² It is understandable that this would be done at this same time, since this was also part of Moses' final arrangements. "After Moses finished writing," cf. 31:9. The emphasis lies not on the writing but on what follows: the giving of the Law to the Levites and the command to place it beside the ark. "The Levites who carried the ark" does not necessarily refer only to the ordinary Levites; rather, the expression refers to both priests and Levites (also elsewhere the carrying of the ark in general is used to indicate the privilege and task of the Levites and hence their unique position, cf. 10:8). Special priests were undoubtedly appointed to place the Law beside the ark.³ "Beside the ark": inside the ark were the tablets of the Law (Exod. 25:16; 40:20). "As a witness against you" ("you" is singular, and refers to Israel as a whole), i.e., with a purpose similar to that of the song (v. 21). The Law testifies against Israel

---

²Some suspect that we should read "song" instead of "law" in verses 24 and 26. If this is correct, verse 24 would be a continuation of verse 22, and verse 28 would also relate directly to the preceding ("these words" of v. 28 are then the same as "the words of this [song]" in verse 24). However, the textual witnesses give no reason to make this emendation. Furthermore, the supposition that both the Law and this song were placed next to the ark is weak (cf. also v. 21, where the song is said to testify because it has been preserved in *tradition*).

³The addition "who carried the ark" is not in conflict with this. According to Numbers 3:30–31 the carrying of the ark was the task of the (nonpriestly) Kohathites (see comments on 10:8), but Deuteronomy does not take this detail into consideration and uses the expression "the Levites who carried the ark" to indicate the tribe of Levi in general. This thus allows for the possibility that *priests* from this tribe were appointed specifically for the task of placing the Law beside the ark.

whenever they sin. This is necessary because of the people's rebelliousness and stubbornness (cf. v. 21), which were already so much in evidence during Moses' life; the Lord knows that these would become even more manifest after Moses' death.

In verse 28 Moses comes back to the song (cf. v. 19). He instructs the Levites of verse 25 to assemble before him all the elders and officials (cf. 1:15); these are the civil authorities who here represent the people and who were charged with teaching this song to the Israelites (v. 19). The phrase "these words" do not refer to the Law but to the song that follows in chapter 32. "Call heaven and earth to testify against them," cf. 4:26; 30:19 (in 32:1 heaven and earth must listen, so that later they may serve as witnesses). The reason Moses gives is that he knows (on the basis of the Lord's words in vv. 16–21) the future of his people, their sin, and the punishment that will follow. "What your hands have made," i.e., idols (4:28).

Verse 30 then states that Moses recited the song (after the people had been assembled as demanded in verse 28). "The whole assembly of Israel": we may say that the people were present in their representatives, the leaders (v. 28), although the command of verse 28 does not preclude that the common people also assembled themselves.

III. The Song of Moses (32:1–43)

This is a song full of poetic beauty. It contains the main themes of prophecy. The train of thought is as follows. After an introduction (vv. 1–4), Israel's gross ingratitude in the face of the faithful care with which the Lord had surrounded them is described (vv. 5–18); then follow the Lord's anger and judgment (vv. 19–25), but the Lord will keep Israel from perishing altogether, lest the enemies pride themselves in Israel's downfall (vv. 26–33). And finally, the judgment on the nations and Israel's redemption are announced (vv. 34–43).

This overview shows that the purpose of the song goes beyond that stated in 31:19–21 (to testify against them); the second part (vv. 26–43) must encourage Israel in their suffering (cf. esp. v. 43). Nevertheless, this promise of redemption contains much to shame Israel (cf. v. 39).

It is clear that the historical perspective of this song reflects a time much later than Moses. In verse 7 it addresses a nation that can look back on "the generations long past." It sees as historical fact not only the wilderness journey (vv. 11–12), but also Israel's settlement in Canaan and their enjoyment of the abundance and blessing in Canaan (vv. 13–14) and Israel's ingratitude for the Lord's blessings (vv. 15–18). We could even say that the judgment is also described as being in the past (vv. 19–25), although this is less clear. Beginning with verse 20, the Lord is described as *intending* to punish Israel. Yet this intent is stated in the past tense ("he said"). And in the announcement of the judgment on Israel's enemies, Israel is presented as already having been struck by the Lord's punishment (vv. 30, 36). It is not until we reach the description of the demise of the enemies that we clearly find a prediction (cf. v. 35).

The critical approach sees in all this proof that the song is not of Mosaic origin but is from an author of a much later period, according to some of the time of the Syrian wars, but according to most of the period of the Captivity. This is unacceptable from a Bible-believing perspective; rather, we would assume that Moses was transported by the Spirit of prophecy to a later time and from this perspective looks back on Israel's history. This is an agreement with the purpose of the song as stated in 31:19–21 (to be a witness).

There are in our opinion insufficient grounds for assigning a specific historical time or period to Moses' perspective. The characterization of Israel's oppressors as a "non-nation" and a "foolish nation" (v. 21) can, from Israel's perspective, be applied to several or all of the nations under whose yoke Israel had to bow. There is no reason to assume that the poet spoke from the perspective of the Captivity, since no captivity is mentioned.

Israel's history is described here in scenes that repeated themselves several times during the centuries of Israel's national existence.

A. ISRAEL PUNISHED FOR INGRATITUDE
(32:1–25)

32:1–4 *Listen, O heavens, and I will speak;*
hear, O earth, the words of my mouth.
²Let my teaching fall like rain
and my words descend like dew,
like showers on new grass,
like abundant rain on tender plants.
³I will proclaim the name of the LORD.
Oh, praise the greatness of our God!
⁴He is the Rock, his works are perfect,

> *and all his ways are just.*
> *A faithful God who does no wrong,*
> *upright and just is he.*

In verse 1, Moses appeals to heaven and earth to hear him—an indication of the extreme importance of his words. Then he expresses the wish that his "teaching" (a term that characterizes his song as containing wisdom based on divine revelation, cf. v. 6) may be like rain and dew that falls on vegetation, i.e., that it may have a refreshing and life–giving effect on the hearts of his hearers (cf. Ps. 72:6; Isa. 55:10–11). This can happen in general because the poet describes the Lord's greatness (vv. 3–4), but should probably be more especially related to the second part of the song, where the judgment on Israel's enemies and the reacceptance of Israel are announced. In verses 3–4 the Lord's greatness, specifically His justice and faithfulness, is said to be the topic of the song. In connection with verse 3, we may think of the redemption predicted at the end of the song, but this greatness also is manifested in the blessings bestowed on Israel in the wilderness and in Canaan (vv. 6ff.). "The name of the LORD" is His greatness and all it encompasses. "I will proclaim," i.e., in what follows. Moses calls upon all (cf. v. 1) to (lit.) "ascribe greatness to our God," i.e., to praise His greatness.

"He is the Rock" (v. 4): this is apparently an ancient name for God (cf. vv. 15, 18, 31, 37). In Psalm 18:2, where the psalmist says, "God is my rock," the idea of refuge is in the foreground (cf. Pss. 19:14; 31:3–4; 71:3). But this is probably a special application of the image; the idea of immutability on which one can depend was most likely originally dominant (cf. below, and also Gen. 49:24, where the Lord is called "the Rock of Israel").

"His works are perfect" (cf. Ps. 18:30) is clarified by "all his ways are just"; this refers to the manner of His rule over the world. In all this He shows Himself to be the God of judgment, who maintains perfect justice, which means especially that He redeems His people by maintaining the law He has given them. This thought of the Lord's unimpeachable justice is again emphasized in what follows and is then linked to His faithfulness. He does what He has promised and does not put to shame those who hope in His promise. In this connection, "does no wrong" and "upright and just" acquire the special meaning of "who does not deviate from His faithfulness."

32:5 *They have acted corruptly toward him;*

> *to their shame they are no longer his children,*
> *but a warped and crooked generation.*

This verse states the dominant theme of verses 5–18, namely, Israel's ingratitude in the face of the grace the Lord has shown His people. Here, as throughout the song, we must remember that Moses speaks from a future perspective and thus looks back on a lengthy stay in Canaan as lying in the past (see above, introduction to this chapter). They have acted faithlessly toward the God who is faithful, upright, and just. "To their shame they are no longer his children" accurately renders the sense of the phrase (lit., "their blemish [is] not His son's"); The Lord made them His children (14:1), but He has rejected them because of their unworthiness; He no longer can or wants to acknowledge them as His children (cf. Hos. 2:1, 3). Indignant, Moses adds that they are "a warped and crooked generation" instead of God's children.

32:6–14 *Is this the way you repay the Lord,*
O foolish and unwise people?
Is he not your Father, your Creator,
who made you and formed you?
⁷*Remember the days of old;*
consider the generations long past.
Ask your father and he will tell you,
your elders, and they will explain to you.
⁸*When the Most High gave the nations their inheritance,*
when he divided all mankind,
he set up boundaries for the peoples
according to the number of the sons of Israel.
⁹*For the Lord's portion is his people,*
Jacob his allotted inheritance.
¹⁰*In a desert land he found him,*
in a barren and howling waste.
He shielded him and cared for him;
he guarded him as the apple of his eye,
¹¹*like an eagle that stirs up its nest*
and hovers over its young,
that spreads its wings to catch them
and carries them on its pinions.
¹²*The Lord alone led him;*
no foreign god was with him.
¹³*He made him ride on the heights of the land*
and fed him with the fruit of the fields.
He nourished him with honey from the rock,

> *and with oil from the flinty crag,*
> *¹⁴with curds and milk from herd and flock*
> *and with fattened lambs and goats,*
> *with choice rams of Bashan*
> *and the finest kernels of wheat.*
> *You drank the red blood of the grape.*

The Lord's faithful care for Israel.—First, Israel is again condemned, briefly and sharply, for responding to the Lord's faithfulness and justice in such a manner; they are called "foolish and unwise" (in the religio-ethical sense—the opposite of that wisdom of which the fear of the Lord is the beginning). Then Moses describes in detail what Israel owes the Lord. He begins with Israel's origins. The Lord is Israel's Father (cf. 14:1; 32:18; Isa. 63:16; 64:8; Hos. 11:1; Mal. 2:10), He created them, and He "formed" (or "established," cf. RSV) them—three expressions for the formation of Israel as a nation. In verse 7 Moses reminds emphatically of "the days of old," of the "generations long past" (lit., "the years of many generations," cf. RSV), i.e., the entire past (concerning the speaker's perspective, see above). "Your father" and "your elders," those responsible for handing down the tradition, must be consulted. Verse 8 speaks of the hoary past, when the Most High assigned the nations their territories. This does not imply that this took place at one specific point in time (which would force us to think of Gen. 11), but should be understood as a poetic summary of all that God has done through the ages to bring the various nations to the territories they now occupy (cf. Amos 9:7). God is said to have determined the boundaries of the nations "according to the number of the sons of Israel," i.e., in such a manner that Israel could receive a land that would accommodate their numbers; Israel is thus the center of God's world rule.

Verse 9 states the reason: Israel, the Lord's "inheritance," is His people and all His dealings with the world are directed toward Israel's well-being (*heil*), and its corollary, the magnification of His name. We must remember that Israel is in deepest essence the church of God; in the new dispensation the New Testament church therefore takes the place of the nation Israel.

With verse 10 begins a survey of all the good things the Lord had done for Israel, first in the wilderness and later in Canaan. "In a desert land he found him": the poet does not mention the stay in and deliverance from Egypt, poetic license designed to achieve a striking contrast between Israel's helplessness in the wilderness and their blessed state in Canaan (cf., also Hos. 9:10; Ezek. 16:4ff.).

"A howling waste": a wilderness where the wild animals howl, an image that accentuates the dreadfulness of the wilderness (and thus the pitiable condition of Israel; cf. Isa. 13:21–22). The Lord took to heart the fate of those helpless people; He "shielded" (lit., "encircled") them with protection and loving care, as expressed in "he guarded him as the apple of his eye" (the object of careful protection; cf. Ps. 17:8; Prov. 7:2).

Verse 11 compares the Lord's guarding of Israel during the wilderness journey to the eagle and its young (cf. also Exod. 19:4; the image is more elaborate here). The eagle "stirs up its nest" in order to force its young to fly; many understand this in the sense that the eagle stirs up the nest to *teach* its young to fly, but this idea is not expressed anywhere in this text. It is in our opinion therefore more likely that the intent of the stirring up here is to transfer the young to another place (because of threatening danger or for other reasons; cf. Exod. 19:4). The stirring up of the nest is not directly referred to the Lord, but it is logical to think here of the Exodus from Egypt. The eagle "hovers over its young" to come to the rescue when necessary. I would render the second half of verse 11, "He spread his wings, caught him, and carried him on his pinions" (cf. NASB, JB); the Lord thus caught Israel like an eagle catches her young and carries them. Israel could not have completed the wilderness journey in their own strength, but the Lord carried them by His power and His love.

Verse 12 still speaks of the wilderness journey and presents the Lord as leading Israel (cf. Exod. 13:21; 15:13)—the Lord *alone* did this, without the help of any other god. This is proof of His greatness, but it also imposes on Israel the solemn duty to serve Him alone. A "foreign" god is a god worshiped by another nation, but the Lord is Israel's God. This manner of speaking does not intend to imply that the other gods are real (cf. v. 17), but rather expresses the strong tie that binds Israel to the Lord.

Beginning with verse 13, the poet moves on to Israel's arrival and stay in Canaan. (Concerning the fact that Moses describes this as having happened in the past, see the introduction to this chapter.) "He made them go over the heights of the land"⁴ (cf. 33:29) refers to Israel's eminence in the land (cf. 33:29; Isa. 58:14; Ps. 18:34, which speaks of David⁵).

Because of this position of eminence, Israel enjoyed all that Canaan offered, which is summarized in "the fruit of the fields" and then detailed as honey, oil, the products of the flock, wheat, and wine. "He nourished him" is literally "he made him suck." "Honey from the rock" means honey found in fissures in the rock, where wild bees collect it. "Oil from the flinty crag" refers to oil from olive trees that grow on rocky ground. The "rock" and "flinty crag" are mentioned purposely to show that in this exceptionally blessed land even those parts from which nothing could be expected yielded wonderful products. "Curds": the Hebrew word refers to thick milk or cream, perhaps also butter (cf. KJV). "Fattened lambs" is literally "fat of lambs"; the fat was considered the best part. "Choice rams of Bashan" is literally "rams of the sons of Bashan." Bashan, with its vast pastures, was famous for its cattle (Ezek. 39:18). "The finest kernels of wheat" means literally "the fat of kidneys of wheat." "Fat" is used metaphorically to refer to what is best, and fat of kidneys was considered the best fat. "Blood of the grape"is red wine.

32:15–18 *Jeshurun grew fat and kicked;*
    filled with food, he became heavy and sleek.
  He abandoned the God who made him
    and rejected the Rock his Savior.
  ¹⁶*They made him jealous with their foreign gods*
    and angered him with their detestable idols.
  ¹⁷*They sacrificed to demons, which are not God—*
    gods they had not known,
    gods that recently appeared,
    gods your fathers did not fear.
  ¹⁸*You deserted the Rock, who fathered you;*
    you forgot the God who gave you birth.

---

⁴The verb is usually rendered "ride" (so most English versions), but the meaning of the Hebrew verb is broader, and we should, in our opinion, not think here of wagons or riding animals (cf. also Isa. 58:14). [Cf. the TEV rendering, "He let them rule the highlands."]

⁵This and similar expressions are used also of God (Amos 4:13; Mic. 1:3). The question whether the expression has been transferred from man to God or vice versa cannot be answered with certainty, although it seems more probable that it originally was used of God and then applied to men (see Amos 4:13 and Isa. 58:14). In our text it may also be a continuation of the image of verse 11 (carried on eagle's wings).

Israel's base ingratitude. Jeshurun refers to Israel (cf. 33:5, 26; Isa. 44:2). The derivation and meaning of the name are uncertain. Some trace it to a stem that means "to be right" or "to be upright." The name then would designate Israel as the upright nation, perhaps especially in contrast to the name Jacob, "deceiver." The name of honor, Jeshurun, would then have been here to remind Israel of its destination and by contrast of its actual behavior.

Jeshurun "grew fat and kicked": Israel is described as a luxuriant ox that has become recalcitrant (cf. Hos. 4:16). Canaan's abundance, instead of filling Israel with gratitude toward the Lord, becomes the cause of its apostasy (cf. 6:11; 8:10; 31:20). Israel abandoned God "who made him" (cf. v. 6) and rejected "the Rock his Savior," the God (cf. v. 4) who was the source of all Israel's *heil*.[6] "They made him jealous": the Hebrew verb indicates a strong emotion, an inner burning that can be either negative or positive (either "zeal" or "envy," "jealousy"). Here it is clearly used in a negative sense and is reminiscent of the jealousy of a man who does not want to share his wife's love with a stranger (this again would reflect the concept of the Lord's relationship to Israel as a marriage). This view is supported by the following words, "with strange gods" (lit., "with strangers," cf. v. 12; Hos. 1, 3). These foreign gods are called (lit.) "detestable things" or "abominations" because the Lord detests them (cf. 7:25; 27:15). "Demons, which are not God" (or, "which are not gods," cf. rsv): the idols are called gods but are not gods. To the extent that they must be considered real, they are nothing but demons, evil spirits (cf. 1 Cor. 10:20).[7] "Gods they had not known" refers to gods who had not helped or blessed Israel (cf. 11:28). They are "newcomers" (jb), who have come into Israel only recently and who were not feared and worshiped by the forefathers—in contrast to the Lord, who was since ancient times the God of the forefathers and of Israel. Thus Israel has deserted its Rock and God, who gave it birth; the poet returns here to the thought of verse 15b. God is not only Israel's Father (cf. v. 6), He is also, so to speak, Father and Mother simultaneously; he is the God "who gave you birth." Israel owes its *entire* existence to Him, and *all* the love a child needs it has received from Him.

[6]See footnote on p. 29.

[7]The Old Testament also speaks of actual demon worship (Lev. 17:7). But here idols are meant, as the following lines show ("gods"). Besides a different word is used in Leviticus 17:7; the word used in verse 17 is found only here and in Psalm 106:37.

32:19–25 *The L<small>ORD</small> saw this and rejected them*
       because he was angered by his sons and daughters.
  ²⁰*"I will hide my face from them," he said,*
       "and see what their end will be;
   for they are a perverse generation,
       children who are unfaithful.
  ²¹*They made me jealous by what is no god*
       and angered me with their worthless idols.
   I will make them envious by those who are not a people;
       I will make them angry by a nation that has no understanding.
  ²²*For a fire has been kindled by my wrath,*
       one that burns to the realm of death below.
   It will devour the earth and its harvests
       and set afire the foundations of the mountains.
  ²³*"I will heap calamities upon them*
       and spend my arrows against them.
  ²⁴*I will send wasting famine against them,*
       consuming pestilence and deadly plague;
   I will send against them the fangs of wild beasts,
       the venom of vipers that glide in the dust.
  ²⁵*In the street the sword will make them childless;*
       in their homes terror will reign.
   Young men and young women will perish,
       infants and gray-haired men.

The Lord's judgment on the ungrateful people. On all these sins now comes God's judgment. Here also Moses is transported into the future. But his emphasis is not primarily on the judgment itself as already having taken place; rather, he shows the Lord as He, angered by Israel, prepares to punish His unfaithful people. Only the phrase "and rejected them" (v. 19) could refer to the judgment itself, but in light of what follows this should also be understood as part of God's intent, by which God, so to speak, detaches Himself from His people. "His sons and daughters": the Lord is the Father of Israel as a nation (v. 6) and thus also of all Israelites individually. There is thus no question of a saving sonship here but rather of the special relationship to Himself in which the Lord had placed Israel as a whole as well as each of its members. This relationship is of an entirely different nature than that in John 1:12; it can be broken, and thus it is more external; nevertheless, it is of great significance. Israel's specific sin is rejection of the grace that was bestowed uniquely on them. It is not insignificant that besides "sons," "daughters" are also mentioned (cf. Isa. 3:16–24; 32:9–12). "Hide my

288

face from them" (v. 20) means "withdraw my favor from them." "See what their end will be": the Lord will leave them to their own devices and watch their destruction without offering help. On "children," see comments on verse 19.

Verse 21 indicates that the Lord will punish according to the principle, "an eye for an eye." The Israelites have aroused the Lord's jealousy by choosing idols over Him; He will arouse their envy by helping a foreign nation so that it will prevail over Israel.[8] And where Israel preferred "nongods" and "worthless idols," the Lord will use a "nonpeople," a "foolish nation." The former means that, compared with Israel, this nation does not deserve the name "people"; they are a nation without understanding (cf. v. 28; Ps. 74:18), they lack true wisdom, of which the knowledge and fear of the Lord is the beginning (4:6).

Verse 22 indicates that it is God's wrath that effects the punishment. It is described as a fire (cf. 29:20; 4:24). "By my wrath": the Hebrew word used here can mean either "wrath" or "nostril"; I would render "a fire has been kindled in my nostrils" (cf. Ps. 18:8; also Isa. 30:28). The image of snorting in anger, as can be observed in animals, is transferred to God, but in such a manner that the hot, snorting breath is represented as a burning fire. The fire is so intense that it reaches down to Sheol, to the realm of the dead, and spreads over the earth and devours the harvest, and even sets fire to the foundations of the mountains. The description of the effects of God's anger here contains elements that were not fulfilled literally in the judgment on Israel as it is described in the rest of the chapter. The description acquires an eschatological character and points beyond the judgment on Israel to the Last Judgment, when God's judgment will manifest itself to its fullest extent and all that is said here will be fulfilled.

Beginning with verse 23, the Lord's judgment on Israel is described in more concrete terms. The Lord will "heap calamities upon them" and (like a warrior, cf. v. 42) shoot all His arrows against them, i.e., strike them in every way possible (cf. v. 42; Ps. 38:2; 91:5; Job 6:4). In verse 24 a list of these calamities begins (cf. Lev. 26:22; Jer. 15:2–3; Ezek. 5:17; 14:21). When the first series of disasters has brought them to the edge of perdition, a second wave will follow. The first series consists of famine, pestilence, and plague, the second of wild beasts, poisonous snakes, and the sword (v. 25), i.e., war. "Terror" also

---

[8]In Romans 10:19, verse 21b is understood in the deeper sense of the calling of the nations.

relates to war: the men able to bear arms are killed by the sword, the women and children will be killed by terror in the home where they hide ("will reign" is not in the Hebrew, cf. KJV). Thus all will be struck, regardless of age or sex.[9]

B. ISRAEL SPARED AND THEIR OPPRESSORS PUNISHED (32:26–43)

Now follows the obverse: the Lord will not let Israel perish altogether lest the enemies boast in Israel's demise. Rather, He will, when the day of vengeance has come, turn against the enemies, publish their folly and sin, and redeem His people.

Another interpretation holds that the punishment and judgment in this section, as in verses 19–25, relate to Israel (specifically, to the ungodly among Israel) while the nations are also included in the judgment. In our opinion, this view is untenable (see footnotes 10 and 12 below).

32:26–33 *I said I would scatter them*
and blot out their memory from mankind,
27but I dreaded the taunt of the enemy,
lest the adversary misunderstand
and say,'Our hand has triumphed;
the LORD has not done all this.' "
28They are a nation without sense,
there is no discernment in them.
29If only they were wise and would understand this
and discern what their end will be!
30How could one man chase a thousand,
or two put ten thousand to flight,
unless their Rock had sold them,
unless the LORD had given them up?
31For their rock is not like our Rock,
as even our enemies concede.
32Their vine comes from the vine of Sodom
and from the fields of Gomorrah.
Their grapes are filled with poison,

9"Make them childless" is the literal meaning of the word; this cannot be the intended meaning here, however, since it would not apply to young men and young women. It must therefore apply to the people of the land, who will be made childless, i.e., the land will be deprived of its children (i.e., inhabitants). The verse then would read, "The sword will snatch them away in the street and terror in the home: both the young men and the young women, infants and gray-haired men."

and their clusters with bitterness.
³³Their wine is the venom of serpents,
the deadly poison of cobras.

Israel kept from total destruction because of the nations.—The punishment the Lord was preparing to inflict in the preceding verses was terrible, but it now becomes clear that they did not bring complete destruction. True, the Lord's anger was severe enough to inflict total destruction (and Israel's sin thus serious enough to deserve it), but there is a reason that keeps the Lord from doing this: the thought of the "enemy," the "adversary," who would "taunt" ("provoke") the Lord by attributing Israel's perdition to their own strength, rather than to the Lord (cf. Isa. 10:5ff.). "Our hand has triumphed," (lit., "our hand is high"): our strength surpassed that of Israel and of Israel's God—not He, but we have done this. Thus they would assail the Lord's honor, and the thought of this becomes the cause of Israel's salvation (cf. 9:28; Exod. 32:12; Num. 14:15–16; Joel 2:17; Mic. 7:10).

Verse 28 further motivates the preceding. The enemies are without sense or discernment (cf. v. 21).¹⁰ It is probably no longer the Lord who speaks here but Moses, although this does not make a significant difference.

Verse 29 continues the thought: the enemies lack true wisdom, which would make them understand "this" (viz., that Israel's demise is due to the Lord rather than to their own power), and they would "discern what their end will be": they would realize that their pride would bring God's judgment on them (cf. v. 20, which speaks of Israel).

Verse 30 brings to light the folly of their delusion by pointing to what happened when the Lord punished Israel (cf. v. 25), which is stated here as something that has already taken place. One enemy could chase a thousand Israelites, and two enemies could put to flight ten thousand Israelites (cf. Lev. 26:8; Josh. 23:10; Isa. 30:17). The battle did not take its usual course—the Israelites could offer no resistance at all, even when faced with a numerically much weaker enemy. All this shows that this was the direct work of the Lord, of Him who otherwise was Israel's Rock (cf. v. 4), but who now has "sold" them, i.e., delivered in the power of their enemies.

---

¹⁰The view that this refers to Israel does not fit in well with the preceding, with which our verse is connected by "for" (cf. KJV; omitted in NIV). Especially decisive are verses 34–36, which in our opinion speak of the judgment on Israel's enemies. But then the description of sin in verses 32–34, as well as verses 28–31, must also apply to the enemies (see comments on vv. 34–36 and footnote 12 below).

Verse 31 further motivates the thought of verse 30. The response to verse 30 could be that it was the "rock," the god, of the enemies who helped defeat Israel. But this is rejected in the statement, "Their rock is not like our Rock"—Israel's God is the One who truly and effectively acts. "As even our enemies concede": not the enemies depicted in the preceding (they would not be inclined to concede anything like this, since they are triumphant, v. 27), but Israel's enemies in general. There are not a few examples of this: the Egyptians (Exod. 14:25), Balaam (Num. 23–24), and the Philistines (1 Sam. 5:7ff.).

Verses 32–33 continue the judgment pronounced on Israel's enemies in verses 28–29.[11] The statement concerning their folly is now expanded by a more general description of their depravity, this to motivate verse 27 (their ascribing Israel's destruction to their own power) and especially as a preparation for the announcement of judgment in verses 34ff. "Their vine" refers to the enemies, viewed as a national entity (cf. Ps. 80:9). It goes back to the "vine of Sodom and Gomorrah," indicating the most profound depravity (cf. Isa. 1:10; 3:9; Jer. 23:14; Ezek. 16:46–49). This is stated here in general terms, although we can also see this in the light of their folly, described in verses 28–29: they do not discern what their end will be, they do not think of the impending perdition, and in this they are like the inhabitants of Sodom and Gomorrah. "Their grapes" and "their clusters" refer to their deeds, which are poisonous and bitter, i.e., evil and harmful to others.

32:34–43 *"Have I not kept this in reserve*
and sealed it in my vaults?
35It is mine to avenge; I will repay.
In due time their foot will slip;
their day of disaster is near
and their doom rushes upon them."
36The LORD will judge his people
and have compassion on his servants
when he sees their strength is gone
and no one is left, slave or free.
37He will say: "Now where are their gods,
the rock they took refuge in,
38the gods who ate the fat of their sacrifices

---

[11]The first word of verse 32 is "for" (cf. KJV; omitted in NIV), which is parallel to the "for" with which verse 28 begins (also omitted in NIV). We could render it here, "Furthermore, their vine. . . ."

and drank the wine of their drink offerings?
Let them rise up to help you!
Let them give you shelter!
39"See now that I myself am He!
There is no god besides me.
I put to death and I bring to life,
I have wounded and I will heal,
and no one can deliver out of my hand.
40I lift my hand to heaven and declare:
As surely as I live forever,
41when I sharpen my flashing sword
and my hand grasps it in judgment,
I will take vengeance on my adversaries
and repay those who hate me.
42I will make my arrows drunk with blood,
while my sword devours flesh:
the blood of the slain and the captives,
the heads of the enemy leaders."
43Rejoice, O nations, with his people,
for he will avenge the blood of his servants;
he will take vengeance on his enemies
and make atonement for his land and people.

The Judgment on the Enemies and Israel's Redemption. [12] The Lord again is the speaker; in verse 36 He is once again spoken of in the third person, while "He will say" in verse 37 introduces another statement by God. "This" is the depravity of the enemies and of their deeds (vv. 32–33), which are "kept in reserve" (cf. Hos. 13:12; Job 14:17). The Lord keeps them in remembrance to execute judgment in His time. "Sealed in my vaults" reinforces the preceding: they are kept with the same care as a valuable and therefore sealed treasure (cf. KJV).

Verse 35 then states the purpose of this storing away: "It is mine to avenge; I will repay" (cf. Rom. 12:19; Heb. 10:30). It is the Lord's prerogative and He will act. Even if this is not yet evident, it will happen at the time appointed by the Lord. It is the time "when their foot will slip." That time is "near" and "rushes upon them." This is said, of course, from the perspective of the time when the Lord speaks,

---

[12]The view that verses 35–36 speak of a judgment on Israel (and that the preceding verses thus deal with Israel's sins) is in our opinion untenable, in the first place because of the content of the verses. The first line of verse 36 may be rendered,

i.e., of the time when Israel will have been delivered into the power of their enemies and when they are about to perish altogether (cf. vv. 25, 36). Then the Lord's zeal will burn against the enemy and for His people, and He will bring punishment and help speedily, even though this may take a long time by human standards (cf. Zech. 1:12).

Verse 36 shows the other side of the judgment on the enemies, namely, Israel's redemption. This verse shows that Israel is kept from complete destruction, not only because of the thought of the enemies' response (v. 27), but also because the Lord has compassion on Israel. The first line of this verse is also found in Psalm 135:14. We would render the word "judge" in this verse as "do justice." The Lord is the Judge, who makes sure that the oppressed receives his rights and who thus delivers him. Israel's oppression was a legitimate punishment for their sins (vv. 19ff.), but it was a wrongful oppression on the part of the enemies. The basis for this doing justice ("vindication," RSV) is His compassion on His servants (Israel; see footnote on p. 289): He sees that "their strength is gone," that they can no longer resist and are about to perish altogether. "No one is left, slave or free," or, "slave and free are both done for." "Slave and free" is a fixed expression indicating all the men (and thus the whole nation; cf. 1 Kings 14:10; 21:21; 2 Kings 9:8; 14:26).

In verses 37–38 the Lord mocks the gods and their worshipers. Those worshipers are (even as in v. 31) the enemies (not Israel; the Lord could not very well say to Israel, "Let them rise up and help you"

"The Lord will judge his people" or "The Lord will render justice to his people" (RSV, "will vindicate"). If the rendering "judge" is adopted and applied to Israel, it is seen as a judgment to purify His people; the ungodly will perish in this judgment, but the righteous will be delivered. The latter are then "his servants" on whom the Lord has compassion. But "his servants" are the same as "his people" (cf. v. 43!), in which case "judge" must also have a meaning similar to "have compassion" and refer to the deliverance from the predicament described in verse 36b, i.e., "judge" must then be taken in the sense of "do justice" (cf. Ps. 135:14).

No less problematic is a comparison of verses 35 and 36; while verse 35 contains only threat, in verse 36 the promise of salvation (*heil*) is dominant. The only natural explanation can be found if it is assumed that verse 35 speaks of the judgment on the nations and verse 36 of the deliverance of Israel implicit in that judgment.

Furthermore, the judgment described in verses 41–42 clearly refers to the nations, and it is highly unlikely that this would be a different judgment from that described in the preceding. The rejoicing of verse 43 also argues for the view that the salvation (*heil*) of Israel described in verse 36 is effected by the judgment on the nations. [For an alternative view, which limits the statement of Israel's salvation to verse 36a, see JB.]

when His compassion on Israel has just been aroused, v. 36). But the Lord does initially address Israel ("their gods"). He mocks the gods of the nations in the hearing of His people to encourage Israel and to teach them to trust in Him alone. On the name "the rock," cf. verse 31. Verse 38 reminds of the offerings that were brought to these gods, of course in the expectation of their help. With "Let them rise and help you" the Lord now turns directly to the nations; this is a rhetorical figure of speech that increases the vividness of the portrayal.

Verse 39 draws the conclusion that the Lord alone is God. Again the Israelites appear to be addressed (as in v. 37); the Lord wants to teach them to acknowledge Him as the only God when He will display His might. "That I myself am He" expresses that Jahweh is the only God (cf. Isa. 41:4; 43:10–11; 48:12), as is also stated in the following line, "There is no god besides me" (cf. 4:35, 39). The next words portray Him in His omnipotence. He puts to death and brings to life (cf. 1 Sam. 2:6; 2 Kings 5:7); He wounds and heals, according to His pleasure (cf. Isa. 43:13; Hos. 5:14). His bringing to life and healing are manifested in Israel's redemption (concerning healing, cf. Hos. 6:1; Isa. 30:26; 57:18); but the emphasis is on the means (the punishment of the enemies) and the conclusion reflects this: "no one can deliver from my hand" (cf. Isa. 43:13).

Verses 40–42 continue in the same spirit. The Lord swears by Himself (cf. Isa. 45:23; Jer. 22:5; Heb. 6:17) that He will punish His enemies. "I lift up my hand to heaven" is a strongly anthropomorphic expression, which presents God as an earth dweller who calls on the God of heaven to be his witness and avenger (cf. Exod. 6:7; Num. 14:30). The day will come when the Lord will sharpen His sword, which flashes like lightning (cf. Gen. 3:24; Nah. 3:3; Hab. 3:11), and execute His judgment. Then He will take vengeance on the nations, who are not only Israel's, but also His adversaries, who hate Him. Verse 42b further describes this: the Lord will use not only the sword, but also arrows (cf. v. 23), which fills in the image of the Lord as a warrior (cf. Isa. 34:5–6; 63:3–6; Jer. 46:10). Accordingly, the entire judgment is depicted here as a battle in which the Lord is the Victor. His "sword devours flesh," a common expression to indicate that the sword kills; His arrows will be "drunk with blood," an expression analogous to the previous one, indicating that the arrows drink blood to excess, i.e., spill blood. The blood is that of those who were slain or taken captive in the battle (the captives are thus also slain). We would expect in the last line of verse 42 a reference to "flesh" to complete the parallelism; instead, one specific part of the body is mentioned, "the hairy heads of the enemies."[13] This is probably an allusion to the custom of letting the hair grow long in war, a custom that likely was connected with the idea of unlimited strength. This "hairy head" of the enemies is thus mentioned as characteristic of their self-confidence and pride, rendered powerless when faced with Israel's God (cf. Ps. 68:21).

Verse 43 forms the conclusion. The nations are exhorted to rejoice with Israel over the impending deliverance; these nations are not Israel's oppressors, but the other nations. This appeal to the nations is in the first instance a rhetorical device to express the greatness of Israel's salvation (*heil*). But in the light of the revelation as a whole, statements such as this acquire a deeper meaning and significance, namely, that in the *heil* that befalls Israel the entire world is involved. The Lord's work is described, in accord with the preceding, as the avenging of the blood of His servants (spilled by the enemies) and vengeance on His adversaries. The idea that He makes "atonement for his land" is based on the concept of blood guilt, which rests on the land because of the "blood of his servants" spilled by the enemies. Atonement is made by punishing the guilty party (cf. 19:13; 21:8–9).

IV. Concluding Exhortation
(32:44–47)

32:44–47 *Moses came with Joshua son of Nun and spoke all the words of this song in the hearing of the people. ⁴⁵When Moses finished reciting all these words to all Israel, ⁴⁶he said to them, "Take to heart all the words I have solemnly declared to you this day, so that you may command your children to obey carefully all the words of this law. ⁴⁷They are not just idle words for you— they are your life. By them you will live long in the land you are crossing the Jordan to possess."*

Verse 44 concludes the report of the Song of Moses (cf. 31:30). "With Joshua the son of Nun," cf. 31:19 (lit., Hoshea, cf. Num. 13:8, 16). Verses 45–47 refer back to Moses' proclamation of the law and add a concluding exhortation. "All these words" refers to all the words of the law. "Idle": the Hebrew word means "empty," and hence

---

[13]The rendering "the head[s] of the enemy leaders," while also possible, is in our opinion less appropriate. If "head" is understood literally, then it is unclear why the blood or flesh is taken specifically from the head; if taken figuratively, in the sense of "most important," then the parallelism breaks down.

"without power," "ineffectual" (note the contrast with "your life"). "For you" is literally "away from you," so that it would not concern you. Rather, these words "are your life": if they are kept, Israel will live long in Canaan.

V. Moses Again Commanded to Climb Mount Nebo (32:48–52)

32:48–52 *On that same day the* Lord *told Moses,* [49]*"Go up into the Abarim Range to Mount Nebo in Moab, across from Jericho, and view Canaan, the land I am giving the Israelites as their own possession.* [50]*There on the mountain that you have climbed you will die and be gathered to your people, just as your brother Aaron died on Mount Hor and was gathered to his people.* [51]*This is because both of you broke faith with me in the presence of the Israelites at the waters of Meribah Kadesh in the Desert of Zin and because you did not uphold my holiness among the Israelites.* [52]*Therefore, you will see the land only from a distance; you will not enter the land I am giving to the people of Israel."*

Now ("On that same day," the day on which he recited the song and spoke the exhortation of vv. 45–47) Moses again is told to go up Mount Nebo to see Canaan and to die (cf. Num. 27:12–14; Deut. 3:27). Mount Nebo (called Pisgah in 3:27) is a peak of the Abarim Range. Concerning Aaron's death on Mount Hor, cf. Numbers 20:22ff. "Because you did not uphold my holiness" (v. 51): the "holiness" is the fullness of His deity—they did not honor Him as God, they did not honor His divine majesty and power.

VI. Moses' Blessing (33:1–29)

Between the announcement of Moses' death (32:48–52) and the report of his death (chap. 34) we find the last farewell of the man of God, the blessing he pronounced on the Israelites.

The blessings proper are found in verses 6–25, while verses 2–5 and verses 26–29 are of a more general nature. The curious element is that verses 2–5 and 26–29, when placed together, make good sense as a unit. The critical perspective therefore assumes that these verses were originally indeed a unit (a song or psalm), while the actual blessings were later inserted between the first and second part. We do not reject this view entirely, as long as what is said below about the origin and content of this chapter is kept in mind.

It is clear that the Scriptures ascribe the content of this chapter to

Moses. However, there is a distinction between this and the preceding chapters with regard to authorship. The Song of Moses (chap. 32) is said to have been written down by Moses himself, but not so this chapter. Rather, we get the impression that this chapter was not written by Moses. Not only does it begin with a superscription (v. 1) whose author appears to distinguish himself from Moses (he speaks of Moses in the third person and calls him "the man of God"), but the individual blessings are introduced similarly (with the exception of the first one). We may therefore assume that this chapter at least was *recorded* by a later hand.

Yet both these introductions and the superscriptions state that Moses spoke these words, which is decisive from a Bible-believing perspective.

The critical perspective assumes a much later date for this chapter (as for Deuteronomy in general). A distinction with respect to date is also made between the blessings (vv. 6–25) and the so-called psalm (vv. 2–5, 26–29). The latter is usually assigned a later date (some think even of the time after the Captivity), while the blessings are believed to be somewhat older (in part because of the force and originality of the images and the traces of great antiquity it is thought to reflect). Many think of the time of Jeroboam II; the northern kingdom (the kingdom of Ephraim) was at that time at the zenith of its power, and it is believed that the blessings reflect this by assigning such an important place to Joseph. Verse 17 is even thought to contain a direct description of Jeroboam II.

We consider this explanation of verse 17 to be incorrect. However, the main issue lies elsewhere. The above view takes as its starting point the assumption that we do not have prophecy here, and that the author could only have described conditions of his own time. Once this assumption is accepted, the Mosaic authorship of this chapter must be rejected. For it cannot be denied (regardless of one's interpretation of various details) that the description of some of the tribes corresponds clearly to what happened in history. But to us this proves only that Moses was led in a special way by the Spirit of prophecy.

We should mention separately the view that assigns Mosaic origin only to the blessings, while relegating the "song" or "psalm" (vv. 2–5, 26–29) to a later period. It is thought that this is possible without violating the Scriptural data: Verses 1–2a would refer only to the blessings of verses 6–25, but not to the song, which was inserted later. But in our opinion this does not do justice to the sense of the Scripture. Verse 1 refers to all that follows and ascribes the content to Moses, although this does not preclude the possibility that it consists of different parts (see above). The claim that verses 26–29 describe Israel's settling in Canaan as a historical fact and must therefore date from a post-Mosaic period does not hold water, since it must also be understood as a prophetic statement (see comments on v. 2).

A. SUPERSCRIPTION (33:1)

33:1 *This is the blessing that Moses the man of God pronounced on the Israelites before his death.*

What follows is called "the blessing" of Moses; this applies not only to the actual blessings (vv. 6–25), but also to the more lyrical portions (vv. 2–5, 26–29), which are joined to the blessings so as to form a unit. "Man of God" is a title frequently used of a prophet; it is used of Moses also in Joshua 14:6 and in the superscription of Psalm 90. "Before his death": Moses is granted a privilege similar to that of the patriarchs immediately before his death (Gen. 27:7, 10; 50:16).

B. INTRODUCTION (33:2–5)

It is at times difficult to establish the meaning of these verses, perhaps due to an inaccurate transmission of the text. It is clear that the blessings pronounced on the individual tribes are preceded and followed by a description of the blessings (*heil*) the Lord has granted Israel as a nation, not only in the giving of the law (vv. 4–5), but also in their settling in Canaan (vv. 2, 26–29). The latter is stated as an accomplished fact; Moses thus sees the future prophetically, as if it has already come to pass (cf. comments on ch. 32).

33:2 *He said:*
"*The* LORD *came from Sinai*
and dawned over them from Seir;
he shone forth from Mount Paran.
He came with myriads of holy ones
*from the south, from his mountain slopes.**

This verse describes a theophany, an appearing of God. This is not the theophany on Sinai, but rather a figurative description of the help the Lord gave Israel in the conquest of and settlement in Canaan (cf. Ps. 18:8ff.). The Lord came *from* rather than *on* Sinai, and He came

---

*Ridderbos translates the last line of verse 2 "at his right hand [appeared] to them burning fire" (cf. RSV).

from Seir and from Mount Paran. Seir (cf. 1:2) is the territory of the Edomites, and Paran (cf. 1:1) lies between Sinai and Seir. Mount Sinai, the mountain where the Lord revealed Himself to Israel, is here presented as His dwelling place, and He comes from there via Mount Paran and Seir to help His people (cf. Judg. 5:4; Hab. 3:3). "Dawned over them" and "shone forth" like the sun (cf. Isa. 60:1-2) describes the appearance of God in glory and splendor (cf. Hab. 3:3-4). This shining light is the manifestation of His divine majesty and also reflects the *heil*[14] that He brings to His people. "With myriads of holy ones" or "from myriads of holy ones" (NIV mg.); the latter rendering would see God as coming from the hosts that are around His throne (cf. 1 Kings 22:19; Job 1:6; Pss. 68:18; 89:8; Dan. 7:10; Joel 3:11; Zech. 14:5) and would also see heaven, the true dwelling place of God, beside the symbolic dwelling place, Sinai. If our rendering of the last line of verse 2 is correct ("at his right hand [appeared] to them burning fire"), then the theophany is described as being accompanied by fire (cf. 4:11; Exod. 3:2), another manifestation of the Lord's majesty and also of the destruction He brings on His enemies ("to them" refers to the Israelites, to whom this manifestation is a source of comfort).

33:3-5 *Surely it is you who love the people;*
  all the holy ones are in your hand.
 At your feet they all bow down,
  and from you receive instruction,
 ⁴the law that Moses gave us,
  the possession of the assembly of Jacob.
 ⁵He was king over Jeshurun
  when the leaders of the people assembled,
  along with the tribes of Israel.

"The people" is literally "the peoples"; here it can refer only to Israel (*'am* refers to a group of people; some versions follow the LXX and read "his people," e.g., RSV). "All the holy ones" is literally "all his holy ones"; "his" probably refers to Israel (although we would expect "their"). The members of the nation are "holy ones" because they belong to the Lord (cf. Exod. 19:6; Num. 16:3; Dan. 7:21ff.). "Are in your hand": here and in the next two lines the poet addresses the Lord; Israel's holy ones are in His hand, protected and safeguarded by Him.

---

[14]See footnote on p. 29.

The text and translation of the next two lines is uncertain; the NIV rendering expresses that the Israelites surrender themselves to the Lord in submission and trust to receive instruction (or direction, cf. RSV) from Him; this may refer to the conquest of Canaan or to the wilderness journey, in which case the author goes back to the time before verse 2.

The latter is even more clearly the case in verse 4, which deals with the giving of the law. Moses gave the law as God's mediator (some would delete "Moses" and read "He gave us," which would fit in well with v. 5). The giving of the law, as well as His manifestation described in verse 2, is proof of His love and grace as shown to Israel; this is further emphasized by the words "the possession of the assembly of Jacob." Israel's riches are the law, because the keeping of this law brings the Lord's blessing and thus life.

Thus the Lord (not Moses) became king over (or in, cf. RSV) Jeshurun (i.e., Israel; cf. 32:15). "When the leaders of the people assembled" refers to the gathering of the people at Horeb (4:10ff.; 9:10; 10:4; 18:16; cf. Exod. 19:17ff.). This, as well as the mention of the law in verse 4, indicates that this being or becoming king refers specifically to the giving of the law, i.e., to the grace the Lord showed Israel by wanting to rule as their King through His law. But also, the Lord's kingship over Israel encompasses all aspects of the *heil* (see footnote p. 29) and redemption Israel received from His hand; indeed, His kingship already revealed itself before the law was given (cf. Exod. 15:18).

C. MOSES BLESSES THE TRIBES (33:6–25)

In verses 6–25 we find the actual blessings, addressed to each of the tribes individually, after the pattern of Genesis 49. Ephraim and Manasseh are combined under the name "Joseph" (vv. 13–17), although they are mentioned separately at the end (v. 17). Issachar and Zebulun are also combined in one blessing (vv. 18–19). The sequence differs from that in Genesis 49 as well as from the usual order in which the tribes are listed. It is difficult to determine a reason for the sequence followed here.

Simeon is not mentioned at all. According to Genesis 49:7 this tribe would be scattered among the others, and Joshua 19:2–9 indicates that Simeon only received a number of cities in Judah's territory. Simeon thus did not acquire a position of independence among Israel; nevertheless, the tribe was not simply absorbed in Judah. Leaders of

Simeon and their genealogies are mentioned as late as Hezekiah's time (1 Chron. 4:34–43).

33:6 *"Let Reuben live and not die,*
nor his men be few."

Even as in Genesis 49, the first blessing is for Reuben, Jacob's firstborn. Jacob had denied him the position of prominence, and Moses also describes Reuben as a tribe that will not be in first position; he limits himself to the blessing "Let Reuben live and not die," i.e., may Reuben continue to exist as a tribe. The second line has been interpreted a number of ways; we would be inclined to understand it as an elaboration on "not die": do not let his men become few so that the tribe will slowly dwindle away and can no longer maintain its independent existence.

33:7 *And this he said about Judah:*
"Hear, O LORD, the cry of Judah;
bring him to his people.
With his own hands he defends his cause.
Oh, be his help against his foes!"

Judah, the tribe from which the king would come, is addressed second (cf. Gen. 49:10). Moses sees Judah in distress and wants the Lord to help Judah and "bring him to his people." This is reminiscent of a period when Judah still lived more or less by itself and had not yet become part of the community of the tribes (cf. the Song of Deborah, Judg. 5, in which Judah is not mentioned), perhaps because it was still separated from the other tribes by Canaanite territory. Note that in these lines the blessing has the character of a request addressed to God (cf. also vv. 8ff.; the blessing in v. 6 is stated as a wish).

The third line reads (if the Masoretic Text is correct[15]), "With his own hands he defends his cause," referring to Judah's position of leadership. This may then refer back to Judah's seeking to be united with his people, a cause that will benefit all of Israel. It is also possible to render, "he will defend their cause," which then refers to Judah's position of leadership in the battles in which Israel will soon be involved.

---

[15]The words are somewhat unclear. Many adopt a conjectural reading, "With your own hands defend his cause" (cf. RSV), which makes this line a continuation of the preceding prayer.

33:8-11 *About Levi he said:*
"Your Thummim and Urim belong
*to the man you favored.**
You tested him at Massah;
you contended with him at the waters of Meribah.
⁹He said of his father and mother,
'I have no regard for them.'
He did not recognize his brothers
or acknowledge his own children,
but he watched over your word
and guarded your covenant.
¹⁰He teaches your precepts to Jacob
and your law to Israel.
He offers incense before you
and whole burnt offerings on your altar.
¹¹Bless all his skills, O LORD,
and be pleased with the work of his hands.
Smite the loins of those who rise up against him;
strike his foes till they rise no more."

In contrast to Genesis 49, Levi is here described as the priestly tribe, chosen and blessed by the Lord. The Thummim and Urim (usually mentioned in reversed order) are found in the breastpiece of the high priest (Exod. 28:29–30). "Your" refers to the Lord: He gave the oracle and He directs it. The tribe of Levi, represented in the high priest, has been given the privilege of wearing this oracle. "The man you favored" is the tribe of Levi as represented in their patriarch. Massah ("testing") reminds of the events at Rephidim (Exod. 17:1–7; cf. Deut. 6:16; 9:22), where the Israelites grumbled because they lacked water; "the waters of Meribah" may point to the same event (the place was called Massah and Meribah, Exod. 17:7) or to a similar occurrence at Kadesh (Num. 20:1–13; the name Meribah is used here also, specifically in the phrase "the waters of Meribah," v. 13). The meaning of the lines is not entirely clear, however. According to the narrative, Israel tested the Lord (Exod. 17:7; cf. Deut. 6:16) and quarreled with Him (Exod. 17:7;

---

* The Masoretic vocalization reads "the man of your devout one." "Man" then would be collective for "men," and "your devout one" would be Moses, so that the Levites are then described as fellow tribesmen of Moses. But this would be an exceptionally obscure description, especially since Moses is nowhere else called "your devout one." Another rendering is "your devout man," which then refers to Levi or to the Levites, but this cannot be justified on linguistic grounds.

Num. 20:13). In this verse, however, it is the Lord ("You") who tested Levi and quarreled with him. This is so different from what is said in Exodus 17 and Numbers 20 that there is reason to wonder if this verse does not allude to something that happened to Levi at Massah and Meribah that is not recorded. If this solution is rejected, then the most satisfactory explanation would appear to be the following. In Exodus 17:1–7 it is not only the people who test the Lord, but the Lord also tests Moses by means of all the trouble the people gave him (similarly, the Lord tested Israel by the difficulties and problems of the wilderness journey; Deut. 8:2). And likewise in Numbers 20:1–13 it was not only the people who quarreled with the Lord, but the Lord also quarreled with Moses and Aaron because they did not honor Him as holy before the Israelites (v. 13). We must then assume that what happened to Moses and Aaron is here transferred to the tribe of Levi, whose most illustrious representatives they are.

A separate question is the reason these facts are mentioned here. The answer may be that the testing of Moses and Aaron (and in them of the entire tribe of Levi) served to prepare them for their task, and that the Lord's quarreling with these men is a reminder of the special responsibility their task brings with it.

Verses 9–10 give an idealistic description of the Levites and the way they carry out their task (no distinction is made between the priests and the nonpriestly Levites). The singular in verse 9a still refers to "the man you favored" (v. 8), i.e., Levi as the representative of the entire tribe. In verse 9b the poet shifts to the plural, which does not make an essential difference. First, the Levites are said not to regard (lit., see), recognize, or acknowledge the members of their own immediate family—they deny the most intimate blood-ties when the Lord's service makes this necessary (cf. 13:7ff.; Matt. 10:37; 19:29; Luke 14:26). This refers in the first place to the fact that, after the sin with the golden calf, the Levites at Moses' command carried out the punishment (Exod. 32:26–29; cf. v. 27, "each killing his brother and friend and neighbor"). But in addition, the (ideal) Levite had to act in the same spirit in the carrying out of his entire task, for example, by being impartial in the administration of justice (cf. 17:8ff.; 19:17; 21:5) and also in the instruction in and explanation of the law mentioned in verse 10. But in all of his official work, the true Levite or priest is deeply aware that he is dedicated to the Lord in a special sense and that no earthly ties may interfere with the carrying out of the obligations incumbent upon him in his sacred service. Verse 9b depicts, in continuation of the preceding and in preparation of what follows, the Levites in their faithfulness to the word and the covenant of the Lord (cf. Mal. 2:6). This covenant may refer to the covenant with Israel, but also more specifically to that with Levi (cf. Mal. 2:5). Their faithfulness to the Lord's law benefits them especially, since part of their task is to teach Israel the Lord's precepts and law (v. 10; cf. Lev. 10:11; Zeph. 3:4; Hag. 2:11). Another aspect of their duties is the bringing of offerings, among which the whole burnt offering is the most important one and is therefore mentioned separately.

The blessing ends in verse 11 with a prayer. "Bless his skills" (lit., "bless his strength" or "substance"; cf. KJV): "skills" would refer to the strength and ability to carry out their task, but this would appear to be less appropriate in connection with "bless" than "substance" or physical prosperity. "The work of his hands" most likely refers to their official work, especially the bringing of offerings; may God be pleased with this, as this will be to Israel's benefit. The conclusion speaks of opponents and foes: may God destroy them. This is a prayer for protection against all those who might want to lay hands on the Lord's priests (cf. 1 Sam. 22:16ff.; Hos. 4:4).

33:12 *About Benjamin he said:*
> *"Let the beloved of the LORD rest secure in him,*
> *for he shields him all day long,*
> *and the one the LORD loves rests between his shoulders."*

Next are Rachel's sons, of whom Benjamin, the youngest, comes first. He is called "the beloved of the LORD." Some attribute this title to the fact that he was Jacob's favorite son after Joseph's disappearance (Gen. 44:20); this relationship with his father then would have been transferred here to his relationship with the Lord. This is not very convincing, however. The reason for this name is more likely to be found in the fact that the Lord dwells in his territory (see below). As the beloved of the Lord, Benjamin enjoys the Lord's special protection. "In him" (lit. "by" or "beside him") again refers to the Lord's dwelling in Benjamin. "And the one the LORD loves rests between his shoulders" (lit., "he shall dwell between his shoulders"): the Lord is seen as carrying Benjamin on His back as a father does his child. However, this imagery is highly unusual, and we would expect "sit" rather than "dwell" and "on" rather than "between." We therefore prefer the rendering "he [the Lord] dwells between his [Benjamin's] hillsides" (cf. JB), referring to the fact that the Lord would have His sanctuary in Benjamin's territory; we can think in this connection of the places in Benjamin where the sanctuary stood for some time (Bethel, 1 Sam. 10:3; Nob, 1 Sam. 21:2ff.; and Gibeon, 1 Kings 3:4), and perhaps also of Jerusalem with the temple (in Josh. 18:28 Jerusalem is considered part of Benjamin, but in Josh. 15:63 part of Judah).

33:13–17 *About Joseph he said:*
> *"May the* LORD *bless his land*
>   *with the precious dew from heaven above*
>   *and with the deep waters that lie below;*
> *¹⁴with the best the sun brings forth*
>   *and the finest the moon can yield;*
> *¹⁵with the choicest gifts of the ancient mountains*
>   *and the fruitfulness of the everlasting hills;*
> *¹⁶with the best gifts of the earth and its fullness*
>   *and the favor of him who dwelt in the burning bush.*
> *Let all these rest on the head of Joseph,*
>   *on the brow of the prince among his brothers.*
> *¹⁷In majesty he is like a firstborn bull;*
>   *his horns are the horns of a wild ox,*
> *with them he will gore the nations,*
>   *even those at the ends of the earth.*
> *Such are the ten thousands of Ephraim;*
>   *such are the thousands of Manasseh."*

Rachel's eldest son, Joseph, is mentioned after Benjamin. Two tribes constitute Joseph: Ephraim and Manasseh (cf. v. 17; Gen. 48:8ff.). The length of this blessing corresponds to the importance Joseph (and especially Ephraim) would gain in the future. Verses 13–16 speak of the riches of the territory assigned to Joseph; these verses are similar to (and in part verbatim) Genesis 49:25b–26. The blessing is described in great detail and includes both the blessings and their indirect causes. The Masoretic Text reads, "with the best of the heavens for the dew" (cf. KJV). We prefer to read *mimma'al* ("above") instead of *mittal* ("dew") (cf. RSV). This emendation finds support in Genesis 49:25 and also corresponds to "below" in the next line. On the other hand, "dew" is mentioned by itself in verse 28. "The best of the heavens" refers then to the rain and the dew, while the land is also blessed with the water from below, the water from springs (this water is seen as coming from the great mass of water under the earth). The territory of Ephraim and Manasseh was considerably more abundant in water than the southern part of Canaan. Also the sun and the moon are mentioned as the indirect causes of blessing; their warmth and light makes the plants of the field grow. "Moon" is literally "moons," perhaps the different phases of the moon or "month" (cf. RSV).

In verses 15–16 the focus shifts to the earth, from which spring plants and trees. First, the mountains and hills are mentioned; we should think here of the forests and vineyards that grow on the hills, but also of grain (cf. Ps. 72:16). The mountains are "ancient" and the hills "everlasting" because they, in contrast to human structures, are permanent (cf. Isa. 54:10). Then, in verse 16, comes the earth in general; "its fullness" is a parallel to "the best gifts." The description culminates in "the favor of him who dwelt in the burning bush." The Lord's favor is the source of all the blessings just described, but it is also that which gives meaning and value to all earthly blessings and surpasses them all (cf. Hab. 3:17ff.). "Who dwelt in the burning bush": cf. Exod. 3:2ff. The section then concludes with the beautiful wish that "all these" blessings may rest on the head of Joseph, i.e., may befall him. Joseph is called "the prince among his brothers." This may refer to the position the tribes that came from Joseph later occupied in Israel; Samaria was in their territory, and the northern kingdom was frequently called Ephraim (also, Jeroboam I, the first king of the ten tribes, came from Ephraim; but Baasha came from Issachar, and the tribal origin of Omri and Jehu is unknown). Another reason may be the high position their patriarch Joseph occupied in Egypt. Most likely both are intended; Joseph's position can be considered a type of the future greatness of his descendants.

Verse 17 is closely connected with the preceding and goes into more detail about the power and greatness that especially Ephraim will have. "In majesty he is like a firstborn bull" (lit., "His majesty is like that of his firstborn bull"): "his [Joseph's] firstborn bull" is Ephraim, to whom Jacob gave the place of the firstborn (Gen. 48:8ff.). He is called a bull to indicate the majesty of his powerful appearance; the image is complemented by "the horns of a wild ox," indicating his strength in battle in which he subdues the nations. "At the ends of the earth" is hyperbole for his power to conquer that no one or nothing can impede. The conclusion is a summary: such are Ephraim and Manasseh, the two tribes of Joseph. The "ten thousands" of Ephraim in contrast to the "thousands" of Manasseh clearly show that Ephraim is the more important of the two.

33:18–19 *About Zebulun he said:*

> *"Rejoice, Zebulun, in your going out,*
> *and you, Issachar, in your tents.*
> [19]*They will summon peoples to the mountain*
> *and there offer sacrifices of righteousness;*
> *they will feast on the abundance of the seas,*
> *on the treasures hidden in the sand."*

The two youngest sons of Leah, Zebulun and Issachar, are also combined in one blessing (the superscription mentions only Zebulun). In the division of the land these two tribes received adjacent territories (Issachar received the Plain of Jezreel and Zebulun the territory north of it), even as in Genesis 49. The imperative "rejoice" means in the context of the blessing that they will rejoice because the Lord's blessing rests on their work. "Tents" is a figurative term for "houses" (cf. 16:7). The two lines of verse 18 should not necessarily be understood to mean that the going out refers only to Zebulun and the tents only to Issachar; the nature of Hebrew parallelism makes it possible that the two lines together express that both Zebulun and Issachar will rejoice, both when they are going out and when they are in their tents: a summary description of all of life. But another explanation is also possible, which connects the going out especially with Zebulun and the tents specifically with Issachar. Genesis 49:14–15 sees the staying at home as characteristic of Issachar, while Zebulun "will live by the seashore" (Gen. 49:13). The latter cannot be taken in a strictly literal sense, since the coastal plain always remained in the hand of the Phoenicians. But it is certainly possible that the proximity of the coast would stir up their mercantile spirit, and thus the "going out" of Zebulun could refer to the fact that merchants from this tribe went out on Phoenician ships on business. In our opinion it is not necessary to make a choice between these two interpretations. It is most probable that "going out" and "tents" apply to both tribes, especially since verse 19 speaks of the two tribes together. But this is not to deny that the choice of words to characterize the two tribes was intentional.

Verse 19 speaks of offerings brought by these tribes, to which they invite the nations. This has been understood in the sense that Zebulun and Issachar would invite pagan nations to participate in the offering meals on the mountain the Lord would choose as His dwelling place (i.e., Zion). But non-Israelites were not allowed to participate in Israel's cultus, and we cannot allow for an illicit cultus in the blessing; besides, the offerings are called "sacrifices of righteousness." "Peoples" here must therefore be taken in the sense of "tribes" (cf. 33:3) and refer to Israelites. Furthermore, this is then not the sanctuary on Mount Zion (these two tribes were not that prominent there), but rather a mountain in or near the territory of these two tribes, e.g., Mount Carmel, where there stood an altar of the Lord (1 Kings 18). The fact that Moses does not condemn the sacrifices indicates that this refers to the time before the building of the temple, when the offering on the "high places" was to some extent permissible. As long as these two tribes have a joint altar there, where they bring the Lord offerings of the rich blessings He has bestowed on them (see below), they invite others from the neighboring tribes to participate in the offering meals or also to bring offerings there themselves.

"Sacrifices of righteousness" are sacrifices that are brought in accordance with the rules, in contrast to various pagan or paganized cults that were practiced in Israel at various times.

The last two lines mention the prosperity that is the basis for these sacrifices. The plural "seas" can also be taken in a singular sense (parallel to the plural "skies" or "heavens"; the plural then serves to express vastness or expanse). If the plural is taken in a literal sense, then it must refer to the Mediterranean Sea and the Sea of Gennesareth. "Feast on" is literally "suck" (cf. KJV); the poetic image indicates that they will "suck" from the sea all that it produces. The "abundance of the seas" is all that overseas commerce and fishing produces. Even though the majority of Zebulun and Issachar did not directly participate in this, they could nevertheless profit from the prosperity of their neighbors, the Phoenicians, by barter. The same is true of the "treasures hidden in the sand" in the last line; the sand is the sand of the seashore, which provided the raw material for making glass and purple.

33:20 *About Gad he said:*
> *"Blessed is he who enlarges Gad's domain!*
> *Gad lives there like a lion,*
> *tearing at arm or head.*

After the last two sons of Leah, Moses mentions Gad, the firstborn of Leah's servant Zilpah. He begins by speaking indirectly of the blessing Gad will receive, by praising the Lord who (lit.) "enlarges Gad," i.e., does not allow Gad to be pushed into a corner by his enemies (cf. Gen.

26:22). Then Moses compares Gad to a lioness (cf. v. 22; Gen. 49:9; Num. 23:24; 24:9), who makes her lair and goes out from there to search for prey; the tearing of (rather than "at") the arm and even the head indicates the complete destruction of the opponent. Others think of the lioness who lies down to leisurely devour her prey, tearing arm and head; this is indeed possible, but the phrases "the arm, yes even the skull" would appear to depict the battle itself. In any case, Moses describes here Gad's prowess and ability to conquer (cf. Gen. 49:19); we think of the battles with the Bedouins who constantly attempted to penetrate the land east of the Jordan.

33:21 *He chose the best land for himself;*
the leader's portion was kept for him.
When the heads of the people assembled,*
he carried out the LORD's righteous will,
and his judgments concerning Israel."

Verse 21a states that Gad chose (lit.) "the first part" for himself; Gad was one of the tribes who, at their request, were given the land east of the Jordan, which had been conquered first. In the following lines both text and interpretation are somewhat uncertain; we follow mainly the Masoretic Text. We take "the leader's portion" to mean the best part, the part that would fall to the leader in battle. The fact that it was "kept for him" justifies his choice. The last two lines may refer to the fact that Gad, like the other trans-Jordan tribes, went with Israel across the Jordan to do battle with the Canaanites. Gad did this (i.e., will do this) "with the heads of the people" (cf. KJV). He "carried out the LORD's righteous will" and "his judgments" in defeating the Canaanites, which was an execution of God's punishment, grounded in justice.

33:22 *About Dan he said:*
"Dan is a lion's cub,
springing out of Bashan."

Dan is called a lion's cub, springing out of Bashan. Moses thus ascribes also to this tribe the power to win in battle (for the image, cf. v. 20). "Out of Bashan": not because Dan would live there (Dan's territory was west of Benjamin), but because Bashan was a habitat of lions.

---

*Ridderbos translates "and he came with the heads of the people."

33:23 *About Naphtali he said:*
> *"Naphtali is abounding with the favor of the LORD*
> *and is full of his blessing;*
> *he will inherit southward to the lake."*

Naphtali "is abounding" with the favor of the Lord, i.e., is full of the Lord's blessing. "Southward to the lake" is literally "the lake and the south." The lake is the Sea of Gennesareth, but what "the south" refers to is uncertain. The expression "the lake and the south" does not give the impression of being a complete description of Naphtali's territory; it may refer to areas that were for some time disputed by the Canaanites, which Naphtali was finally able to conquer.

33:24–25 *About Asher he said:*
> *"Most blessed of sons is Asher;*
> *let him be favored by his brothers,*
> *and let him bathe his feet in oil.*
> *²⁵The bolts of your gates will be iron and bronze,*
> *and your strength will equal your days.*

Finally, Asher is mentioned, and his portion is described as especially rich. He will be "most blessed of sons" (i.e., most blessed among the sons of Jacob); "let him be favored by his brothers" expresses the same thought. "Let him bathe his feet in oil": his land will be so rich in oil that it is possible, so to speak, to wade in it. Indeed, Galilee, Asher's territory, was rich in olive trees.

Verse 25 adds protection against the enemies: may his cities be well fortified and may he live in peace in these fortified cities as long as he lives (as long as the tribe exists).

D. CONCLUSION (33:26–29)

The conclusion of Moses' blessing is closely related to the introduction. Even as in the introduction, Moses described here the blessings (*heil*) that Israel will receive from the Lord, especially through the settlement in Canaan (cf. v. 2); here also he speaks of the future as if it were already in the past.

33:26–27 *"There is no one like the God of Jeshurun,*
> *who rides on the heavens to help you*
> *and on the clouds in his majesty.*
> *²⁷The eternal God is your refuge,*

and underneath are the everlasting arms.
He will drive out your enemy before you,
saying, 'Destroy him!'*

No one is like the God of Jeshurun (i.e., Israel; cf. v. 5 and 32:15) in greatness and goodness. He helped Israel (when they settled in Canaan, see above[16]) and He did so by displaying the full extent of His greatness and majesty. The image used to convey this is that of the Lord riding through the heavens on the clouds (to rush to the place where His help is needed; cf. Pss. 18:9; 68:33; 104:3).

Verse 27 further elaborates this. The Lord is Israel's refuge (lit., dwelling), where they can hide from all danger. He, "the eternal God" (cf. Ps. 90:1; Hab. 1:12), who has existed from of old; this expression serves to emphasize the greatness of this God and thus also the efficacy of His help. "And underneath are the everlasting arms": this is another way of describing the help offered Israel. In all their struggles and difficulties, Israel was carried by "eternal arms," the strong arms of God. The qualification "eternal" again serves to emphasize the power and majesty of God's arms.

Finally, the preceding statements are focused in the concrete promise, "He will drive out your enemy before you": He drove out "the enemy" (the Canaanites) before Israel and commanded Israel to destroy them, i.e., He gave Israel the strength to destroy them.

33:28 *So Israel will live in safety alone;*
Jacob's spring is secure
in a land of grain and new wine,
where the heavens drop dew.

Thus Israel received Canaan as a land where they could dwell in safety. "Alone" (cf. Num. 23:9), i.e., in their own land where their enemies cannot reach them. "Jacob's spring" is a rather unclear expression; it probably is synonymous with "Israel," "spring" being understood in the broader sense of the water or stream that flows from a spring. The people are then seen as such a stream that flows from the patriarch Jacob. Canaan is praised for its abundance of grain and new

---

*Ridderbos renders "He drove out. . . ."
[16]The statements in verses 26–27a could be rendered in the present tense and thus be understood as having general application (cf. RSV). But "he drove out" in verse 27b is clearly past tense, and Hebrew idiom requires that it be connected with a past tense (consecutive imperfect).

wine (cf. 8:8) and its dew (cf. v. 13)—Israel is secure and has abundance.

33:29 *Blessed are you, O Israel!*
   Who is like you,
   a people saved by the LORD?
   He is your shield and helper
    and your glorious sword.
   Your enemies will cower before you,
    and you will trample down their high places.

Thus Israel is blessed above all other nations: because no one is like Israel's God (v. 26), there is no nation whose lot can be compared to Israel's. "Saved by the LORD": cf. Isaiah 45:17. He is (lit.) "the shield of your help," the Protector who is always prepared to help, and (lit.) "the sword of your excellency," the Warrior who effects your greatness. Thus the enemies will surrender and Israel will "trample down their high places," i.e., triumph over them (cf. 32:13).

VII. Moses' Death
(Chapter 34)

The Book of Deuteronomy ends with the story of Moses' death. Since ancient times, many Jewish and Christian exegetes have held that this chapter was written by someone other than Moses (most think of Joshua, some of Eleazar or Ezra). And rightly so. Although others believed that Moses himself wrote this chapter on the basis of prophetic inspiration, there are in our opinion insufficient grounds for this view, since the scriptural data do not force us to conclude that the entire Book of Deuteronomy in its final form was written by Moses. In view of the historical character of this chapter, it is on the other hand logical to assume that the narrative dates from the period immediately after Moses' death and not, as many have held and still hold, from a much later time (in the past this view was held by those who thought of Ezra as the author, and more recently by adherents of the critical school in general). There are insufficient grounds for assigning a late date to this chapter. We do consider it probable, however, that the final words in verses 10–12 (especially "Since then, no prophet has risen in Israel like Moses") look back upon a long history, and are thus of a much later date. But nothing prevents us from assuming that this is an addition made by a later inspired author. The name "Dan" in verse 1 must perhaps be explained in a similar manner.

On the other hand, "to this day" (v. 6) and the description of Canaan proper in terms of tribal territories (which would not have been possible before the division of the land) in verse 2 can be from the hand of Joshua or one of his contemporaries. These particulars thus do not force us to assign a later date, but they do indicate that this chapter was not written by Moses but was composed after his death, and then not immediately afterward; if Joshua is thought to be the author, we must think of his later years.

But Joshua (or whoever the author may have been) could not have written this narrative without divine inspiration. Israel saw Moses climb up Mount Nebo, and they knew from Moses' own statement that he went up to die (cf. 3:27). But the details reported here concerning Moses seeing the land, the Lord's speaking to him, and his burial in "the valley" could only be known to the author through a special illumination of God's Spirit.

34:1–4 *Then Moses climbed Mount Nebo from the plains of Moab to the top of Pisgah, across from Jericho. There the LORD showed him the whole land—from Gilead to Dan, ²all of Naphtali, the territory of Ephraim and Manasseh, all the land of Judah as far as the western sea, ³the Negev and the whole region from the Valley of Jericho, the City of Palms, as far as Zoar. ⁴Then the LORD said to him, "This is the land I promised on oath to Abraham, Isaac and Jacob when I said, 'I will give it to your descendants.' I have let you see it with your eyes, but you will not cross over into it."*

After Moses has blessed Israel, he goes to fulfill his final earthly task. In accord with the Lord's command of 32:48–51 (cf. 3:26–27; Num. 27:12–13), he climbs Mount Nebo to die. Nebo lies "across from Jericho" and is the highest peak of the Pisgah mountains, the northernmost part of the Abarim Range (mentioned in 32:49 and Num. 27:12). There the Lord shows him the entire land. The question is whether we should understand this as a natural seeing; from Mount Nebo one can indeed see the mountains from Hebron all the way to Galilee, the Dead Sea and the entire Jordan Valley, and in the distance even Mount Carmel and the Hermon. Nevertheless, the words "the LORD showed him" seem to indicate that God sharpened Moses' vision so that he saw the land more clearly and completely than he would have been able to otherwise. The sacred author takes us with Moses through the various parts of the land. First he mentions Gilead, which here apparently refers to all the land east of the Jordan. The words "to Dan" (the phrase reads lit., "Gilead to Dan"; "from" is not in the Hebrew) present problems. We would most naturally think of the city of Dan (in ancient times called Laish), situated east of the Jordan on one of the sources of Jordan. But this city was not called Dan until the time of the Judges (Judg. 18:29), and we would prefer to assign an early date to this chapter. In view of this, some have thought here (as well as in Gen. 14:14) of Dan Jaan, mentioned in 2 Samuel 24:6, or of another place called Dan. But we do not know of a third Dan, and the location of Dan Jaan is uncertain; besides, this text speaks only of Dan, without any addition. Furthermore, the location of the well-known Dan of Judges 18:29 fits this context very well. The objection that this Dan was not situated in Gilead proper has little force, since Gilead apparently refers here to the entire region east of the Jordan, and Dan's location in the far north of this region would make it an eminently suitable reference point. As for the name, we may assume that the author (e.g., Joshua) wrote Laish, which was later changed to Dan when the name of the city was changed.

In verse 2 the description moves to Canaan proper. The various regions are identified by the names of the tribes to which these regions were later allotted. It must therefore be assumed either that the narrative was written down after the division of the land or that the geographical references were later adapted to the then-existing conditions; there are insufficient grounds for the latter supposition (see above).

First, the three main divisions of Canaan are given; Naphtali refers to what was later called Galilee. "The territory of Ephraim and Manasseh" is the central part, while "all the land of Judah" is the southern part of Canaan. Moses sees all this "as far as the western sea" (the Mediterranean Sea), i.e., the entire land to its far border.

Verse 3 then mentions separately "the Negev" (the steppe south of Judah) and the Jordan Valley. That which is nearest is mentioned last, since this is where Moses' eye finally comes to rest. "The Valley of Jericho" refers to the part of the Jordan Valley north of the Dead Sea, while "as far as Zoar" indicates that the Dead Sea is included (Zoar was located on its southern shore). Jericho is called "the City of Palms" because of the palms that used to grow there in the Jordan Valley (Judg. 1:16; 3:13; 2 Chron. 28:15).

The Lord then says to Moses that this is the land He promised to the forefathers. Moses may see it but not enter it; the latter is punishment for his sin, the former a manifestation of God's gracious favor, which mitigates the punishment.

34:5–8 *And Moses the servant of the LORD died there in Moab, as the LORD had said. ⁶He buried him in Moab, in the valley opposite Beth Peor, but to this day no one knows where his grave is. ⁷Moses was a hundred and twenty years old when he died, yet his eyes were not weak nor his strength gone. ⁸The Israelites grieved for Moses in the plains of Moab thirty days, until the time of weeping and mourning was over.*

Then Moses, "the servant of the LORD," dies. This is the first time he is called by this title (in 3:24 Moses calls himself "your servant"), which is frequently given him after his death (Josh. 1:1, 13; 8:31, 33; et al.). The title does not only express his *calling* to the Lord's service (a very special service in Moses' case), but also the *privilege* of a special and intimate relationship with Him (comparable to a valet or personal servant who is allowed to serve his master directly and who is allowed to be continuously in his presence). "There" is on Mount Nebo, probably not on top of the mountain but in "the valley" mentioned in verse 6. He died in Moab, not in Canaan. "As the LORD had said" is literally "according to the mouth of the Lord"—hence the rabbinical explanation that Moses died "by the mouth of the Lord," i.e., by the Lord's kiss (a view mentioned only as a curiosity). "He buried him" (v. 6): the rendering "he was buried" (NEB) is grammatically possible (idiomatically, English uses the passive voice to express the impersonal pronoun; lit. the phrase would read "one buried him"), but is precluded by the statement "to this day no one knows where his grave is." "The valley" is probably a saddle or col near the top of Mount Nebo; we may assume that Moses, after seeing Canaan from the top of Mount Nebo, went down to this valley at the Lord's command and died there. The idea that Moses' grave was unknown to prevent that the Israelites would be tempted to superstitiously venerate his body is unlikely. The Israelites never showed any tendency toward the veneration of dead bodies; indeed, this tendency could scarcely have developed among them, since to them dead bodies, bones, and graves were sources of uncleanness. There must therefore be a different significance in this. In the first place, the Lord, by burying Moses Himself, wanted to honor His servant in Israel's eyes, so that they might continue to value his work more. Part of this was that the grave remained unknown, since it served to emphasize the mysterious and wonderful nature of his death (and thus, by implication, also of his life work). But can we say more? We know that on the Mount of Transfiguration the three disciples saw Moses and Elijah speaking with Jesus (Matt. 17:3). This would appear to suggest the view (also held by the Jews) that Moses' body was reunited with his soul after death. Support for this might also be found in Jude 9, where the archangel Michael disputes with the devil over Moses' body, which can be understood in the sense that Michael rescued Moses' body from the power of the devil ("who holds the power of death," Heb. 2:14) and thus from destruction.

At his death, Moses was 120 years old (cf. 31:2); verse 7 states that nevertheless "his eyes were not weak nor his strength gone." Thus the Lord had strengthened His servant in spite of all the difficulties he experienced (cf. Isa. 40:31). The Israelites mourned Moses for thirty days (as they did Aaron, Num. 20:29).

34:9 *Now Joshua son of Nun was filled with the spirit of wisdom because Moses had laid his hands on him. So the Israelites listened to him and did what the LORD had commanded Moses.*

Joshua, the son of Nun, succeeds Moses. He was "filled with the spirit of wisdom"; this wisdom is the practical understanding that enables one to do what is right. We would capitalize "Spirit," because it refers in our opinion to the Spirit of the Lord who gives Joshua this wisdom. Already before he was commissioned to be Israel's leader, Joshua was called "a man in whom is the spirit" (Num. 27:18), and now he possesses this gift of the Spirit in special measure, to make him fit for his task (cf. 1 Sam. 16:13). "Because Moses had laid his hands on him": an act by which Moses, following God's instructions, makes Joshua his successor and equips him for his task.

34:10–12 *Since then, no prophet has risen in Israel like Moses, whom the LORD knew face to face, ¹¹who did all those miraculous signs and wonders the LORD sent him to do in Egypt—to Pharaoh and to all his officials and to his whole land. ¹²For no one has ever shown the mighty power or performed the awesome deeds that Moses did in the sight of all Israel.*

Finally, the unique place Moses occupies in sacred history is emphasized. No prophet like Moses has risen in Israel since then. This is explained further in the following statements, which describe in what ways Moses towered above all. The Lord knew him face to face. Exodus 33:11 states that "the LORD would *speak* to Moses face to face, like a man speaks with his friend." The expression "face to face" thus indicates the very intimate and familiar way in which the Lord revealed Himself to Moses (cf. also Num. 12:6–8). The word "knew" in our text also includes speaking but is broader and refers to association and fellowship in general; it also includes specifically the giving of power to perform the miraculous signs and wonders that were part of Moses' task.

This ability is indicated in the last three verses. The Lord knew Moses (lit.) "in regard to all those miraculous signs . . ." (cf. KJV), i.e., the Lord gave Moses all that he needed to perform those signs and wonders. Mentioned are the signs and wonders of Egypt and in general all the "awesome deeds" he performed in the sight of Israel (which refers in the first place to the crossing of the Red Sea).

This further elaboration also shows that the phrase "no prophet . . . like me" does not contradict "a prophet like me" of 18:15. The latter statement was made in the context of the contrast between Israel's prophets and pagan divination and thus speaks of the *essential nature* of Israel's prophetism, while this statement speaks of a *difference in degree* between Moses (whose prophetic office laid the foundation of the covenant with Israel, of which he was the mediator) and the prophets who came after him (who all had to build on this foundation).

Finally, these verses give the impression of having been written at a time when all or most of Israel's history was in the past. We consider it therefore probable that they were not written by Joshua or by someone else from the early days of Israel's history, but by a later inspired author (perhaps Ezra). In any event, they apply to the entire history of the old covenant. But their application is also limited to the old covenant. Christ, the Son, is greater than Moses, the servant (Heb. 3:3–6); He is the Mediator of the new and eternal covenant of grace and reconciliation.